The Seduction of Place

"*The Seduction of Place* is an engaging ramble through the history and character of cities around the world ... A rewarding jaunt through urban history."

D0793054

"This is a necessary book. . . . Few aut[hors] ... vincing, rigorous and enjoyable journ[ey] ... to an electric-aided sunset over Manha[ttan]." —*The Guardian*

"The breadth of this little book is overwhelming, it is a compact tour de force." —*World Architecture*

"Rykwert treats his chimerical subject with a delightfully wide-ranging scholarship. . . . *The Seduction of Place* sets an agenda that brings compassion, and an involvement founded on 'humane discipline,' to a singularly important debate." —*The Independent*

"*The Seduction of Place* seamlessly combines the usually irreconcilable elements of factual information and narrative thrust into a most pleasurable read about cities and who and what has shaped them ... inventive, edgy and witty."
—*The Art Newspaper* (Book of the Year)

"A complexly argued, beautifully written and provocative meditation on the nature of cities." —*Publishers Weekly*

"Rykwert's passionate account of contemporary cities in relation to those of the past . . . offer[s] an elegant synthesis of those individuals whose visions of new cities have shaped urban planning around the world." —*Blueprint*

"A[n] idiosyncratic tour of modern architecture and urban design."
—*Art in America*

"The best whither-the-city book I have come across in ages."
—Hugh Pearman, *Sunday Times* (London)

JOSEPH RYKWERT

The Seduction of Place

Joseph Rykwert is Paul Philippe Cret Professor
of Architecture Emeritus at the University of
Pennsylvania. He is the author of ten previous books, including *The Idea of a Town*,
all of which have been widely translated, and
is a provocative and stimulating writer on
architectural and urban subjects.

Also by Joseph Rykwert

The Idea of a Town:
The Anthropology of Urban Form in Rome, Italy, and the Ancient World

On Adam's House in Paradise:
The Idea of the Primitive Hut in Architectural History

The First Moderns:
The Architects of the Eighteenth Century

The Necessity of Artifice

The Brothers Adam

The Dancing Column:
On Order in Architecture

The Seduction of Place

The History and Future of the City

JOSEPH RYKWERT

OXFORD
UNIVERSITY PRESS

OXFORD

UNIVERSITY PRESS

Great Clarendon Street, Oxford OX2 6DP

Oxford University Press is a department of the University of Oxford.
It furthers the University's objective of excellence in research, scholarship,
and education by publishing worldwide in

Oxford New York

Auckland   Cape Town Dar es Salaam   Hong Kong   Karachi
Kuala Lumpur Madrid Melbourne Mexico City   Nairobi
New Delhi Shanghai Taipei Toronto
With offices in
Argentina Austria Brazil Chile Czech Republic France Greece
Guatemala Hungary Italy Japan South Korea Poland Portugal
Singapore Switzerland Thailand Turkey Ukraine Vietnam

Oxford is a registered trade mark of Oxford University Press
in the UK and in certain other countries

Published in the United States
by Oxford University Press Inc., New York

ISBN 978-0-19-280554-6

Printed in the United Kingdom by
Lightning Source UK Ltd., Milton Keynes

To Zoë and Gaia and my severest critic

No man ever knew, or can know, what will be the ultimate result to himself, or to others, of any given line of conduct. But every man may know, and most of us do know, what is a just and an unjust act. And all of us may know also, that the consequences of justice will be ultimately the best possible, both to others and ourselves, though we can neither say what *is* best, or how it is likely to come to pass.

—John Ruskin, *Unto This Last*, 1862, p. 8

Contents

Acknowledgments

THIS BOOK HAS BEEN all too long in the making—if not so long in the writing. My first debt is to the many students and colleagues at Cambridge, at the University of Pennsylvania, and at the Jagiellonian University in Kraków with whom the ideas that inform it were discussed. My research assistants at the University of Pennsylvania, Nathaniel Coleman and Taha al-Douri, have helped in more ways than they know.

Andrew Motion (then still a publisher) first suggested that I might write a book on this subject. Many friends with whom the book was first discussed encouraged me to go on and warned me of pitfalls: George Baird, Marc Baraness, Czesław Bielecki, Mario Botta, David Chipperfield and Evelyn Stern, Jean-Louis Cohen, Charles Correa, Françoise Choay, André Corboz, Hubert and Terry Damisch, Balakrishna Doshi, Aurelio Galfetti, Antoine Grumbach, Vittorio and Marina Gregotti, the late Panos Koulermos, Paul Levy, Richard Sennett and Saskia Sassen and Ivan Zaknić. I owe an even greater debt to busy friends who have put their work aside to read the manuscript: Dennis Cosgrove, Graham Howes, Paul McQuail and Gwen Wright. They have raised problems I had not considered and saved me from some of my grosser errors. I was also lucky enough to be able to call on the specialist knowledge of two members of my family, Christian Devillers and Julien Studley.

To Desmond Hui I owe the possibility of three trips to China as well as his companionship there. Lawrence and Andrea Nield welcomed us in Australia.

My agent, Bruce Hunter, helped me give shape to the book, and Shelley Wanger has been a ruthless yet considerate editor. Alice van Straalen gave a new form to the paperback edition. I owe them all a great debt. The staff of the London Library has been courteous and patient, as have those of the University of Pennsylvania and of the Elmer Bobst Library at New York University.

My wife, Anne, urged me to write this book, tried to keep me to the argument, and trimmed some of my more wayward sallies. The book is as much hers as it is mine. What mistakes of judgment and fact it nevertheless contains remain my own.

My two granddaughters were born while this book was in the making. The future of the city will be in the hands of their generation, and so I dedicate this book to them.

The Seduction of Place

Finding Some Place in All the Space

BY 1945, MOST OF EUROPE and much of Asia was in ruins. Planners and architects, their attendant sociologists and engineers seemed absolute masters of a situation in which they would have to work very quickly. A vast proportion of the housing in Japan, China, Burma, and Europe had to be rebuilt.

These professionals had sharpened their ideas and worked out their proposals during the inter-war period, and many of them had spent the war preparing for its aftermath. They believed that they could guarantee that rationally planned and freshly designed cities of a new civilization would rise from the smoking and cruel ruins and would ensure the happiness of the survivors and the veterans. These professionals were seen as the pioneers of a new and better world: their work was to be based on statistical inquiry and on technical efficiency. History had nothing to teach them—it spoke only of the bad, old times. Theirs was an optimistic vision. Building became the highest social priority: in the first half of the century, any young man in a Latin-speaking country, whether in Europe or South America, who needed a university degree but had no special interests, often studied law; but after 1945, many of them gravitated to architecture. In Britain, a Labour administration was sponsoring not only new forms of urbanization, but meticulous research into the details of housing.

By 1965, the situation had changed radically. Many of the new projects turned out to be less satisfactory than had been expected: in the United States, returning veterans were not housed in visionary architect-designed cities, but in vast suburbs provided by developers on the old speculative basis. Society came to regard architects with disdain; the schools of architecture had to refocus and the satirists sharpened their pens. Gustave Flaubert's jibe: "Architectes: tous des imbéciles, oublient toujours les escaliers dans les maisons" (Architects, such fools; they always forget the staircases in homes) was translated and revived.

Still, the architects who began practicing after the war were not all convinced of the rationality and efficacy of their older colleagues. It seemed to them that the housing estates that were going up at a fast rate left a lot to be desired. Perhaps the city was not, after all, an assembly of well-planned housing units, but something that required a different kind of inquiry. The International Congress of Modern Architecture (CIAM), the organization that had promoted the ideas which motivated most of the planners and architects of the immediate postwar decades, came under attack from within. At its tenth meeting in Dubrovnik in Yugoslavia, it broke up.

I grew up during the breakup of CIAM. Even as a student, I had been dissatisfied with the teaching I had received, which was entirely colored by the rationalist heritage, even in its coy British redaction. The fiddly sociologism seemed both churlish and misleading. I began looking to historical precedent and at alternative approaches to the way many related to their environment, particularly to those which were being investigated by anthropologists. For reasons too tedious to recount, I decided to concentrate on the Roman city, which had always been held up as an instance of rational order, since it was modeled on a standard military camp and organized on a grid. As I looked more closely at what Roman writers had said about it, though, I discovered that the conventional view was entirely misleading. It was the military camp that was based on the town, since it was intended to provide more than a temporary home for soldiers. Like the town, the military camp could be occupied only after an elaborate series of ceremonies had "explained" its form to its inhabitants. Even its rectangular and gridded plan was an image of the Roman beliefs about the world and their place in it.[1]

This led me to question the whole received teaching about the rational/economic nature of settlement, as it also led me to question another idea—that the town is shaped by impersonal forces. It seemed to me then—as it still does now—that other notions, feelings, and desires governed the makers and builders of towns, that the city did not grow, as the economists taught, by quasi-natural laws, but was a willed artifact, a human construct in which many conscious and unconscious factors played their part. It appeared to have some of the interplay of the conscious and unconscious that we find in dreams.

The principal document and witness to this process was the physical fabric of the city. Of course, a city can never be a unified work of art or a beautiful object—all sorts of things buffet and push human intentions about—so it is difficult to think of a close parallel to it among artifacts. Or as Calvino put it: ". . . cities believe themselves to be the work either of the mind or of chance, but neither the first nor the second suffices to maintain their walls."[2] The Greeks, who used the word *polis* for the city, used the very same word for a dice-and-board game that, rather like backgammon, depends on an interplay of chance and rule.[3] The players' skill is shown by the way they improvise on the rule after every throw of the dice. If the analogy works, it would follow that we are agents as well as patients in the matter of our cities. Cities and towns are not entirely imposed on us by political or economic direction from above; nor are they quite determined from below by the working of obscure forces we cannot quite identify, never mind control. I say "cities" and "towns" because in England the two are distinct entities, and towns are made into cities by incorporation based on an arbitrary government decision; in the United States any urban grouping can take it upon itself to assume the "city" title. In any case, both words translate into German as *Stadt* and into Italian as *città*. In French the word *cité* signifies something like "the old city," "the nucleus of the town." Spanish has *urbe,* with its Roman ring—and gave us the science of urbanism—as well as *ciudad,* another word with an antique sound, like our "city," while *población* refers to the community rather than its walls. *Villa*—like the French *ville* and the English "town"—carries a whiff of country origin.

Cities, like their inhabitants, are a mix of good and bad. Since writing was invented, some five thousand years ago, literate critics of the city have been clamorous. Nevertheless, people have always crowded into cities, and their praises have also been sung vociferously. "Every nation has the government it deserves"[4] is an aphorism that has long been accepted as a truism. Do we have the cities we deserve as well? Sociologists, traffic experts, and politicians have all written at length about the city and its present problems. Economists and futurologists have prophesied its demise. Reading them I have always been struck at how little the physical fabric of the city—its touch and smell as well as its sights—occupies their attention.

At the risk of appearing superficial, I will therefore consider the city as it presents itself to our senses, and attempt a reading of what that surface might reveal, as well as what it conceals. It seems to me that the treatment we accord urban space—particularly the public part of it—can be usefully related to how the city displays itself in its public buildings. Dominant buildings have long ceased to be those in which political and public power resides but are rather those of private finance and corporate investment. Rental offices, apartment buildings, and corporation headquarters crowd the skyline. Such seats of political power as have been built in the last few decades—you need only consider the Pentagon building in Washington (reputedly the building with the largest footprint in the world)—are not showy or overpowering. They present themselves as physically remote and isolated behind barriers of parking and security, precautions which make their impact on the passerby, or even the driver-by, one of abstraction or alienation—as majesty once masked and isolated rulers.

My view of such matters is probably conditioned by my disability—I am not, nor have I ever been, a driver. It may make me more indulgent than some of my motorist contemporaries toward projects of pedestrianizing city streets. Still, my view of the institutional building removed behind its vast buffer-zone of parking areas must be shared by driver and non-driver alike. Whether you pass the car park from an outer gate, or whether you enter it to park your own car, the buffer effect is not very different.

Public institutions have therefore been muffled, yet the feel and the fabric of the town or city is always present to the citizen as it is to the visitor. Appreciated, seen, touched, smelled, penetrated, whether consciously or unconsciously, this fabric is a tangible representation of that intangible thing, the society that lives in it—and of its aspirations. A representation, a figuration—not, I insist, an expression. That word "expression" always makes me think of something involuntary, instinctive and therefore passive, like paste squeezed out of a tube. Or something that happens whether we will it or not, something unintended like the expression on our faces, which our feelings may compel before reason and intention have a chance to take over. Representation, on the contrary, suggests reflection, intention, even design in this context: a project. Since it is always willed fabric and image (however unsatisfactory we may think them), a town or city can never be quite passive, and because there is constant interaction between society and the urban fabric, we cannot tinker with our cities without making some adjustments to society as well—or vice versa. Perhaps it would be closer to the truth to say that a change to one must imply, presuppose, a change in the other.

The modern city is a city of contradictions, however; it houses many *ethnes*, many cultures, and classes, many religions. This modern city is too fragmentary, too full of contrast and strife: it must therefore have many faces, not one. The very condition of openness is what makes our city of conflicts so attractive to its growing crowd of inhabitants. The lack of any coherent, explicit, image may therefore, in our circumstances, be a positive virtue, not a fault at all, or even a problem.

However much the way we live in the city is conditioned by our antecedents, it is always the same physical fabric to which we respond: and again, even if the mottled, fissured, discontinuous modern cities were all that they should be (and not many of their inhabitants think they are), they will not stay that way. Cities change constantly—whatever their virtues or their faults. That is the one certain thing we can learn from the cities of the past. The speed of change has been on the increase over the last century and a half, and it is accelerating even more as globalization affects the whole urban fabric. We must therefore assume that our cities are malleable, and that we—citizens, administrators, architects, planners—can do *something* to make our preferences clear, and that we have only ourselves to blame if things get worse rather than better. Though the powers ranged against them seem crushingly vast and wholly impersonal, ordinary citizens are sometimes able to intervene—and some have already engaged in such action.

As we consider possible forms of this action and the effect it has had in the past on the fate of cities—their economic success, their drawing power and population movements—it is worth keeping in mind that the pride of citizens in their home does not seem to follow rational or even commonsensical criteria. Yet we need ways of understanding what makes some cities stable and desirable, while others empty or degenerate. Many critics who explain how modern world cities—whether established old metropolises like Mexico City or London, or relatively new ones, like New York or the recently ascending Kuala Lumpur—came to be the way they are, only take account of the impersonal economic forces that shaped them. Yet in spite of its vast area and its equally vast population, the center of Mexico City is urban in the old sense. It retains the features of a Spanish colonial town around the Zócalo, the main square, which Cortés laid out just after the Conquest. The arcaded surrounding buildings, the "National Palace" with the president's (once the viceroy's) residence, the law courts, town hall, and cathedral, are there but not the parliament buildings, and that absence is also part of the Spanish heritage. Mexicans perceive the Zócalo as the hub of their city—even of their country—and it remains the focus for post-election rallies as well as protest meetings. The out-of-scale sprawl has not effaced the drawing power of that configuration. The success of a city therefore cannot be measured in terms of financial growth and of a share in those markets it may have managed to capture, or even of its place in the process of globalization which is the inescapable phenomenon of our time—but depends on the inherent strength of the fabric and its availability to the social forces that mold the life of its inhabitants.

Globalization is the most powerful of the economic forces operating in the city of the present and of the immediate future. It has produced a concentration of economic power in certain capitals, now conventionally called world cities: New York (the most powerful), London, and Tokyo—with Shanghai waiting on the sidelines to play that role as well. As the effective world or globe capital, New York will occupy much of my attention. The economic argument for this dominance has often been set out, but the status of Manhattan is not merely economic.

The very word "globalization"—a buzzword nowadays, though it has been about for a long time—has a masking effect, suggesting that what is happening all over the globe is beyond the control of any one country or government or city, and that we might as well make the best of the situation we have. Some even go so far as to assure us that what we have are the very best possible conditions (for all the contrary evidence) and that what we really need is more of the same, but richer. Against these triumphalist and often impersonal estimates, other journalists, sociologists, and economists have constantly aired the failures and the defects of the modern city, commented on their causes and prescribed remedies. These critics—the sociologists especially—are accurate and perceptive accountants of the loss in immediacy, in a sense of community, in security, which recent changes in the city have involved, but they do not seem able to help those of us who suffer such loss.

Urbanists, economists, and historians divide, very roughly, into two main groups. There are, first, the chroniclers of the vast movements of history, which those who work in Hegel's wake—from Karl Marx to Joseph Alois Schumpeter, and right down to Francis Fukuyama and Jean Baudrillard—have seen as shaping our fate, and which we need to scry if we are to act in harmony with their dynamic, since any attempt at change and reform may act against history. Extremists in that camp have despised piecemeal remedies. Social conflict, they thought, should be sharpened. When conditions became unbearable, a revolution would establish a just society. All conflict could then finally be resolved. Somewhat different in their diagnoses on the other hand are the paladins of the free market, who tell us insistently how powerful and unpredictable these forces are, and how akin to the irresistible forces of nature; our choices in dealing with them are therefore limited, since our prosperity within the city is conditional on their untrammeled operation. Any regulatory constriction might stunt the free growth of the market by defying nature, and make us all—and our cities—poorer; perhaps ruinously so. Tampering with the forces of history and with the economy in particular is likely to land us with problems of an almost ecological kind.

Both schools are only marginally concerned with the fabric of the city and our experience of it, and both seem to be preaching a form of impotence—either before the forces of history or before those of the market. I propose to suggest, on the contrary, that these vast and seemingly impersonal historical and/or economic "forces" have always been the aggregate products of the choices that were made by individuals. If you think of any historical process in graphic terms as the vector resulting from any number of forces acting in different directions, you will see that any alteration in their alignment will deflect the angle of the vector.

Moreover, the motives of the agents—of the developers, the administrators, and the politicians—in manipulating the urban fabric, even when they would seem to be calculating and rational, often turn out to be obscure and sometimes quite willful, nor are they always articulated. The canny, sober, logical desire for profit and/or power may be balanced by much less rational machinations for prestige and status, which can be tempered by social responsibility and even genuine, disinterested benevolence. Of course, the most carefully calculated actions may turn out to be misguided or misdirected however determining their circumstances may have been. Each one of us has a measure of freedom to weigh some of his or her motives against others—and is therefore free to act in a particular way, but also to act otherwise.

That is why irrationality and miscalculation—sometimes ruinous miscalculation as I will need to recall later in the book—are as much an inescapable part of the history of urban development as they are of the story of banking or of the industrial economy or, even more explicitly, of stocks and futures trading. However inept or farsighted the calculation, the consequences of my action may be what I wanted or foresaw, but may also turn out to be entirely different from what I or anyone else could predict. As we make our history or even history *tout-court*, Marx pointed out, we do not choose the circumstances in which we do so, since the past always conditions our present as it determines the patterns of our thinking and feeling.

The risk of miscalculation and failure are attendant on freedom; and freedom inevitably presupposes responsibility. Although no town or city I live in can possibly be exactly as I wish it, even in the best of all possible worlds, yet the way it looks and the way it works has been determined by people like myself, not by impersonal forces: you and I also made the decisions, however small—how to fence the garden, what car to buy, which way to vote in the local elections—that go to make up the physical shape of the city. What sometimes looks like an impersonal force is often a vector such as I have described, resulting from all our decisions, whose exact angle or direction as well as impact we inevitably modify by our everyday activities, however subtly.

Of course, labor economics, market movements, traffic planning, or even natural disasters are much more powerful in forming the city than any private decisions can ever be, though these public moves are also determined by individuals. Acting in an official role, some of us may concern ourselves with matters which modify or impinge on the city's image, like the planting of tree avenues or the preservation of old buildings. Politicians and economists tend therefore to dismiss any concern with the image of the city as a superficial and transitory worry. The notion that "adjusting" this image might have an impact on the whole social framework is alien to them. Of course "image" is a word we tend to consider in the context of public relations. The citizens' view of a city is discussed in terms of the success of baseball or football teams, the growth or fall of the crime rate, royal or presidential visits, and other press-worthy events, while any talk of the physical shape is mostly considered too old-fashioned, too "aesthetic" and therefore too frivolous to merit serious attention. After all, it seems barely to impinge on the "quality" of the citizens' life. For all that, any description of a city's shape that can be gathered from a citizen's or inhabitant's comments—or just a pattern of movement—represents a constant and intimate dialectic between the citizen and the physical forms he or she inhabits; this may influence its image as radically as the city's economic and political life, which also determines its fate. You need only consider the impact of the Guggenheim Museum on Bilbao or the Opera House on Sydney. When talk of the physical shape and the city's image is dismissed as being merely concerned with the "dressing" for it, with façade, a "facing" for the underlying realities, it is worth remembering that we all get the faces we deserve.

My face has certainly had its effect on my fate, since fate and face are linked in a constant two-way process.

To conceive of the city as a producer of space seems to me another (and very subtle) way of denying responsibility for its fabric even though "the production of space" has recently become an important factor in any discussion. Space is no thing—it cannot ever be instrumentalized (reified, some critics would say) or deliberately shaped any more than the Manhattan skyline. It is, we are told, secreted by society as the shell is secreted by a snail. Like a style, it is meshed with the society that produces it and therefore cannot change until society has itself radically altered. Being primarily concerned with form, I am inevitably worried by the use of the term "space" as the common currency in city discourse.

It seems equally mistaken to me to consider the city as an "organic," a "quasi-natural" entity.[5] Too much of it is consciously manipulated by the assorted planners, developers, financiers, even architects. The fabric does not grow smoothly—as the notion of producing space implies. On the contrary, it seems to me to develop quite unnaturally by jumps, by fits and starts, and—as the old saw says—nature does not work by skips or jumps.[6] The abrupt and uneven jigsaw of conscious and unconscious workings is exactly what I have always found both fascinating and perplexing.

The critics of urban life are sometimes dismissed as the misguided successors of those many intellectuals who, over the millennia, have detested and mistrusted the city.

"The mobs of great cities add just so much to the support of pure government as sores do to the strength of the human body," wrote Thomas Jefferson in his "Notes on the State of Virginia." The damage that cities would do to the manners and spirit of the relatively innocent, land-loving American people seemed such a threat to him that he preferred to bear the expense of transporting raw materials for manufacture in Europe across the Atlantic and have them return to the United States as finished goods than have urban industries exert their corrupting influence: "Let our workshops remain in Europe," he argued. With time he recognized that cities were necessary for the economy—even in the United States—though initially he would only allow them if planned as checkerboards: a square of building alternating with one of woodland.[7]

Cities have always been viewed as instruments of luxurious corruption—parasites on the virtuous and fruitful occupations of country folk, as Jefferson thought, but also extolled as a powerful stimulus to economic and intellectual development. That contradiction, with many others, has even seemed a guarantee of their vitality; the prosperity they offered through their markets, the powerful physical presence that their defenses granted as a shelter to the weak—all this made them magnets that drew people and sustenance from the surrounding countryside, as well as people and goods from more remote places.

People first made cities some ten thousand years ago; or if not quite cities, urban settlements at any rate. How these first coagulated from other kinds of habitation is not at all evident. Economists like to identify their sites as trade crossroads, though it is not quite clear what the termini of these roads might have been. The concentration of the first cities in river valleys—the Nile, Tigris-Euphrates, Indus, the Huangpu—is a recurring theme, even though the ancient cities of Mesoamerica and South America were founded without the assistance of any river traffic, and many of the urban centers in Mesoamerica seem to have been gigantic sacred complexes surrounded by low-lying villages. Still there is no doubt that points of exchange—markets—are very ancient. The goods exchanged there may even have some forms of conventional valuation: there is plenty of evidence that there was an "international" trade in which cowrie shells were some kind of token at the end of the Paleolithic age. However, there is at present no generally accepted account or model of how settlement was fixed anywhere.

In the Old World, towns seem to have started somewhere in the Near East. Currently sites such as Çatal Hüyük in southern Turkey and Jericho in Palestine are reckoned the oldest—more or less urban—settlements that archaeologists have recovered. Markets were attached to even the earliest towns, and markets require accounts and even records, which were first kept by memory and tally. Oral traditions, supplemented by gesture and music, may—as we know from the example of modern non-literate peoples—transmit and maintain ideas of great sophistication and complexity. Yet at a certain point markets came to demand some form of literacy. The Inca Empire seemed to do without it and its origins are much disputed. True literacy, in the form of syllabaries, is thought to have begun independently in China, India, and the Near East sometime in the fourth millennium, about the time that constituted cities are first recorded, and that has identified the beginnings of history with that of the city. But this also had an obverse effect from the beginning, in that the scale and articulation of even the first cities invited the division of labor and of authority.

As they grew, they attracted strangers who may have differed in language and religious belief and civic custom, even in skin color, from the locals. Such hybridities, tolerable in times of growth and security, may become sharp and painful when the economic climate changes. Strangers quickly turn into scapegoats. "Ethnic cleansing" is a late-twentieth-century term for a procedure that has been carried out, sometimes with great cruelty, in many countries and cities over the centuries. Indeed, Scripture already carries a warning about the city: "God the first garden made, the first city Cain." Thus wrote the seventeenth-century English republican poet, Andrew Marvell, commenting pointedly on a passage in the Book of Genesis:

And Cain . . . builded a city; & called the name of the city, after the name of his son, Enoch. (Gen. 4:17)

So Scripture tells of the foundation of the first city by the first murderer in the land of Nod, the land of exile and vagabondage (that is what the name "Nod" means in Hebrew), as a shelter for humanity driven out of the garden of Eden. Many traditions—Chinese, Indian, African, European, Mesoamerican—speak of an analogous coming into settlement out of wandering, out of the nomadic condition. All these traditions reassert how dangerous that passage was, and insist that the beginning of every settlement had to be accompanied by rituals and sacrifices to placate the power of the place. Elaborate procedures were followed in accordance with divine creation, so that what was "taken out of" nature physically and appropriated for human use could be restored to her as image and metaphor. Every city had its own gods, its own religion and calendar, and reckoned its own time from its foundation. In any given place time began when the city was founded.

Poets sang, and later wrote, about the passage from the nomad settlement to the permanent, temple-and-market–oriented and defended town. And they recorded the sense that something was lost in the process when the enclosure of a piece of ground broke the texture of nature by cutting it out of the continuity of landscape. However, as we learn more about such origins, both from archaeologists and from ethnologists, it becomes clear that the conceptual diagram of a settlement may be incorporated in its customs, its marriage regulations, its rituals, and even the outlines of its plan, all of which a modern observer may be hard put to find in the ruins of these ramshackle villages.[8]

The sense of loss and the constant threat of the outside world are even recorded in some of the oldest of all surviving written texts. In the Sumerian epic of Gilgamesh, which was popular all over the Near East since the third millennium at least, and exists in Babylonian, Assyrian, and Hittite versions besides the original Sumerian, the plot of the story turns on the fight, rivalry, and later friendship between the urban tyrant Gilgamesh of Uruk, or Warka, and his "opposite number," the wild nomad, Enkidu, who loses his power over plants and animals after being taught urban, courtly ways by a harlot (prostitution is an urban profession), whom Gilgamesh sent to seduce him. Such themes were not limited to epic and legend, but were actually built into the very fabric of the town, almost as a criticism of their rising fortunes, by reminding the rulers of their often humble beginnings and the impermanence of their power. Ancient cities often had relics of their remote and rural origins at their center. In Mesopotamia city rulers were regarded as divine bailiffs and were ritually humiliated by a priest, only to be restored to their authority by a sacred marriage in a thatched reed hut; in Athens, the highest court, the Aeropagus, sat in a thatch-and-clay-roofed building; in Rome, the wood and thatched hut of its first king and founder, Romulus, was piously maintained on the Palatine Hill, close to where the emperors later built their vast marble palaces.

Once professional literary men begin to earn their living in Greece—unlike the salaried Egyptian or Mesopotamian temple scribes and annalists—the contrast becomes more pointed, as Hesiod shows in his *Works and Days*. The poet tells his farmer brother how things have declined from the Golden Age to his own times: either because of the poisoned gifts that Pandora has brought humanity in her famous box, or because the legendary first men, that virtuous golden generation—mortal but diseaseless like the gods—have simply died out. They were replaced, Hesiod insists, first by an inferior, then by the foolish, tarnished silver generation, which was followed by a fierce bronze one. It is only in the following fourth age, that of the heroes, the half-gods, that specific cities such as Troy and Thebes appeared, in whose wars many of these heroes killed each other off. Finally came the modern age; Hesiod, who has offered the most explicit version of the legend, calls his own generation one of iron:

> And I wish that I had no part
> in the fifth generation
> of men, but had died before it came,
> Or been born afterward:
> For here now is the age of iron. Never by daytime
> will there be an end to hard work and pain
> nor in the night
> to weariness.[9]

The Greek legend of an age of gold was also reflected in another account, a more "historical" one, which told of an "ideal" city (or at least, a model one) in a mythical past, which could in some sense be remade. The city of the ancient Athenians—*autochthones* (born of the earth)—in that remote past, was already divided into three classes, had a circular central Acropolis, and had resisted the powerful and rich city called Atlantis, situated somewhere beyond the Pillars of Hercules—the straits of Gibraltar—which, in turn, had been eroded by its excessive imperial ambitions. Both cities were to vanish in a great cataclysm. Atlantis, like Athens, was a circular city, unlike most of the settlements of Plato's contemporaries. Its physical division among the various Athenian tribes was, within the city, a miniature version of the land division in the surrounding landscape.[10]

While Plato offered the archaic city as an example of both urban virtue and urban decay, some Greek writers poured scorn on the city and its ways. Aristophanes, for instance, in the *Birds* and in the *Assembly of Women* mocks the pretensions of urban planners and legislators. The Roman satirists—Horace, Martial, Juvenal—made much of their hatred of Rome, of its jostling crowds, its filthy streets, its corruption, and, by contrast, of their love of the rural life, even if Ovid in his Dacian exile pined after big-city pleasures.

The Atlantis of legend, the Athens and Alexandria of history, were models of what a city should be for the ancients. Pausanias, the traveler who wrote a guide to the Greek world late in the second century A.D., makes clear what a town is not. As he comes to an ancient and fortified but largely ruined one called Panopeus on the road from Delphi to Athens, he notes: "If you can call it a town—when it has no town hall, no gymnasia, no theater or market square, nor any public fountain with running water."[11] He writes dismissively, using the common Greek word πολισ, which means both city and its farm hinterland, as well as the city dwellers; for him it is not the houses and the walls, but the public spaces and the physical presence of institutions that raises any settlement to the status of a city, a *polis*.

City-centered though the Greek world was, it never had a capital—or as we would say—a metropolis. The many Greek colonies all over the Mediterranean and the Black Sea were always sent by some mother-city, which is what *metro-polis* actually means. Athens did have that role, but only for Ionian Greeks; their terminology was equivocal on this point. It was sometimes just called αστή (*asti*), the town, while *polis* in Athens itself was only the ακρο part of it, the "high" city, its fortress, which we call the Acro-polis. Not until the time of Alexander the Great and his successors, late in the third century B.C., did one city impose itself on the whole Greek-speaking world as its hub, and not so much for its political, but for its economic and cultural importance—Alexandria in Egypt.

When Hellenistic Greeks spoke of *"the* City," it was Alexandria they usually meant. Speakers of Latin never had any problem about a capital. While the Latin word *urbs,* despite being related to the word for plowing (since the Romans ritually plowed around the outline of a new city), really meant a built-up and bounded enclosure like the Greek *asti,* the plain and unqualified *Urbs,* the City, could only mean Rome itself. And for all Romans—and I mean the citizens of the ancient Empire, as well as modern Italian ones—it carried the sense of "world center," since, proverbially at least, all roads still lead to Rome.

Atlantis, like other ancient cities, had been a "closed" community, in the sense that the city demanded religious as well as political allegiance of its citizens, and the presence of other races was regulated—when it was tolerated. Contradictions in the inevitable conflicts of city life were absorbed if not altogether eliminated. No city, in any case, claimed a monopoly over the calendar or the world hypothesis of all its subjects outside its walls. That is where Rome introduced a new factor: her imperial success was marked by her imposition of her own calendar in all her territories.

The Early Christians, who saw the cities of the Roman Empire as irredeemably corrupt, offered no such historical or exotic utopias in their polemics as Plato had offered in describing Atlantis and the earliest Athens, descriptions which were certainly intended as pamphlets against contemporary conditions. For all that, the ideal to which the Early Christians looked turned out to be urban: it was the New Jerusalem that Saint John the Apostle describes at the end of the Book of Revelation. Later many other models of an ideal or unrealizable city would provide texts for sermons. Saint John's heavenly Jerusalem in the form of a cube—as opposed to Plato's Atlantid circle—with three gates in each of its four sides, is a promise of bliss that only direct divine intervention could bring down to earth. But more terrestrial, semihistorical ideals also appear in medieval literature, like the Camelot of Welsh or Breton Arthurian romances.

Such imaginings were given an architectural and almost buildable representation in the project for the city of Sforzinda, which—shortly before 1500—the chief architect of the Milanese Sforza princes, Antonio Averlino, who called himself Filarete ("lover of virtue" in Greek), offered to re-create in his treatise, an architectural handbook in the form of a dialogue novel. His city was a long-lost one like Atlantis.

The social paradigm was almost always offered in urban terms by reformers. When the saintly Thomas More's narrator-hero, Ralph Hythloday, chanced on the island Utopia, he found a perfectly integrated city, whose laws, dress, manners, and appearance all corresponded to a model of tolerance and harmony remote from the chaotic and violent urban agglomerations of his contemporaries. He first published the book in Latin—it was to have an international appeal—and in doing so he incidentally also founded a new literary genre, since utopias—in which the problems of society may be discussed by reference to some fictional ideal and remote city or country—are inevitably a criticism of current urban practice and a polemic about policy.

Utopia is an ambiguous notion. It is, of course, no-place, and that is how More's title is often read—but it can also be understood as the good place, and that is perhaps the way the title had originally been intended. The first English translator thought it was "about the best state of a publique weale." Like More's Utopia, the circular "City of the Sun," about which the south Italian philosopher, Tommaso Campanella, wrote a century later, offers another variant on the urban fabric. Sporadic essays of this kind become a flood of suggestions in the nineteenth century: from practical and applicable proposals such as the centralized and centrifugal satellite city described by the English planner Ebenezer Howard, which became the model for many garden cities and new towns all over the world, to the extremely elongated *ciudad lineal*—"the linear city"— which the Spanish engineer Arturo Soria y Mata dreamed of building over vast stretches—from Cádiz to Saint Petersburg or Copenhagen to Naples.

Believers in continuous, linear economic growth have, over the past century, also repeatedly insisted that the city—as we know it—has no future. Thirty or forty years ago, futurologists asserted that by the year 2000, cities—particularly the North American city—would have spread so as to amalgamate into long, extended (but unlike the *ciudad lineal*, completely amorphous as well as vast) sprawls: they talked about Bos-Wash (Boston-Washington—swallowing up New York therefore), on the East Coast of the United States, Chipitts (Chicago-Pittsburgh) in the Midwest, and San-San (San Francisco-San Diego) on the Pacific. The arrival of information technology and the consequent communications explosion of the conurbations would produce a much lighter—perhaps even continuous—low-density population spread, which was named "the

Global Village."[12] The global village of the futurologist's imaginings is, note it well, a village, not a town or city. Computerized workers would not need physical contact with each other or any controlling central organization, and would be able to operate from their homes, which could simply be dotted about the countryside. Writing in 1967 Daniel Bell quotes a number of other forecasts:

> Dr. Glenn T. Seaborg, Chairman of the U.S. Atomic Energy Commission . . . holds out a promising future for women: "By the year 2000 housewives . . . will probably have a robot 'maid' . . . shaped like a box [with] one large eye on the top, several arms and hands, and long narrow pads on each side for moving about." Dr. Isaac Asimov . . . foretells . . . that by the year 2000 man will be exploring the limits of the solar system and living underground. . . . Even the beauty industry has clambered aboard: "The chic woman of the year 2000 may have live butterflies fluttering around her hairdo . . . attracted by a specially scented hair spray. . . . [She] will control her body measurements by reclining on a chaise-longue with electronic bubbles that massage away problem areas . . . she will have available silicones for filling in frown lines and wrinkles on aging faces.[13]

Bell was not altogether convinced by such prophecies, quite correctly as it happens, and opines that:

> Considered from the point of gadgetry, the United States in the year 2000 will be more *like* the United States in the year 1967 than *different*.

Information Technology (IT for short) is now bringing about the "radical redesign" of office space and of working conditions, but its effects are not yet measurable, nor is the impact on the city of on-line shopping and home-video entertainment.

At the time of writing the conurbations have not amalgamated, however, and many of the other prophecies made thirty years ago now seem comical. It is New York—even more specifically, it is Manhattan—that is the capital of the globalized economy, not Bos-Wash. On the other hand, other developments in the world have taken the forecasters by surprise. No one quite expected that Mexico City would become the world's biggest one (the current projection for its population in 2000 is twenty million, more than three times that of all Denmark), nor the catastrophic expansion of Cairo. Nor yet the third or is it fourth agricultural revolution which caused this influx into Third World developing cities.

But my starting point is different from that of such admirable predecessors, since my polemic is not against the disordered, even chaotic city, but against the anonymous and alienating one as it has grown in the nineteenth and twentieth centuries, and for which the term *dystopia* has been coined by its most hostile critics. My polemic is also against the more recent image of the city that has developed in the last two or three decades: the city as an image of social inequity.

Consider the game we have, as the Greeks did, to play about the city: Monopoly. It was copyrighted in 1935, celebrated its jubilee triumphantly in 1985, and spawned many accessories—T-shirts and suchlike, even a special museum. Although at first the snakes-and-ladders board on which it was played had locations in London or New York, it has gone through countless editions in many languages and the boards have been adapted to many lands. I certainly played at it as a child in Poland, and I dare say most of my readers have done the same. The city on the board is always presented in terms of real-estate values, and like a developer you can build up to so many houses on each location, and if you can afford it, finally a hotel. And like the developer's real-life situation, its hazards and pitfalls include both bankruptcy and jail. That rather social game has now been replaced by the inevitable computer one, Sim-city, in which the solitary player has a hypothetical landscape on which to place his buildings—and they are all separate object-buildings which he cannot modify. But the game is again a money game. The player has to carry out developments within cash limits, and to show a balanced budget and a growing cash flow to win a reward—though unlike Monopoly, Sim-city does not punish. Because the computer has to quantify, success and failure cannot be measured in more complex terms.

Those are the terms, however, that I wish to consider: what strategies are open to citizens who wish to shape their habitats in ways that would conform more closely to their wishes. A budget constrains any city authority: but—and there the computer game may have its uses—a budget may be manipulated. Balancing the budget reflects the conflicts of expenditure, but also the conflicts of demand. Any measures worth taking must, I suggest, start from the assumption that no ideal resolution of all those conflicting demands can ever be achieved. To take an obvious instance: most urbanites would say that a private house with a garden was their ideal dwelling, though they might also admit that a high-density urban life has its rewards, even if it excludes the possibility of individual home ownership for all but the very richest. Take another instance: pollution and crowding. Traffic problems were among the detailed complaints of the Roman satirists. They have been listed in

many a litany of attacks on the city and its shortcomings which literature has offered ever since cities began. Whatever the sources of energy, a
measure of pollution is inevitable in larger cities, as are occasional acute
traffic problems. Of course, pollution could be, but obviously is not,
kept within tolerable levels. What that limit might be and how to
achieve it is, inevitably now, a matter of heated and often acrimonious
debate. Certainly, visitors to London in the nineteenth century found
traffic congestion offensive. The stench of horse dung and urine was
overpowering, and a century ago the novel automobile seemed, ironically enough, to provide the decisive antidote to urban pollution.

That is perhaps why the critics of the city, economists particularly,
have recently moved to a more radical argument: Were cities, after all, a
real stimulus to economic and social growth or were they rather a parasitic excrescence on market economies that would have flourished even
more without them? Was not the necessary racial and religious mix of
urban society a solvent to social conventions and social cohesion? Would
humanity have done better without cities altogether? And are they worth
having and sustaining? Or should we find ways of dismantling them
institutionally even before the Global Village becomes a reality?

You may ask the same question in another way. Have cities not come
to the end of their useful contribution to the world's well-being, and
should they not be allowed to diffuse, dissolve, or implode—or suffer
whatever process of decomposition they seem to be undergoing with the
help of the shopping mall, the amusement park, the ex-urban corporation headquarters, and the computer simulation? Whatever happens to
world capitals, you may not expect such a dissolution imminently. Globalization has brought with it a new form of urban density and concentration. Even if it presents itself daily—because the disappearance of the
city is still part of our journalistic fare—that question is unreal.

Many writers—satirists, social reformers, and utopians—have taken
up such themes, and offered a destructive criticism of the city by holding
a distorting mirror up to urban life. My aim is quite different: to show
that the city is a precious, essential and inalienable part of the human
achievement—and sometimes a splendid setting against which human
actions are played out—and to suggest some rules of the game which
direct that play.

1. How We Got There

TWO HUGE, SUCCESSIVE WAVES of dispossessed rural populations rose over the cities of the world, flooding the urban fabric and swelling it to breaking point. It was the first of these waves, at the end of the eighteenth and in the early nineteenth centuries, that shaped the urban fabric that we know. The recent and much bigger one that billowed up at the half-century has not subsided: we are still floundering in it and cannot yet read its modalities or estimate its impact accurately. It has transformed Cairo and Moscow, Bombay, Kuala Lumpur, Jakarta, São Paulo—but most of all Mexico.

Any account of the response to those two waves must take into account the forces that brought about the first one. I am writing this not because I am a revivalist or historicist, but because the past is all we know.

What the shrewd Austrian economist Joseph Schumpeter[1] wrote fifty years ago or more about economic life is also true of the urban fabric:

> . . . only detailed historic knowledge can definitively answer most of the questions of individual causation and mechanism. . . . Contemporaneous facts or even historic facts covering the last quarter or half a century are

perfectly inadequate. For no phenomenon of an essentially historic nature can be expected to reveal itself unless it is studied over a long interval.

The first of these two waves hit British cities first and then French ones, spreading to the rest of Europe—and then the world beyond. What resulted in England and France was very different, though there were many parallels. The French monarchy had for two centuries (but especially in the reign of Louis XIV) managed to concentrate the landed nobility around the court by a system of favor and intrigue so that Paris became a center of political and economic power as well as of culture. The newly urbanized nobility were seen—notably by Voltaire—as the civilizing leaven of the capital. Other brilliant and influential writers such as Rousseau hated the city, and Paris in particular. As a young man, Rousseau had arrived there from Turin, the small, neat handsome capital of the dukes of Savoy, and the dirt and squalor he encountered in the Paris suburbs set him against the big city for good. He only went there, if one is to believe his *Confessions,* to earn enough money to allow himself long absences.[2]

Voltaire, despite the Parisian triumphs of his last years, did not think of it as his preferred city either: he found the values of the old and urbane aristocracy too constricting. As Rousseau admired Turin, so Voltaire admired London as the model of a truly meritocratic city. And he was right, since even the pre-Hanoverian English crown never succeeded in establishing a powerful centralizing court, though the Stuart kings tried, and one of them, Charles I, lost his head in the process. Their failure was clearly represented by the ramshackle modesty of the palaces at Whitehall and Saint James's, which were never aggrandized, despite plans to do so and reconstruction after fires. This was the great age of European palace building when very modest sovereigns indeed, like the prince-bishops of Würzburg, built themselves residences the British Empire would never equal—not even in the nineteenth century. British magnates, on the other hand, did build themselves palaces grander than the king's, as the duke of Marlborough did at Blenheim, the earl of Carlisle at Castle Howard, or the earl of Leicester at Holkham. Meanwhile, Charles II's attempt in the 1670s to build his own Versailles on borrowed French money, an out-of-London palace at Winchester, was frustrated by Parliament.

The Whitehall court of the Hanoverian Georges—who took over England in 1715 but had rather grander quarters in Hannover which they retained—was too skimped and mean to have any political or cultural hold over status-seeking British magnates, who were themselves riled by a newly rich banking class that was aggressively buying titles and climbing through intermarriage. Landowners were therefore thrown back on the resources of their mismanaged estates, where they were irked by their dwindling incomes, which they attempted to bolster—usually unsuccessfully and sometimes disastrously—in various financial speculations of which the South Sea Bubble of 1720–21 was merely the most notorious. The more intelligent among them realized that the husbanding of their neglected estates might throw off a much better income. In increasing numbers they became enthusiastic farmers, and much ingenuity and capital were applied to improvement. Two noblemen were leading reformers: Charles Townshend and Thomas Coke (great-nephew of his namesake, the builder of Holkham). Lord Townshend (1674–1738), who had been ambassador to Holland, is associated with the refinement of crop rotation, a skill he first learned from the Dutch. On withdrawing from administration, he devoted himself to the cultivating of his extensive but rather neglected lands by developing root crops—swedes (rutabagas), beets, turnips (he was even nicknamed Turnip Townshend)—and promoting the selective breeding of cattle.

Improved breeding of farm animals had already been practiced in Holland—which, being land hungry, had the most advanced agriculture in Europe—and in Germany, though it would not become systematic until Gregor Mendel published the results of his genetic experiments in 1865. Yet the new supply of root crops in Britain provided excellent cattle fodder in the winter, as did clover (which Townshend also grew as part of his crop rotation), and thus prevented the usual large-scale slaughtering of farm animals in the autumn. Two generations later, Thomas Coke vastly improved cattle, sheep, and pig breeds; he also managed to fertilize the light and sandy soil of his unpromising Norfolk estate to produce wheat instead of the rye that had been grown there previously.

Jethro Tull, a Berkshire gentleman-farmer, introduced even more radical reforms: he devised the first semi-mechanical, horse-driven sowing drill and an analogous hoe. Accepted slowly, his inventions were soon well known in Europe and improved. Voltaire had used them on his farm at Ferney on the Swiss border. Independently, a new form of plow seems to have been developed by a number of manufacturers in western Europe: a Dutch form, adapted in Yorkshire, became the most advanced type until the revolutionary development of steel plows at the beginning of the nineteenth century; it required only a horse or two to draw it, instead of the several oxen that were used to draw the old square ones.

The changes in tillage revolutionized animal husbandry: cattle were no longer bred to be brawny for drawing power, but smaller-boned and smaller-headed for meat; sheep were also bred more for meat than for wool. Imported fibers took over from homegrown, especially Australian wool, but above all cotton—imported first from Egypt and India, and later from the United States. Export trade was irreversibly transformed as cotton, the primary raw material of the textile industry, replaced wool which had, since the Middle Ages, been the most important British product.

Other factors led to changes in the scale of agriculture, especially in Britain. Until then most land in Europe had been under strip cultivation, each owner farming a number of (sometimes widely separated) strips. Commons were shared by several owners or tenants, which furnished pasturage as well as fuel and hunting rights.

"There was nothing particularly English about this: a traveller met with it from Andalusia to Siberia . . . on the Loire and on the plains of Moscow," wrote a Scots agricultural expert and landholder soon after 1800.[3] Enclosure gradually "privatized" open lands—waste and heath—first in Britain, but increasingly all over Europe. Such measures deprived the rural poor not only of the fish and game on which they had relied for their protein intake but also of cooking fuel. Their troubles were further exacerbated by the British Game and Night Poaching laws that sharpened and extended the ancient "Laws of the Forest." The same land produced bigger yields while requiring fewer hands, but enclosure required parliamentary sanction to be legal. Between 1714 and 1730, an act a year passed through Parliament, and they snowballed quickly; in the decade 1750–60 there were 156 such acts; twenty years on, between 1770 and 1780, 642. After a slight falling off, 906 were passed from 1800 to 1810, when legislation was simplified and the pace increased. An analogous development occurred in France before the Revolution. Some of the French nobility, first humbled and then impoverished by the domination of the increasingly centralized and increasingly powerful court of Louis XIV at Versailles (though partially emancipated during the minority of Louis XV), turned to the English gentleman (or even magnate) farmer for a role model. But French laws that had allowed free grazing on common lands were not withdrawn until the royal edicts issued after 1764; they established the legal procedure for the enclosures which—as in Britain—benefited the large-scale landowners.

Enclosures raised yields, but they also depressed and impoverished some of the rural population. If some economists are to be believed, the rural population in parts of Britain was reduced to a bread-and-cheese diet in the second half of the eighteenth century. Historians do not always agree about the effect of enclosures on welfare, though some sharp observers at the time reported the evils it brought with it. The radical Tory propagandist William Cobbett (who was perhaps the most explicit, brilliant, and the most widely read) insisted on the negative effect of the new agriculture on the rural poor as well as on the landscape. Many writers of the time echoed his sentiment:

> *Inclosure came & evry path was stopt*
> *Each tyrant fixt his sign where pads was found.*
> *To hint a trespass now who crossd the ground*
> *Justice is made to speak as they command . . .*
> *Inclosure thou'rt a curse upon the land,*
> *And tasteless was the wretch who thy existence planned . . .*

Or briefly and more vehemently:

> *Inclosure came and trampled on the grave*
> *Of labours rights and left the poor a slave.*

So the Northamptonshire farmer-poet, John Clare, himself the son of a farm laborer and an admirer of Cobbett.[4]

Others, such as the economist and traveler Arthur Young (much admired by King George III), took a more nuanced view, though as a firm advocate of enclosures, he was not worried by the pauperizing of the rural population:

"Everyone but an idiot knows that the lowest classes must be kept poor or they will never be industrious," he wrote; but after 1800 he, too, became a violent enemy of enclosures and one of the few articulate protesters against it.[5]

Protests were violent. The removing of boundaries on the newly enclosed commons became a capital offense—one of the many economic "crimes" punished by death in Britain. For all that, the areas of variegated strip, divided by grass verges and interspersed with hazel and fruit trees, were soon replaced by broader, hawthorn-hedged, squarish rectangles and wide, open pasturage, with occasional oak, ash, and elms. The appearance of the countryside changed gradually but completely, and on this ground the English fox hunt developed. By the time one of

Oscar Wilde's characters expressed his distaste for "the English Gentleman galloping after a fox—the unspeakable in full pursuit of the uneatable," he was deriding a commonplace.[6] Within three or four generations, this enclosed, "rolling" landscape came to be perceived as "traditionally" English—and the great agricultural depression of the first decades of the nineteenth century, with its attendant disturbances, arson, cattle- and sheep-stealing and -maiming, the hangings and the transportations that paid for it, was largely forgotten. The resulting landscape was seen as quintessentially picturesque.

The much more conservative French landowners were slower to adopt agricultural reforms, and that is why analogous developments proceeded more gradually and rather differently in France and southern Europe. In any case, France lacked large-scale cattle farming, which provided the British farmers with abundant manure. There were recurrent famines, one of which was the immediate cause of the 1789 events. The redistribution of church property after the Revolution—though it did not benefit the poorest farmers—did put more land under the plow. Still, the largely victorious fight against the laws of mortmain (which had allowed the accumulation of large estates as church property) had occupied Enlightenment agricultural reformers in southern Europe and profited the very same yeoman class, *franc-tenanciers*, which enclosures had impoverished in Britain.

All over Europe food production still remained the largest and most labor- and capital-absorbing activity well into the nineteenth century. But in Britain agricultural employment declined sharply. It occupied only a quarter of the working population by 1850; this had gone down to a tenth by 1900, and was a mere 5 percent by 1950. In France the agricultural population was still at 45 percent by 1900 and had only fallen to 30 percent by 1950; in Russia agricultural employment went from 85 percent to 80 percent between 1850 and 1900, down to 45 percent by 1950. The forecast and warning that the poet and essayist Oliver Goldsmith had made about 1750 that:

> ... *a bold peasantry, their country's pride,*
> *When once destroy'd, can never be supplied.*[7]

was fulfilled very fast.

Inevitably, such economic changes and such laws separated the peasant (where the term was still applicable) from his obligations as well as his privileges, and turned him into a wage earner. Inevitably, too, they caused hardship, often famine and always resentment, and reduced the numbers of those working the land. By the middle of the nineteenth century farming had become a manufacturing industry.

The very word "industry," which in Latin had signified diligence, energy, and purposefulness, and was treated as an aspect of the virtue prudence, had come in the eighteenth century to indicate a group of people who applied themselves to some form of production. "Arts, manufactures, and commerce [are] the industry of towns . . . agriculture, the industry of the country," says Adam Smith.[8] By the mid-nineteenth century the meaning changed again: it was used almost exclusively for mechanized manufacture, such as cloth production—and gave its name to the revolution about which I have been writing in this chapter. The term "manufacture," too, changed sense. From its original "hand-working" it came to mean factory production by the mid-nineteenth century. The word "industry" was not applied to all forms of energetic and nonproductive moneymaking (as in "service" industry—advertising, tourism, etc.) until the late twentieth century.[9]

During the seventeenth century and well into the eighteenth much fiscal and productive activity continued to be based on the economics of special groups, on wealth being a by-product or the companion of power; and like power, it needed to be protected and guarded, so that trade was sometimes regarded as a kind of warfare. The economic thinkers of the mid-eighteenth century separated their discipline gradually from politics: the first chair of political economy was established (in Naples) in 1755. Political economy, they thought, should be studied as part of the natural order, and it could be understood in much the same way as biology or physiology. The leading economic doctrine of the time, that of a group of scientists and politicians known as the Physiocrats, is sometimes summed up in the slogan *laissez-faire, laissez-passer;*[10] free trade was best, because that was nature's way. Trade and industry must not be fettered by taxation, and since farming is the ultimate producer of wealth, revenue must come from land rents alone. The Physiocrats relied for the success of their policies on a return to agrarian values. Their most effective disciple, Anne-Robert-Jacques Turgot, Baron de l'Aulne, made some of their ideas his policy when he governed the Limousin province, very effectively, from 1761 to 1774.[11] As a result he advanced to the post of comptroller general of the whole kingdom for an abortive two-year stint, when he successfully abolished conscripted labor (which took farmers off the land), and handed public works, especially roads, to contractors paid from public revenues. This produced a notable improvement of both road network and road surface.

In the last year of Turgot's brief ascendancy, Adam Smith published his *Wealth of Nations*. Smith had spent some years in France, where he was very much in the Physiocratic circle, and made a particular friend of Pierre-Samuel du Pont de Nemours, who was to play a very important part in the establishment of American institutions through another friend, Thomas Jefferson. *The Wealth of Nations* has remained a brilliant account of the nature of market forces and the division of labor, and has provided a much more sophisticated and articulated view of the economy as a mirror of the natural world than anything formulated by the Physiocrats, though, like them, Smith asserted the primacy of agriculture as the essential productive process.[12]

For all this insistence on the land, technical ingenuity in France was directed more toward automata and manufacturing than to agricultural machinery, as had been the case in Britain. Jacques Vaucanson (1709–82) devoted much of his life to making robots—notably a drummer and a flute player. A mechanical loom, similarly controlled by a revolving drum and studded with pins whose movement released its heddles to weave elaborately figured silks, turned out to be his most momentous invention. But Vaucanson's experiments were frustrated by the corporate organization of the silk weavers. His machines were deposited disassembled in his own collection, which was eventually absorbed into the Conservatoire des Arts et Métiers after his death. There another weaver-technician, Joseph-Marie Jacquard, reassembled and improved the machine in 1805 and gave it his name. The Jacquard loom has been the basis for all mechanical weaving machinery in the nineteenth and twentieth centuries—until it was replaced by the computer.[13]

In England the fly shuttle had been devised by John Kay, a weaver-turned-mechanic, who was an older contemporary of Vaucanson's, probably in 1733. It consisted of a number of commonplace and familiar devices: hammers and springs, and wooden guide-rails, all of them combined in such a way as to enable a single workman to produce much wider pieces of cloth much more quickly than had been possible before. The invention soon provoked protests from local weavers in East Anglia, but was gradually adopted by manufacturers who refused to acknowledge Kay's rights in the invention—and he died ruined by legal recriminations. During the next thirty years the fly shuttle became a standard piece of cloth-making equipment and put critical demands on the spinners.

Even though the required spinning machine was patented five years after Kay's bankruptcy in 1748, James Hargreaves, who perfected it twenty years later, suffered the same fate. In spite of Vaucanson's and Kay's inventions, weaving lagged behind the other cloth-making trades: the first workable mechanical loom did not appear until 1785. The British inventors were consistently pirated by greedy manufacturers, while in France Vaucanson was stymied by the power of organized craftsmen.

French innovations were known but not much publicized in Britain, yet textiles were the second largest employer after agriculture. Numbers are difficult to estimate, since much of the work—wool spinning and carding particularly—was the secondary activity of farmers and farm laborers. As in textiles, so in agriculture, eighteenth-century machines did not involve any radically new materials or devices. Their components were made of wood, leather, and brass; water and animals provided the power. In America water-powered engines were developed much more rapidly than in Europe, as labor was very scarce and no powerful labor organizations agitated against their use. In the 1780s, a Pennsylvania miller-engineer, Oliver Evans, devised the very first complete assembly belt in his mill, using gravity, bucket wheels, transmission belts, and Archimedean screws—all powered by water—to turn sacks of grain into sacks of flour. His invention was immediately copied by many American millers, yet Evans and, after his death, his widow were refused any profits from his patent, since it was considered a mere assembly of familiar devices. Evans later adpated his invention to steam; but, after all, the water power on which he first relied had been harnessed since antiquity. The windmill was the greatest technological innovation of the early Middle Ages, even if wind was too inconstant a source of energy for the earliest industrial processes. Refined though they were, wind and water engines probably provided less than a tenth of the energy an agrarian society required, yet the early factories were called "mills" precisely because they worked by rotary motion dependent on water power.[14]

Evans therefore shared the fate of the many eighteenth-century inventors who were the true creators of modern industry. Vaucanson, Kay, Hargreaves—and many others—for all the ingenuity of their devices, did not seem to their contemporaries to have made any radical innovation, even to such a technological sophisticate as Thomas Jefferson (whose opinion was solicited in 1813, when the millers of Pennsylvania denied Evans's widow protection of her husband's patent before Congress). When faced with what was to become the essential device of the Industrial Revolution—the conveyor belt—even the best informed and the most farsighted saw only the familiar pieces of which it was made up, not the novelty of the process or the organization. That is also why the Industrial Revolution caught them unawares.

The creation of the steam engine from the mining pump, and the changes in iron smelting, are usually considered the primary motors of that industrial revolution which led to the absorption of the newly dispossessed rural populations into the urban proletariat. But that is not what really happened. The revolutions of the eighteenth century had little to do with coal and steam, and everything to do with the new agriculture (which provided the manpower for the factories) and the mechanizing of cloth making. Heavy industry, metalworking, and mining, where conditions of employment were even worse than in farming or textile work, lagged behind.

The changes produced by mining and metallurgy, brought about by the shortage of fuel, were much more obvious and striking, though less revolutionary. By the sixteenth century, the forests of Europe had disappeared as populations rose and more land was farmed. Tree-planting enthusiasm was prompted by the need for locally self-sufficient shipbuilding in many countries. Although Spain had no shortage of timber for exploration and warships, Tudor England already had severe problems—as did the Low Countries, which were too water-logged and too intensely farmed to have extensive woodland. The Dutch would therefore buy whole forests in Scandinavia as "futures" for their shipbuilding during the seventeenth-century English wars.[15] Britain also became one of the main importers of building timber from eastern Europe, through the Baltic. There were serious shortages of ship timber again during the Napoleonic wars and the problem remained until the mid-nineteenth century, when metal ships displaced wooden ones.[16]

Coal and later coke became the alternative source of fuel as a result of deforestation. After 1650 the English surface mines—which had been the richest source of coal in the sixteenth and seventeenth centuries— were gradually exhausted so that ever deeper shafts and galleries had to be dug to extract it. They were often flooded, and the conventional horse-powered bucket-machines could not cope with such a problem. New and powerful machinery was needed.

The possibility of combining water and fire to power mechanical devices by steam was even known to the engineers of late antiquity, though an industrial application was not considered until the seventeenth century, when a military engineer, Thomas Savery, devised a rough steam pump to cope with mine flooding (the "Miners' Friend"), which he patented in 1698. Many such rough pumps were made, and many improvements effected. Although such engines used steam power, they still had wooden beams, copper boilers, and brass cylinders, and all they were good for was controlling flooding in mines.

Shortage of wood affected all metal production, but iron especially, since charcoal was essential as fuel for smelting, and processes using coal never succeeded. As a result, Britain had to import much of its iron during the post-1650 fuel crisis. Another inventor, Abraham Darby, a Yorkshire-born Quaker of Coalbrookdale, devised a process for making iron using coke—and the higher temperatures this produced led to an improvement in iron foundering throughout the century. The increasing use of coke and the improved ventilation through high-chimneyed smelting furnaces brought about the grimy mineheads that became one of the most striking features of the northern English industrial landscapes, already littered with the relics of open-cast coal mining.

Iron deposits happened to be close to the coal mines of northern England in Lancashire and Yorkshire. By 1750 smelting produced pig iron in industrial quantity, but hand-forging was still the accepted way of working it into use. After 1800 cast iron became the staple in many industrial applications: rails, and also the structural parts of industrial buildings, as well as bridges. At Coalbrookdale itself and over the Wear at Sunderland, bridges were made up of ribs assembled of iron sections that were treated like the voussoirs of an arch. Although nothing was known of the molecular structure of iron, it had long been clear that forging would produce tensile material, while casting would only result in brittle, compressive metal. A more decisive change was introduced when hand-wielded hammers were replaced by steam-powered rollers in the 1780s as part of the slow transformation of circular into reciprocating motion in machinery.

A quite different fuel crisis changed manufacturing conditions decisively in favor of ever larger concentrations. Early industrial installations had relied on wind and animals of burden, but above all on water, and this determined their location. They were more or less cost-free, but coal had to be paid for. Steam engines were not only expensive to buy but also to run and maintain; they had to be fired continuously, which imposed strenuous shift working conditions which were completely unacceptable to the older incorporated workers.

It was Matthew Boulton, a Birmingham manufacturer of metal goods and pioneer of mass production, and the Scottish engineer James Watt, who produced the first rotary engines for mining pumps that made it possible to harness steam for production. However, Watt had realized its potential early, and his first rotary double-action engine powered an all-metal London flour mill in 1786. Such steam engines were initially bulky, but smaller, more precisely made versions were soon also being turned out, and within twenty-five years of the Boulton and Watt patents, they would become sufficiently adaptable to replace horsepower in the drawing of heavy weights. Boulton and Watt were luckier at patenting than their contemporaries in the cloth industry. By 1800 three hundred of their iron engines were working in various capacities, and they were soon unable to satisfy the rapidly growing demand. However, even when the Industrial Revolution was in full swing, the impact of the steam engine on British industry remained marginal, since the great change in the methods of production had been ideological and managerial, not technical or scientific.

The devising of the factory system needed the organizational genius of one man, Oliver Evans's near-contemporary in Britain, Richard Arkwright (1732–92), a barber from Preston in Lancashire, who was responsible for creating the factory system used today. He, too, was dogged by patenting difficulties as Kay, Hargreaves, and Vaucanson had been, since his "inventions" were even more obvious rejiggings of familiar devices; but his business acumen made him one of the first, if not *the* very first, factory masters. His main enterprise, a cotton-spinning mill, was horse operated, but he moved to water power in his second establishment, still called "mill." It was only shortly before his death in 1792 that he had his machinery harnessed to a steam engine.

The rapid growth of industry required a quick expansion and more efficient transport. In the middle of the fifteenth century[17] the invention of the lock in Italy made it possible to move vessels up and down hills, transforming water transport. In 1487, the Naviglio canal, which encircled Milan, was joined to the Naviglio Grande, which ran down to the Ticino at Pavia and into the River Po; Leonardo da Vinci apparently perfected the device.[18] Canals were used both for transport and for irrigation of the surrounding fields. But it was the Canal du Midi with 119 locks, finished in 1680 between the reigns of Louis XIII and Louis XIV, that became the great achievement of Europe. Three thousand miles of canal were added to the French waterways and contributed to the much greater volume of French trade, and even industry.

The state of British roads was recognized as a serious impediment, being far worse than might have been expected from the degree of wealth and civilization which the nation had even then attained. Some of the labor force that the process of enclosure had thrown on the market was absorbed by road building, which underwent a rapid change in the second half of the eighteenth century. Many better seventeenth-century roads in Italy, Spain, and France were in any case based on those traced by the Romans. To the east and north of ancient Roman Imperial boundaries (the *limes*), as well as in Britain, gravel roads or cobbling had been adopted during the Middle Ages as cheaper alternatives to the Roman method, which provided a long-lasting surface of polygonal stone blocks. These newer roads were inadequate for freight vehicles, and British waterways had also been neglected.

By the end of the seventeenth century, the glass-windowed, leather-sprung carriage had made coach travel more comfortable. Paved roads were now in demand for both commerce and diplomacy. This also coincided with the quick growth of postal coach services—to carry both mail and passengers. All over Europe—and of course, in England—regular relays of horses and accommodation provided a combination of post office, railway station, and hotel. The French government was even able to publish a tariff and timetable for the whole of Europe annually from about 1780.[19] This meant that the roads had to be constantly maintained and improved. Edward Gibbon's admiring account of the march of Septimus Severus from his headquarters in the province of Pannonia, near Vienna, where he was elected emperor by his troops in A.D. 193, to Rome—800 miles in forty days—presupposes a much better state of road than was to be found in Britain when Gibbon began publishing his *Decline and Fall* in 1776.[20]

Since the sixteenth century certainly, wooden beams had been laid in wheel ruts to help with the transport of coal and iron in the north of England and in Scandinavia. About 1750 the building and postal contractor Ralph Allen constructed a funicular railway—worked by pulleys and gravity—to transport stone from the quarries at Combe Down to the rapidly growing city of Bath, which he was helping to finance, and even for export via the River Avon. Rails came to be made up of iron in the late 1760s, and locomotives with steam engines were first used at that time both in the mines and as freight carriers. From 1825 the first passenger carriages, between Stockton and Darlington in the north of England, were included in such trains. It is worth noting that the Stockton-Darlington railway tracks had been originally planned in wood, and the first passenger carriage—dubbed "the Experiment" by George Stephenson—was a separate horse-drawn wagon, run on the same rails and only eventually incorporated into the locomotive-drawn "trains."[21] The standard European railway carriage was to become a steel-sprung chassis of three or four post chaises mounted together on a buggy, and these jointed coaches became the compartmented and later corridor-connected railway carriage of the 1860s and 1870s. In North America, the trains of unsprung, covered wagons were later reconfigured as long, open railway carriages.

The first regular steam railway passenger service from Manchester to Liverpool opened in 1830 and was an immediate and runaway commercial success. George and Robert Stephenson's "Rocket," which pulled it, became the model for all subsequent locomotives. Within a few years railway lines were laid in France and Austria, and in the following decade in Germany, the Low Countries, Russia, and Italy. Switzerland and Scandinavia also had their first lines in the 1840s; Spain in 1848, Portugal in 1853. Greece and European Turkey did not have railways until the 1860s, when the idea of global railway "networks" was beginning to develop in western Europe, though the trans-Siberian railway was not finished until 1905. So light did the steam engines become that a steam flying machine—not yet an airplane—became a serious proposal.[22]

The laying of railway lines required complex legislation very like that needed for enclosures but involving a much bigger investment, which was forthcoming. The British Parliament authorized it exponentially, increasing capitalization from £4,500,000 a year in 1842 and 1843 to £17,750,000 in 1844; £60,000,000 in 1845, and £132,000,000 in 1846, by which time it was only a fraction of the sums requested. There was such enthusiasm for railway investment that the speculation of railway shares in the 1840s was almost entirely responsible for the financial crash in 1847. The 1840s and 1850s were the great decades of railway growth, the mileage increasing by about 50 percent a year.

Steam revolutionized manufacturing and transport, but agriculture resisted steam power, though, like other productive processes, it became increasingly mechanized. The climax of enclosure had been reached and passed by the 1840s with the intensification of manuring (which came to be known as "fertilizing") and the industrializing of reaping and harvesting. Natural manures—animal droppings mixed with straw, seaweed, blood, and ground bones—were replaced with nitrogen and potash compounds which were more manageable, if less beneficial to the soil, and this produced a second agricultural revolution requiring much more complex and efficient machinery. Already in 1783, the Society of Arts—soon to become "Royal"—offered a prize for a machine that would "mow and reap," though such a machine was not patented until 1811. Inventors persisted until one Cyrus McCormick, a Connecticut farmer, devised a successful combination in 1834. He moved to Chicago, and the many improved versions of his machines dominated grain harvests in the midwestern prairies for many decades; he showed them at the Crystal Palace exhibition in London in 1851. European critics found the machine cumbersome, but it was quickly accepted in Europe and North America—not in South America or in Asia. Finally in the 1880s a full combine-harvester was created.

All such machines were horse-powered until the end of the nineteenth century; steam could not be harnessed to them usefully, and the internal combustion engine, which would take them to another stage of development, was in a remote future; horse-free combine-harvesting became a possibility only after 1890, when Gottlieb Daimler and his associates produced the first internal combustion, gasoline-powered carriage.

All this progress took place as farming incomes became increasing depressed. Some of the cheap labor created by the enclosures had been absorbed into the new large-scale farms, but more gravitated to the new industrial centers. The recently mechanized spinning mills were first set near rivers, later near coal and iron mines, partly to be near the sources of cheap power, but equally because the labor force, particularly in the older towns—Norwich, Bristol, York, Lincoln—was both corporate and protectionist, hostile to new workers, and insistent on a minimum wage. The weavers' organized hostility meant that weaving—unlike spinning—was not mechanized until about 1800, at the very time when William Blake's resounding line about the "dark Satanic mills" (now associated with fire and steam and iron) was written—even though practically all existing factories were in fact water-powered "mills."

Other poets could provide appreciative commentary on the sublime aspect of industrial "improvements":

> *From the germ of some poor hamlet, rapidly produced*
> *Here a huge town . . . and there,*
> *Where not a habitation stood before*
> *Abodes of men irregularly massed . . .*
> *O'er which the smoke of unremitting fires*
> *Hangs permanent, and plentiful as wreaths*
> *Of vapour glittering in the morning sun . . .*

wrote Wordsworth in *The Excursion;* not that he had any illusions about the economic reality that caused that vapor to glisten in the morning sun. The "darker side of this great change" was very much on his mind, and a little later in the same poem, he describes the "many-windowed fabric huge," which he observes at the evening change of shift:

> *Disgorged are now the ministers of day;*
> *And, as they issue from the illumined pile,*
> *A fresh band meets them at the crowded door—*
> *. . . men, maidens, youths,*
> *Mothers and little children, boys and girls,*
> *Enter, and each the wonted task resumes*
> *Within this temple, where is offered up*
> *To gain, the master idol of the realm*
> *Perpetual sacrifice . . .*[23]

Such large mills, the first factories, brick and wood structures with wooden machinery, frequently caught fire. When steam power took over from water, the fire hazards increased, and in the 1820s building regulations were tightened, requiring the displacement of structural wood with iron. Yet the very word "factory" was a novelty just before 1800, as is clear from the text of a proposed protectionist bill of 1795: "Of late, several merchants have become manufacturers of cloth and, for the better carrying on of such manufactory, have erected very large Buildings which are called factories. . . ."[24]

These new multistory buildings required powerful support; timber was not only a fire hazard, but also not strong enough to carry the new equipment. Iron was the answer, and again it was Boulton and Watt who first realized its potentialities. By 1801[25] they produced a project for a seven-story factory building with an internal structure of columns that were cast-iron hollow tubes and could support large spans despite the small diameter of the columns. Their project was not executed, but many similar and more elaborate ones were. Long and six- or seven-story buildings could now house banks of steam-powered machinery. The grimy effusions of their coal-stoked furnaces were accepted as a condition of industrial life. Until the invention of smokeless fuel in the late 1940s put an end to them, the pea-soup fogs of London—also fed by domestic coal-heating—were considered a natural phenomenon.

Cast iron had already for some decades before that been combined with another updated material, sheet and plate glass, to create such large glass hot-houses as the Palm Stove at Kew, where exotic climates could be simulated on a large scale. In 1851 Joseph Paxton, one of the most remarkable gardeners of the time, used the technique to make a vast hall for the very first of many international expositions of trade and industry. This building was regarded with amazement by his contemporaries and was soon dubbed the "Crystal Palace."[26] Metal and glass were to play a major part in all these displays, which became a biannual event for the introduction of novel forms of construction, particularly when they happened in Paris—and I will have more to say about all this further on.

In the late 1850s metal construction was advanced yet further when Henry Bessemer devised the steel smelting process. But even before that the first, slightly cumbersome cast-iron cage buildings appeared; the most famous was the Menier chocolate works at Noisiel-sur-Marne, devised by an architect-engineer, Jules Saulnier, and built in 1871–72. The four-story cross-braced skeleton of cast iron is clothed in terracotta—perhaps the first curtain wall ever. The main factory building spans three stone piers set in the River Marne, which was, and remains, its main source of energy.

Saulnier's iron cage and curtain walls had little direct impact in Europe; in the United States iron cages, less refined than Saulnier's, had been built twenty years earlier, and this kind of construction was to be replaced by much more spare and elegant steel frames. At the same time, the American inventor Elisha Graves Otis devised a safe passenger elevator, which became the prototype of all subsequent lifts; Bessemer and Otis in the 1850s provided the two essential ingredients that were to make possible the tall buildings that transformed the urban landscape some decades later.

As steam-powered factories—often huge buildings with their attendant, usually squalid housing for the workers—multiplied, the population rose; the absence of major wars and epidemics is sometimes given as a reason. France was the most populous state in Europe; in about 1750 it had an estimated 22,000,000 inhabitants, 26,000,000 at the time of the Revolution. Paris may have reached a million at that time, and was certainly the largest city in Europe. France, and to some extent Italy—known since the Middle Ages as the "land of a hundred cities"—were more urbanized countries than Britain, where in 1750 only Norwich and Bristol exceeded 20,000 inhabitants. They were overtaken in the next fifty years by Manchester, Liverpool, Newcastle, Leeds, Sheffield, and Nottingham. It was a time when the British population also grew rapidly. In 1760 it was reckoned at 6,500,000; at the first census of 1801, it was 9,000,000 and by 1831, it was 14,000,000. These figures were not really affected by immigration, which was more or less balanced by emigration. They seem to indicate a sharp rise in the birth rate balanced by low life-expectation. Moreover, by the 1820s, machinery had become sufficiently developed to require only unskilled operators. Factory masters in fact distrusted and would not employ skilled workers, whom they considered self-willed and contrary, a danger to the discipline of the unskilled worker. To the workers all this seemed both menacing and provoking. During the 1810s and 1820s a series of violent machinery-wrecking attacks—of which the most famous were carried out under the command of a mythical "Captain Ludd," a kind of Robin Hood *redivivus*—paralleled those on farming property. Both ended in many executions. The first attempts to set up trade unions also ended in a spate of hangings and many "transportations" to Australia. Fear of the French Revolution had led to the instituting of a system of spies and informers among the semiorganized workers, and to the formation of militias. The famous attack by an armed and mounted militia on a vast unarmed crowd, estimated at between 60,000 and 100,000 participants assembled on Saint Peter's Field outside Manchester on August 16, 1819, came to be known as the Peterloo massacre (to rhyme with Waterloo). On that occasion many of the workmen had marched under the banners of their old guilds and corporations. Peterloo effectively changed the nature of working-class protest in England for some time, though it is a mystery why it did not provoke an armed rising or a revolution. This has generated much debate but defied conclusive explanation. In France, under the old regime, the economic theorists of laissez faire disapproved of any protectionist corporations and guilds, which were therefore abolished by the Republic. Any attempt at forming even the most elementary labor unions or controlling the excesses of bourgeois profit making was repressed with the guillotine in the name of the General Good. The French unions did not achieve any real power until the strike year of 1834.

At first the mass move into the towns was accompanied by a brief rise in life expectancy. The enforced closing of gin shops reduced street violence, and the spread of inoculation virtually abolished smallpox after 1800.[27] Though economists were perplexed, they could only deduce that a greater consumption of meat and vegetables, the substitution of wheat for other cereals, improved drainage and construction, and greater personal hygiene due to cotton underwear and the use of soap, as well as general medical progress, caused this phenomenon. These latter factors certainly affected the middle classes, yet they left the old rural and the new urban proletariat open to three (or four—historians number them differently) virulent epidemics of cholera between 1830 and 1860. Lower-income urban dwellings were made of brick and had roofs of slate rather than of wood or thatch as they did in rural areas, thus making them less vulnerable to many parasites. These houses were also unencumbered by the presence of any dust-producing industry, but primitive sanitation—a marginal hazard in the country, where domestic refuse and human waste would have been dispersed in the fields—is always deadly in the crowded town. Here it became a festering source of infection in stagnant urban quarters in which houses were packed back to back and the sewage drained sluggishly down interior alleys that could neither be effectively ventilated nor cleaned.

The heavy pollution from coal-fired industry replaced the dust-producing spinning wheels and looms. Tuberculosis increased catastrophically, though it was the successive outbreaks of typhoid and cholera—a threat to all classes—that finally mobilized public opinion. The epidemics coincided in England with the Reform Act of 1832, which widened parliamentary franchise and allowed some reforming voices to be heard, however feebly at first.

It is now clear, as it was not, perhaps, to earlier historians, that these revolutionary and irreversible changes were not initiated by scientists and their discoveries or even innovative technologies, but were at first a reordering of older, sometimes ancient bits of machinery by clever artisans, exploited by the managerial and organizational skills of the manufacturers. Even the factory mill and the railway had been put together from preexisting features of the industrial process. The harnessing of steam and the large-scale manufacture of cast iron were important but later catalysts of change. The demand on technology and for new materials barely kept up with the requirements of managers and builders.

The positive, even heroic aspect of these changes received scant notice from "high" culture; even the strange, entrancing, and often terrifying spectacle that was offered by the achievements of industry did not seem to inspire the best artists of the time. Yet landscapes had already become a dominant painting genre. True, William Gilpin, the theorist of the new kind of "picturesque" landscape painting, found the view of the iron furnaces on the River Wye in Gwent more inspiring than their neighbor, the ruins of Tintern Abbey, surrounded as they were by wretched cottages inhabited mostly by the idle beggars he despised:

> The country . . . has been described as a solitary, tranquil scene: but its immediate environs only are meant. Within half a mile of it are carried on great iron-works; which introduce noise and bustle into these regions of tranquillity.
>
> The ground, about these works, appears from the river to consist of grand woody hills . . . a continuation of the same kind of landscape as that about *Tintern Abbey;* and are fully equal to it.[28]

Wordsworth, visiting Tintern some twenty years later, saw only the beauty of the landscape—and by then industry did not have quite the anodyne and benevolent aspect that Gilpin had noted.

Arthur Young, whom I quoted earlier on enclosures, found "the flames bursting from the furnaces with the burning of coal and smoak of the lime-kilns . . . altogether sublime." Philippe de Loutherbourg, a Franco-Swiss painter who had come to London as a theater designer for David Garrick, but had also been a mesmeric healer and an associate of the charlatan Cagliostro, had painted the sublimity of the Coalbrookdale works[29] at night. He also recorded some forges and casting shops. Joseph Wright of Derby, who was both very interested in representing the strange effects of scientific experiments and in the mechanical transfer of his work to porcelain plaques, did paint Richard Arkwright's mill by night in 1780 and was to do so again by day some ten years later. Very few other painters approached industry, though there are one or two exceptions. John Constable only took an interest in semi-industrial subjects, such as the chain pier at Brighton or the locks on the River Stour. J. M. W. Turner, the artist most obviously susceptible to the effects of Wordsworth's "vapour glittering in the morning sun," painted Newcastle, with the Tyne crowded with tall-masted ships in a smoggy haze.

Other artists were horrified by the effects of industry: John Martin, best known for his mezzotint illustrations to Milton's *Paradise Lost*, was no Luddite, but a friend of engineers and actively involved in industry and such urban developments as the embanking of the Thames and improved drainage. Yet he told his son after a visit to the north of England that "he could not imagine anything more terrible, even in the regions of everlasting punishment" than the Black Country, the intensely industrialized region of the northern Midlands. On his return he painted a vision of the Apocalypse based on his experience.[30]

With very few exceptions, there was no visual equivalent of Wordsworth's denunciation of the new human misery in *The Excursion,* yet one very elegiac picture might be taken as a perhaps autobiographical celebration of the old order passing. Turner's *The Fighting Téméraire* shows the proud old sailing ship—which had fought at Trafalgar—all tall and stately, lit by a sunset glow, being towed by a much smaller black steam paddle-tug to its last docking at Deptford. Turner certainly witnessed the scene and was so attached to this picture, which he called "my darling," that he refused to sell it or even lend it for exhibition. Contemporaries found that there was something ominous about it, though John Ruskin considered it the last fully accomplished work among his masterpieces. Turner's biographers, on the other hand, have seen it both as a lament for the Old World before the coming of the machine or even as an allegorical account of Turner's career, unrewarded by honors. The artist, as ever, kept quiet about any symbolism. Some years later, in 1845, he showed another picture, which recorded the new environment created by the industrial process: *Rain, Steam and Speed—the Great Western Railway*. The black, fire-spewing engine is shown rushing over a bridge at the spectator, and the golden background—with girls dancing on the riverbank and the plowman on the hill beyond—has been read as a similar nostalgic comment on his time. The picture is a primary piece of evidence—it may well be the first account by a major artist of the truly revolutionary effect rapid movement has on perception. "The world," wrote a hostile contemporary, "has never seen anything like this picture."[31] Ruskin, Turner's most enthusiastic and voluble admirer, was also wary of this painting; he once noted that Turner had probably done it to "show what he could do with an ugly subject."

Most "high" artists of the nineteenth century shunned the subject of industry in spite of all its sublimity. Insofar as they dealt with it, they did so in allegories and allusions. The exceptions are notable, because they are so few. William Wylde's watercolor of the smoking chimneys of Manchester, commissioned by Prince Albert in 1857 to commemorate his visit there on the occasion of an exhibition of the country's art collections, is virtually unique. This disregard is paralleled by the architects, who took little interest in the design of factories or in the housing of the poor.

Yet there was a general hunger for industrial imagery: the industrial achievements of the country called for celebration. There was a profusion of popular prints, in woodcut and copper plates, but also in new techniques more suited to mass production, such as steel and hardwood engraving, lithographs, and transfers on china of industrial subjects. Later there were also photographs, but all these were regarded as visual journalism, ephemera, not the stuff that got exhibited in galleries and academies.

Even the Impressionists, when they did look at the railway, saw the shimmer of steam and glass, not the effects of transparency or speed. Edouard Manet's *Chemins de Fer*, also known as *Gare Saint-Lazare*, for instance, is a double portrait with a train standing in the background. Claude Monet's series *Gare Saint-Lazare* shows stationary trains and the effects of light through glass roofs. He also painted the bridge over the railway lines just outside the station, *Le Pont de l'Europe*; again it was the shimmer of steam that fascinated him: the engines appear to be static or moving slowly. Gustave Caillebotte's variations on *Le Pont de l'Europe* also show glimpses of the train and puffs of smoke, but concentrate on the bystanders. Even "realist" painters, Gustave Courbet, Honoré Daumier, Jean-François Millet, who showed the miseries of the rural worker and celebrated moments of social protest, seemed unconcerned with either the grandeur or the squalors of the industrialized landscape. Gustave Doré, the most prolific illustrator of that prolific century, and fascinated by the cities of his time, took no interest in the new landscape. Camille Pisarro, who considered himself an active anarchist, did paint a train drawing out of Norwood Station in London, and the Crystal Palace at Sydenham, and he made some pictures of a factory at Pontoise near Paris, but these were very much incidents in a rural or semirural landscape; the factory chimneys are like the poplars of his earlier work, and the Crystal Palace is there for its atmospheric effects. Not until the last quarter of the century did painters engage with working industrial installations. True epic images of industry and its achievements were not made until then, and they were not really celebrated until the Futurists concentrated on them in the twentieth century.

By that time, the marshaling of energy had made its inevitable, irreversible impact on the landscape and on the town: first came the replacing of animal and human labor by the harnessing of wind and water; that was followed by steam, gradually supplanted by gas and oil; both were partially displaced by electricity after 1900. During that time, the move of populations into cities, which was accelerated by enclosures in Britain, became a European phenomenon. In France, and as the century went on, in Germany and central Europe, Scandinavia, and the other Latin countries (notably north Italy and Catalonia), the younger industrial machine was already operating, railway trains were running, and the new proletariat had invaded and bloated, swamping and bursting the city fabric. Urban crowding and urban poverty, which had always coexisted, now reached an unprecedented scale. But a cultural transaction with the machine never mediated the impact of machine work on the body politic. That shock was never entirely absorbed.

2. First Aid

THE HIGH SOCIAL COST of enclosure has been counted repeatedly even by the many who recognized its economic benefits. The social cost of industrialization, glaring and painful though it was from the outset, seemed more acceptable because its long-term benefits were obvious and promised to be universal.

When the nineteenth century began, industrial labor was wretched and city dwelling had become unacceptably congested, polluted, and grimy, but not even the most acute contemporary critics of the first capitalist-industrial society and its inequities—Comte de Saint-Simon (1760–1825), or Robert Owen, Charles Fourier, Pierre-Joseph Proudhon, Peter Kropotkin (1842–1921), or Marx and Engels, whose lives span the century—thought that the process could or should be halted. They, like many other social thinkers, saw radical economic reform and/or social revolution as the proper cure for the evils of a society dominated by the profit motive rather than by the public good. Nor did they have a sense of the problems that the failure of the cultural transaction with the machine might imply.

John Ruskin was perhaps the most vociferous critic of the process itself, but although he was heard respectfully by crowds—he was an enormously popular lecturer and read so widely that he was considered a best-seller in his day—his exhortations were treated more as literary exercises than as calls to social action. Outside observers, such as the dominant Prussian architect Karl Friedrich Schinkel—who toured industrial Britain on behalf of his government in 1826—was as impressed by the superabundant energy of the new industrial society as he was appalled by the urban squalor from which it sprung.[1] In 1835 the equally brilliant French social observer Alexis de Tocqueville found Manchester horrifying:

> Smoke, thick and black, covers the town . . . 300,000 human creatures move ceaselessly through that stunted day. A thousand noises rise endlessly from out of this dark, dank maze, but they are not the sounds usually heard in great cities. The steps of scurrying crowds, the cranking of wheels grinding against each other, the scream of steam escaping from furnaces, the regular beat of looms, the heavy roll of waggons. . . . You will not hear shouts of joy or sounds of pleasure, nor the music of instruments which announce a holiday anywhere. You will not see easy, relaxed people taking their leisure or going out into the nearby countryside for their simple pleasure. . . . Yet out of this stinking drain the most powerful stream of human industry springs to fertilize the whole world. From this filthy sewer pure gold flows.[2]

A year after de Tocqueville's journey, another critic, the feverishly productive British architect Augustus Pugin, who died at forty in 1852, published *Contrasts,* a book that puts forth his condemnation of the industrial city, contrasting it with a romanticized version of the same setting before the Reformation. Neither de Tocqueville nor Schinkel would propose remedies, and Pugin's prescription of a wholehearted conversion to the beliefs and practices of the age of faith, which for him meant A.D. 1450 or thereabouts—as well as a return to what would soon come to be termed an "organic" or "closed" society governed by a landowning nobility (while a commercial and manufacturing middle class would "know their place")—was not even popular with most of his coreligionists. The other side of Pugin's belief, that a return to the kind of building and furnishing, to the physical environment that existed in the fifteenth century, just before the Reformation—the manner most commonly labeled Perpendicular Gothic—would bring about the changes he demanded seemed more acceptable. From what he wrote, it was not clear whether a different architecture would produce social change, or whether the change was necessary to renew the environment.

Nor did Pugin explicitly advocate a social revolution or a return to craft
methods and guild organization—and in this he was very unlike some of
his contemporaries in France, as well as in Britain. John Ruskin and his
most powerful disciple, William Morris, both despised him and deni-
grated him as a tin-pot architect. Yet he managed to develop a consistent
approach in the detail of those church buildings in which he was personally involved—like Romsey Abbey in Hampshire (where he is buried)—
and much more conspicuously, in the Houses of Parliament, the Palace
of Westminster, where he conceived and had executed all the surfaces of
the building, outside and in.

The protests and projects of these preachers—of Pugin (1812–52)
and Ruskin (1819–1900) as well as Ruskin's mentor Thomas Carlyle
(1795–1881)—against present social evils were conditioned by the aftermath of the French Revolution. The Revolution had caused almost as
much terror in the Britain of their youth as it did in the rest of Europe,
not only because of the specter of violence evoked by the Peterloo massacre, for instance, but also because of the confusion that followed the
collapse of the *ancien régime* and the ascent of the new bourgeoisie to
real political as opposed to economic power. The dominance of rising
industry by market forces implied, or so it seemed to them, a whole new
social modality about which Friedrich Engels, writing in 1877, approv-
ingly quotes Carlyle's ringing denunciation that it has made "cash pay-
ments increasingly the sole nexus between man and man."[3]

Protests against the evils of society came from those who saw the
inequalities of the old world perpetuated in the postrevolutionary order,
as well as those who thought that the destruction of a hierarchical society in France and the dissolution of the links that the guild system had
imposed presaged near-apocalyptic disorders in the rest of the world.
While a number of "conservative" and "recusant" political movements
furthered such views, many more protest organizations sprang up in the
first half of the nineteenth century to challenge the emerging economic-
industrial status quo by attempting alternative social groupings—communities that aspired to a more or less ideal status. Not since the
breakdown of the church-inspired unity of northern Europe after the
Reformation, when millenary movements promised paradise on earth,
had there been such a profusion of projects on offer. Their very proliferation in postrevolutionary Europe seems a symptom of the unease, even
anxiety, provoked by the breakdown of the old social order. Nor was it
just a matter of social unease: to some, new evils seemed more glaring
and menacing than the older inequities, since the rising urban popula-

tion and the laborers—particularly children—now lived in conditions that many thought much worse than those of the slaves on West Indian and southern American plantations.

Towns and cities therefore had to be reorganized in the face of the existing urban turmoil. There were several differing models to which planners could appeal. The growth of cities had been affected by the increasing amount of earthworks necessary to combat the power and accuracy of artillery introduced after 1500; their outlines had taken on a more or less polygonal shape to provide emplacement for cannons. Polygonal walls did suggest alternatives to the grid: streets radiating from the center to a gate in each side of the polygon. Such plans were often engraved and published, though very rarely built. Nine-sided and radial Palmanova was established by the Venetians as a fortress against the Empire at the end of the sixteenth century. A few years earlier, the French had built Philippeville and Rocroi on their Flemish borders. Glykstad on the Elbe, south of Hamburg, was laid out as two radiating half-hexagons early in the seventeenth century. All these were admired and visited by princes and engineers—but they were few in number and small in scale. The grid—implying a rational division of land—was still the dominant urban plan, however elaborately polygonal the defenses. And the grid plan, which goes back to the very oldest settlements, has remained the underlying scheme for most towns, promising not only order and clarity but equality in property distribution.

An obvious precedent for housing artisans was the asylum town built either to shelter Protestants fleeing persecution or to welcome foreign craftsmen. The most famous was probably the square, Freudenstadt, founded as a refuge by Duke Frederick of Württemberg about 1600. Different, but also manifestly ordered towns, such as the Sicilian towns of Noto, south of Syracuse, or hexagonal Grammichele, were built in the seventeenth century to settle refugees from earthquakes. The implication of all these enterprises was that the order established in the plan would in some not quite explicit way promote a rational social functioning among the inhabitants.

That had also been the motive of the many princes and builders who in the late sixteenth and the early seventeenth centuries produced various projects for more or less regularly planned, orthogonal and radial polygonal fortified towns defended by earthwork ramparts. Their orderliness, obsessively repeated, was in itself a utopian polemic against the messy and cramped towns in which their contemporaries lived. Unlike such exotic seventeenth- and eighteenth-century utopias as Bacon's *New Atlantis* or Campanella's *City of the Sun*, these projects were not just provocations; many of them were actually built. Mannheim, on the confluence of the Neckar and the Rhine, in western Germany, was laid out as a chessboard within oval ramparts over an earlier foundation that the French had razed in 1689. Its north side was a huge palace, while each row of blocks was identified from the palace southward by letters, the blocks numbered east and west in each row. In America streets, not rows, were so numbered. Also planned in that way during those two hundred years were Livorno in Tuscany, Vitry-le-François, Göteborg, Zamość in Poland, Valletta on Malta—also Pondicherry in India, and Batavia (now Jakarta) on Java. Many older towns had in any case to be modified, since the old city walls of stone or brick were no defense against the new weapons, which used gunpowder and iron projectiles instead of slings, catapults, and stones.

Louis XIV and his minister, Jean-Baptiste Colbert, were energetic builders of star-shaped fortified towns on the edges of the kingdom, for which they had the services of one of the great military geniuses of all time, Sébastien Le Prestre de Vauban, who laid out Neuf-Brisach, Montdauphin, Colmar, Longwy, and Saarlouis, always as grid layouts within the polygon; only at Charleroi did Vauban toy with a radiating layout. For all their commitment to fortification, Louis XIV and Colbert realized that the old walls of Paris were of no use in modern warfare, while their distrust of the Parisians did not make refortifying the capital a priority. The defenses were therefore dismounted in two campaigns, in 1670 and 1676, and the ramparts replaced by continuous tree-lined avenues. This *cours*, which was to encircle the city, came to be called *boulevard* later. Vauban had wished to replace the old Paris defenses with much more extensive ones; but this was carried out only in the 1840s—a century and a half later—in the reign of the bourgeois king, Louis Philippe.

The Parisian innovation of the boulevard gradually became an important element of the modern city all over the world, and a general term for wide, tree-lined streets in many languages. Where surviving earth ramparts in other towns were not dismounted, they became peacetime promenades. The example of Paris was followed all over Europe— notably in Vienna, where the *Ring* of encircling boulevards became, after 1830, the most important feature of the city. The Parliament, the University and Town Hall, the Opera and the Court Theater, the Palace, Museums, the Law Courts, and many other public buildings—each with its own open space—were sited there.

In the Spanish New World, meanwhile, the very first urban plan was Hernan Cortés's rebuilding of Mexica-Tenochtitlán, which he had conquered and destroyed in 1521. He had it reconstructed a few months later on the grid plan of the Aztec capital, and it remains the basis of the present city. Ten years later Francisco Pizarro recorded that when he founded the town of San Miguel in Peru, which did not prosper, he laid it out "according to the rule, with a central square." Other conquistadors founded colonies, almost all planned orthogonally, whether on earlier native foundations like Cuzco or on virgin land like Buenos Aires, Lima, Guatemala, or Santiago de Chile. King Philip II had promulgated the "Laws of the Indies," based on ancient Roman surveying practices, to guide such foundations, and these royal decrees specified a grid plan as the standard layout of any new settlement. Even before the laws were issued it was quite usual in many Spanish towns to site such important institutional buildings as the main church, law courts, mayor's or governor's residence— and a place for public executions—around a central square. The French followed a similar plan with New Orleans and St. Louis. An echo of those regulations can be found in the plans of the *reducciones,* the cooperative villages with collective housing that the Jesuits established throughout Paraguay and Bolivia to shelter Indians from the rapacious, overbearing Spanish landowners and the oppressive authority of both church and state. The *reducciones* were disbanded when the Jesuits were expelled from the Spanish empire in 1772, but their shells, many of which are still inhabited in Argentina, Chile, Peru, and Bolivia, survive.

The English-speaking settlers of North America had neither the historicizing nor the ceremonial pretensions of the French or the Spanish. The cities of Latin America had not only been planned, they were tightly controlled by the government and the church, which put their mark on the town and brought learning. Between 1550 and 1600, universities were founded in Lima, Mexico, and Bogotá, and Córdoba in Argentina. The University of Mexico, which taught both the Nahuatl and the Otomi languages, had a library of ten thousand volumes—bigger than many European universities at the time. The Puritans who arrived in New England in the seventeenth century and the royalists who settled in Virginia had meager ideas about building or planning or institutions. The Indians of North America, however, unlike those of Central and South America, had not only built orthogonal settlements but large collective dwellings—mounds—which are strewn over a vast area south of the Great Lakes. These mounds were up to a thousand feet in length or diameter and they were of a very different plan: some were square or circular, others in the shape of birds or quadrupeds or serpents. They seem to have been abandoned by the time the Europeans arrived. The Indians of the Plains, whom the European settlers did encounter, were mostly nomadic, though perhaps descended from the mound builders. At any rate, these settlers never took any interest in the mounds, and certainly never considered taking them over.

Though the English-speaking settlers had left their home country in protest, they were inevitably influenced by conditions there. And London provided the one outstanding exception in the great European effort at rationalization. When much of the City burned in the Great Fire of 1666, several, mostly rectilineal, plans were drawn up by prominent experts. The most famous one, by Sir Christopher Wren—in which an orthogonal grid is broken by oblique radiating avenues—proposed a plan for rebuilding the City, which interweaved avenues in the way the French had perfected in the park context as at Chantilly and Versailles. The citizens' ferocious attachment to their property rights ended any possibility of "rationalized" improvement, so all attempts at planning were abandoned. The City of London therefore remained a medieval warren.

Avenues radiating obliquely to the right-angled grid of older street-layouts had in any case become the model for all later urban projects after the grandiose and much publicized replanning of Rome carried out with unprecedented speed by Pope Sixtus V during his brief reign from 1585 until 1590. He linked the main monuments of the city with wide, straight roads and marked their junctions by monuments—mostly columns and obelisks, such as the one in the Piazza del Popolo—which were crucially situated, not necessarily at the center of an open space, to provide focal points for vistas, and marks that pilgrims could easily identify. The pope meant those fixed points to organize movement—specifically the path and processions of pilgrims between the seven most important Roman basilicas. But his roads also had to be sauntering streets, and part of Sixtus's policy was favoring builders with the offer of considerable tax inducements for new shopkeepers and craftsmen.

Planners of cities as well as of formal gardens—witness Wren—increasingly adopted the papal approach of associating oblique vista avenues with orthogonal plans. Versailles and Marly and their emulations all over Europe were newly planted in Wren's lifetime, but were fully grown a century later. "Whoever knows how to lay out a park," wrote Abbé Laugier, one of the most popular and influential of mid-eighteenth-century architectural theorists, "will have no trouble in drawing up the plan according to which a town is to be built with regard to its extent and the site. . . . It will need regularity and fantasy, associations and oppositions, random incidents to introduce variety, great regularity in the detail, and confusion, clash and ferment in the whole."[4] He could write this, confident that his readers knew exactly what sort of park he was talking about. The combination of orthogonal and oblique would then become the basis of L'Enfant's Washington project thirty years later and consequently one of the commonplaces of modern urban planning.

But this relaxed approach to the city received a sharp jolt from the group of engineers and architects who were trained by an institution founded just after the French Revolution to provide France with essential technicians at a time of crisis but which has endured until now to form very many of its technocrats, the Ecole Polytechnique. The School at first only prepared students for specialized engineering, but quickly became one of the most powerful and exemplary teaching bodies in the world, like the Ecole Normale Supérieure which was founded about the same time to teach humanities and social sciences. Their alumni, the *Polytechniciens* and the *Normaliens,* became the nucleus of the French intellectual elite and have remained so ever since.

For nearly thirty years an architect called Jean-Nicolas-Louis Durand taught the *Polytechniciens* architecture as part of the engineering course. His pupils were all state-funded, uniformed, noncommissioned officers and the method he taught was clear and very schematic: it depended on his belief that all building forms fell into three classes. The lowest were those determined by the "nature of materials" and the process of manufacture. The highest were those of geometry, among which the cube and the sphere were the most perfect. In between, and providing a bridge and a mediation, were those derived from history, and they included all ornament. Chinese, Arab, Indian, and Gothic forms were allowed equal validity, though the architecture of Greco-Roman antiquity was given tacit preference. Nothing about these forms, Durand insistently told his students, could be considered as having value other than that of satisfying the demands of habit: any account of their origins or implications was indifferent to the architect; they were to be treated as the paper over the crack between the perfection of geometry and the contingencies of material. This detached, abstract view of ornament coincided with the first attempts to mass-produce it cast in metal, in various synthetic stones, plaster or terra-cotta as a commercial proposition.

More important for the future of urban form was Durand's teaching about how to design. It was a clear method, reduced to a diagrammatic four-step procedure:

1. You examined and analyzed the client's demands first.
2. You then drew the main cross axes of the plan and whatever the program you had analyzed.
3. You set out the elements your analysis provided as a grid pattern oriented on the axes.
4. Having done that, you set columns first and then walls on the grid lines.

This procedure also became the basis of teaching at the Ecole des Beaux-Arts, where two of Durand's associates and Napoléon's court architects, Pierre Fontaine and Charles Percier, made it their own, and that of their colleagues and successors, and it became the model for architectural schools in the Old World and in the New.

Durand's approach was already implicit in the *Plan des Artistes*, the revolutionary project for the transformation of Paris that was drawn up by a committee that sat from 1793 to 1797 (through the Reign of Terror, 1793–94). It suggested the piercing of a number of avenues, as well as the creation of traffic circles: one at the Bastille, now the site of a bronze memorial column and a new opera house, and another at the Etoile where the Arc de Triomphe now stands. The biggest one was to be to the south of the city, where the meridian of Paris—as in Greenwich—passed through the local observatory and was to be crossed over by two avenues. It was part of a bid to make Paris the geographic world center. Although the plan was drawn up before Durand began his teaching at the Ecole Polytechnique, the Plan des Artistes demanded exactly the sort of architecture that he was inciting his students to design.

The burden of this teaching—the declared purpose of the whole Polytechnique project of social betterment through technology—required the rationalizing of urban planning so that the whole building process could become the medium of the social engineer. In that sense, the enterprise was implicitly utopian. The methods that the Polytechnique taught were so clear, simple, and almost self-evident that they have remained the tacit and unquestioned assumptions of many planners and architects. Even if acceptance was not universal—and there was disagreement, particularly from historians—Durand's doctrine is still implicit in much urban planning and urban design. His name is no longer familiar, and the origin of his ideas is often forgotten, but the impact remains and is therefore systematically underestimated.

This obsessional interest in axial planning had another effect on urban space. In the past, many open gathering places—squares and other public areas—would have a central decorative object placed in them. Occasionally, elsewhere, as in the Parisian Place Royale—renamed des Vosges by Napoléon—a statue of Louis XIII would be so set that Henry IV's commercial and ceremonial intention for that square was traduced. Louis XIV reared his horse at the center of the circular Place des Victoires; a modestly sized statue of his great-grandson, Louis XV, became the focus of what eventually turned into the extensive Place de la Concorde in the eighteenth century, and was replaced by the figure of the Republic that faced the guillotine during the Reign of Terror. An Egyptian obelisk and fountains took their place there under Louis Philippe.

These are not the type of open spaces that appear in the kind of axial planning instituted by the *Polytechniciens*. Their wide roads were arteries (this anatomical term moved to transportation in the nineteenth century) only for circulation. The buildings that lined them tended to be elevated and colonnaded—forbidding and isolated objects, not participants in a city pattern or city texture. Besides, the columns that decorated these buildings provided the kind of masking surface which Durand demanded. Using conventional ornament as a masking agent (sometimes to a quite overwhelming degree) was to be important throughout the nineteenth century, which was also the great age of new building types: the factory and the railway station, the department store, the grand hotel, and the office building, which turned into the skyscraper. Ornament often disguised intrusive novelty, as Durand suggested, and he only allows its presence to satisfy habit and convention.

The Polytechnique doctrine had a utopian dimension and was formulated in a city that had pretensions to stately grandeur, even if it was not altogether ordered. Ironically enough, it was in chaotic, property-obsessed London that Sir Thomas More had, a century and a half before the Great Fire, initiated Utopia as a literary genre, and any number of emulations were published between his time and the Industrial Revolution. In these writings on religious and ethnic tolerance, cleanliness, and safety, a great deal of attention is devoted to the exact organization of society. However, the fabric of the ideal city was not often given close attention, but when it was, its shape was almost always regular. More's own Amaurote, the capital city of Utopia, was "almost four-square"; Tommaso Campanella's *City of the Sun* was circular; Valentin Andreae's *Christianopolis* square again. Francis Bacon's *New Atlantis* does not have a definite outer shape, though much attention is devoted to the individual buildings and even the dress of the inhabitants; but François Rabelais' *Abbey of Thélème* is hexagonal. Gabriel de Foigny's *Terra Australis* has square cities,[5] and there were several more shapely utopias written during the eighteenth century—located in Africa, Australia, the

Pacific, and even in some chronologically unspecified future. Yet these books were not really written with any definite idea of providing particular plans for future settlements, nor were colonies founded to emulate them.

These writers were primarily concerned with a return to nature, which they often presented as an account of an idealized society discovered in some remote part of the world. The "state of nature" meant freedom from social convention, irksome labor, and often sexual inhibitions, and it even licensed promiscuity. They rarely considered actually applying their ideas in an experimental settlement; their societies already existed in some ideal and perfect exotic place, no doubt in the South Pacific, where travel writers had implied the most appetizing fruit grew on every tree and equally appetizing maidens were to be had for the asking. Utopian writers recognized that the resulting unions would produce children, however, and education in social skills without the trammels of family life was one of their principal concerns. It made them reflect on the difference between nature and nurture.

Without wishing to imitate any utopias, some reformers thought that the distance that the ocean crossing guaranteed would provide the condition for establishing an ordered, rational, and benevolent settlement that might in the end improve society in general. Land seemed unconfined in North America, while religious toleration, in short supply in the Old World, might be the one great benefit of all this openness. Many more or less religious groups followed the first Puritan emigrations, as did many secular settlers (and even some convicts, before some of that traffic was rerouted to Australia and Polynesia). The newly founded towns required some form of regulation, though this rarely indicated their general shape, but were concentrated on such matters as distances between single buildings and their relation to the street. Of course, some of these new towns also brought with them the constricting attitudes of sectaries who established their own rules of intolerance in this new context—witness Salem in Massachusetts.

The English Quaker statesman and philanthropist William Penn founded Philadelphia, which means "brotherly love" in Greek, in 1682 as an enclave of religious toleration and of peace with the Indians. Penn and his surveyor, Thomas Holme, planned a whole new city as an elongated rectangular grid stretching from east to west between two rivers, the Delaware and the Schuylkill. There were to be buildings fronting both rivers, so that the city edges would be defined from the outset, and its fabric might grow inward. The central square, at the crossing of the two main streets, was to have the town hall. A subsidiary wooded and parklike square would be at the center of each quarter. Detailed planning of the blocks in this grid was not provided, though many of them were to be articulated by terrace houses of various sizes with gardens between them. As it was, the city started growing from the eastern end, and the first city hall was located there, near the Delaware. Though Penn and Holme intended to build it on one side, it was moved in 1871 to occupy the whole central square when the city had grown further. A large public space was not a requirement of urban life in the United States at the time. On the other hand, the founders' intelligent land policy, which involved a parceling out of the surrounding territory and the planting of a village at the center of each circumscribed lot on the very fertile Pennsylvania soil, ensured a measure of prosperity, as did the excellent port in the estuary of the Delaware. The toleration that its very name proclaimed attracted a number of quasi-independent religious or ethnic groups into the city and its dependencies, so that by 1800 Philadelphia was the second-largest city of the English-speaking world, after London.

In contrast, further south, in Carolina, Sir Robert Montgomery of Skelmorlie was given vast lands and named governor of the province in 1717/18. He planned a square colony, which he called the margravate of Azilia: a fortified square, twenty miles to a side, of low-density housing and plantations surrounding a square town, which was in turn cut by diagonal avenues in the middle with a palace for the "margrave" or governor. It was a beautifully engraved and monstrously ambitious scheme, but his grant of land lapsed. In 1733 Samuel Johnson's friend Colonel James Oglethorpe was commissioned by King George II to found Savannah in Georgia as a refuge for British debtors and paupers, though it was also to act as a defense against the Spaniards and the Indians and later the French. In Oglethorpe's Savannah, blocks were internally planned with two rows of terraces separated by an area of gardens and a common square. Savannah was given a long-term development plan, which was maintained for over a century, and it remains a showpiece. It was almost coincidental that Oglethorpe took the Wesley brothers (Charles as his secretary) with him. Although neither Charles nor John found him at all easy to get on with, and they returned to England after a few years, the journey out led to a contact with some Moravian Brethren—whose impact proved essential to the development of Methodism, which the Wesley brothers founded on their return.

The Moravian Brethren, who moved from Moravia to Saxony, were a factious Episcopalian Protestant group persecuted by the Imperial authorities. They were led by a carpenter, Christian David, who became the architect of the sober, dignified buildings in Herrnhut, where the local landlord, Count Nicolaus Ludwig von Zinzendorf (1700–60) welcomed them. Zinzendorf reconciled their differences, gave them his own theological beliefs, and was therefore regarded as the new founder of the group. Since they considered themselves missionaries to other churches, as well as to the heathen, rather than a sect, their small numbers are not an indication of their influence. They came to America in 1741 and settled over much of Pennsylvania, New England, and Carolina. They also settled in the Midwest, where missions to the Indians were an essential part of their work, as well as in Mexico, Alaska, Greenland, and Surinam.

Throughout the eighteenth century, many other more or less extreme religious groups looked to the wide open spaces of a New World. Moravian settlements were emulated. Whatever their religious or political beliefs, they did have one thing in common: their towns and villages were intended to last, and that made many of these settlers model agriculturalists and horticulturalists; since some felt that they were re-creating paradise on Earth—a garden of Eden—they became very assiduous orchard keepers. This was in strong contrast to the more secular farmers who, in moving slowly westward, practiced a form of slash-and-burn cultivation, and relied on the resale value of their exhausted land for profit to bolster any income they might obtain from their farm produce.

Of the many sectarian groups of this period, one of the most famous followed Mother Ann (Lee) from Manchester, England in 1774 to settle at Mount Lebanon, near Albany, New York. Known as the Shaking Quakers, or Shakers, they preached a public confession of sin, and advocated community of goods and total sexual abstinence, with separate dormitories for men and women. Their ecstatic prayers involved energetic dancing (hence the sect's name) and meetings that were so persuasive that by 1800 they had six thousand members scattered in settlements in New York state, Massachusetts, and Kentucky. In the twentieth century their numbers fell, and although the last faithful died out in the 1970s, the fine, spare buildings and the equally spare but very well made furniture and household objects are testimony to a century and a half of productive activity. Their conviction that each believer is a "living building," and their practice of "social architecture," show the importance they attached to the formal discipline of their design as a part of religious practice. A parallel ambition of many sects was the re-creation of the temple in Jerusalem—attempted twice by the Mormons, for instance—or even the building of the "New Jerusalem," according to

Saint John's specification in the Apocalypse, which suggests one reason why many of these communities had such a strong preference for grid planning.

Many other religious groupings of various inspiration were to move to the New World: in Pennsylvania there were settlements of German Anabaptists (or Pennsylvania Dutch—nothing to do with Holland, "Dutch" here being merely a corruption of *Deutsch*), some called Mennonites, others Amish after their sixteenth-century leaders. They have maintained their language and forms of dress and the old farming methods, rejecting all nineteenth-century technology (particularly agricultural machinery), as well as artificial fertilizers, and will have nothing to do with steam and combustion engines, though some will accept electricity. They hold extreme views about worship, predestination, and purity of life and doctrine, so that excommunication is an important feature of their social life; some groups avoid any contact with the outside world, whereas others are happy to mix, on their own terms, and provide a link and outlet for the others. Because of the rising taste for "organic" foods in the last two decades of the twentieth century, their produce has been in constant demand and their commercial success has provoked the jealousy of neighboring conventional farmers. Through the nineteenth century many other groups arrived to found settlements: there were Zoarites in Ohio, Hutterites in South Dakota (after 1870), and Inspirationists in Ohio, who founded a series of rectilineal villages. There were Spiritualists in upstate New York, Harmonists—and many others. Several thousand pacifist Doukhobors, persecuted in Russia for several generations, were allowed to leave for Canada in 1895 and settled at various points of Saskatchewan. Many of these settlements were intended to set an example to others, being missionary, even if they did not always claim to have achieved a fully preconceived or even a clearly outlined utopia.

But the political pamphlets or "science fiction" of secular utopian agitators of the industrial age show how eager they were to work out their projects in practice. Their optimistic calculations were based on the notion that once centers of a new social order were established, on however modest a scale, they would act as a leaven to the whole social body whose many problems they would resolve. Their agitation often took on the allure of a missionary endeavor, and in that they emulated some of the character of those religious settlements that tended to have a more extended and settled life. The communities that they founded looked for an asylum that could free its inhabitants from social constraint as well as from the pressures of the market economy. Although they had no taste for eighteenth-century "naturist" exoticism, it seemed to many of them that in order to succeed they had to settle on virgin territory, free of the shackles and limitations imposed by the dysfunctional society about them.

Some reformers were so daunted by the vastness of the problem as well as by the confusion and the complexities of the various remedies that were being proposed that they concentrated their efforts on remedying one or another of the most obvious defects of the city. A rationally conceived social order incorporated in a city plan, for instance, seemed to offer a rather old-fashioned cure for conceptual chaos. In 1848 the traveler, parliamentarian, and temperance agitator James Silk Buckingham drew up a plan for a type of mile-square town, zoned outward by square streets, some of which were to be glazed arcades: power and riches were to reside in the center, so that both class and income decreased toward the perimeter. The cheapest and socially lowest ring would include workshops and open out to the country "which is favourable to their health, and, being close to their workshops, is also favourable to the economy of their time and labour." This clear and ordered arrangement would outlaw such vices as gin shops, beer halls, and brothels, and limit—perhaps even remove—social tensions altogether.[6]

More realistic reformers, appalled by wretched housing, the rising incidence of tuberculosis, and other epidemics, felt a healthy environment was more important. Already in 1827 the prolific architect, planner and landscape designer John Buonarotti Papworth had proposed a residential town on the other side of the Ohio River from Cincinnati, to be called Hygeia, after the Greek goddess of health—but this came to nothing. Some fifty years later, Sir Benjamin Richardson, a pioneer of anesthesia, humane slaughter, cremation—and generally of public health—published a proposal for a city of one hundred thousand inhabitants, also to be called Hygeia, that was strictly regulated to prohibit smoking and the consumption of alcoholic beverages. The population density was to be low—twenty-five persons an acre—and the sanitary provisions and the planting very generous. Wall-to-wall carpeting and overfurnishing was banned, Turkish baths and tiled bathrooms would be introduced; although the proposal started life as a paper at a conference, it was published as a pamphlet and widely debated. Sir Ebenezer Howard, the father figure of the garden city movement, was inspired by it when he drew up his project.

These rather naive ideas for reforming housing were overshadowed by thoroughgoing proposals to reconstitute the whole socioeconomic structure to make it easier to deal with the impact of the new industrial forces. The revolutionary thinkers of the second half of the nineteenth century read such proposals assiduously and had to come to terms with them. Marx and Engels singled out Robert Owen and two French "utopian socialists," Claude de Saint-Simon and Charles Fourier, for special attention. These were indeed the most prominent proto-socialists, though the solutions they advocated were very different. Their ideas were linked to fostering associations that would transform society, while Marx and Engels were concerned with the working class assuming power. It is perhaps not surprising that, like Marx and Engels, Prince Peter Kropotkin, one of the founding fathers of the anarchist movement, saw the trio as the progenitors of the different workers' movements of his own time: Saint-Simon of Social Democracy, Owen of the trade union movement, and Fourier of anarchism.

The first of these three offered to reorganize society as well as industrial production. Robert Owen, the son of a Welsh craftsman-shopkeeper, was born in 1771, and turned out to be a managerial infant prodigy. By age nineteen he was running a large mill near Manchester, where he improved both the conditions of his workmen and the spinning process to produce, reputedly, the best cotton in England. On a working visit to Scotland Owen met and in 1799 married a Miss Dale, whose father, banker David Dale, had started a mill in 1784 with Richard Arkwright at New Lanark on the Clyde. Owen bought the mill, which was powered by the falls of the river, and attempted to apply his ideas about organization to it. He limited working hours, improved the housing, started a nonprofit company shop, and contributed to its commercial success by creating a cooperative workforce. However, when he attempted to reduce the returns on investment, his shareholders protested, prompting him to buy the shares and form a new company with the utilitarian thinker Jeremy Bentham and the Quaker physicist-politician William Allen. These early experiences turned him into a theoretician and a propagandist. A philanthropic as well as a great commercial success, New Lanark soon received a stream of visitors: statesmen, social reformers, even Grand Duke Nicholas, later known as the "Iron Czar" Nicholas I. Owen was often consulted on economic measures and legislation, and his pamphlets were widely read by kings and their ministers, by the president of the United States, and even by Napoléon in exile on Elba.

Despite all the warnings, Britain and its government were unprepared for the economic crisis after 1815, at the end of the Napoleonic wars. A vast national debt had to be fed by recurrent taxes, and the returning soldiers and sailors encountered an army of the unemployed, farmers, spinners, and weavers. Owen offered a solution to the problem: a plan for model settlements based on his New Lanark experience. He designed one himself for twelve hundred inhabitants, which he thought should have between one thousand and fifteen hundred acres, primarily of agricultural land, to make it self-sufficient. Each family would have a four-room house without a kitchen, since eating was communal. The houses formed three sides of a square and on the fourth side were dormitories for the older children, an infirmary, and a guest house. There would also be houses for the teachers, the doctor, and other officials, as well as a cooperative store. A long central building articulated the square: it was for the administration, kitchens, and refectory; adjoining it to the left was a school building for infants (children after the age of three would be communally raised, though with access to their families), with a lecture room and a chapel on an upper floor. To the right was the school for older children, with committee and meeting rooms as well as common rooms and a library. The interior of the square was planted with trees as a park. Separated from the main square by more plantings were industrial buildings, a slaughterhouse, stables, and so on.

Started as a project for the abolition of pauperism, Owen's scheme was soon advocated as a general solution to the problems of the modern city. He himself took an extreme position about the influence of nurture over nature; the "formation of character," he believed, was always imposed by environment, so that schooling was the primary concern of his organization, and it made him one of the founders of the infant school movement in Britain. Together with his enthusiastic disciples, he soon set about realizing the scheme: the first was at Orbiston, near Glasgow, and immediately afterward at New Harmony in Indiana, where he bought thirty thousand acres of land, farm equipment, and the cattle of a small Protestant group called the Rappists after their founder, George Rapp, or the Harmonists after their ideals. But Owen had greater ambitions, and engaged a youngish architect, Thomas Stedman Whitwell—who died in 1840, but is now remembered chiefly for having built an iron-roofed theater, the Brunswick at Whitechapel in London, which collapsed after three days, killing several people—to design a new central-square building. While it does not quite correspond to Owen's specifications, it gives a stronger indication of what was intended than did Owen's own rather schematic drawing of the physical appearance that he sought.

New Harmony stood for the emancipation of women and slaves, as well as humane working conditions and equal schooling for all children. At its high point, there were about a thousand settlers. Unfortunately many of them were scientists, literary men, and educationalists rather than craftsmen and farmers. Much discussion and even dissension ensued; some settlers seceded to found their own enclaves, and after two years Owen had to admit ruin (he had invested much of his capital there) as well as defeat; but even though he returned to London, three of his sons stayed in America, one of them, Robert Dale Owen, becoming a congressman responsible for progressive legislation.

Although some later short-lived communities were founded on his model—in Hertfordshire, in Galway, and about thirty more in the United States—he himself settled in London, and attracted a circle of political and literary figures. It may well be that in this circle the term "socialist"—as a cant synonym of "Owenist"—was first used sometime before 1835; the word appears in 1832–33 both in France and in England. When Owen had been in America, a group of his Lancashire followers had started a cooperative store in Rochdale, usually regarded as the origin of the cooperative movement that is sometimes called the working-class equivalent of the joint-stock company, though it soon lost any revolutionary coloring and survived as a great commercial enterprise. Owen's immediate impact was on education and on factory legislation; his permanent achievement was this cooperative movement.

The second of Marx and Engels's trio, the Comte de Saint-Simon, was a kinsman of the equally famous duke of the same name who had written the sparkling, very spiteful account of the court at Versailles a century earlier. In his late teens, Saint-Simon had fought in the American Revolutionary War (to defend, he later said, industrial liberty), and unlike most French nobility not only welcomed the Revolution, which ruined his family, but on being released from prison at the end of the Reign of Terror, actually made a large fortune by speculating in mostly church land—enough to live extravagantly and to support scientific research as well as his own generally short-lived schemes. As for his family background, he had little nostalgic interest in it, though he did think that being a descendant of Charlemagne suited him particularly to the job of uniting Europe. The concept of social class was really first formulated in his circle, and Saint-Simon looked to the enterprising manufacturers, bankers, scientists, and technician-engineers to rule the new industrial society. The lawyers and "metaphysicians," he thought, having done their useful work of destruction, had ruined the 1789 revolution, which they had created, by neglecting finance and industry and prattling on about liberty. The newly powerful, the scientists and technicians, would be a different clerisy and politics would be "reduced" to a science based on their methods. Instead of fighting, the two great industrial powers, England and France, should associate, and be joined, when the time came, by a united Germany governed by a European parliament. Saint-Simon's munificence and his experiments so impoverished him that in old age he was penniless; an attempted suicide led to the loss of an eye (and to an allowance from admirers for the rest of his life). He then moved on to a quasi-religious conviction—which he set out in his *Nouveau Christianisme,* published in 1825, the year of his death—about the nature of human sympathy. It was, he maintained, the only possible basis for all human association. Although Saint-Simon sometimes thought of himself as a religious leader, it was a group of his followers that set up a semi-monastic community first in central Paris, then at Ménilmontant, led by Barthélemy Prosper Enfantin, who, like another of the disciples, Saint-Amand Bazard, assumed the title of *Père* well after the founder's death. The coming scientific age was a divine revelation and would bring untold blessings to mankind; only the vesting of power in a clerisy-elite could result in beneficent social change. These disciples turned Saint-Simonism into a theosophic system with strange excrescences, like a forthcoming female messiah, and actually began promoting ideological settlements, mostly in Germany.

Like his contemporary, Hegel, Saint-Simon constructed a historical system and always maintained a belief in the gradual perfectibility of society. Of the "utopian socialists," to use Marx's label, Saint-Simon was the most accurate forecaster of the politics and economics of industry. Rational, worldwide territorial planning is implied in Saint-Simon's system, and it was that which his followers and particularly the most devoted secretary, "Père" Enfantin, enthusiastically advocated. There were two groups: the first, like Enfantin and Saint-Amand Bazard, were graduates of the Ecole Polytechnique. The other was a small coterie of Jewish bankers who applied Saint-Simon's doctrines to their fiscal policies in midcentury and under the Second Empire of Napoléon III. Without their manipulation of credit, the rebuilding of Paris under the Imperial prefect, Baron Georges-Eugène Haussmann, would not have been possible. They remained faithful to the master and paid for the publication of his complete works and for the maintenance of his tomb.

In the course of his travels, Enfantin met Ferdinand de Lesseps, a French consular official in Egypt, who was already familiar with Saint-Simon's ideas. They discussed a plan for a canal to link the Red Sea and the Mediterranean, through Cairo and Alexandria, which Lesseps tried to sell to the Vali of Egypt, Said Pasha, though it was finished under the first khedive, Ismail. The canny diplomat then carried the canal over a shorter route, supported by the Turkish government and other Saint-Simonian financiers. Lesseps later became involved in Saint-Simon's other proposed canal, linking the Atlantic and Pacific. Such a scheme had been discussed desultorily since the sixteenth century, but was initiated through Panama by French enterprise; it was not finished until 1915, having been ceded to the United States.

Many of Saint-Simon's projects have been accomplished—the canals he proposed, for instance, were built. Many of his prophecies have been fulfilled—more or less—and we live in the meritocratic, managerial, free-market society that he foresaw. Which leaves a real problem in describing and commenting on his teaching nowadays—since all that has not brought us the social harmony and the universal prosperity that this fulfilment promised.

Auguste Comte, the most influential of Saint-Simon's disciples intellectually, had been his secretary for some years and was another *Polytechnicien*. As he had been very close to the master, with whom he broke just before Saint-Simon's death, there followed a generation of recrimination about influence and even plagiarism between Comte and the Saint-Simonians, who certainly held a number of beliefs in common, like the tripartite division of human history into animist, theological, and scientific phases. Comte had a much more systematic mind than Saint-Simon and is often considered the founder of sociology, the "scientific" study of society. This was to be a new kind of science, quite unlike the other physical ones. Biology was to be the model that differed from the older analytic sciences, which studied things by taking them apart. Comte's new science would be synthetic: it acknowledged that plants, animals, or society could not be separated into their parts, could not be dissected without radical alteration, and that observations had to be carried out on complete organisms.

Like Saint-Simon, Comte also believed that industrial and financial power had to be moderated by and sublimated to the spiritual. This led him to found a church of the Great Being, with ministers and services, which had missions in Britain and even more successful ones in Russia and Latin America, particularly in Brazil. That religiosity, which T. H. Huxley called "Catholicism without Christianity," grew from Comte's conviction that the exercise of power in society was inevitable, that it must be tempered by encouraging altruistic impulses, and that the social peace essential to progress depended on the acceptance by the body politic of a socioeconomic hierarchy and everybody's place in it.

Even though Comte had founded a philosophy and a church, he had not founded any settlements. His contemporary, Charles Fourier, the third of the Marx-Engels utopian socialists, had very different social concerns, which stemmed from his withering contempt for his own chaotic and barbarous times in general, and French bourgeois society in particular. He felt that the two most odious things about the civilization in which he lived were: first, the free market; and second, the institution of marriage.

Fourier's primary reforms are divided into two areas: the political (to do with duties), and the domestic (to do with pleasure). The distinction was crucial, since it was his principal contention—from which all his utopian strivings depended—that pleasure, *not reason,* must be the only sure basis on which any moral system can be built. He called pleasure "positive happiness," and it was primarily of two kinds: gastronomic and erotic—but they were always social, since sharing was part of the pleasure. Human passions—which he defined as the seeking of pleasure—are divided first into the five standard appetites, which correspond to the senses, but also into four simple affects of ambition, friendship, love, and parental feelings. There were, moreover, three distributive passions, which he called the cabalist, the composite, and the butterfly or alternating, basing his social organization on them. The cabalist passion is for intrigue and rivalry; the composite or interlocking is a desire for satisfaction, both of a sensory and spiritual kind, while the butterfly is passion for change and novelty. Properly articulated, 810 subcategories could be identified and that gave him the ideal number of interrelationships.

Something similar had been suggested by a slightly earlier polygraph and utopian, Nicolas Restif de la Bretonne, also known as "the Rousseau of the gutters." He had imagined himself flying to his eighteenth-century exotic realms in his *Découverte Australe.*[7] Like Fourier, Restif also loved categories and neologisms, as did another quasi-utopian, the infamous Marquis de Sade: everything had to be categorized and catalogued with a naturalist's thoroughness. The failures of business and marriage were, for instance, subdivided into thirty-six kinds of bankruptcy and forty-nine of cuckoldry.

All this cataloguing was essential, since Fourier believed men would not undertake work that they might otherwise find irksome unless organized into competing groups (cabalist passion) and working in short shifts (butterfly passions). Even the most disagreeable jobs could be managed pleasurably in such a society, as he shows in the much-quoted example of how trash would be collected. Children, who were, of course, to be socially nurtured and educated, he argued, love muck of all kinds. In the new society they might therefore be organized into what he calls "small hordes"—in brilliant uniforms, armed with fife and drum, mounted on ponies—to collect trash as an elaborate game. Their education would be varied; they would be taught gastronomy in the kitchens, particularly in the pastry kitchens, while social virtues would be taught by the performing of a total work of art, such as opera.

Future society would be organized to satisfy all appetites and passions, including those sexually "perverse," so no one would need to be repressed. It was to be based on the interplay of all the catalogued diversities, and therefore could not be egalitarian. In any case, a variety of income and status was necessary, since the participants would include a large proportion of craftsmen and farmers, and a much smaller number of artists, scientists, and financiers. Such an attempt to accommodate all possible stations and appetites, as Walter Benjamin has pointed out, would require interlocking with a machinelike precision.[8]

Fourier's view of history was also extremely precise: it covers a period of eighty thousand years, articulated into thirty-two clearly labeled and demarcated historical epochs. Fourier saw the time in which he lived as the end of the ascendant epoch, between the fifth epoch, which was a period of barbarian competition and conflict, and the sixth, guarantism, which will begin the era of complete social harmony. During this epoch, whose arrival he thought it his duty to hasten, men—he deduced from his premises—would develop extraordinary faculties: they would reach a height of seven feet, reach the age of one hundred forty-four years commonly; they would also develop an extra limb, a tail ending in a third eye. The passage from social chaos to harmony would, as he himself wrote, lead to thirty-five millennia of human well-being, after which the world would descend by a symmetrical sequence to the original chaos and misery. In the meanwhile, harmony would have astonishing ecological effects. With breathtaking scientific optimism, Fourier foresaw that the extension of agriculture would warm the globe and cause the expansion of the northern lights. The aurora borealis would become a much more extensive and near-permanent phenomenon, which would alter the chemistry of seawater, precipitating its "bituminous" component, neutralizing the salt, and turning it into something tasting like *aigre-de-cèdre* (a kind of citron drink, popular in France at the time). Marx admired Fourier's organizational proposals, but had no time for the vast cosmological system into which his utopian speculations had to fit.

Fourier was precise about the process of history and its environmental consequences, and equally precise and assertive in his prescriptions for the physical environment of the new society. The cities on which his vision depended were therefore specified in the greatest detail. He is the only one of the "secular" utopians who made his reforms integral with urban planning and the detailed design of his buildings, since the future organization of society was bound up with the provisions for its housing. His visionary project owed something to his childhood in Besançon, in eastern France, where Claude-Nicolas Ledoux—arguably the greatest single architect of the late eighteenth century—had been very active. The theater he designed for the town was built between 1778 and 1784, begun when Fourier was six and finished when he was twelve. In the preceding years Ledoux, as the architect of the royal salt works, had built a model factory half-circled with worker housing at Arc-et-Senans, just over ten miles south, as the first installment of a circular "ideal" town. As someone who in his later years used to go about with a tape measure to size up any building that interested him—and who wrote admiringly about Ledoux's buildings in Paris—Fourier could hardly have missed any of it. It is therefore not surprising that the city built at the passage from civilization to guarantism, the period which was just beginning, was planned in three circles: the center, which includes the public buildings, a second circle of large dwelling units, and the outer suburbs with farming. These circles were to be divided by green-belt planting, and the relation of building height to street width and the separation between buildings were precisely regulated and under the control of special town councillors who were given the pseudo-antique title, *édiles*. Old monasteries or palaces could be adapted for the smaller settlements at the initial stage of guarantism, but even large palaces or monasteries, such as Versailles or the Escorial, would just not be large enough to contain the true phalanstery, since each one would need to accommodate some fifteen hundred inhabitants as well as workshops and offices. Each building was planned as a recessed central block with advancing side wings, like Versailles. It was to be 360 fathoms long (2,160 feet—710 meters—almost twice the length of the palace at Versailles), and made up of five-story buildings, enclosing planted courtyards. The façades of the long blocks were broken at intervals by porticoes of giant columns as high as the whole building. The ground floor was for vehicular traffic and workshops; a mezzanine housed children and the aged, and above that were the common rooms and two stories of dwellings. All apartments, two rooms deep, were on the inside of the building, facing into the large, parklike private courtyards, while the outside of the building above the mezzanine was the glazed and heated public street, a kind of arcade rising the full four floors, which—in the full harmony period—was to be thirty-six feet wide. Noisy workshops, practicing musicians, and children's activities would be in one wing of the main building, the hostelry and other management quarters in the other. The main block had a "rich" section, various officers' quarters, and the exchange—where activities and passions, not stock or bonds, were traded. A theater and a church each had its independent pavilion. There was to be a large square before the phalanstery, while the outbuildings—stables, stores, workshops, poultry houses, and other utilities—were on the other side of the square, but connected to the main building by underground streets. It would not have been an architectural showpiece, if the published engraving is to be believed, though its organization is fascinating.

Finances were to be based on agriculture, chiefly market gardening, and secondly on industry—and here he differed from his utopian contemporaries. Production and economy were not the primary aim of the phalanstery, since Fourier insisted that *all* work should be both agreeable and voluntary. It was the notion of a society wholly organized for pleasure that, paradoxically perhaps, endeared him to Engels, as did his brilliant style. Engels thought him one of the greatest, if not the greatest satirist of world literature, and particularly enjoyed the phantasmagoric vocabulary of neologisms he devised to cover all the varieties of passion and human relations. His language games have nearly all been forgotten, and the only one of his terms to survive in French and Italian common parlance, phalanstery, has, ironically enough, come to mean a vast and barracklike building rather than the highly articulated pleasure palace of Fourier's proposals.

His first phalansteries were to have been set up by volunteers opting out of conventional society and would therefore be expensive. It was calculated that the contributions of his followers would need to amount to forty million francs (approximately £16,500,000 as against Owen's £96,000 in the currency of the time) if they were to buy the terrain, build and equip the phalanstery, and make it self-sustaining. For the jump start, Fourier, unlike the more modest Owen, looked to the great and the good of his time: the dukes of Devonshire and Northumberland, or the bankers, as Baring and Hope; such European princes as Czartoryski, Esterhazy, or Medina-Celi were also mentioned, but Fourier died before any financing came forth.

Fourier despised the Saint-Simonians for what he considered their joyless managerism. He never met the master, but having made one or two approaches to the followers, soon realized they were not going to go his way. He learned of Owen's experiments from the press, and soon established contact, though he and Robert Owen met only briefly at an official reception in 1837, the year Fourier died. There were certain similarities in their proposals: the scale of the settlement, the source of income, the planning of the terrain; and Fourier originally saw the work of Owen, who was only one year older, as a precursor of his own work. Fourier soon became disillusioned with Owen as well, since his program seemed too monastic and too egalitarian. The undifferentiated square plan of the Owenite settlements threatened to create both the chaos and tedium that his own project avoided. He condemned Owen as a charlatan.

A number of Fourier's followers continued to work toward some realization of his ideas. The subject was widely discussed, and the very popular novelist Eugène Sue, a Fourierist sympathizer, made the foundation of a phalanstery the theme of one of his novels. Victor Considérant, another *Polytechnicien* who left the army engineering services, led the Fourierists after the master's death. He interested a steel manufacturer, Jean-Baptiste Godin, who had a foundry at Guise, in Picardy just south of the Belgian frontier, and in 1859 the first stone of a modified phalanstery, the *familistère,* was laid. As its name implied, it did not aspire to the full gamut of Fourier's sexual exuberance, but limited itself to housing workers' families. Following Fourier's model, it was made up of three blocks, of which the center one was recessed, while the very long internal streets and parklike courtyards were replaced by a rather modest glazed internal square. The apartments now had kitchens, presupposing the family groupings that the new title promised, though baths, showers, and latrines were still shared. When Godin died, he left the building and the factories—which were producing heating equipment—to the workers as a cooperative, and it is still active. Though it has been much extended, it has retained its old buildings.

Like New Lanark, Guise attracted pilgrims and the curious—as well as emulation. Fourier had a strong following in America. Alfred Brisbane, who had met the Parisian Fourierists in his travels, came back and argued the Fourierist cause daily in the *New York Tribune.* As a result of his teaching, the "North American Phalanx" was founded in 1843 in Red Bank, New Jersey. It lasted for twelve years—plagued by fires and financial problems—since its tiny jump start was contributed by members and not by outside magnates. In Southport, Wisconsin, the "Wisconsin Phalanx" had an even shorter existence. In all there were thirty or more Fourierist foundations, which achieved various measures of success or failure.

There were also many "utopian" settlements of native American inspiration. Celebrated by Emerson and Hawthorne, Oneida in upstate New York had both a political and a religious tendency. It called itself bible-communist, preached "complex marriage" and the community of goods, as well as discipline by "mutual criticism" in regular meetings. Its market gardens prospered, and the invention of a new form of animal trap by one of the members led to a very successful hardware line. Oneida did have employees as well as members but it would not allow them to unionize, though it consistently paid higher wages and offered much better conditions than could be obtained elsewhere. It became a great financial success. Communal marriage was given up "in deference to public sentiment" in 1879, however, and in 1881 Oneida became a joint-stock company.

These settlements were the most famous and successful, but there were many others—some forty between the United States, Latin America, and Europe; Fourierist settlements, proto-phalansteries, went on being founded well into the twentieth century. Between 1910 and 1920, the first European electric steel mill at Ugine in the Savoie, on the French side of the Italian border, built a housing scheme for its workers run on cooperative principles. Although it was called the "phalanstery," and contained dwellings as well as a great deal of public space and communal enterprises, the management principles were only a pale reflection of Fourier's great project.

Of all their predecessors among the utopians, Marx and Engels were kindest to Etienne Cabet, whom they regarded as a proto-communist, while the others were mere socialists. His program involved the total control of land and an egalitarian view of society about which his fictional hero is lyrical in the *Voyage to Icaria*, which was published in 1840 in Paris. Cabet's novel had an impact similar to Fourier's writings. The circular city of Icaria, which his utopian society occupies, is traversed by a river with a central island much like Paris; unlike Paris it is laid out on a regular plan, and made up of standard housing units, their elements mass-produced, an early appeal to the efficacy of prefabrication. The economy is organized on the basis of universal conscription, standard wages, uniform clothes, and a complex credit system for those who wish to practice the nonconscript work of journalism, painting, and medicine. Cabet himself found France hostile after the July revolution of 1830, and he exiled himself to England, where he fell in with Owen, who, in spite of his own setbacks, encouraged him to settle in America. Cabet negotiated favorable conditions with the state of Texas, and in 1847 some fifteen hundred "Icarians" set out for Red River territory in the north of the state. The revolution of the next year in France, and the wretched conditions of the terrain, soon drove many of them back.

Undeterred, Cabet himself led another group to the United States in 1849. On finding that after the assassination of Joseph Smith the Mormons had vacated their bombarded settlement at Nauvoo, Illinois, on the Mississippi near Fort Madison—which already had a grid plan and a number of public buildings, including the first Mormon temple—the Icarians settled in the old buildings; but this venture was not much more successful than the Texas one. Cabet himself moved to Saint Louis, where he died in 1856. The Icarians went on to found more settlements, three in Idaho and another one in California: the last one to close its doors in Idaho did so in 1896.

Meanwhile the "associationist" utopians had come near the centers of power in France. Considérant, a number of Saint-Simonians, and other more or less socialist leaders were elected deputies after the fall of Louis-Philippe in 1848: under the leadership of the most energetic of the reformers, Louis Blanc, various measures, such as the creation of Cabetian nationalized workshops—employing, at one point, one hundred thousand workmen—were justified. Most of these radical programs were frustrated after the coup d'état of 1851 and the advent of Louis-Napoléon, the future Napoléon III, known as "the Little," even though he presented himself as "the workers' friend" and took a real interest in worker housing. Considérant, having lost his parliamentary seat, was invited by Brisbane and encouraged by Godin to travel to Texas to found another phalanstery, La Réunion, outside Dallas, but that also had a very short life.

Clearly the construction of utopias was a highly popular nineteenth-century occupation, especially in the United States:

> We are all a little mad here with numberless projects of social reform. Not a reading man but has a draft of a new community in his waistcoat pocket. I am gently mad myself, and am resolved to live cleanly,

wrote Ralph Waldo Emerson in 1840 to Thomas Carlyle, just before entering Brook Farm.[9] Some two hundred known model communities are recorded, involving about a hundred thousand persons directly. Many more went unrecorded, and most were started with the view of reforming society in general.

After the failure of the Second Empire and the cruel, disastrous end of the Commune of Paris of 1871, the writing of utopian solutions to social problems took a rather different turn. The commune had been the climax of those movements that had stirred public conscience and worried the heads of state of Europe and America in 1830 and 1848. The vision of violent social change to resolve the tensions and inequities of industrial society then receded. In the second half of the century, political and scientific utopias were composed, some by major authors: Samuel Butler considered a society in which crime was medically treated, while disease was punished—and music instead of money kept in banks. Jules Verne wrote a number of visionary accounts of what scientific developments would allow humanity to accomplish. None of these prophetic visions—from which the more recent "science fiction" descends—was intended as a model for improved new settlements.

In the 1880s, an American writer, Edward Bellamy, had taken up the eighteenth-century narrative device of waking up his contemporary observer in some hypothetically remote and future time to provide an account of society in the year 2000. His novel *Looking Backward* (1888), tells of the hypnotically induced dream of a Bostonian of his own time, who wakes up after a century's sleep to find himself in a society that is technologically advanced but morally and politically inert. The United States, Bellamy foresaw, would have constituted itself into a corporation owning the land and all means of production, with all work based on a system of conscription, all payment being standard, while merit would be rewarded with honors and rank. This working society he likens to a well-drilled army when it is commanded by a great general like von Moltke. Deserters would not be tolerated; those "opting out" would find themselves in solitary confinement on bread and water until they were "reintegrated." The sexes were to be equal, since technology would have delivered women from household chores; all cooking would be done centrally and delivered to homes, while cleaning was to be done by contract workers. And there were other technological innovations: music would be piped directly to houses, money abolished, and all exchanges effected by credit cards. Bellamy was eagerly read, and societies were even founded to make his vision real. Of all Bellamy's readers—and he was a popular, if not a very engaging writer—the most important no doubt was William Morris, the one man whose vast energy welded Ruskin's notion of work, more specifically manual work, to Marx's economic teachings. Within months of the book's appearance in the United States, Morris had reviewed Bellamy's book rather negatively in *The Commonweal,* the organ of the Socialist League, which he edited with Edward Aveling, Karl Marx's son-in-law. Morris hated the militaristic analogy, the conscription, the technological wizardry, and his *News from Nowhere*—which was serialized in 1890 and became a book in 1891—was his response. Again it is a future, but in England this time. The visionary is a young nineteenth-century socialist from Hammersmith in London, where Morris lived at the time, who sees the end of the twentieth century. It is an England transformed by a violent and bloody and—by the time of the narrative—only vaguely remembered revolution in 1952 (Bellamy's revolution had been gradual, peaceful—and long). Capitalism and parliamentary government have been overthrown (the Houses of Parliament have been turned into a dung heap) in favor of a loose federation based on local democracy—a free-exchange market and social ownership of land as well as the means of production—all of which Morris called Communist. The problems of overproduction and consequent market fluctuations are dealt with by a drastic reduction of work hours. This combines to produce a beatifically happy and beautiful world—or at any rate does so in England—a world of handsome and healthy artist-craftsmen. Morris's book may have been less accurate as a forecast, but was—and has remained—much more popular than Bellamy's, though Bellamy, now forgotten, was a best-seller in his own time and his book did go through several editions.

Morris himself was a great artist-craftsman and a prolific, if not always successful, entrepreneur. A convinced Marxist, he collaborated with Engels and was familiar with past utopian literature. He admired Owen and New Lanark, where the workmen regained their natural dignity and which seemed to him a foretaste of the society he depicted in *News*. With Fourier he shared the principle that all work was to be play, though he learned it from Ruskin and Carlyle, and to Marx he owed above all the idea of the class struggle and his theory of value. He also read Henry George, the American disciple of the French Physiocrats. They are welded together in the vision of a society more anarchic than socialist, where work as play inevitably results in a beautiful environment, and children are discouraged from writing too early,

> because it gets them into a habit of ugly writing. . . . You understand that handsome writing we like, and many people will write their books out . . . I mean books of which only a few copies are needed—poems and such like.[10]

Morris never founded a settlement, though he did have highly organized work teams as well as shops in which his products were sold. But there were many spin-offs, like the relatively long-lived "simple-life" craft community at Chipping Campden in Gloucestershire, led by Charles

Robert Ashbee, and the various attempts at forming a guild socialist political movement, which nonetheless never entered the mainstream of labor politics.

On the other hand, one of the last truly optimistic utopians, Theodor Hertzka, did propose that a settlement be founded based on his principles. Hertzka was already a distinguished and highly placed Austro-Hungarian economist when he published *Freeland: A Social Anticipation* in 1891. It described a city and state in which a laissez-faire economy would be based, as it was for Bellamy, on the state ownership of the land and the means of production. His proposal, translated into English within a year by Arthur Ransome, remembered now chiefly for his teenage sailing novels rather than his Russian adventures and his friendship with Lenin, aroused wild enthusiasm. Freeland associations were founded in many towns and a periodical was started to spread Hertzka's ideas. Land was "offered" in equatorial Kenya for a settlement practicing his economic policies; it was in the lands of the nomadic Masai so as not to involve any expropriation. In the end, the settlement never "got off the ground," and the offer of land was withdrawn. It did, however, direct the attention of a number of Zionist leaders to the possibility, also frustrated, of a Jewish settlement in Africa known as the "Uganda Scheme." Theodor Herzl did read Hertzka, as is clear from his own utopian pamphlet, *Altneuland,* which provided indirect inspiration for the kibbutz movement.

The relatively new science of biology—the word was not coined until 1802—from which Auguste Comte had developed his notion of sociology—percolated another idea into utopian thinking: that of arriving at perfect human beings and therefore ideal or at least harmonious, non-conflictual societies by selective breeding. It came to be regarded as a separate discipline, eugenics, a term coined by Sir Francis Galton in the 1880s.[11] Selective breeding that had long been practiced on animals, he thought, could be applied to human beings equally well, an approach diametrically opposed to Owen's and that of many nineteenth-century reformers' belief in the dominance of environment over inheritance. It owed more to Herbert Spencer's pessimistic version of evolution—he coined the formula "the survival of the fittest"—than to Charles Darwin himself. The impact of this diluted and vulgarized aspect of Darwinism was taken up by many writers, most popularly by Edward Bulwer-Lytton, in his last novel, *The Coming Race* (1871). What Lord Lytton only implied was explored by H. G. Wells in a number of books. *The*

Time Machine (1895) was published only four years after *News from Nowhere* and *Freeland*. In it, Wells provides a picture of humanity divided into two races, since the eugenic formula was taken to mean that selective breeding could work down as well as up.

Any political and economic changes discussed in these books were to be brought about by biological engineering and selective human breeding; social reforms were irrelevant. The impact of the racist, political ideologies of the 1920s and 1930s gave eugenics a really bad name. It is commemorated most dismally by Aldous Huxley in his *Brave New World* (1932). Huxley wrote when utopia was no longer credible, since the foreseeable future was turning into *dystopia*—or even, as others would have it, *kakotopia*.[12] To Huxley the idea of breeding an inferior race of servile semihumans, which would be taken up as a serious project by the Nazis, is merely a nightmarish vision. For all that, throughout the second half of the nineteenth century utopia fascinated many writers on both sides of the Atlantic, but divorced now from the idea that their proposals might be acted upon. The ultimate dystopia was political, not biological: George Orwell's *1984* showed an ultratotalitarian society, near enough in time and space.

Walden Two (1948), the only widely read recent book about a utopia to describe a satisfactory society achieved by a system of habit-forming rewards and punishments, rather than either political or eugenic tinkering, is by B. F. Skinner. He developed the biologist Pavlov's primitive attempt to work out the relation of stimulus to reaction in animals into a systematic account of human behavior. *Walden Two* is an account of a harmonious community peopled by a completely conditioned group. It has not led to any experiments.

The enormous impact that utopian models had on social thinking and urban planning needs to be affirmed. The idea that work—all work—might be pleasurable and so undo the curse on Adam is an undercurrent in many of these projects. It was shared nostalgically by Fourier, Ruskin, and Marx. That notion seems as remote and irrelevant in the postindustrial city as it had been in the days of the conveyor belt. Yet such a hope, however modified, is the only possible source for any urbanist's energy and application. That is why, in spite of the poor record of squabbles and bankruptcies, and the short life of so many utopian settlements, the impact of utopian writings has been—and I think will continue to be—enormously powerful. For all Marx and Engels' dismissive examination, utopias became a great force in the protest movements, and an agent in the ferments provoking the social transformations that followed each of the two world wars.

That the nineteenth-century city was confusing, congested, and unhealthy, as well as dangerous, is a truism. Action to remedy the defects was constantly stymied by an underlying belief in the liberal concept of the free-floating value of money and the ultimately benevolent, "natural" working of industrial development. Nor has this changed.

3. House and Home

THE CHAOTIC AND OFTEN WRETCHED nineteenth-century city was a constant challenge to the passion and energy of the utopians, but their reforming zeal and their optimism did have a constant impact on policy. Even so, the solutions that they and a few benevolent manufacturers advanced to solve the most urgent social problems turned out to be inadequate. The great utopian hope that ideal and organized communities could act as a leaven upon the urban masses was repeatedly disappointed. The cities of the industrialized world went on growing uncontrollably, and their problems inevitably multiplied.

The figures are telling. If they do not always take account of various boundary moves, they show how the populations were counted. Paris, the biggest city in the western world early in the eighteenth century, rose to 581,000 in 1801 and to 935,000 by 1841. In 1870, when the Second Empire fell, it had reached 1,852,000; and in 1900 it stood at 2,714,000. A relentless centralizing drive which was initiated by Cardinal Richelieu and Louis XIV to fortify the monarchy at the expense of aristocracy made Paris "the Capital of the Nineteenth Century" in Walter Benjamin's memorable phrase.[1] It also made the brilliant and trend-setting city politically unstable, so that it suffered radical changes of government in 1815, 1830, 1848, 1852, 1870, and again in 1871. London, on the other hand, which had had its revolutions two centuries earlier (1642, 1660, 1682), grew more slowly than some other British cities; yet it grew steadily through the eighteenth century. By 1801 the County of London had increased to about 864,000, gradually overtaking Paris in both numbers of inhabitants and in economic power. It was not only larger than Paris but also larger than all the other populous cities at that time: Constantinople/Istanbul, Beijing, or Edo; in 1841, Greater London was counted at about 2,500,000 and rose to 3,890,000 in 1871, and 6,586,000 by 1901. It was not only the biggest city in the world by then, but also the most powerful financially, and absorbing new inhabitants so fast that by the beginning of World War I a fifth of the population of England and Wales had gathered in London. Nevertheless, London remained a horizontal town, while European cities had begun to move upward.

The demand for houses became voracious and insatiable. Houses had been more or less taken for granted by architects in the past: they were produced by builders who followed a rule-of-thumb practice. In a walled city houses were the infill between its two public constituents, the walls and the institutions. From antiquity until the eighteenth century, craftsmen had their workshops; merchants, even bankers, had their warehouses and counters in their houses. Apartment dwellings as tall as ten floors had existed in the late Roman Empire, but as the Empire declined, and ancient cities became depopulated, these were gradually abandoned. Yet the Tuscan or Venetian three- and four-story family palaces are simply the best-known housing types in which the combination of living and working quarters is established and fixed. From the fourteenth century onward, even the grandest Italian families would divide their town palazzi, with shops or warehouses on the ground floor and mezzanine, as in the Roman *insulae;* the best quarters on the first and second floors; and apartments for lesser familiars, retainers, or even lodgers above.

Renaissance architects—always concerned to find an antique precedent for any type of building—had problems not only finding them for housing (little was known about ancient *insulae*), but even for palaces. Ruins were not much help in this matter since not enough of any famous palace had survived to provide material for a reconstruction. Vitruvius, who wrote the only architectural treatise to survive from antiquity, did not provide an account of a real palace of his own time, though he did describe the permanent backdrop of the theater. Tragic plays always dealt with the fortunes of heroes, kings, and princes; the stage therefore represented the kind of palace mythical kings might have occupied.

Vitruvius's description—adopted by Renaissance architects as their model—could be tested against surviving theaters, such as the one at Orange in southern France. By the mid-seventeenth century the grander kinds of houses, such as the country house in England, or the *hôtel particulier* in France, were given some attention. But interest was thin for the poorer sort of housing, though here and there were notable exceptions, usually in the form of tied housing—housing owned by an employer and reserved for employees; the powerful Augsburg financiers the Fugger family, for instance, developed a part of the town as tied housing for their employees in the mid-sixteenth century.[2]

Paris, so much more compact than any Anglo-Saxon town or city, had, since the seventeenth century, grown accustomed to purpose-built, middle-income apartment buildings. Apartments within big town houses—called *hôtels*—and even apartments in royal palaces were considered quite usual private quarters for the powerful and rich as well as for their social and political inferiors. What was true of the French royal and princely courts was also true of Germany, Austria, and Spain. Like many European cities, Paris was surrounded on its outskirts by small industries, warehouses, and very substandard housing clustered around them, which stemmed the spread of residential suburbs, as did the refortifying of Paris around 1840. Much more concentrated than London, Paris was also socially stratified vertically. An apartment building might contain shops and workshops at ground level, over which there would be lordly high-ceilinged apartments on the first floor. The cost fell as one went up in the building, and the variously indigent occupied the roof space, or mansards; they took their name from the great seventeenth-century architect, François Mansart, the popularizer of the two-slope curb-roof that dominates the roofline of most French and many other European cities.

The population of London, meanwhile, was increasingly zoned outward from its rich center in vast rafts of two-story housing. Parisian suburbs on the other hand were either made up of squatter shacks or "flatted" apartment blocks. Horizontally stratified, they provided for a more complex social mix than the terraced London estates. The social and rental gradation of apartments according to height was modified by the invention of the safety elevator—the first one was installed in Mannheim in 1880—though it was not until the electric passenger elevator became a fixture of the middle-range Paris apartment buildings after the Second World War that the rigid stratification was finally transformed.[3]

Berlin, with a population of 197,000 in 1816, went from being a *Residenzstadt,* or capital of the electors of Brandenburg, to the third most powerful industrial capital in Europe in the second half of the century. In 1841, it had a population of 431,000, which doubled in the next thirty years as a result of an enclosure system by which the Junker estates grew at the expense of yeomen farmers, much as in England, but a century later. By 1871, as the capital of the new German empire after the victory over Napoléon III, it was already a *Weltstadt,* with a population of 826,000, leaving the other German cities, Hamburg, Munich, and Vienna, way behind. It was almost as big as Paris in 1900, with 1,900,000 inhabitants. Housing in Berlin and some other cities of central and eastern Europe was grim. The *Mietskasernen* of Berlin, the Rhineland, Vienna, and later Hamburg and Munich, Warsaw, Prague, and Saint Petersburg were block-size buildings, often five to seven stories high, with several interior courtyards to act as light-wells, though they were usually too narrow to admit much light. Most of these buildings were put up at the edges of old urban areas, where the lower floors facing the street were indeed the better and more expensive ones. For all that, there was hardly any real social diversity. As their name implied, they were built to maximize rents, even if their exteriors were often stuccoed and molded to maintain the more or less civilized patination of city streets.

Eighteenth-century Berlin, largely controlled by the Hohenzollern court under Frederick William I, III, and IV, developed in a stately and planned way; Frederick II, the Great, had been notoriously mean about building. The French-style avenue, lined in lime trees, became its axis; the squares and gardens opening off it led to the Pariser Platz, and beyond the Brandenburg Gate to the Tiergarten. This had been a hunting ground (not a zoo) but was turned into a French-style park by Frederick William I, who also imposed a varied geometry on the plan of his capital, making open spaces that ranged from square to oval and octagonal; the biggest was the circular Rondell, later Belle-Alliance and now Mehringplatz. It all made an urban ensemble that could rival that of any other city, though it was quickly engulfed by the rapid population rise. While the numbers nearly doubled, Karl Friedrich Schinkel, who controlled Prussian planning and patronage until his death in 1841, was involved in designing monumental buildings (the hugely porticoed New—now Old—Museum, the Werdersche Kirche, and Potsdam cathedral as well as several palaces, the Building Academy, and monuments) rather than in planning for expansion, as Berlin was turning into the most densely populated city in the world. In 1808 the independent administration and boundaries of the old city had been legally confirmed; but this move was used to increase the height of the tenements by landlords and was further reinforced by police fire regulations that fixed street width to building heights, with an absolute limit of 25 meters (about 82 feet), based on the 22-meter (72-foot) height of the fire engine ladders; this was copied in many other European cities. An attempt to provide an urban plan concerned primarily with road surfaces and with drainage in 1862 turned out only to aggravate the problems and concentrate high-density housing even more within a new railway ring completed in 1877. The war and the victory of 1871 stimulated the greatest expansion of Berlin. In spite of insistent calls for decentralization, the planning policy remained unchanged, and the few concerted plans for *Siedlungen,* or planned suburbs, led to a series of bankruptcies. The only relief was provided by a kind of green belt of agricultural and park land surrounding the city, created by the two rivers, the Spree and the Havel, as well as the lakes Müggel and Tegel and the canals which connected them.

The problem of housing the rural poor who had crowded into cities arose in Britain that much earlier and much more grievously than elsewhere. The new urban masses would accept almost any form of roof over their heads. British towns and cities had already absorbed half the population of the country by midcentury in a way that was without precedent anywhere. Workers crowded around the new mills and factories and as industry grew most manufacturers depended on local landlords or builders to put up such housing for their workmen as they could. Although poverty was grinding and seemed irredeemable, even the poorest could be squeezed for some rent. Nothing was done nationally or locally for several decades to improve or even regulate conditions, given the climate of relentless laissez faire.

At the centers of some older towns such as in Manchester—where the conditions graphically described by Engels in great detail seemed even worse than those that had already shocked de Tocqueville ten years or so earlier[4]—neglected and derelict properties were overrun and densely crowded. On the urban edges and out of the centers, around the new mills and factories where they escaped any municipal control, new houses provided minimal sanitation or space while still producing profitable rents. They took the form of interminable square miles of wretched shacks, usually of brick with tile or slate roofs, their drainage and accommodation only improving slowly and marginally as legislation imposed rising standards and the mechanism for enforcement became more efficient. Things were, however, worse in the "stews" or the "rookeries," as the slums in the center of London were called. Overcrowding had become a constant preoccupation of the builders as it was for the authorities. Epidemics and accidents produced panic reactions: schemes of forced emigration were advocated as a remedy, and some, of orphans and vagrants to the dominions, seem to have been more or less covertly carried out.

The situation was deteriorating. In the eighteenth century the occasional factory master would realize that something had to be done, that they would have to build near the more inaccessible mills or mines if workmen were to be attracted there. Moved partly by self-interest and partly by benevolence, manufacturers began to think that decent tied accommodation could provide a solution to many pressing social and sanitary problems. Most of the early industrialists did not care what housing they built for their employees, but potter Josiah Wedgwood built himself a house surrounded by workmen's cottages at Etruria, outside Burslem, Staffordshire, in 1769–70, while other mill owners such as Richard Arkwright provided his workmen with cottages at Cromford in Derbyshire; they are two early and exceptional examples. In Glamorgan, at Merthyr Tydfil—the largest Welsh town in the mid-eighteenth century—the Guest family financed terrace houses near their iron mills, analogous to Robert Owen's in New Lanark, though much more modest and without any of his reformist program. Unfortunately the pollution from the nearby mine and the iron mill was such that within about a decade the estate fell into neglect, and any substantial move to provide "model" housing had to wait for another century. These efforts were minuscule in comparison to the vast stock of slum housing being built all over the country.

The horrors of working-class housing may seem glaring now, yet action to reform conditions was unbelievably slow. The masses had been of little interest to engineers and architects. In the first half of the nineteenth century slum landlords, who cared neither for the plan nor the design, wanted their builders to do the simplest job possible: a stripped-down version of the Georgian brick terrace house. Such public buildings as churches or schools were not part of mass-housing "developments." They would be planted among such housing only as an afterthought, the result of private benefactions or institutional intervention.

The first English Public Health Act, which attempted to regulate both drainage and water supply, was not introduced until 1848, and only as the result of the pressure orchestrated by a civil servant, Edwin Chadwick. Since the authorities were lax in enforcing it, several decades of parliamentary and local government action were needed before it had any real effect. And it was met with strong opposition—not only from the landowners whose profits it cut, but also from liberal economists. The reluctance of politicians and industrialists was clearly stated in their journals in *The Economist* at the time:

> Suffering and evil are nature's admonitions: they will never be entirely eliminated and the impatient attempts of benevolence to banish them from the world by legislation . . . have always produced more bad than good.[5]

Meanwhile the seventh earl of Shaftesbury, a contemporary of Chadwick's, who had also been an energetic proponent of an act limiting the industrial working day and the banning of child labor (which also became law in 1848), had energized a "Society for Building Model Lodging Houses" to sponsor some such housing in 1846–47, and since their residents turned out to be less vulnerable to cholera epidemics, an act controlling such accommodation was passed in 1851. But inertia meant that

> the Act has remained a dead letter. Either the municipal authorities of our large towns know little, or else they care nothing, about the actual conditions of the lowest classes[6]

as a contemporary witness complained.

Still, Shaftesbury had the ear of Albert, the Prince Consort, who, against government advice, involved himself in the agitation for better working conditions as well as for improved housing. He had built cottages for workers on the royal estates and at the time of the Great Exhibition had a couple of "model" cottages, of no great architectural distinction but fireproof and soundly drained, built near the Crystal Palace; they may still be seen on a site at Kennington in south London to which they were moved. Their designer, Henry Roberts, acted as surveyor to the Society for Improving the Conditions of the Labouring Classes, the first of several such bodies, which built an estate in Clerkenwell, on land given them below market price by the duke of Bedford. Associated with Lord Shaftesbury, Roberts had come to prominence by winning a competition. Wealthy and pious, he turned his attention to low-income housing and designed several estates in Bloomsbury and Gray's Inn Road in London. His work and his first book, *The Dwellings of the Labouring Classes,* in 1850, advocated multistory tenements as the only appropriate form of low-income housing. The book was eagerly read throughout Europe, but Roberts retired to Italy "for his health" in 1856. The American philanthropist George Peabody, who had settled in London, founded an analogous society for building working-class housing around the same time, though he employed a less distinguished architect, Henry Darbishire, who also worked for Baroness Burdett-Coutts, another philanthropist interested in the improvement of working-class housing.[7] Roberts and Darbishire were the first architects who considered working-class housing as a central professional problem.

At the height of the Chadwick-Shaftesbury agitation, in 1855, Parliament had established the Metropolitan Board of Works as the controlling authority over inner-city building. Although it appointed an architect and allowed him an office, the main figure in its operations was a French-born engineer, Sir Joseph Bazalgette, who was appointed in 1853 to be responsible for the construction of a sewer system even more ambitious than the one in Paris, and for the embanking of the River Thames. The permanent cess-pits built after the Great Fire of 1666 were by then overflowing into the streets. The multiplication of water closets and the random laying of sewers by developers had made the river stiflingly fetid; in 1848–49 there was another cholera epidemic. Yet reform was slow and finance for the new sewers was hard to come by. A crisis came in the very hot summer of 1858, when the fetid air wafting in from the river meant the drapes in the Houses of Parliament had to be soaked in chloride of lime to make the air in the debating chambers tolerable, but to no avail. *That* finally spurred action.

The Metropolitan Board was destroyed by accusations of peculation and corruption in 1889, when it was replaced by a rather different body, the London County Council, reorganized when London outgrew the county boundaries, in 1965, as the Greater London Council. In a near century of existence it made a huge impact on urban housing before it was dispatched by Margaret Thatcher in 1985. In its time it controlled the old Metropolitan Board of Works—the sewers and the parks—as well as the water supply, and finally the transport system of the city. By the 1950s it also had the world's largest architects' office, with some five thousand professionals, and most of them were concerned with the design of housing estates.

The healthier middle classes were also multiplying, and faster, because of their lower mortality. Two London family firms, the Burtons

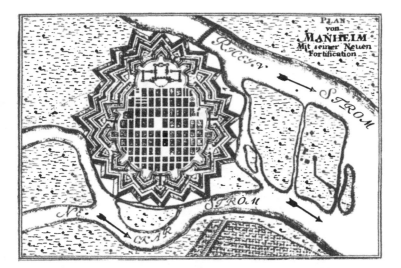

Mannheim, on the confluence of the Rhine and Neckar rivers. Destroyed by Louis XIV in 1689, it was replanned in 1695. The grid layout suggested the first numbering of streets in one direction, and labeling by letters in the other. Anonymous print.

Palmanova was a nine-sided fortress, right, built in 1593 with a hexagonal central open space, focused on a flagpole and a cistern.

ykstad, near the mouth of the Elbe,
rth of Hamburg. Designed in 1616
by François Pacherval, it is a half-
exagon, with streets radiating from
the main square, reflected on the
other side of the canal by a similar
ut incomplete half-hexagon; one of
the few north European fortified
plans with radiating rather than
gridded streets.

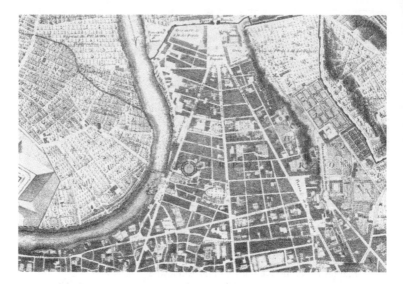

Giambattista Nolli's plan of Rome published on twelve sheets in 1784. This section is the northern gate, the Porta del Popolo, and the Piazza del Popolo, the main processional entry of the city, which was transformed when the two hemicycles were added by Giuseppe Valadier after 1813.

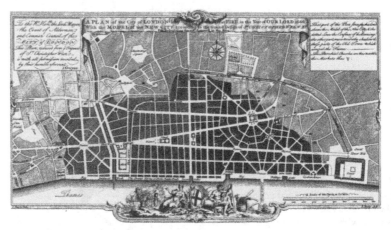

Plan for London by Sir Christopher Wren, the first of several submitted to King Charles II within a few days of the Great Fire of September 1666 and the one he favored. The varied grids of the streets are broken by wide, oblique avenues, the crossing points used to locate the main open spaces and institutional buildings; it was almost immediately rejected by the Lord Mayor and the Council. Drawn by John Gwynn and engraved by E. Rosker from Stephen Wren's *Parentalia*, 1750.

The Turgot "plan" of Paris, commissioned in 1734 and engraved by Louis Bretez, was a projection on the survey that had been drawn up by a surveyor-geometer, the Abbé de la Grive; its 20 plates measure ten feet by seven when assembled. The section above shows the square Place des Vosges, laid out under Henry IV, and the Bastille, also the Arsenal, created by Francis I and destroyed in 1871, the Ile St. Louis as well as the Louvier Island, which was joined to the right bank in 1844 by filling the river channel. The section below shows the Marais, occupied by many noble houses, and the circular Place des Victoires.

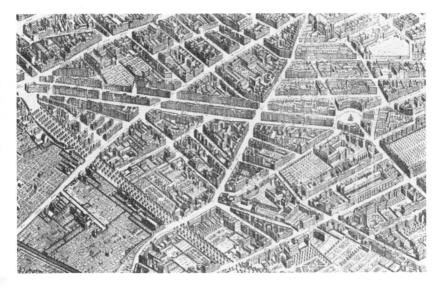

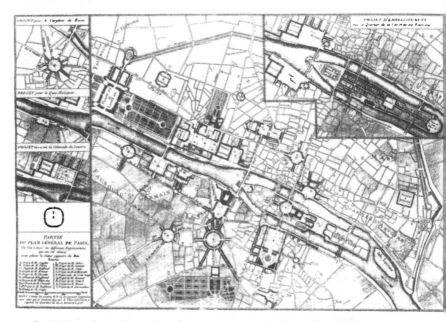

Paris. Pierre Patte, Competition for a monument to the glory of Louis XV, 1765.
The most ambitious of the projects, which is shown in the inset, proposes a symmetrical
Louvre on the left bank of the Seine and a vast new domed cathedral on the tip of
the Ile de la Cité.

Mexico City. The Zocalo or Plaza de la Constitución, opposite right, at 269 yards
square is the second-largest public paved space in the world; only Red Square in
Moscow is larger. It is laid over the market of the Aztec capital and a section of its
temple precinct, Tenochtitlán. The Palacio National, the Presidential Palace, was built
originally for Hernán Cortés, the conqueror of Mexico, from the stone of the ruined
palace of the last Aztec sovereign, Montezuma. It became the residence of the Spanish
viceroys as well as of the unfortunate Habsburg Emperor of Mexico, Maximilian.
Despite the amorphous growth of the city, the Zocalo, the Cathedral, and the Palace
remain the center of the city, together with the town hall and the Supreme Court.

The Cathedral, above, a compilation of various designs, which took more than two centuries to complete, was begun in 1525, though the present structure was built after 1563, on the site of the Aztec temple of the Sun, using some of its stone; on the right is the very ornate—Churrigueresque—parish church of the city, the Sagrario Metropolitano, designed by a Spaniard, Lorenzo Rodriguez, who was probably a pupil of the manner's originator, José Benito de Churriguerra.

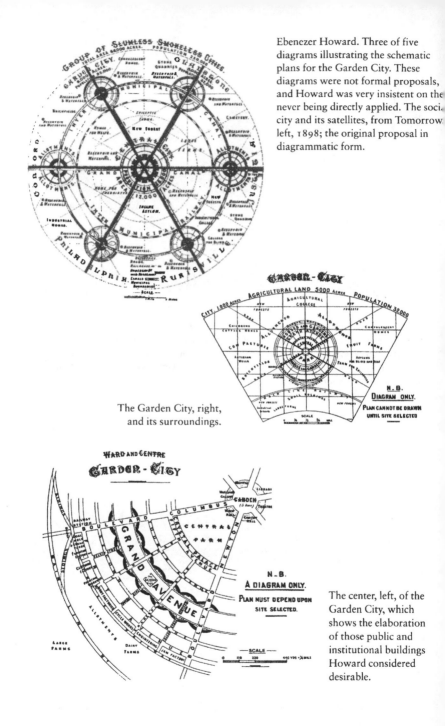

Ebenezer Howard. Three of five diagrams illustrating the schematic plans for the Garden City. These diagrams were not formal proposals, and Howard was very insistent on them never being directly applied. The social city and its satellites, from Tomorrow, left, 1898; the original proposal in diagrammatic form.

The Garden City, right, and its surroundings.

The center, left, of the Garden City, which shows the elaboration of those public and institutional buildings Howard considered desirable.

ondon. Hampstead Garden Suburb, right, proposed in 1903 but not planned until 1907 by Barry Parker and Raymond Unwin, favorites of he Garden City movement. Although the founders' intention was that the suburb have a largely working-class population, it has, in fact, become something of a middle-class enclave.

London. Hampstead Garden Suburb. The Free Church, left, adjoining it was also begun by Edwin Lutyens in 1911 but not finished until 1960. The founders of the "suburb" insisted that the churches should stand in an open space. The Anglican/Episcopalian church of St. Jude, on the right, was also designed by Lutyens, 1909–1911.

London. The Queen Anne style. Richard Norman Shaw's own house in Ellerdale Road, Hampstead, designed in 1874 as an isolated building and finished in 1876; within a decade it was surrounded. The compositional asymmetries associated with Queen Anne become idiosyncratic in the architect's own house, in which he also experimented—successfully—with a novel drainage system.

The wished-for union of Brooklyn and Manhattan into Greater New York, symbolized in 1893—in the run-up to a referendum on the subject—by the two mayors mimicking the Brooklyn Bridge by holding hands, though the consolidation of the city was not achieved until the new year of 1898. Anonymous woodcut.

and the Cubitts, made vast fortunes from design-and-build enterprises and covered large, adjoining tracts of Highbury, Islington, Bloomsbury, and Belgravia with middle-class housing, much of which is still occupied. The senior Cubitt sibling, Thomas, became a vastly influential figure, a member of Parliament like his brother William, who also became lord mayor of London. Thomas agitated for the improvement of London drainage and for the control of air pollution, as well as for the embanking of the Thames. One of the main movers in the establishment of Battersea Park, he acted as one of the guarantors of the Crystal Palace when it hit financial troubles, much as the elder Burton had bailed out the enterprise of building Regent Street two decades earlier.

In spite of their conspicuous success, the manner in which this middle-class housing was built was not regarded with enthusiasm by the Burtons' and Cubitts' contemporaries, and certainly not by the next generation. The young Benjamin Disraeli reflected on the monotony of the London estates in his novel *Tancred, or the New Crusade,* which first appeared in 1847:

> Those new districts that have sprung up in the last half-century, the creatures of our commercial and colonial wealth, it is impossible to conceive anything more tame, more insipid, more uniform. . . . This amount of building capital should have produced a great city.

Nor are the middle classes only to blame:

> In our own days we have witnessed the rapid creation of a new metropolitan quarter, built solely for the aristocracy by an aristocrat. The Belgrave district is as monotonous as Mary-le-Bone . . . at the same time insipid and tawdry.[8]

A more "interested" observer of the housing scene, George Gilbert Scott, echoes Disraeli. Writing in 1855, he exhorts his reader to

> look . . . at the rows of miserable houses in the suburbs of our country towns and at the wretched creations of speculating builders in the neighbourhood of London: are they not vile beyond description?

These violent condemnations are not of the pitiable conditions of the working classes in the slums, but rather of the execrable taste of builders like the Cubitts, while the poorer indeed display the vernacular style of house-building more truthfully than the forced production of persons of more ambitious notions.[9]

Scott, like many of his contemporaries—in France, they complained about the tedium of the rue de Rivoli—wanted variety of outline and surface and abhorred the uniform stuccoed terraces of the Burtons, the Cubitts, and their innumerable imitators. He preferred the lumpier if unadorned artisan dwellings of less renowned builders, though the acres of slum were below his notice, of course.

For all the acknowledged, wretched squalor of workers' housing, the half-century had, paradoxically, also been the great period of pattern books for small rural houses and cottages, some even for the very poor, though housing the proletariat was of no real interest to these pattern makers.

There is no sense, in all these arguments and publications about building, that something unprecedented and threatening had taken place. But there was great unease about the momentous political shift that had resulted from the gradual extension of the vote throughout the industrialized world. Some of those newly enfranchised in Britain found that they could exert pressure on the rich and powerful. The government reacted. Disraeli, aware of the franchise extended to the urban poor by his Reform Act in 1867, backed legislation introduced by his home secretary, Sir Richard, later Lord, Cross, also a close friend of the Queen. In 1874 Disraeli was prime minister again, and an Artisan Dwelling Act gave local authorities compulsory purchasing power to develop property so acquired. However, as the middle-class housing estates extended and "metropolitan improvements" were run through some of the more insalubrious quarters, slums were pushed a short distance beyond them. The government of the day finally took this matter seriously enough to establish a Royal Commission on the Housing of the Working Classes; their long report, published in 1884–85, reported that:

Rookeries are destroyed, greatly to the sanitary and social benefit of the neighbourhood, but no kind of habitation for the poor has been substituted. . . . The consequence of such a proceeding is that the unhoused population crowd into the neighbouring streets and courts . . . and when the new dwellings are complete . . . the tenants are not the . . . persons displaced [so that] those whose need is greatest suffer most acutely.[10]

About midcentury the horrors of the situation turned the minds of some individual industrialists to housing improvement, and they looked back to forms of "tied" colonies of the *ancien régime* and of the early factory masters. The mixed motives of these patrons who provided housing, in whatever form, only to workers in a particular employment was evident. Often the buildings were owned outright by the employer, who exchanged the benefits of better housing for restrictions on rebellion, strikes, unionized organization, even "undesirable" behavior such as drinking alcohol. In some cases finance would be offered on restrictive terms to buy leases. Radicals considered all these efforts as attempts to dampen class fervor by turning workmen into small property owners— and Engels damned such moves as an antirevolutionary practice.[11]

These "tied" villages, and even the Refuge cities of an earlier time, had been sporadic incidents. Toward the end of the eighteenth century, at the outset of industrialization, some grandees initiated proto-industrial housing. Ferdinand IV of Naples, mostly remembered by historians as a cowardly, vengeful renegade, founded a silk-weaving town, San Leucio, as a kind of cottage industry factory, just north of the vast palace at Caserta that had been built by his father, Charles III, in 1786. He endowed it with elaborate regulations, including a dress-code: clothes for each sex were to be standardized, and any display of vanity or wealth discouraged. Education after the age of six and smallpox inoculation were compulsory; sons and daughters were to inherit in equal parts. Since wills and dowries were disallowed, the king provided a house for each new married couple, who had to be matched freely and could not be constrained by parents. In spite of these restrictions the population doubled every ten years in its first half-century, and the village became the center of Italian silk weaving; although it was privatized in 1870 it still prospers as a silk factory today.[12]

A more notable and extensive *ancien régime* establishment was the old "royal" iron- and glass-works at Le Creusot in Burgundy. Since the site was rather isolated, it included workers' housing in a multipurpose building. After the Revolution the works went through various hands and transformations. The Brothers Schneider, who bought them in 1836, found the crowded apartment housing inadequate, as it invited unionizing, and thought that the tied "barracks" in which most workers lived might at least be augmented by terrace houses.[13] Collective dwellings were supplemented by private developments, though in spite of the manufacturers' encouragement, the majority of new houses in the rather disorganized growth was mostly put up by local small investors.

The royal saltworks monopoly provided tied housing at Arc-et-Senans, not far from Besançon. The works were sheds in which the saline water was evaporated; two of them stretched on either side of a cubical manager's house, and the complex was completed by a hemicycle of housing. The apartments for the workers were grouped in several buildings, and in each one the bedrooms were planned around a pavilion with kitchen, dining room, and communal services. The whole complex was designed and built by the great architect Claude-Nicolas Ledoux between 1775 and 1780. Ledoux barely escaped the guillotine, but built nothing after the Revolution. He spent the remaining few years of his life elaborating a complex "ideal" village around his original "tied" village of Chaux. Although many of the engravings he prepared were not published until 1847, and some are still unpublished, his vision of the highly articulated complex of pavilions, in which each social function will have its own building whose form would declare its purpose, has been fascinating to nineteenth- and twentieth-century architects. Though, of course, its very complexity makes Ledoux's a utopian endeavor.

In England there was a new crop of tied housing about the middle of the nineteenth century. Among them was a pioneering "model" estate for the workers of a mill, with a library and school, built at Copley near Halifax by a worsted manufacturer, Colonel Edward Akroyd, between 1849 and 1853. He employed George Gilbert Scott, who had been trained by Henry Roberts, to provide a "village character" to the square around which the gabled cottages had been built. They were back-to-back, unventilated, and unsanitary, and Akroyd improved on them at Akroyden, with another mill and tied village nearby. Though not from an old landed family, Akroyd had inherited a fortune and could at least partially fulfill the role that the young Benjamin Disraeli advocated as "ideal" in his most widely read novel, Sybil, published in 1845. The model settlement he described, which included a school and an institute, was built around a textile mill by a Mr. Trafford, the younger son of an old local landed family turned highly successful industrialist. Trafford had a sense of responsibility toward his workmen, which (Disraeli implied) should inspire the new industrialists as it had the old landed gentry.[14]

Sir Titus Salt, a highly successful inventor and manufacturer of even humbler origins than Akroyd, moved his mohair and alpaca works out of Bradford in 1851, and, stimulated by Disraeli's account, gradually built his model town, Saltaire, around it. Although he employed Sir

William Fairbairn, a well-known engineer who had collaborated with George Stephenson, to design the structure of his factory, its exterior, as well as the grid-plan housing in Saltaire, was in fact done by a Leeds office, Lockwood and Mawson, who followed Italianate handbook patterns but did enliven it with public buildings. Twenty-five years later, and a mile or so away from Copley, William Hesketh Lever, a successful grocer turned world-scale soap manufacturer, founded Port Sunlight on the Mersey in 1888, not far from Liverpool. He also funded the first chair in town planning and urban design at the University of Liverpool, while Cadbury's chocolate works built Bournville, outside Birmingham, a few years after that.

The situation developed rather differently in the United States. The first American water-powered cotton mill was founded by Francis Cabot Lowell in 1814 at Waltham, Massachusetts, on the Charles River, but it was moved after his death by Boston Associates, the industrial group with which he worked, onto the Merrimack, also in Massachusetts. The town was renamed Lowell. Since there was no large pool of rural dispossessed or poorhouse inmates, the textile workers had to be attracted by the conditions of work, and were practically all female. Pay was fairly good, and they were lodged in large, but relatively salubrious, boarding-houses. Lowell was a model for a number of other such water-powered mill towns: Chicopee Falls and Holyoke in Massachusetts, Manchester in New Hampshire. Lowell was still booming when Charles Dickens visited in 1842; he was struck by the liveliness and cleanliness of the girls who made up the transient workforce, by the lending libraries and the journal the girls published, and by the presence of a piano in the common rooms.[15] The tight regulations forbade not only the sale of alcohol but even of "frivolous" candy. With the rise of steam power and the increase of the labor force through immigration, these conditions soon changed, even though cloth continued to be manufactured there until 1929.

But "company towns," as they were called in America, were relatively rare. The fifty houses built by the owner of Howland Mill in New Bedford, Massachusetts, in 1888 were considered notable, perhaps because the mill owner, having reduced his tenants' rents when times were tough, seems to have been ruined by his generosity in the financial crisis of 1893. Most manufacturers who provided tied housing imposed much tougher conditions. The best known, George Pullman, the maker of "parlor cars," imported an eclectic New York architect, Solon Beman, to build both his own house and the nearby "tied" town called after himself, which included the unusual facilities of not just a school and a park, but a library and theater, churches, a sports center, and a hotel. He was inspired by the Krupp villages around Essen. Pullman proved an inflexible landlord: his workers were not allowed to associate or to buy leases on their houses and could be evicted at ten days' notice. Critics see the amenities as a mask for the inherent conflict between the workmen and the employers, and, in any case, the stringent conditions led to a series of unrests in 1882, 1886, and 1888 that culminated in a violent strike during the 1893 financial crisis which threatened to spread, but was broken by the federal militia dispatched by President Grover Cleveland. Pullman was described as a "modern Lear."

There were other disturbing incidents. At Dayton, Ohio, the National Cash Register Company built a "model" town where the workers were encouraged to decorate their houses, and in 1890 Frederick Law Olmsted was brought in to design a clubhouse. Nevertheless, the inhabitants struck and exacted considerable concessions. The town at Dayton remained, but Pullman was sold in 1895, and thereafter many manufacturers offered their workmen financing to find their own quarters. Company towns suffered a fate similar to that of utopian settlements. Indeed, a curious superimposition occurred when the failed utopian community Hopedale, near Milford, Massachusetts—which had adopted and extended phrenological ideas to include the beneficent effect of octagonal building—was taken over in 1856 by a textile mill to house its workers, turning the ideal, "closed" community into an equally closed bit of capitalist patronage.

Still, company towns continued to be built, certainly up to 1914, not only for the steelworkers at Bethlehem, an old Moravian Brethren town, and near Pittsburgh, but for the rubber workers at Firestone Park and Goodyear Heights in Ohio. "A housed labor supply is a controlled labor supply" was a conviction that many manufacturers shared.[16] But they had been warned of potential trouble, and increasingly even the more controlling manufacturers preferred to support more or less cooperative housing schemes or to provide subsidies for their employees; some also provided welfare schemes of various kinds.

Cooperative enterprises, branching out from the Owenite Rochdale experiment, had set up a network of friendly societies and savings banks emulated in America as well as in western Europe. Mortgages were virtually unobtainable and housing investment was not a priority. In Germany, Victor Huber, who held a chair in romance philology in Berlin, had become a leading propagandist for housing reform. He argued for the virtue of such housing cooperatives, but many of them ended in bankruptcies in spite of noble and even royal support. The attempts to interest Berlin architects in working-class housing after 1840 was explicitly rejected as being unworthy of their attention. It took another fifty years before they directed any serious efforts to the matter.[17] In any case, these efforts make a miserable showing in a century of riotous building.

The housing situation of the poor in Germany and in France had become as alarming as in Britain. There had already been housing agitation in France after the great cholera epidemic of 1831–32. Louis Villermé, a physician, embarked on a survey of conditions that related to public health, and his report was published in 1840. Henri Frégier, a police official, was more concerned with criminality than with health, and he published his parallel findings in the same year. Yet, inertia reigned: neither of these much-read reports led to any action.

It was industrialists rather than public authorities who organized the earliest French attempts at housing reform. A group of philanthropic and evangelical Protestant Alsatian manufacturers created a Société Industrielle in Mulhouse, which was to finance design, textile, and chemistry schools, as well as the very first French business school in 1825. Just after 1850, inspired by Henry Roberts's book, they sponsored a philanthropic agency, the Société des Cités Ouvrières, which set a standard for worker housing in France based on single-family dwellings and offered them to the occupiers at very low mortgage rates, though they also required a down payment. This arrangement was soon imitated by other French institutions, while a Catholic group, the Société d'Economie Charitable, of which Villermé was a member, initiated a rate-paying society in 1853, though it did not become involved in building low-cost housing until about 1880. A state-aided *caisse d'épargne* was suggested as a possible financier of low-cost housing in the 1880s, but that project also failed.

Before he became Napoléon III, Louis-Napoléon, as prince-president, had sponsored the translation of Henry Roberts's book on the dwellings of the laboring classes within a year of its publication; a German translation followed a little later. After the coup d'état of 1851, which had turned the prince-president into the emperor Napoléon III, the new sovereign donated the confiscated fortune of his predecessor, King Louis Philippe, to stimulate, as it happened, without great success, workmen's housing. An isolated incident is the building of the Cité Napoléon, a block of 190 apartments designed by Gabriel Veugny, an architect, for the Société des Cités Ouvrières off the rue Rochechouart, which runs between the Gare du Nord and Gare Saint-Lazare. Organized on four floors around a glazed internal street, it included shops, a crèche, baths, and a surgery. It was immediately welcomed by the Fourierists and was condemned as encouraging promiscuity by moderate reformers such as Louis Villermé and for its half-heartedness by the extreme left. It remained unique.

The new emperor himself had ambitious ideas about what was to be done in his capital, and had, even before his accession, himself drawn an elaborate plan for cutting new streets and avenues through the old urban fabric and providing the city with parks. As his executant, he chose a junior but firmly Bonapartist civil servant, Georges-Eugène Haussmann, who immediately began revising the Imperial project; he realized moreover that this could be carried out only if both the Parisian water supply and drainage system were entirely reorganized. New interconnected major sewers took effluents into the Seine, well below the city boundaries, while new aqueducts increased the water supply greatly. Meanwhile the street pattern was completely transformed, not by additions to the existing fabric, but by driving wide and often tree-lined avenues through the center, connecting its main institutional buildings and promoting traffic in the ring they formed analogously to most of the larger cities of the industrial world.

Those new Parisian streets were soon lined with buildings whose organization was quite different from Napoléon I's rue de Rivoli. Although their façades were neither built nor financed by authority, tight planning regulations meant that materials, cornice heights, rooflines, balcony projections, and other salient features had to conform to a norm. The economy of the street piercings and the public works—an important source of employment for new immigrants—was financed on a deficit basis, a form of financing much recommended by Saint-Simon. The Pereire brothers, bankers who had been part of Saint-Simon's inner circle, were closely associated with Haussmann's enterprise.

The provision of urban parks was the emperor's personal concern rather than Haussmann's, and it was carried out with the help of a brilliant gardener-organizer, Alphonse Alphand, in collaboration with Haussmann. They presented Paris with parks ringing the city, whose picturesque and elaborate variations accentuate the achievements of the English "picturesque" gardeners: the Bois de Boulogne, the Buttes-Chaumont, and the park at Vincennes. The reorganizing of the canals, with the old lock emplacements turned into miniparks to provide an added theatrical element to the business of transport, was part of the project, but, of course, it was the joint enterprise of Napoléon and

Haussmann that contributed vastly to making Paris the "capital of the nineteenth century." Many of these projects had been fully realized when Napoléon III fell after his catastrophic defeat by the Germans in 1870.

The urban park was not an altogether new institution. Royal and princely gardens had been opened to the public since the sixteenth century: the Tuileries and the Luxembourg in Paris, and in London, Saint James's, Hyde Park, and Kensington Gardens. The first public park, however, bought, specially planted, and arranged for the public and at local public expense was begun at Birkenhead, near Liverpool, by Joseph Paxton in 1834. Calvert Vaux and Frederick Law Olmsted had known it well. Like Central Park, Birkenhead was the result of determined advocacy by individuals, often against indifferent authorities and hostile press campaigns. Much the same course was followed by many American cities, and public parks became essential amenities of the urban scene. In France the provision of public parks became an official priority, following the example of Napoléon III in Paris.

Plagued though he had been by fiscal and political problems throughout his twenty years' reign, Napoléon invested much of the empire's energy and some of its finances in the Paris project. No doubt economic and cultural prestige was his principal motive, though both the emperor, after his fall, and Haussmann are often credited with less honorable ones: financial greed, of course, and the planning of straight avenues as a method of crowd control (artillery could fire down them at barricaded masses). There had certainly been some associated and very profitable speculation in land values, but no proof was ever found that Haussmann had benefited privately. As for crowd control, it may have been a real, though certainly an ancillary, motive. Haussmann's and the emperor's primary aim seems almost certainly the one stated: to provide a salubrious and orderly bourgeois capital. Nothing on a similar scale was attempted in Rome when it became the capital of Italy after 1870, or even in Berlin when it became the capital of the new empire a year later. The avenues, such as Kingsway, that were pierced in London had neither the scale nor the urbanistic ambitions of the Paris works. In these terms Britain, in spite of its financial and commercial primacy and stability, lagged behind France, or at any rate London lagged behind Paris. But the defeat and the commune that followed were a damper on the growth of Paris; the crowding in the 1860s was followed by a fall in the population after the siege, and an economic crisis which followed it. By 1880, however, the numbers had caught up. Many of the bits of old Paris wedged between Haussmann's improvements became overcrowded tenements housing workers who needed to be near the city center. Cheap overpopulated lodging houses, *garnis,* replicated the unsanitary situation that thirty years earlier Shaftesbury had tried to remedy in London with his "model lodgings houses." An estimate of construction for 1879–84 suggested that lower- and lower-middle-class housing grew by 15 to 20 percent, while more expensive housing, of which there was a surplus, increased by 30–40 percent.[18] As a result of the discussion around the World Exposition of 1889, the Société des Habitations Bon Marché was founded early in 1890 as a powerful pressure group to reform housing, and its first important action was to sponsor an architectural competition for low-income dwellings. HBM blocks, later joined by HLM, Société des Habitations à Loyer Modéré, became the dominant preoccupation of later French architects.[19]

Since the industrializing and urbanizing of Germany, and the housing problems that came with them, were certainly behind France and nearly half a century behind Britain, things went at a different rhythm there. Germany produced no Owen, and no Fourier, either. But Britain and even France did provide lessons. The first housing reformers, in the 1840s, were definitely improvers of the early *Mietskasernen.* A number of early estates in the Ruhr adopted the Mulhouse precedent, which had passed to Germany after 1870. In the 1860s, when steel production became an important factor in German industry, the Krupp company began, on a small scale, to build model, tied settlements for its workers—both blue- and white-collar—around Essen, where they had begun smelting just after 1810. For nearly a millennium that small town had been the fief of a Benedictine nunnery and was ruled by its princess-abbess, but it was incorporated into Prussia about the time the Krupp Works started smelting there, employing about ten workers. The Krupps' fortunes seem to have been turned by their exhibit at the Crystal Palace in 1851; by 1860 they were employing nearly 12,000 workmen and not only were they the main employers of the town but also its effective masters. By then they had become the main steel supplier in the world—including Canada and the United States—until American industries caught up. Essen armed Germany for the French war, so that the workforce stood at 25,000 by 1890 and was to rise to 70,000 by 1912.

The Krupps needed to attract and hold their large, growing workforce, but like most of their contemporary industrialists they were slow to see the importance of housing. By the 1850s the small town was already overcrowded and unsanitary. In the 1860s the first, minimal, and more or less temporary houses for managerial staff inside the old

city were built as an emergency measure, but soon more elaborate, varied quarters—terraced, flatted, single-family dwellings, some with gardens, others with adjoining parks—were built. Elementary institutional
buildings were gradually added: schools and libraries, churches, bath-
houses and theaters. The standard of housing was very high, but control
was correspondingly tight. Trade union activity was actively discouraged, and rubbish bins were regularly inspected for seditious political literature. Real growth came after 1871. By then the Krupps had become
the main movers in the matter of German worker housing.

At first the plans of the Krupp settlements were conventionally rectilineal, but they softened to accommodate topography as well as the
"biological" imagery and aspirations of fin-de-siècle planners. In the
largest, the Margaretenhöhe, designed in 1906 by Georg Metzendorf, a
young architect who specialized in housing, the full formal development
of the *Siedlung,* the lower-income suburb that became a feature of the
interwar years in Germany, had been achieved.

Metzendorf was representative of his generation, and the business of
housing came to occupy architects increasingly. By the 1860s, a few had
begun to accept housing as a legitimate interest and increasing attention
to the plan types and their detailed layouts in the use of space, ventilation, and hygiene tended to push problems of style into the background.
Many architects found that the new housing types could not usefully
wear any of the old stylistic uniforms. Horizontally planned dwellings,
recommended by architects (such as Robertson and Darbishire) and
philanthropists, were even (reluctantly at first) accepted by the English
middle classes. The first Parisian-style "flatted mansions" were built in
London—at Grosvenor Gardens, overlooking Buckingham Palace—in
the 1860s. About the same time, they first became fashionable in New
York, where they were called "French Flats."[20]

Compared with Berlin, Vienna, or other world cities, all of them
expanding, Paris was in fact less densely populated. Not only did world
cities suffer from such unmanageable expansion, but a number of smaller
ancient cities around the Mediterranean were growing very rapidly out
of their medieval urban centers as well, sometimes multiplying their area
in a few decades. Provincial backwaters found themselves transformed
into the capitals of new nation-states—Athens, Sofia, Belgrade—even
Florence was the capital of Italy for a while, to be replaced by Rome
after 1870. Such towns tended to develop "rationally"—that is, in rectilineal patterns of streets and squares, added to their old, often irregular,

center. Barcelona, though not a capital, was the most clamorous instance of such growth, since unlike the rest of Spain, Catalonia was industrializing rapidly. The population of Barcelona moved from 35,000 to 115,000 during the eighteenth century and stood at about 175,000 in 1854, a large part housed in slums as crowded as any in Manchester or Liverpool; it was the most densely populated European town with a very high mortality rate as a consequence. When the walls of Barcelona were torn down during a constitutional crisis, the municipality declared a competition for the city's expansion. The winning project—which had much in common with those in Athens and Rome, though more rigidly zoned according to income and social class—was set aside by the government in favor of one that had not been submitted to the competition. It was by Idelfonso Cerdá y Suñer, who was a graduate—like some of the politicians and civil servants of the liberal government of 1854—of the Madrid Engineering School, modeled on the Parisian Ecole Polytechnique. Cerdá's project was very much an essay in social engineering. A politician of the liberal left, he moved to a moderate anarchist position later in life even though his project was imposed on Barcelona by royal decree. As a man of powerful conviction who held that any proposal could be algebraically evaluated, he set his grid plan out confidently to the north and east of the old city, and crossed it by diagonal avenues, one being the exact north-south axis.

In this scheme, the city has two principal functions—dwelling and movement—and each function must be given its separate role. Cerdá's primary concern was with dwellings and road surface, or more grandly stated, housing and communication. Communication, as he rightly and forcefully foretold, would transform the future city. It had to be studied, he insisted, on the model of the anatomist or even physiologist as a body made up of tissues and enlivened by its functions, its processes. In this matter he was in advance of some of his contemporaries, who would make a strong appeal to biological models as prototypes of both plans and of ornament. Every block in his project was to be a square with lopped corners, therefore making all crossings octagonal, to ease traffic flow. Occupation was to be at relatively low densities: Cerdá envisaged building along two sides of the block, with gardens in the center strip, though he also considered several permutations of this geometry. He was also definite about social provisions: a social/religious center for every region of twenty-five blocks, a market every four regions, and a park every eight. The Spanish word *ensanche* meant swelling or enlargement, but has become more of a technical term, meaning a planned enlargement of a city. In Barcelona it was to provide for 800,000 inhabitants, though its present population stands at 1,700,000. These figures, and the realities of land ownership, meant that Cerdá's rules would soon be broken: all the blocks are by now built up to twelve stories high with internal courtyards, much like urban blocks in the rest of Europe, though the general layout retains some of its appeal. It is his plan that provided the basis for the revitalizing of Barcelona in the last two decades of the twentieth century.

The plan and its projection into the future were justified after the fact in Cerdá's *Teoría General de la Urbanización* of 1867, his incomplete masterpiece, published in the same year as volume 1 of Marx's *Das Kapital*. The book first launched the word "urbanism" and the notion of a separate discipline concerned with both the making and the study of towns.[21]

Cerdá was conscious of breaking new ground: his terms and the study would introduce his reader to material that was *completamente nueva, intacta, virgen*:[22] a science relying on statistical evidence and on physical survey. He formulated the notion of "survey before plan"; that survey had to be both historical and statistical-geographic. It has become commonplace and is now associated with more empirical Anglo-Saxon planning procedure, though it was certainly a fresh principle when he formulated it. It ushered in notions which were still relatively novel: that planning—as later architecture—had to be regarded as a scientific activity, and that solving problems was the essential task of planners and architects. By that token what had been called composition—all that was concerned with the formal side of the project—was in some way superrogatory—or aesthetic.

Cerdá's concern with future communications pointed to an urgent and actual urban problem: traffic. The horse—whose ammoniac droppings produced some insistent complaints about urban pollution—was crowding out the urban street. Hackney carriages—taxicabs, in effect—had long circulated in both London and Paris. In 1635 they were limited to forty in London, but by 1700 there were seven hundred of them. In Paris, where they multiplied equally quickly, they owe their name, *fiacre*, to the first ever taxi stand—at the inn sign of Saint Fiacre, or Fiaker, a seventh-century Irish missionary in France. Carriages, packhorses, and wagons were augmented by the omnibus—the earliest urban public mass transport vehicle. The great philosopher-mathematician Pascal is reputed to have started the first urban carriage company in 1662 in Paris, but it did not flourish then, and the first effective omnibuses between Porte

Saint-Martin and the Madeleine began operating in 1828; by then there were some 17,000 other vehicles on Parisian streets, and omnibuses were imitated in London within a few months. They were an immediate success and in the first ten years there were 62 operating in London, though by 1850 they had gone up to 1,300 and 250 of those operated to and from the Crystal Palace.

The new omnibuses added to traffic jams and to the horse traffic pollution. In the traffic-ridden cities of the end of the century, the internal combustion engine and the automobile that it powered were seen as offering relief from the horse dung that infested the streets. Social reformers as well as architects saw these developments as a challenge and an inspiration. Some urbanists hoped that they could resolve all urban problems by isolating one, such as traffic, and then they would be taking the first step toward treating the city as a whole. Henry-Jules Borie may be taken as the Parisian forerunner of a trend. He was only marginally interested in social organization or social inequities. Communication and transport were the focus of his concerns, and he considered transport a public service. In the 1860s, Borie proposed raising both the areas occupied by traffic in the city and the population density by building urban blocks higher—up to twenty floors—than the six or seven that were customary in Paris and roofing the internal courtyards with iron and glass. Vertical circulation would be provided by "moving rooms," which were in fact huge steam elevators. The roofs were to be used for schools and colleges as well as for roof gardens. Although Borie's proposal, published in 1865, was more closely related to the exhibition buildings of his time than to everyday habitations, it is more important as a symptom than as an influence. He was the harbinger of many of the proposals and some of the realizations of the twentieth century.[23]

At about the same time, Joseph Paxton looked at analogous problems in London just after he had become a member of Parliament. Already in 1855, he proposed the "Great Victorian Way," which would link the London railway stations by a glazed arcade, which I shall discuss when I come to consider the glazed arcades as an urban proposition. Five years later the first tunneled London "Metropolitan" (later "Underground"— though *metropolitan* became the international word for urban rapid transport: as witness the Paris *métro*) railway was planned on a stretch of Paxton's project between Paddington and Farringdon Road. It was run on steam in 1863 and for some time later, but that caused obvious ventilation problems. Yet, the London Metropolitan Railway, in spite of official skepticism, was an instant success. Tracks were laid on the short stretch between Baker Street and Euston; within months other lines were planned. An alternative system using compressed air to move mass-transport vehicles was tried in New York in 1868, but was abandoned almost immediately, though the elevated steam railways running at the same time were to become the first American rapid urban transport system.

In Paris the first move to mechanize transport was the putting of the double-decker horse-trams on railway lines, following the American model, since in New York horse streetcars had been tried in 1832 and successfully run since 1852. They were then adopted both in Philadelphia and, in about 1860, in London. Although they worked so well that they were soon supplemented by steam, yet in Paris horse streetcars ran until 1913. Much of the last quarter of the nineteenth century in Paris was devoted to debates between the various forms of new mass transport. The New York elevated model, which included monorails, and the London-modeled underground were both proposed. Finally, in preparation for the World Exposition of 1900, a combined-transport system, which used single-decker buses and metropolitan—subway—railways, was continued into overground suburban commuter trains. Vienna, still an Imperial capital, built its very opulent *Stadtbahn* during the last decade of the nineteenth century. In Berlin, a similar battle between elevated and underground public transport ended in the victory of the underground system in the first decade of the twentieth century, though it was later supplemented and partly superseded by a high-level system. The New York subway system was the last to be organized in a world city, since the rock of Manhattan Island was not favorable to tunneling.

Toward the end of the century, but well before the introduction of the automobile, and in spite of the innovations, reformers fixed on traffic chaos and perpetual jams as the true urban plague. A Spanish engineer, Arturo Soria y Mata, familiar with Cerdá's theoretical writings, radicalized his ideas into what may have seemed the ultimate traffic solution in 1894: a *ciudad lineal* of tightly defined section, but infinitely extendable plan; a central roadway through which an electric railway line passed, and a bicycle and a carriage lane to be lined by two hundred meters of low-rise, but quite high density housing on either side. Beyond them was a belt of agricultural land, at least four kilometers wide. His aim, as Soria himself put it, was "to urbanize the country and ruralize the town" and provide rapid access to workplaces located in the old urban centers.

Although Soria foresaw a city running from Madrid to Saint Petersburg or Moscow, only some five kilometers, outside Madrid, were actually built and operated in 1897. In that same year he also founded a quarterly, *La Ciudad Lineal,* which may have been the first periodical concerned with planning matters—and which lasted long enough to give publicity to his project, but also time for alternative proposals to be considered. His ideas were taken up by the French urbanist Georges Benoit-Lévy, who even addressed the League of Nations on the subject in 1927. In the United States various adaptations were made, notably by Edgar Chambless, who proposed to concentrate urban populations into extremely long, snakily curving multistory buildings; it was a ribbon of repeated elements, as Soria's was, but Chambless's one was to be multistoried and had a monorail link running through its foundations. All public institutions were included—as episodes—within the structures, which were set sheerly in agricultural land. The most powerful impact of Soria's ideas came in the twenties. In 1929–30 the linear city reappears in Le Corbusier's plans for Rio de Janeiro and Buenos Aires as well as in the much-discussed plan for Algiers, to which he returned several times.[24] In Germany the idea was taken up enthusiastically as well. Ludwig Hilberseimer, architect and prolific urban theorist, had been called to the Bauhaus in Dessau in 1929 and immediately mobilized the students to turn out plans of Dessau as a linear city. After the Bauhaus was closed he moved to Chicago with his friend Ludwig Mies van der Rohe in 1938. In the plans he and his pupils developed for Chicago and the neighboring towns where main street is effectively a chaotic form of linear city development, the linear idea was elaborately developed, though there was surprisingly little direct application in practice.

In the Soviet Union this planning notion was taken up by a prolific sociologist, Mikhail Okhitovich, and was much favored by a number of Constructivist planner-architects, who called themselves "Disurbanizers" and saw the "linear city" as the remedy for urban chaos and sprawl. They produced a number of linear projects, the most famous being the plan for a "greening" of Moscow. Nikolai Miliutin, a politician and journalist, not an architect, headed the team, which produced a linear plan for Stalingrad and also took part in the 1929–30 competition design for the new heavy industry city of Magnitogorsk near the Ural iron mines.[25] Another team was led by Ivan Leonidov, perhaps the most brilliant designer of his time. The publication of his plan led to accusations of "Leonidovism" and more dangerously of petit-bourgeois tendencies. Leonidov was suspended from teaching and given humble jobs; he managed to survive until 1959. Okhitovich was made a scapegoat, was arrested in 1935 and disappeared. It was the last gasp of the "linear city" in eastern Europe.

An imported team of German architects under the leadership of Ernst May drew up a plan for Magnitogorsk. Having been the chief planner of Frankfurt, May produced a number of other Soviet plans on "rational" principles, of which Magnitogorsk was perhaps the most important. In 1933 the decision against the plan was taken at the highest level: the variants were proposed by G. K. Ordzhonikidze,[26] who was also present at a conference of the Presidium at which Stalin himself denounced the linear city as well as the relatively low density plans associated with May. He called for high density, six- and seven-story buildings, and more of them stone-faced. Fortunately, May had left the Soviet Union for Africa by 1933, and Magnitogorsk did not live up to the great investment of talent and energy devoted to it. It never became a great city, for all its mineral riches.

We shall never know whether the linear city would have finally solved all urban traffic problems as Soria promised, but at any rate, by the first decade of the twentieth century, the traffic pattern of the modern city was in place, even though vehicle numbers were increasing exponentially. Automobile production on an industrial scale only became possible just before 1900, but as that first decade drew on, it became clear that its impact on traffic movement would be great. Some urbanists became concerned, even alarmed. In 1906, a French architect, Eugène Hénard, whose brother and father were (like himself) trained at the Ecole des Beaux-Arts and who had invested a great of energy in the care of ancient monuments in an urban environment, proposed a number of simple devices to solve the intractable traffic problems. He was an indefatigable writer and published (1903–9) a number of pamphlets publicizing his ideas.

One device was a form of proto-cloverleaf crossing for busy central city roads. Another—more complex and expensive—was the construction of multilevel roads that would carry various forms of traffic underground, as well as provide public elevators. The most popular proved the roundabout or traffic circle (*ronde giratoire*). Vehicles entering the circle would move around it in one direction, and leave it on reaching the appropriate exit. Hénard wanted to create a focal point in these circles by setting an obelisk or a pavilion or even a column, lamppost, or fountain in the middle. Pedestrians would reach the center by underground passages.

Since he had first made his name with a detailed and conscientious study of Parisian buildings to be preserved, it was ironic that Hénard had such faith in the roundabout as a solution to traffic problems that he proposed planting one in the middle of one side of the Palais-Royal, a proposal that was never considered seriously by the authorities. In fact Hénard's device was taken up in Germany and Britain—where it became much more popular during the twenties and thirties than it had been in France—almost as soon as it was published. The traffic roundabout was not a new idea, of course; the *Plan des Artistes*, drawn up just after the Revolution, had suggested a number of them. Following it, the first large Parisian circle had been placed at Napoléon's behest at the Neuilly gate (the Barrière de l'Etoile)—since a number of roads converged on it— with a vast triumphal arch commemorating the ill-fated Grande Armée at the center. It was organized as a commerce-free monumental zone under Napoléon III.

Circular spaces were something of a novelty and very rare in urban layouts before then, even in theoretical ones. There had been curved the-aters and amphitheaters in antiquity, but no circular pedestrian or traffic spaces. In the seventeenth century circles do appear increasingly in park layouts. And one of the earliest circles in a city to have traffic circulating around a central statue, that of Louis XIV, was Place des Victoires, planned after 1685 in the west of Paris. The competition for the monu-ment "to the Glory of Louis XV" yielded a number of circular plazas, including proto-roundabouts on the left bank, at Buci and at the Odéon, though Ange-Jacques Gabriel's winning, executed project was the rect-angle that is now the Place de la Concorde.[27] Circular spaces appeared in other towns about this time, such as the Belle-Alliance Platz in Berlin, planned in 1734–37, or the Circus at Bath in 1753; ten years later the Royal Crescent was planned. There had been some earlier instances like Schloss-rondell at Schloss Nymphenburg outside Munich, planned in 1728. The most obvious of them, the Piazza del Popolo, which opens within the most stately, northern gate of Rome, received its central obelisk from Sixtus V in 1589, but did not get its oval form until 1824, though there were earlier plans; it did not become a one-way circulatory system until after 1950.

The circle as a plan form becomes enormously popular at the time of the Revolution. Many space-hogging circular *places* turn up in Polytech-nique projects. In any case, circulation would take up an ever greater percentage of the urban surface in response to the rising volume of traf-fic. This increase did not occur as a result of observed changes, but in anticipation of them. That is why I am tempted to conclude that it is concerned with something different: with the change in the nature of public space. The roundabout is primarily a space to move through, not a space to be or dwell in.[28]

If you look at older town plans this change in the nature of public places is clearly illustrated. The churches and civic buildings of a town are almost always shown in some detail in them, as if their floors were continuous with the street surface; the floor patterns both in and out are registered, and their internal columns or features have the same presence as the monuments and wall of the city. This continuity is graphically evident however impervious and elaborate the screening walls of palaces or façades of churches. Giambattista Nolli's plan of Rome, published in 1748, is perhaps the last clear instance of it. But even if you look at the splendid so-called Turgot Plan of Paris—which is more a projective aerial view than a plan proper, published in 1739—you might note how explicit the planning of parks and gardens appears, and the volumes of public buildings against the rather anonymous volumes of the houses. When in 1810 the Atlas of Paris was begun by two architects, Vasserot and Bellanger, all walls and all interior volumes were given the same weight. This kind of cadastral survey was continued throughout the nineteenth century. But from that time on, the city plan becomes a graphic but also a legal and fiscal summary of solid and void, not of public and private.

This internal visibility of the private realm is the product of another, very different change brought about by some utopian writers and the housing reform movements that I have already mentioned. From the mid-nineteenth century onward, middle-class and even working-class housing occupied architects increasingly; so much so that by the twentieth century it became their chief preoccupation, if one were to judge by publications, at any rate. The plans of houses and apartment blocks proliferate and are the subject of many competitions. It is as if, in the course of half a century, the whole building profession and industry had geared itself around to a new aim. From about 1900 onward the schools of architecture, the competitions, the building periodicals, and the government agencies concentrate on housing as their primary concern. This means that the way the history of architecture is written has to undergo a gear shift when it reaches 1875 or thereabouts; any historian looking at architecture after that has to concern himself or herself increasingly with housing. But there is another building type that challenges the architect's ingenuity: the factory. As the typology of housing is constantly discussed and refined, so a new attitude develops toward the place of work. When worker housing engulfs the factories, they become part of the urban fabric and their monumental possibilities are realized: the reputation of the manufacturer and the advertising potential of the factory as a part of the city. These two types of building, which earlier architects hardly considered, now become their main preoccupation.

4. Style, Type, and Urban Fabric

HOME OR THE PLACE OF WORK had never been the architects' main concern. They preferred to operate in the public realm. Before 1875 they were much more likely to have designed Railway Stations, Town Halls, Churches, Banks, Palaces and Private Mansions. Even the factory was not very interesting to them until the closing years of the century.

The most acrimonious and extended discussions of the nineteenth century were devoted to problems of style. It may seem frivolous to consider city fabric in such terms from the beginning of the twenty-first century, and yet not only nineteenth-century architects but also their clients devoted a vast amount of attention and energy to the discussion. The disputants also included many philosophers, historians, and social thinkers: Goethe, Ruskin, Chateaubriand, even Victor Hugo took sides. There were those who saw the inability of the nineteenth-century architects to achieve a unified "style for the age" as a reproach and a challenge. Inevitably, therefore, various claims were constantly being made that such a style had finally been achieved.

In these discussions, style referred to the surface of a building. It could be identified by ornament, which in turn seemed to have a more or less direct relation to material and to methods of working. But it was ornament, not the plan or the massing, or the interior volumes, that determined the style of a building. Yet style was not only about surfaces, it was often also a semiotic device.

Until the nineteenth century you "read" the building as a type—a town hall, a church, or whatever—by the way the masses were organized, certain precedents invoked, and the ornament selected. This relationship, based on an old metaphoric understanding of building, had been banished with the *ancien régime,* and was replaced by the idea that a building might declare itself to its users by historical, even narrative reference, or even more blandly by actually being labeled in large letters. This was one of the most rooted, yet the most diffuse aspects of historicism. Two main issues were disputed in this battle. Did style signal *what* the building was to be used for, or was it the style or the themes of the ornament that signified usage? And was the style to be dictated by ethnic and even political loyalties?

The discussion of style was, in any case, a novelty. In the sixteenth century, travelers returned with accounts of faraway societies whose manners and building styles were completely unfamiliar, yet coherent and admirable. In the West the notion of style was very much influenced by Giorgio Vasari, who thought that the development of art followed the same course as human life—childhood, youth, maturity, old age—and a new beginning. He had no doubt that this gave a true account of modern times, which were dominated by Tuscan art; his teacher, the "divine" Michelangelo, was its absolute master, and therefore this Tuscan work was the climax of all art; everything before Michelangelo had been a preparation for that climax, while everything after him had to be considered a decline. This quadruple division of infant gropings, rough youth, "classic" maturity, and degenerate aging was proclaimed as an absolute doctrine by the antiquarian-historian Johann Joachim Winckelmann, the founding father of neoclassicism, working from Rome. Goethe and Hegel took up Winckelmann's scheme; for Hegel it provided the structure of his historical vision, the philosophy and history of the whole century, and through him it made its impact on Marx, and provided the scheme which many writers on art then followed. It was inevitably taken up by later writers on architecture; one instance was Thomas Rickman's *Attempt to Discriminate the Style of Architecture in England,*[1] which in 1819 provided the terminology of the Gothic revival. Romanesque architecture became an antecedent, which he called "Norman," and was followed by a sequence of early English "decorated" or "perpendicular." Between early English and perpendicular, "decorated" became the perfect Gothic style.

That revival was slow in starting, since however vocal they were about this matter, nineteenth-century architects were not always very stringent. The style of the enormously prolific and successful John Nash, for instance, tended to a relaxed, even somewhat slapdash version of Italianate-archaeological. He took his turn at contracting and even at property development, and he was prepared, as were most of his contemporaries, to vary his style according to the occasion: for the prince regent, later George IV, he designed the generically "oriental" Royal Pavilion in Brighton, freely mixing Turkish, Arab, and Indian motifs; nor was he averse to Gothic when it seemed appropriate for the odd castle or cathedral, like Saint David's in Pembrokeshire, or a prison; he even experimented with a "primitive hut" style, producing a whole development in that manner at Blaise Hamlet near Bristol, which included an imitation druidical altar; and he managed all this while being quite adventurous in his use of new materials, particularly iron, and vastly enterprising in his major London undertakings, like Regent's Park and Regent Street.

Unlike Nash, the other major British architects of the time, John Soane, James Pennethorne, and Charles Barry, took this matter of style more seriously. But even they were affected by the capacity of industry to mass-produce ornament. All this coincided with the development of a hard, linear drawing technique with which even the best architects rendered surface. At the same time the conventional and abstract character of "historical" ornament taught by Jean-Nicolas-Louis Durand at the Ecole Polytechnique, as well as the Ecole des Beaux-Arts, was well known in England, France, and the United States. Durand's belief in the marginal nature of ornament was ancillary to his teaching about methods of design and his dogmatic concern with grids and axes. It is not clear how or why his views became so pervasive, though certainly French planners and architects in the wake of the Napoleonic engineers—many of whom had been trained by Durand—saw the axial planning as the only possible method of designing in cities. Through them it became the most influential hidden planning doctrine—its full influence is still not fully appreciated by historians of the city. Not only engineers and architects, but also financiers and developers swallowed it wrapped up in the sweetening of Saint-Simon's fiscal and technological teaching. The Chicago Plan of 1911 and the new capitals of Brasília and Islamabad show how the hidden hand of Durand went on controlling the planners' endeavors.

Ornament that is meant to work by historical association can never be specific and unequivocal. Town halls might be Gothic—evoking guildhalls and medieval free cities—but if they were Classical, they could refer to Roman or even to Athenian civic pride and primitive democracy.

In fact, Gothic suggested religion to some, even if the perversity of adopting medieval ornament for Lutheran and Calvinist liturgies did not escape some commentators. Financial institutions tended to prefer Classical trappings—which suggested stability and endurance. History was called in when questions of style had to be settled by reference to function: museums, banks, ministries, and palaces tended to be "Classical," on ancient Roman or Renaissance precedent, while churches might be Gothic, Romanesque, and even Byzantine.

All this allowed for a certain laxity in application: there was no need to commit oneself to any specific style, not even in the one building. Projects in more than one style were not unusual. In 1854 Edward Barry, whose father, Sir Charles, had designed the Houses of Parliament with Pugin, shocked some of his contemporaries by submitting four designs for the same plan in different styles for a competition. When Schinkel designed a rather opulent "Classical" church in the Werdersche Markt at the center of Berlin, King Frederick William IV of Prussia suggested that a Gothic church on the same plan might not only be "more Christian" but cheaper and more appropriate for parsimonious Prussian Lutherans. For the same king, Schinkel had designed a neo-antique opera house, and his most famous building, the Neues Museum, now Altes, was intended to evoke the stoas of ancient Athens where philosophers might perambulate in the colonnades of the new Athens, Berlin. In old Athens itself, the rapidly growing capital of the recently constituted Greek monarchy, once the birthplace of democracy, the issue of style caused polemics, as there was some doubt as to whether the style appropriate to the new state should be pseudoantique recalling ancient glories, or Byzantine and, therefore, a Christian style.

The most combative and committed Gothic paladins, however—such as Augustus Pugin and Eugène Viollet-le-Duc—were not content to revive the Gothic style, but wanted to return to what seemed to them a great historic moment in architecture, in order to find a way out of the decadent present and discover a new, nonhistorical style. Pugin's doctrines were surprisingly straightforward and free of any pedantry. He taught that (1) there should be no features about a building that are not necessary for convenience, construction, or propriety; and (2) that all ornament should consist of the essential construction.[2] He also emphasized that pointed, i.e., Gothic architecture was the only one (though he had the grace to add "strange as it may seem at first sight") in which these "great principles" were fulfilled. Viollet-le-Duc, secular and rationalist where Pugin was an enthusiastic convert to the Roman Church, was a very influential theorist and restorer. He forcefully advanced the notion that French thirteenth-century architecture was the most lucid of all the historic styles. The structure of a Gothic building was to him a representation of weights and tensions in balance and therefore provided the clearest example of a new architecture in which stone would be perfectly counterbalanced by iron and steel. Another innovation—large areas of industrial plate glass and the new wide spans of metal construction—would determine the modules and scale of a new urban order.

Gottfried Semper, the architect of the Museum and Opera in Dresden as well as of the museums in Vienna, believed something analogous about the Roman architecture of the sixteenth century, though he, too, was prepared to exercise Byzantine-Romanesque options. For all three, Pugin, Viollet, and Semper, the adoption of a specific historical precedent was only a preliminary step, and could provide the key to a future architecture. By returning to an ideal, or idealized, style, a way forward could be found to a different and better way of building than that prevailing in the unfortunate present.

In Britain, where the style battle had perhaps been fiercest and most pedantic, the term "the battle of the styles" was formulated by the young George Gilbert Scott, who would become the most successful of all the "Goths."[3] And the style question was given a new direction in 1836, when the competition conditions for the future Houses of Parliament explicitly demanded that they be designed in a "national style." This "national" style was identified as Gothic or Elizabethan. And that not altogether "pure" style was adopted for the winning project by Charles Barry and the same Augustus Pugin whose rather Spartan views on ornament I have just quoted. Pugin, in spite of that, provided Barry with his winning and coruscating surface of which Big Ben has become the most familiar fragment. Such "impurity" would be echoed in France and Germany. The vast cathedral of Marseilles was designed by Léon Vaudoyer in 1852 with "evocations of the domes of Byzantium, the marble-clad cathedrals of Tuscany . . . and the radiating chapels of French Romanesque pilgrimage churches. . . ."[4] Sometimes stylistic readings may have seemed perverse—as when some English Catholics, once they were allowed to build in central London, rejected Pugin's identification of Gothic with their faith. To them Neo-Renaissance or even better, Neo-Baroque—as of the Brompton Oratory (1878–1884), which was their principal church until the Byzantine Westminster Cathedral opened in 1902—proclaimed their loyalty to a modern and papal Rome, and this was more important than the invocation of some remote age of faith.

The most single-minded architects of the time—Soane and Schinkel—had already begun to search for a personal style that would owe only an indirect debt to history. Soane, who had little use for Gothic but was very judicious and knowing in his historical and archaeological references—sometimes using medieval motifs in a generally "Classical" framework—arrived, in his later designs of the 1820s and 1830s, such as the Dulwich Art Gallery and his own London house in Lincoln's Inn Fields, at a stripped and simplified classicism, which many of his contemporaries did not find acceptable at all, but architects such as James Stirling, Norman Foster, and the followers of Ludwig Mies van der Rohe a century later admired it. Mies van der Rohe was a constant admirer of Schinkel. In one of Schinkel's last buildings, the Bauakademie in Berlin, the architectural school in which he had a sumptuous apartment, and which was finished in 1836, he was praised for having achieved his own resolution by developing a wholly new style "out of the nature of brick."

The return to an idealized period in order to advance to a new style was also attempted in painting. In Germany the revival of medieval style and practice to include mosaic and fresco was sponsored by an energetic group which came to be known as "the Nazarenes" and were later emulated by the Pre-Raphaelites in England; architecture, some said, lagged behind. A young architect, Heinrich Hübsch, addressed a group of them in 1827, proposing a new style for the epoch, which he himself went on to practice. The address was published and became the focus for extended and acrimonious discussion. The style he advocated was to incorporate new metal construction, allowing large spans and the use of plate glass. He called it the *Rundbogenstil,* and the label stuck, though it was not an instant success. In 1850, on the order of King Maximilian II of Bavaria, the Academy of Fine Arts in Munich actually declared a competition to "invent a new style"; but although that also provoked a long debate, the prize was not awarded.

Inevitably some found this obsessive concern with style, even with the creation of new ones, unsatisfactory. John Ruskin did not believe that a new style was possible in his time, but went on preaching that an architecture that did not bear the mark of the inventive and even anarchic artist-craftsman who imitated nature in his ornament was not worth having. Beauty was not available without savagery. Although he made an impact on the universities and on some church builders, his voice—brilliant, seductive, and resonant—was one crying in the wilderness of heavily machine ornamented buildings.

A new factor in these discussions was the sharpening of scholarship and the proliferation of handbooks, of which Ruskin's own *Stones of Venice* was one of the most bulky.[5] In the decades before, and using the new printing techniques, aquatint, steel-engraving, and lithography, a great many designs were published for picturesque cottages destined to be a part of the "improved" landscape. Some were merely variants on the *cottage orné,* while others did propose structural and sanitary improvements. Humphrey Repton and John Claudius Loudon wrote very popular gardening handbooks that included advice on, and specimen designs for, houses. The Italianate landscapes of Claude Lorrain and Poussin were viewed as the ideal, and the most popular of the house pattern books, Charles Parker's *Villa Rustica,*[6] provided instructions on how such houses were to fit into landscapes. Enlightened patrons followed his recommendations: the bibliophile sixth duke of Devonshire removed the village of Edensor out of sight of his windows at Chatsworth and had Joseph Paxton (still acting as ducal gardener) design it "picturesquely," in the *Villa Rustica* manner. And this "style" could be fitted to more exalted uses. Prince Albert adapted it when he designed the private royal residence, Osborne House on the Isle of Wight, with Thomas Cubitt, whose firm built it. It was visible to anyone leaving or arriving by transatlantic ships in Southampton. The design was much published and became extremely influential, particularly in the United States.

Parker's Italianate style became a staple of this pattern book genre, spread from Britain to Europe and the United States through the publications of the father of American landscape architecture, Andrew Jackson Downing, and his English-born associate, Calvert Vaux. Downing had corresponded with Loudon, and Vaux made his career in the United States where he was to work on the design of Central Park in New York with Frederick Law Olmsted. As Vaux pointed out, the services of architects were not always easily available in the New World,[7] which gave the pattern books their special importance and paved the way for the much more extensive and very profitable possibility of buying designs, and later, whole prefabricated houses from catalogues by mail order. In fact, the plans and surfaces of suburbia still owe a great deal to the nineteenth-century pattern books. The mail-order house continued to be popular until relatively recently.

In England, the way in which the new styles were applied was evident in the very different railway stations built in less than twenty years within five minutes' walk of each other. The first metropolitan railway station ever was Euston, built in 1836. Robert Stephenson, working with architect Philip Hardwick, conceived a kind of propylon for the city, a huge Doric gateway, behind which the railways drew up directly as on a forecourt.[8] Ten years later (1846–49) the bare forecourt was separated from the street by a large entry hall designed by Hardwick's son, Philip C., and so instituted the railway station "type," in which the railway lines, almost always covered by a more or less adventurous metal structure, were sheltered from the street by a substantial and usually monumental entrance hall. A couple of years later, the new railway station at King's Cross was designed by Lewis, the youngest of the Cubitt brothers, in a version of *Rundbogenstil,* modulated by the kind of Italianate, pattern-book detailing the Cubitts had used in their housing. Contemporaries even spoke of an "Italian style, more properly called English railroad style."[9] Between King's Cross and Euston, the other northwest London railway station, Saint Pancras, answered their classic and *Rundbogenstil* inspiration with Gothic cast iron (1865–67 by Sir George Gilbert Scott).

The story of the origin of the Saint Pancras project has been told often. It illustrates both the importance of style and its ambiguities. Commissioned to design a new building for the Foreign Office overlooking Saint James's Park, the young George Gilbert Scott at first produced a Gothic building that was rejected by the overbearing Whig magnate, Lord Palmerston, who had become Prime Minister just then. Palmerston said that "he must insist on . . . a design in the Italian style," which (he felt sure) Scott could do equally well. Mortified, Scott translated his original project into a Ruskinite Byzantine-Venetian manner. But the minister found the revised version to be "neither one thing nor t'other— a regular mongrel affair." He wanted the "ordinary Italian." Scott thought of his fee and his family, bought "some costly books," and complied, and the outcome was the rather flabby building that still overlooks Saint James's Park. He adapted the modified Gothic project to Saint Pancras's Station, "though divested of the Italian element," and Scott confessed that he considered the design "too good for its purpose," presumably because its exalted Gothic manner should not serve such base utilitarian needs as railway travel.[10]

The quarrel between architect and client was public, widely discussed, and even reported in the popular American magazine *The Crayon. The Crayon* also employed the young Moravian and Vienna-trained Leopold Eidlitz, newly arrived in New York in 1845, as a writer who set out the doctrine of *Rundbogenstil* for America, though the architecture he practiced was very Ruskinian, as one of his earliest and most successful independent designs, that for the Dry Dock Savings Bank in New York of 1857, clearly shows. But Eidlitz would also collaborate with Henry Hobson Richardson on the State Congress in Albany, New York, while Richardson's design for Trinity Church in Boston may be the most accomplished of all *Rundbogenstil* achievements. Eidlitz's friend and apologist Montgomery Schuyler became the most celebrated American architectural writer of the century, and through his advocacy the *Rundbogenstil* made a powerful contribution to the Chicago style of the 1870s and 1880s.

The business of the battle of the styles was played out in the first International Exposition of 1851. The idea of such a fair had been rejected in France, but it was an English civil servant, Sir Henry Cole, backed by the authority and energy of Prince Albert, who created the project, and it summed up the excited enthusiasm of the mid-Victorians for the unprecedented achievements of their own time. The artists and reformers around Henry Cole had formed a pressure group, the Art Manufacturers, to "promote public taste" through "beauty applied to mechanical production." Cole, under the pen name Felix Summerly—he could not involve himself in "commercial" activities as he was a civil servant—had published popular guides to monuments and designed china and metal objects whose forms were based on plants, while a group of artists associated with him reformed art education in England beginning with elementary schools. Unexpectedly, it was the not as yet knighted former gardener, Joseph Paxton, who provided shelter for the Exposition in the form of the Crystal Palace, inspired by his greenhouses of Chatsworth. It turned out to be a brilliant public success and inspired much enthusiasm as well as some opposition. John Ruskin dismissed it as "a cucumber frame," but he was in a small minority. The world applauded the vast, translucent, iron-and-plate-glass monument. Ironically enough, Turner—the painter Ruskin most admired—observed it with great interest a few weeks before his final decline:

> It looks very well in front because the transept takes a centre like a dome, but sideway ribs of glass frame work only towering over the galleries like a giant.[11]

The long nave of 1,851 feet, the transept, and the double aisles filled with exhibits, were recognizable "elements" of a public building. The relatively small structural bits and pieces may have been familiar from greenhouse as well as shopping-arcade construction, but their combination was unexpected, unprecedented; above all, the organization of the building, with all the metal pieces cast and finished in various Midland foundries—mostly in Birmingham, and assembled on-site in record time—seemed prodigious. The style, too, could not be identified, though the cast-iron columns and the arched ribs were certainly quite elaborately ornamented—even if the excessive transparency had to be shrouded in scarlet drapes to make the building more "substantial" at ground level. The success led to instant imitations: in New York, in Munich, in Dublin.

The impact on the city fabric was quick: soon there were many proposals for providing sheltered public and communication areas. The schemes varied from sensible and manageable to the phantasmagoric. The possibility of covering a whole street with glass had first been exploited in Paris, toward the end of the eighteenth century, in the Palais-Royal, then the residence of a junior branch of the royal family. The shopping arcades around the palace garden, which provided much-needed income for the minor royals, were supplemented by a glazed wooden structure that crossed the gardens, to be replaced after 1828 by the glass-roofed masonry building which became a model for such constructions. In the second half of the century there followed many schemes for glazing-in not just pedestrian streets, but entire boulevards, even tree-lined ones, and a number were actually built, but only for the use of pedestrians. The longest arcade remains the Gallery of Saint Hubertus, built in 1847 in Brussels, four years before the Crystal Palace. The tallest were built in Cleveland, Ohio, and in Naples, though the grandest and perhaps the most famous was that of Victor Emmanuel II in Milan of 1865–67. The roomiest must be the GUM, the New Trade Hall in Moscow. More recently, after 1950, the type was revived in the context of the urban shopping center: the Eaton Center in Toronto and the Galleria in Houston are directly modeled on the Milan prototype.

There were those who wanted to extend the glazed arcade even further. A Mr. Gaye, then director of the Italian Opera House at Covent Garden in London, proposed a vast brick viaduct supporting a glass-and-iron arcade seventy feet high, which would include a pneumatic postal service and connect the Bank of England to Trafalgar Square, a distance of some eight miles. That was in 1845, but within a few years, a much more ambitious project for encircling central London with a viaduct-arcade was presented to the now constituted Commission for Metropolitan Improvements. Paxton, by now a member of Parliament, proposed to connect all the London railway stations with a ten-mile mixed-use and multilevel gallery, sixty feet wide and ninety high. The lowest roadways were to carry railway lines, both slow and express;

higher levels would be lined with shops and heated in the winter. Although Paxton (being a realist) worked at the project in great financial detail and inspired great enthusiasm from Queen Victoria and Prince Albert, and everyone generally, yet the money could not be found to carry out the plan.

While the glass-and-iron-covered street was being built all over the world, the Crystal Palace made its own contribution to the discussion of style. The architect-publicist-ornamentalist Owen Jones, close to Henry Cole's circle, provided the sharp color scheme of the iron structure, and based it on the complementaries purple and orange. It brought him the international fame that his book *The Grammar of Ornament*, published in 1856, confirmed and extended. At first sight the book might seem an invitation to eclecticism: Chinese and Japanese, Greek and Turkish, Arabic, and even African ornaments are presented in varying numbers of brilliantly colored lithographic plates. His book was part of a new genre, since the old Eurocentric manuals were now set aside for surveys of the exotic. Chromolithography became the preferred medium for these publications.

Yet the real pith of Jones's book are the ten closing plates in which a variety of plants are presented with such fidelity that they almost look as if they were real leaves and flowers pressed between the pages. These are to be, Jones suggests, the true models of the ornament of the future—and not all the exotic and historical examples of which his book is full. His book went through many editions and was pored over by architects and designers all over the world. It helped further the notion that new ornament, derived from natural forms—and therefore a whole new style—might be altogether separated from one grounded in historical reference: an idea that came to full fruition in Art Nouveau. More generally, Jones, like Cole, was interested in breaking down the barrier between "high" and "popular" or even "industrial" art. These concerns had obvious economic implications. International exhibitions showed up flaws and promoted competition in taste and design, and this concerned politicians and industrialists who worried about the appeal of their industrial goods and the share of the foreign markets their own countries could command. Education was considered an effective remedy for shoddy design and for the alarming decline in what the manufacturers produced. Taste was obviously becoming an important commercial factor, and various institutes and academies, which therefore taught design to the lower orders, who would work in industry without aspiring to the status of artists, were opened in England and Germany—

though they had in fact existed earlier in France. These schools were required to offer examples on which the pupils formed and improved their taste.

The improvement of taste was to affect not only the mechanical draftsmen working on ornament, but even the "higher" artists and the general public. The importation of—and sometimes the battle for—the best antiquities can be read as attempts to remedy the deficiencies of public taste and of industrial production. The purchase of the Elgin Marbles by the British government in 1806 was supposed to stimulate a lasting revival of British art, which was to come to fruition, thirty years later, in the project to decorate the Houses of Parliament with frescoes illustrating British history, and make its chambers a gallery of great new British art. Industrialists were busy founding collections of art for public display, and endowing the buildings to house them, which they saw as magnets for prestige and publicity. The explosion of museums in the late twentieth century, though it was based on these tentative beginnings, is an entirely new phenomenon.

Jones and Cole were totally convinced of the benefits that industry would ultimately bring, and themselves designed objects and patterns for industrial production; John Ruskin and his followers, of whom William Morris was the most prolific and important, on the other hand, expected a new civilization and a new style to arise from a violent attack on the whole industrial-capitalist social framework, and therefore saw the revival and maintenance of craft standards as their prime social responsibility.

For all their political and ideological differences, Morris drew on those ten plates in Jones's *Grammar,* as did many of his contemporaries, and a move in the same direction as that of the Cole-Jones circles was made by their most articulate opponents, the Pre-Raphaelite painters and other friends of Ruskin—Edward Burne-Jones, Holman Hunt, and Dante Gabriel Rossetti—who began decorating furniture and other "everyday" objects, designing tapestries and embroidery—all of which culminated in William Morris's splendid and, virtually, one-man effort to revive medieval craft production for domestic consumption. Morris's copiously hand-made products—wallpapers, textiles, furniture, metal-work—and the publications that accompanied them, were enormously popular among the "swinish rich" whom, as an active socialist, he despised; many who did not necessarily have much sympathy with his political attitudes—and who are collectively known as the Arts and Crafts movement—emulated him.

The architects of the Arts and Crafts movement managed to combine the "picturesque" attitude found in earlier pattern books with an attractive and curious mix of medieval brick outlines framing eighteenth-century sashes and casements—something they considered "vernacular" and therefore timeless. This mix came to be known as the Queen Anne style.[12] Philip Webb, who designed the "Red House" for Morris at Bexley Heath, on the Kent edge of London, provided the prototype for it in 1859; Norman Shaw was its most successful and best-known practitioner, and William Godwin the most refined; it was he who came closest to incorporating "aesthetic" Japanese-type details and ornament into the style. Godwin, too, was the first architect to work on a new kind of enterprise, a suburb offering housing alone, therefore called a "dormitory" suburb. One of these, Bedford Park, to the west of London, was developed when a new railway station was opened at Turnham Green about 1875. A different developer from the time of the Cubitts and the Burtons had had the district laid out by an obscure surveyor, and the architects—Godwin first, then Norman Shaw and his disciples—designed the public buildings: a church, an "institute" (or club), and an inn. They also provided basic house designs, which both builders and patrons were at liberty to vary. It was a commercial success, catering to a "refined" and "progressive" public, as a contemporary ballad, "spoken" by the developer, explains:

> "Here trees are green and bricks are red
>   and clean the face of man,
> We'll build our houses here," he said,
>   "in style of good Queen Anne" . . .
> Now he who loves aesthetic cheer
>   and does not mind the damp
> May come and read Rossetti here
>   by a Japanese-y lamp.[13]

G. K. Chesterton set his *Man Who Was Thursday* in Saffron Park, a thinly designed version of Bedford Park:

> The stranger who looked for the first time at the quaint red houses could only think how very oddly shaped the people must be who could fit in them. . . . Even if the people were not "artists," the whole was nevertheless artistic.[14]

This publicity witnesses to the enormous interest that Bedford Park stimulated, and indeed it soon became the one modern site that any young architect coming to London would visit. With its wholly middle-class population, it turned out to be the ancestor of an infinite number of such suburbs in Anglo-Saxon countries.

Soon after 1870, Shaw designed the first really prominent mansion apartment block in London based on Parisian precedent, Albert Hall Mansions overlooking Kensington Gardens and facing the Albert memorial where the Crystal Palace had once stood. Using relatively cheap materials, it managed the "Queen Anne Style" blend with an irregular, picturesque grouping. Many of the architects employed by the London County Council both on housing and on public services—schools, fire and police stations—were followers of Norman Shaw. In the last decades of the century, the LCC finally conceded that organized working-class housing was not just the thin wedge of state socialism. The first—or at any rate the pilot—public housing scheme, Boundary Street in Bethnal Green of 1890, involved slum clearance and was cast in the new style.

As the century drew on, the issue of style and ornament paled; somehow technical achievements seemed to transcend these quarrels. The immediate impact of the first World Exposition was that it provoked competition between London and Paris, and Paris had won. In 1853 the vast iron-and-glass market, Les Halles, was built on the emperor's insistence that the buildings be "vast umbrellas," in fact a huge "arcade." There had been earlier iron-and-glass markets, of course, but nothing on the scale of Les Halles. Hector Horeau, an engineer, who had won the first prize for a cast-iron hall for the 1851 Exhibition in London, proposed a vast, single-span building; Eugène Flachat, yet another Polytechnician and a follower of Saint-Simon—and the first major French railway builder, responsible for the stations at Saint Lazare and Montparnasse—proposed a more complex and articulated but also very wide spanned hall. Such projects frightened the authorities, who preferred Victor Baltard's more sedate solution for Les Halles.

After the first big bang of the Crystal Palace, the London fairs were not structurally ambitious, unlike the later Parisian ones; important fairs thereafter, and until 1937, were all held in Paris. This is at least in part due to Napoléon III's, and his successors', faith in deficit financing, which Haussmann called *dépenses productives*. For the first Parisian 1855 fair, the nave of the main hall had a vast span of forty-eight meters, 160 feet, more than twice that of the seventy-two feet of the Crystal

Palace. It was not adventurous though, since it was buttressed by great masses of brick and lead. But in 1867, a huge glazed oval structure covered most of the Champ-de-Mars in Paris and proved the last world's fair to be contained in one building. It was ringed by a Halle des Machines in which Gustave Eiffel and his associate J. B. Krantz accomplished spans of astonishing elegance. They also introduced the very first hydraulic elevators: a cabin set on a telescopic rod that was raised by pressurized water, quite common later in Paris, Lyon, and Marseilles and even tried in New York in the Flatiron Building. Gradually these were all replaced by Otis's electric safety elevator so that by 1950 few hydraulic elevators were operational. Around the same time central pressured air was also supplied to work an alternative system of telescopic elevators, also seen for the first time in Paris, as well as the pneumatic postal service that ensured the delivery of Parisian mail at telegraphic speeds. It was in operation until the 1950s, so that the ubiquitous blue *pneumatique* forms still appeared in post–World War II French literature.

At the Universal Exposition of 1878 the use of glass curtain walls and another highly inventive steel-and-glass machine gallery confirmed a France returned to prosperity after the defeat of 1870, though the really spectacular exhibition was the one of 1889—for the centenary of the Revolution—whose (by then the third) Galerie des Machines was the largest span ever roofed, 115 meters (nearly 350 feet—seven times the span of the Crystal Palace nave). The hall was covered by a series of steel three-hinged arches and was even more remarkable than the 300-meter tower adjoining it, designed by the now celebrated Gustave Eiffel. The Eiffel Tower is the only reminder of that great triumph of French engineering.

It was taken for granted that all these buildings, however structurally adventurous, would carry ornament, which could be very obtrusive. The vast arches that connect the piers of the Eiffel Tower, and their repeated palmette motifs, have no structural function at all, but serve to "bind" the structure visually. Nor was there any call for such ornament to be of a piece stylistically. Usually it was conventional and eclectic, though on the whole engineers preferred simplified classic ornament to the less spiky and less amenable Gothic.

Such problems of style were exacerbated and diffused by the reproachful presence of grand but crumbling medieval structures. Many of the restorers of these buildings held some form of the tripartite Winckelmann-Hegel notion of style, by which the middle period was always the superior one. In England this meant that "Early English" buildings could be brought up to their "Decorated" potentiality, while the decadent "Perpendicular," never mind "Tudor," accretions could be stripped out. George Gilbert Scott, of Saint Pancras and Foreign Office fame, was a radical, if not an ignorant restorer, and it brought down on him the wrath of William Morris and his friends. The Society for the Protection of Ancient Buildings was founded in 1877, specifically to protect Tewkesbury Abbey from Scott, but it soon widened its activities and remains a force in historical preservation, partly responsible for the preference for that term over "restoration." There was no equivalent movement in France, or in Germany and Austria until much later, but the French restorers' work had government and even Imperial backing. Viollet-le-Duc, a personal friend of Napoléon III, resurfaced many of the French cathedrals, notably Nôtre-Dame in Paris. He, and others, believed that medieval monuments should be set free from the "accretions" that had gathered about and onto them. Nôtre-Dame, Milan Cathedral, that of Chartres, and Saint Stephen's in Vienna, were isolated from surrounding buildings and—as in Milan—provided with a large new square, often with a statue in the middle. This is certainly not how they were conceived by their builders. A great medieval church was primarily a façade within the city, a front. It also towered over its town as a landmark; yet within it was a soaring vault and a glittering, luminous array of stained glass, hanging as though it were a curtain, to enclose and define the volume, which is the primary function of such a building. The rest of the structure stretching back from the façade is a kind of exoskeleton—a carapace from which the vault is in turn suspended, and which is of secondary interest. That is why in the great abbeys and cathedrals, the cloisters, even when they are built in one continuous campaign, nestle between the buttresses of the abbey church, as at Westminster Abbey, Durham, or Canterbury; or in France, at Cluny and Rheims; Salamanca and Burgos in Spain; Batalha in Portugal. The great church is embedded in the close texture of the monastery or of the town, and opens within it. You see the bulk of the main building only in glimpses, but denuded of its accretions and barnacles, of the workshops, the shops and stalls that clung to it, it is impoverished, and, in a way, also betrayed.

These misunderstandings of the restorers reached breaking-point when a new "Gothic" building, the Votivkirche in Vienna, was centrally placed in a newly organized urban space. It touched off an important protest. The Votivkirche commemorated a failed attempt on the emperor Franz Joseph's life (in 1853—though the building was not finished until 1879) and was designed by one of Vienna's leading architects, Heinrich Frestel. It is more important for the reaction it produced than for its wholly conventional appearance. It provoked a Viennese painter-architect, Camillo Sitte, who had been a pupil of Frestel's, to propose a different setting for it, and justify this in a pamphlet, *City Planning According to Its Artistic Principles*,[15] which first appeared in 1889 and was immediately reprinted. It was translated into French in 1902, into Russian in 1925, Spanish in 1926, though no English translation was published until 1945. The enormous popularity of the book was paradoxical, since it went directly counter to much very pragmatic current planning practice. Sitte's opposition to and contempt for the sanitary and traffic engineers who were the masters of the city plan had an immediate appeal—the excessive technologism of the engineers and the greed of the developers was as unpopular then as it is now.

Sitte denounced the tendency of contemporary planners to pin and erode central public space with monuments, and appealed to the example of both the ancient and the medieval city where such monuments were used to outline public areas so that their centers were left open for assembly and free circulation. He was sarcastic about the roundabout as a planning device, and used the Parisian *rond-point* at the Etoile, and its triumphal arch, as the prime negative example. But his ultimate enemy was the overexploitation of the city block by developers; he also cordially disliked the uniform and straight avenues that the planners of his day often laid out, and justified his disapproval of such planning by citing the awkward traffic-crossing that was the inevitable result. Above all, he praised the beauty and commodity of the medieval city. He is now more often associated with his secondary concern, the charm of winding streets and the exploitation of vistas, rather than with his primary one: the integrity of open spaces—plazas rather than squares—since he liked them irregular and interconnected. He insisted that they were civic "rooms" and should be left open; any statues and buildings should outline, not occupy the space.

And Sitte's book was not just a success with the public. Joseph Stübben, whose handbook for town planning was probably the most popular manual on the subject, and who had won the competition for the replanning of Vienna in the year of Sitte's publication, was one of his most useful converts. That handbook, which also quotes Sitte, and first appeared in 1890 as part of a very popular German series of building manuals, was also called *Städtebau*, as was the periodical founded by Sitte, which was widely read. He found himself much in demand as a consultant and juror of competitions while being given several important commissions. Sitte's principal English convert, Raymond Unwin, quotes Sitte repeatedly in his *Town Planning in Practice*, a book that went through many editions from 1909 onward. Sitte's influence was to have the most impact on the planners of the English Garden Cities, in Scandinavia and Holland, on the design of many American suburbs through Clarence Stein, as well as on German *Siedlungen*. Le Corbusier read the French translation of Sitte's book, probably in 1910, and was immediately seduced by it. He planned a book on Sittean principles, and returned to it several times, though when he finally published his *Urbanisme* in 1925, it was an explicit rejection of Sitte's willful preference for medieval-type irregularities. Modernity, Corbusier said, required the grid and the straight line, though if you look at the drawings and the plans that illustrate his arguments, the debt to Sitte is evident.[16]

Sitte makes an even more uneasy appearance in some recent books on the city: his love of Richard Wagner associated him, somewhat arbitrarily, with the *völkisch* architects and planners who served the Nazis.[17] Yet his own ideal of the mixed-use city with agora-like public spaces would not have accommodated the marches and rallies of the Nazis nor even the regimentation of the *Kraft-durch-Freude* party settlements. His medievalism is corporate, that of the Meistersingers, and it was diametrically opposed to the Speer-Hitler axialities of their unrealized Berlin plan, which goes back to the worst inanities of Durand's disciples and successors.

Sitte's contemporary, the enormously successful Viennese architect and planner Otto Wagner, who designed the Viennese underground railway, and was another winner of that Viennese planning competition of 1893, had quite a different view of the future city, which he also published, and fragmentarily applied. Although he was more sanguine about modernity than Sitte, he also wanted a controlled and contained city. His *Grosstadt* was Vienna, and it was to grow on a network of circular and radial roads by discrete units of some 100,000 to 150,000 inhabitants; each unit would have mixed-use public buildings and a center, but unlike Sitte's town, it would have wide, straight, tree-lined avenues, and uniform-height apartment blocks.

Sitte was stylistically consistent; Wagner was more volatile and passed through many different styles. From his early neo-Renaissance efforts, which he shared with Sitte, Wagner moved through an exuberant Art Nouveau phase to an emphatically geometric and classicizing modernity, although he claimed to have no interest in style himself. Stylistic change, Wagner thought, was a product of change in behavior and in construction; it is only when they have been absorbed that a new style will inevitably result. Different though their approaches were, Wagner and Sitte start from an analogous dislike of the Viennese Ringstrasse. Wagner despised its masquerade of historical styles, Sitte its windy and excessive open spaces which leave the monuments isolated in the traffic and makes them unapproachable. Whatever divided Wagner and Sitte, however, they both considered the city a collective work of art.

Wagner died in 1917, having projected a victory/peace church for Vienna. Yet Vienna after the war was not the capital of an empire, but of a small republic. It had a socialist administration, which considered working-class housing as its prime duty. Karl Ehn, a pupil of Wagner's, became its technical director and served first as a socialist, then, after 1938, as a Nazi. He is most closely associated with the building of the block-size apartment housing estates, the *Höfe*, of which the most famous was the Karl-Marx Hof, built in 1927, which became a bastion of the left during the disturbances of 1934. Between the end of the war and those troubles, sixty-four thousand housing units had been built, and they can, in some sense, be regarded as the beginning of the realization of Wagner's *Grosstadt*.

The different styles discussed here had been more or less historically derivative, however carefully refined. They did not obey Owen Jones's injunction to derive style and ornament from nature alone. "Nature" at this time had a specific cultural weight. Charles Darwin was the paradigm of the scientist and nature was therefore the nature of biology, but it is difficult to estimate the effect of biology on design. As I have suggested, it seems to underlie Cerdá's understanding of urbanism, as it does the increasingly "organic" nature of the *Siedlung* plans such as those for Krupp. It is essential to the understanding of the wholly new style, whose ethos owed much to Ruskin and Morris, but whose structural methods owed more, perhaps, to Viollet-le-Duc. Its full ornamental panoply was rapidly achieved in the late 1880s and was hailed as the style for the forthcoming, the twentieth century. As its predecessors and heralds demanded, it made much use of exposed metal and much glass. Its ornamental forms, if not based directly on nature as Owen Jones and John Ruskin had both decreed, were linear and abstract, though always curvilinear.

This new style seemed both fresh and popular when it finally appeared, and its names in different languages—*Art Nouveau* in English, *Style Métro, Yachting Style* in French, *Jugendstil* in German, *Stile Liberty* in Italian—all carried overtones of exoticism, new flowering, spring, of popularity, and of commerce. A number of its practitioners were involved in left-wing politics, and one of its principal monuments, the

Maison du Peuple in Brussels, designed by Victor Horta in 1896–99 and destroyed by a developer in 1963, was a trade union headquarters. The style was promoted in aspiring provincial centers rather than the world cities: Brussels, Nancy, Glasgow, Turin, and Barcelona saw its most brilliant manifestations. It left its mark most obviously on Paris in the extravagant Métro stations that one of its most brilliant exponents, Hector Guimard, designed at the time of the World Exposition of 1900, and which were the only contributions of any great architectural distinction to that opulent show. Guimard's stations were designed in a very floriated, linear, and energetic style. Art Nouveau owed much to Jones and Morris, but also something to the Japanese example, which had become extremely fashionable in the last decades of the nineteenth century. The exotic element was an important ingredient at a time when the whole of Western civilization seemed to be in decline or in radical transformation.[18] The 1900 Exposition had been a great triumph of public relations, like the 1937 World's Fair was to be on the eve of World War II. But that 1937 Fair could give only three more years of life to the image of Paris as *ville-lumière*. After Hitler marched down the Champs-Elysées, Paris never did recover its status, and New York "stole modern art."[19]

And yet that very optimistic style had no lasting power. The 1900 Exposition had not given it wider circulation, while in 1902 a world exhibition of Decorative Art in Turin, which was to have been its triumph, turned out to be its winding up. Clearly, Owen Jones's hope that a style could be deliberately developed, with a whole ornamental vocabulary based on natural forms, was simply not going to be realized. Although a few designers and architects went on bravely developing its themes for a year or two, its energy had flagged after a mere decade. The century whose style it was meant to be did not want to know about it. There followed a time of some confusion, which ended violently in 1914. Historical styles, even in their mixed and modified versions as practiced by the Anglo-Saxons, did not engage the best architects or designers. The very successful practitioners who had exhibited in Turin—Peter Behrens and Bruno Paul in Germany, Josef-Maria Olbrich and Josef Hoffmann from Austria, as well as the Frenchman Auguste Perret—all attempted forms of simplified, austere, and often quite unadorned "classical" architecture reminiscent of Schinkel and Soane in their "astylar" modes, experimenting with the control of geometry to achieve harmonious proportions. Concrete was used rather than steel.

Peter Behrens was appointed chief designer to AEG, the most powerful electrical producer in the world in 1907: he effectively "styled" that huge enterprise—from trademark to factory buildings—and controlled all the products from electric bulb filaments to powerful turbines. All AEG's publicity was printed in a typeface he designed. His Viennese contemporaries also turned to the manufacture of everyday things, though they had no such industrial backing, so that the Wiener Werkstätte produced a stream of more or less "astylar" geometrical and sumptuous objects into the 1920s by old craft methods.

The defeat of 1918 and the financial crisis that followed it played havoc with any notion of style in Germany. Architects reacted to a change of circumstance and a lack of commissions by withdrawing from the orderliness of the last Imperial period. Vast utopian schemes, "Cathedrals of Humanity, Mountains of Light," were drawn and published. The highly successful classicizing architects and designers of the prewar times, Peter Behrens among them, experimented with dramatic, fluid forms that depended on the plasticity of poured concrete and sharp colors, the transparency of glass. Some architects identified their approach with that of Expressionist painters, a movement that had originated before the outbreak of the war, and demanded the deformation of perceived forms in the interest of greater faith to emotion, an approach they had absorbed from "primitive," particularly Polynesian art.

Having produced a few remarkable buildings—the Einstein Tower in Potsdam of 1919, designed by Erich Mendelsohn, is perhaps the best known—the architects most immediately affected by the movement—Walter Gropius, Ludwig Mies van der Rohe, Bruno Taut—shifted their attention to *Sachlichkeit,* a concern with common-sense and a matter-of-fact approach to building. It was to dominate German architecture before the advent of Hitler in 1933. However, the influence of the Expressionist movement, first over the European art of the interwar period, and later over American art—as the very term "Abstract Expressionism" shows—remained powerful and is still with us.[20]

The quick stylistic changes that had occurred after 1900 reflected another very important shift. Ornament and even style came to be seen as beside the point when the new city was being discussed, particularly when the needs of mass-housing were so urgent. Great urban constructions that had been given prime attention in the nineteenth century were no longer of interest; factories, dams, hangars, silos, warehouses, and high-rise buildings seemed the challenging types.

There was a radical shift in the visual arts: Realist and Impressionist painters may not have celebrated the industrial worker and the factory, as they did peasants and manual laborers, but they saw their contemporaries, particularly their working contemporaries, as heroes. The epic mode, which for centuries had been the appropriate manner for representing antiquity and sacred history, was extended in the nineteenth century to the Middle Ages and was evident in Rossini's and Donizetti's (but, above all, in Wagner's) operas, as well as in Nazarene and Pre-Raphaelite painting. By the end of the century, the epic mode was appropriating everyday life. The domesticity of the kitchen and the bedroom, which had been at home in the novel and the still-life, now invaded the canvas aggressively. Actual newspaper clippings and pieces of cheap machine-printed wallpapers appeared as abrasive fragments in Cubist paintings: Collage was born.

"You read the handouts, the catalogues, the posters which sing so loud. That is your poetry this morning and for prose you have the daily papers. . . ." Guillaume Apollinaire, a great poet who was also the chief apologist of Cubism, wrote ruefully,[21] aware of the cost that negotiating the broken breach between high-culture and the machine involved, a breach handled so awkwardly in the nineteenth century. It may be accidental that the first illustration of his book on Cubism is Picasso's painting of a factory at Horta del Ebro, which is dominated by the faceted solid of its tall chimney.[22]

Yet some Cubists still thought of their art in terms of a style; Raymond Duchamp-Villon, brother of the much more famous Marcel, designed Cubist ornament for an otherwise conventional and rather ungainly house, which was exhibited in the Salon d'Automne of 1912. It was also published in Apollinaire's combative Les Peintres Cubistes the following year, and even if it was considered a maverick exercise, its consequences were surprising.

The 1912 Paris Salon exhibition had been organized by the Belgian critic and architect Frantz Jourdain, and he was responsible for introducing decorative art into that yearly and very academic show. Together with his son, Francis, he developed Duchamp-Villon–type ornament. At the same time, the rather different geometrical manner that Peter Behrens and Bruno Paul, Josef Hoffmann, and Charles Rennie Mackintosh had developed out of Art Nouveau absorbed it, and by 1920 a new style, involving jagged lines and angles, fancy glass and mirrors, and lush surfaces was formulated; called Art Déco after yet another Paris exhibition, that of the Decorative Arts in 1925, it now seemed to encapsulate the brilliance of the "cocktail" or the "jazz age," the exuberances of the nineteen-twenties. Its very brief (and somewhat camp) flowering seemed to offer a cheerful and occasionally urbane way of dealing with the austerities that modernism imposed by combining a geometricized version of Art Nouveau motifs with a suggestion of "scientific" streamlining. It provided splendid opportunities for fashion designers—for Paul Poiret,

Jeanne Lanvin, and later Coco Chanel. It is also associated with the French furniture of the period—Ruhlmann, Mallet-Stevens, Henri Sauvage (the last had, before 1914, been one of the pioneers of low-cost housing) and seemed ideally suited to the interiors of transatlantic liners. It was adopted quickly in the United States and became the accessory of hotel and skyscraper designers. Some of the biggest buildings just before 1930—40 Wall Street, the Chrysler Building, and the Empire State Building in New York, as well as the Merchandise Mart in Chicago (not a skyscraper perhaps, but until the construction of the Pentagon, listed as "the world's largest building")—appealed to it. In the event, it turned out to be even more ephemeral than Art Nouveau and was killed off by the 1929 stock market crash.

Duchamp-Villon himself died in 1918, having survived a wartime gas attack. His most memorable work, the large bronze sculpture *The Horse*, with its implications of mechanical complexity and of movement, was associated with Cubism but perhaps even more with another group, the Italo-French (later also Russian and English) Futurists. They claimed to have devised an epic way of making music, painting, sculpture—even food—celebrate the current conditions: new forms of locomotion and manufacture, a catastrophic increase in speed, the view of the earth from the air. Their city, proudly vaunting much that we now consider the curses of modernity—cacophony, fumes, the speeding vehicles, ever-present airplanes—did not have a universal appeal. But the Futurist manifestos, beginning in 1909, spawned many aggressive publications from different movements that were closely interrelated and often shared membership. Together, they constitute "the avant-garde" of the twentieth century and had an intimate but uneasy relation with the architecture of their time.[23]

Architecture is very capital-intensive, and patronage, however forward-looking, could not accept the extremes of environmental experiment that the theories of the avant-garde sometimes demanded. The creation of a new style for the coming twentieth century had turned out to be too brittle and remote an exercise. Its failure suggested that since historical styles offered no key to the future, and the making of a new style based on nature had proved impossible, the whole century-long business of working a style out and of inventing ornament was a futile exercise; perhaps the buildings of the future should have no style at all. Forms might be projected out of a statement of human needs. They could simply be fitted closely around what went on in a building—its "functions"—or they might be derived from the process of construction or even the "nature of materials," particularly now that a building could be industrially produced. Geometry could simply be taken for granted. In any case, the new architecture did not need to cater to habit or convention, which ornament had satisfied in the past. In fact, architecture, with all its trappings of artifice and style, was irrelevant: what was needed was a *Baukunst,* a building art. As it turned out later, that doctrine would have its dangers too.

These dangers were not obvious at first. To some, clean lines and smooth surfaces seemed very attractive after the fussy linearities, the clutter of preceding decades. Ornament was not only useless, it was also extravagant—as the great Austrian architect and popular journalist Adolf Loos began to point out already at the end of the nineteenth century, appalled as he was by the Viennese excesses of Art Nouveau. Inventing ornament could only be the business of "primitive" people, he declared. We moderns could appropriate it, as we do when we use Persian carpets or wear embroidered peasant dress, but we cannot, in spite of what the designers of the 1890s believed, ever create new ornamental forms.

Loos's argument was forcefully and wittily stated. After its first appearance in German, his essay was taken up in French by Le Corbusier's periodical *L'Esprit Nouveau,* and the title "Ornament and Crime" was often corrupted to "Ornament Is Crime." A century separates us from the first appearance of his essay, and it is often forgotten that it was a polemic against Art Nouveau. Historic ornament—not just Persian carpets and Chippendale chairs, but even classical columns—Loos himself used freely, since they seemed to him perfectly legitimate objects for emulation and even appropriation.

Nor did Loos quite foresee the ornamented modernity of Art Déco. On the contrary, he saw a French return to classicism as a sign of mankind coming to its senses. An architect, he says, is a mason who has learned Latin, while modern architects seem to speak Esperanto.[24] The return to classicism that Loos applauded was more generally known as a "return to order," and Auguste Perret's, as well as Le Corbusier's architecture of the time, could also be interpreted as part of that movement. Unlike their German contemporaries, both of the French masters, and in particular Le Corbusier, provided historical justification for their designs. Corbusier's most famous projects then were deliberately provocative and polemical, so that their "classical" associations are often overlooked. His "City for 3 million inhabitants" was a rectangle of high-rise (sixty-story) cruciform skyscrapers surrounded by a carpet of housing made up of recessing and projecting blocks set in parkland, while the "Plan Voisin" of 1925 applied the same approach to Paris as a whole, filling the center of the Right Bank with a grid of skyscrapers, among which the main monuments of the city (the Louvre, Nôtre Dame) were left standing as a scatter of incidents. Although he prepared many more urban projects, some obviously polemical, others intended for immediate realization, Corbusier's urban planning schemes were not adopted—even after the war. The Plan Voisin, for all its ruthless application of the grid and its Saint-Simonian extolling of an administrative and entrepreneurial elite, makes its obeisance to an urban and historical context that would become even more marked in Corbusier's postwar work.

Meanwhile, the Nazi assumption of power provoked the move of a number of European architects to the United States. Walter Gropius, who headed the architecture program at Harvard, had founded the most important design school of the time, the Bauhaus—first in Weimar, then in Dessau—and it condensed much that was most exciting in the art of the time. It was to have a powerful impact all over the world, though it was closed by the Nazis in 1933. Through his teaching at Harvard, Gropius championed the view that the architect was just another member of the building team, that his discipline was based on first principles and had no need of any historical dimension; what the architect did was to solve problems—those of his clients. Ludwig Mies van der Rohe (who had in fact been the last director of the Bauhaus), the principal champion of *Baukunst* against architecture, settled in Chicago, where he designed and structured the Illinois Institute of Technology and built a number of large and, to some, exemplary buildings: the Lake Shore and Commonwealth apartments, Lafayette Park Housing, the Federal Center, as well as a number of buildings in Canada. All of these demonstrated his total devotion to his much-quoted motto, "Less is more" (later lampooned as "Less is a bore"), but also his belief that order was the only saving bulwark against pervasive social decay. He also claimed that his work derived its virtue from the use of the simplest geometries and the visible statement of the technology by which the building was put together.

Still, Mies had prejudices and procedures that he kept to himself: the formal methods by which he arrived at the proportions of his buildings and their parts, and which he had learned from such masters as Bruno Paul and Peter Behrens, for whom he had worked before 1914. Many huge and growing architectural offices developed in the United States after 1945, and they turned to Mies for inspiration. Mies's obsessional concern with the building technique as the controlling factor in design resulted in a style that seemed easy for other architects to try to imitate, though in doing so they often removed his formal refinements as irrelevant. The concentration on production, on the manufacturing process, also pushed Mies and his followers to think of each building as an individual object, never as part of, never an event in the urban fabric. The effect is exemplary in New York: Mies himself designed the Seagram Building on Park Avenue, whose refinement of detail is in sharp contrast to its corrosive defiance of its urban context. And the same effect is even more obvious in the series of high-rise buildings built between Forty-ninth and Fifty-ninth Streets on Sixth Avenue in New York. The developers, and the architects who built them, took over his total disregard of urban form, with none of the virtues of Mies's obsessional care over detail, and between them produced one of the more devastating urban landscapes of the century.

At first, the devastation they had caused was not at all obvious either to patron or architect. As it became evident, architects became the useful butt of jibes, which could even be given a xenophobic spin—almost as if those ascetic designers that the Nazis had expelled from Europe had corrupted good native developers into putting up faceless buildings.[25] Many of these foreign architects were associated with the constantly reiterated proposal that the problems of the city—particularly its housing—could be resolved by the grouping of slab-blocks in parkland to provide high-rise but relatively low-density dwellings. Gropius, Ernst May, Mies, Corbusier, and many others produced versions of such a scheme, and many of them were built in Europe and in Asia, as well as in the United States. This whole enterprise has turned out to be disappointing, an enemy of urbanity and of social cohesion, provoking the most destructive criticism of modern architecture. At times the criticism and jibes turned to destructive rage. In St. Louis, the Pruitt Igoe apartments, designed by the well-known Japanese American architect Minoru Yamasaki, was dynamited and destroyed in 1972—the event was filmed and has often been shown in schools of architecture. But this did not stop Yamasaki, who went on to do a vast number of big and eclectic buildings: the World Trade Center in New York, the International Airport in Boston, and the Federal Reserve Bank in Richmond, Virginia, being the most visible. And although he has adjusted his stylistic mannerism, Yamasaki has been heavily criticized for the way in which the access and movement in these buildings was organized.

Until it was superseded by the Sears Tower in Chicago in 1974, the World Trade Center (1966–72) towers were briefly the tallest buildings in the world but have none of the thrust of the Empire State Building about them—a wag even said that they look like the boxes in which the Empire State came wrapped. Like Pruitt Igoe, the World Trade Center attracted explosive rage, but its bombing, unlike the controlled dynamiting twenty years earlier of the St. Louis apartments, killed six people, injured thousands, and broke much glass, miraculously leaving the structure unscathed.

At his most eclectic, Yamasaki, too, was primarily concerned with the building as an object separate from its surroundings. The relationship of tall buildings to the street remains one of the great problems of twentieth-century building. This is not the "fault" of architects, of course, though they do bear responsibility for having created a functionalist discourse from which all formal considerations may conveniently be banished. The objectionable featurelessness of much postwar building is, however, willed by developers and accepted by their employees and clients with alacrity.

Rather different and sometimes vociferous protests were to appear, and the fertile growth of the graffito is one of its visible signs: "We are the writing on your walls," a famous London graffito at Hyde Park Corner proclaimed.[26] The graffito may not always rise to Norman Mailer's heroic vindication—that it is the "quintessential marriage of cool and style . . . [when] you write your name in giant separate living letters . . . lithe as snakes, mysterious as Arabic and Chinese curls . . . and do it in the heat of a winter night when the hands are frozen and only the heart is hot with fear . . ."[27]—but it is not just an undirected urban environmental protest practice, and often involves acrobatic feats of climbing, mostly by teenagers and those in their early twenties. It has been absorbed by advertising as well as by the art galleries, even museums. Graffiti have appeared all over the world, and their style, dependent on the strip cartoon, has been surprisingly homogeneous: I have observed them in California and Poland, New Jersey and Italy, England and China. To write on walls may be instinctive and ancient: the advertising, political, and commercial messages written on the walls of Pompeii are an accidental survival of an early practice. The new technique of spray-can painting, however, has given it all another dimension, and its scale has grown in competition with advertising, even if no graffitist has yet been able to rival the ten- to fifteen-story images of teenage bottoms that "mass-designer" clothes manufacturers plaster on the side of Manhattan high-rise buildings. The protest element of the graffito has also been absorbed into commercialized radical chic imagery. Jean-Michel Basquiat may have been the first spray-can painter who actually copyrighted his graffiti (SAMO ©—for Same Old Shit), but unlike most true graffitists he always made his writing legible. His friend Keith Haring publicized his art by patently masochistic exhibitions. Where the genuine graffitist eludes capture, Haring, sometimes accompanied by photographers, would produce his gear ostentatiously in subway stations, inviting public manacling as a defacer of public property.

Still, the dissatisfaction with bare walls that the graffito reflected was so general that various palliatives were tried. There was another attempt to return to some form of modern, invented ornament in the fifties, with the use of geometric patterns on ceramics or stamped aluminum. Stone and concrete filigree was used by Edward Durrell Stone on some prominent buildings, such as the Gallery of Modern Art at Columbus Circle in New York, now the New York Cultural Center, or the Kennedy Center in Washington. This turned out to be even more evanescent than Art Déco.

By the late sixties a concerted drive for a more or less "ironic" use of historical precedent—it adopted the label "postmodern"—seemed very seductive to some architects. In any case, the old modernist argument that ornament was an unnecessary extravagance no longer held: computer-drawn and machine-made ornament was no more expensive than any other kind of finish and could even help to camouflage cheap materials and shoddy workmanship.

Postmodernism has now been given a rather different implication and weight by sociologists and geographers, who are concerned with the way categories of knowledge develop within late capitalist society in harness with power and privilege. The excuse that such "uses of history" in building are ironic does not really seem convincing when irony rises forty stories high. Many postmodern buildings look very much like the wholly unironic historicist buildings of social realism as it was practiced in eastern Europe, about which I will have more to say later. The "movement" may not have been either lasting or very significant in Western architecture, but it was troublingly symptomatic in that its rapid promotion represented the recognition on the part of developers and financiers—not just of architects—that the architecture of the previous decades had somehow failed society.

The mode was abandoned almost as quickly as it was taken up in Europe as well as North America—since developers were prepared to modify the surface of the buildings, but not to cut the returns on investment that any concession of space for public use might involve. Postmodernism may have been sidelined in the West, but it has suddenly, since 1997–98, become the dominant design mode for fast-growing high-rise housing in China, an environment where rampant capitalism is promoting the overproduction of rentable space. The Chinese are now the biggest patrons of pure-housing cities: public, institutional building is forgotten.

This commercial Chinese postmodernism—spiny (as in the fun-palaces) or blunt (as in the housing)—is very different from the folkish and bookish, neo-Ruskinian (absurdly so, because "classical") Anglo-French version or the populist "decorated-shed" American variety. Such unity as postmodernism has springs from the mood of reappraisal that afflicted the most thoughtful modernists within a few years of the war. Already about 1950 there was much talk of the need for a "new monumentality." At its 1951 Congress in Hoddesdon in England, the main modernist organization, CIAM, which would break up a few years later, took the nature of public space as a theme. Some of its leading figures produced a report, *The Heart of the City*, in which the very notion of the city dominated by housing was put to the question—and although for a while there was much talk of new monuments and even a new monumentality—no definite answers or recipes were forthcoming, though these discussions did have an immediate impact on some of the best architects of the time. Clearly, there had been even more modernisms than there would be postmodernisms, and indeed neither "movement" could really be constituted as a style. In any case, the real problems of the city would have nothing to do with such matters, even if both architects and their patrons would go on talking about them.

5. Flight from the City:
Lived Space and Virtual Space

A CITY WHOSE DOMINANT buildings are housing—and I mean housing for offices as well as apartments for people—will inevitably be short on public spaces and on monuments, whether the city develops horizontally or vertically. Monuments will be dwarfed by their surroundings.

Such a city will therefore also be short on places that might serve its inhabitants as landmarks, orientation guides, and "points of interest," or any other striking, easily identifiable features to use as meeting points. That is why even the most grasping developers will talk about "identity points," if only to allow a visitor to orient himself.[1]

People tend to select something prominent, something that has played a role in the life of their city, for a landmark: a town hall, a market cross, fountains, monuments, theaters, church porches, and the like. The nineteenth century added the enclosed spaces of railway stations, as well as glazed-in streets—arcades—to the repertory of such places. In stations, huge standing or suspended monumental clocks were useful signposts, as they were in department stores. This changed radically when clocks and indicators became digital and multiple, so that specially designated "meeting points" at stations and airports have to be labeled as just that to help disorientated air travelers. Airports, which are isolated from the city fabric, tend, in any case, to be as uninflected as the cities that they serve.

Points of orientation are essential for any sane urban or rural living. Without them a citizen cannot "read," let alone "understand" his home. "A distinctive and legible environment not only offers security but also heightens the potential depth and intensity of human experience,"[2] wrote Kevin Lynch. Some forty years ago, Lynch pioneered a study of how such "readings" were arrived at—a study that has never been superseded nor, unfortunately, developed. He and his team in the planning department at MIT in Boston were not only interested in landmarks but in the whole repertory of those features that make an urban environment: boundaries and limits, how people constituted "their" districts and quarters, and how paths were marked out through the city. Lynch and his associates recognized that the notional map of the city— the way people reconstituted it in their minds—might be very different from any "objective" survey that could be provided by cartographers. Any town, district, or quarter will require not only markers that inflect it, but various more or less discreet places of semi-public, semi-private meeting—as well as such places of tryst as taverns, restaurants, cafés, and public bars that were so amply provided in the nineteenth-century bourgeois city (nor did they cater to one class of person only).

Within the twentieth-century city of housing, the identifiable places of meeting have been drastically reduced. Many of the restaurants and bars have by now been turned into nearly identical fast-food franchises, selling chips (G.B.)/French fries (U.S.A.),[3] hamburgers, fried chicken, pizza in various forms, the omnipresent sweet fizzy drinks, and so on, which are distinguishable from each other only by their shrill trademarks and advertising, and are designed for quick turnover and takeaway. Seats tend to be hard, cutlery and crockery often disposable, and the environment garish but bare—quite unlike the plush-and-cut-glass gin palaces, pubs, bars, and cafés of the bourgeois town. The homogenized nature of the fast-food franchises means that their outlets can never be site-specific, nor can they offer alluring points of reference, since only the abstraction of their logos marks them. As in most of the institutions of late capitalism, unvaried repetitions convey the message that space has been standardized, that its inflections and associations have been ironed out, even if occasional ones may be adopted as corner cafés.

A closely related phenomenon has affected our public perception of time, which is now measured very exactly by cesium atom clocks to less than a millionth of a second in laboratories. Yet time's public face is increasingly abstract—as signified by the digital timepiece—and that in turn affects the way we live the experience of space. Old two-handed clocks often measured accurately enough for everyday purposes, but much more figuratively.[4] The most famous of them is probably the blue-and-gold mosaic one that was set up in the tower overlooking the Piazzetta of Saint Mark in Venice round 1500; not only are the minutes and hours indicated—and the quarter-hours struck on a bell by gigantic bronze figures above it—but the days and months, as well as the phases of the moon and the position of the sun in the Zodiac, are shown. Such elaboration—sometimes with the addition of the dates of church festivals—of the calendar was quite usual in those clocks that were set up in cathedrals and town halls from the fourteenth century onward in much of Europe, and they were usually enlivened by ringing bells as well as shows of automatons.

Public time has been measured since antiquity; we owe the Babylonians our twenty-four-hour day and the 360-degree circle, while predynastic Egypt devised the 365-day year. The regularities of nature were already being noted by people in the Old Stone Age, who notched records on antler or bone implements, which archaeologists have called "ceremonial scepters" or *bâtons de commandement*, ancestors of the tally-sticks that are still the common reckoning instruments among nomads and pastoralists.

The reading of the length and direction of the sun's shadows to mark the points that we now call "of the compass" is certainly preliterate. As soon as there were cities, they were also thought of as sundials. In Republican Rome a herald would announce "official" sunrise and sundown, and later noon as well, by observing the sunlight in relation to certain buildings: legal business could be only transacted in the official daytime he determined. The vast sun clock set up by the first emperor, Augustus, in the Roman Field of Mars had a tall Egyptian obelisk for a needle. But by then there were more or less public sundials all over the city:

> My belly was my only timepiece. It was
> As reliable and more accurate than any of them

Plautus makes one of his hungry toady-parasites complain;

> But now I can't tuck in unless the sun allows me to
> As the town has those wretched sun-dials everywhere.[5]

Time was also measured publicly by *clepsydrae*—sand or water clocks—which probably originated in Mesopotamia. The Roman Agora in Athens housed its public water clock in a splendid and porticoed octagonal shrine, topped with a large bronze weather vane and adorned with reliefs of the principal winds, which is still one of its landmarks. All that was before the mechanizing of time.

The city conceived as a sundial suggested a correspondence of place and time that may be taken to imply that the clock of complex dials and moving figures relates a regular and precisely measurable time to the varied, elastic duration of experience—which is universal and commonplace. Everyone will have noticed how much longer it seems to take to get to an unknown destination than to return from it. That is analogous to the deformation of space by our occupation of it, a space that the eye can reckon by markers and monuments. When that mesh is torn, the work of the artists and the architects operating in the public realm becomes increasingly difficult, particularly when they are called on to make permanent installations—public buildings and places—monuments in short. It is also true that as monuments (in the narrow sense: commemorations of persons and events) have been dwarfed in space, so they have become more difficult to devise and slow to attract validation by the public. That is why many artists who are invited to commemorate something or someone turn to light displays or temporary installations.

A much bigger and more important problem is the design of the public building, home to some important and powerful institutions. The difficulties became obvious a hundred years ago, and in a crucial and quite novel situation—the devising of "housing" for a global authority. In the relatively calm period around the turn of the twentieth century, various sites were being considered for an international authority even before any form of world government was constituted. The Hague, where the International Peace Conference had been called in 1899, was to become the home of the international courts of arbitration and justice, the first such world institution, and a competition for the buildings to house it was won, in 1903, by an otherwise very little known nor very distinguished Lille architect, Louis-Marie Cordonnier. The Palace of Peace opened, in one of the typical ironies of history, just a year before the First World War broke out, and so it was not occupied until 1922. Meanwhile, in 1913, two architects, the Norwegian Hendrick Christian Andersen and a French Rome prizewinner, Ernest Hébrard, had published an atlas of designs for a center of world government. This was to be a city of a million inhabitants, which they provisionally set at the mouth of the Tiber because they both loved Rome. The project was technologically advanced, with a rapid transportation system and centralized heating, though as a planning exercise it never went beyond the voluble Beaux-Arts commonplaces. It evoked much enthusiasm, particularly in Belgium, where an alternative plan to build it as a satellite to Brussels—and so provide a counterpoint to the Hague—was debated in the Belgian parliament. World government, a world capital, was very much on people's minds long before globalization became a buzzword.[6] At the same time, the League of Nations, which grew out of the Versailles Treaty of 1919, began meeting in Geneva in 1921, though it did not declare a competition for a "palace" to accommodate both its assembly and secretariat until 1926. The position chosen was a suburban, well-wooded park along the lake, at the northern edge of the town, just off the road to Lausanne. Only one of the competition entries, that of Le Corbusier, really took up the challenge of that site, and he articulated the buildings among the trees, setting both debating chamber and the secretariat at the edge of the lake. His project was also one of the earliest that included an underground car park for a public building. The winning projects did not make such provisions, but then the other "avant-garde" scheme by the Swiss Hannes Meyer—who was to succeed Walter Gropius briefly as director of the Bauhaus in 1929—did not do so, either. Meyer's project—more aggressively machinelike, yet entirely additive—makes an interesting contrast; he neither tried to exploit the lyrical possibilities of the site nor to bind the elements into a rhetorical unity. Corbusier's design, on the other hand, has an obvious climax: the fan-shaped debating chamber, its narrow end coming down to the water's edge. In front of the end wall the president's suite is a low, curved, quasi-independent pavilion, reflected in the lake and accessible directly by boat. Its importance was to be emphasized by a large sculpture, which declared its public and rhetorical intention. Corbusier's project was among the six *ex aequo* first-prize winners but was eliminated on a technical quibble about the drawings. In the polemic justification of the scheme published after its rejection, when functionalism was a new slogan, Corbusier more or less deliberately concealed this narrative intention by insisting that his project was not for a palace, but for a home—an efficient and wholly rational housing for a new world government. Did Corbusier feel that his gesture to the more conventional understanding of the public nature of a building was somehow "unmodern"?[7] Neither he nor his apologists have been very explicit about it. These projects of Le Corbusier's have had a mixed reception. Even though the designs were rejected by juries, some of his critics from within the modern movement have described them as neoclassical—at the time a disparaging term. There seemed no other way to explain their being so appealing yet so out of joint with their time than the stylistic one, and their very unfamiliarity makes them seem, paradoxically, reactionary.

The building that did go up by the lake in Geneva, a ponderous, committee-designed palace, was not finished until 1939, by which time the League was in any case irrelevant: the Second World War was beginning. The building's style is very much *pompier* and "classical," which by then was associated largely with totalitarian regimes. It is surrounded by fenced formal gardens and screened from the town by areas of above-ground parking. In 1931, having won another competition, this time in Moscow—for the central Trade Union building—Le Corbusier entered a third competition, and again unsuccessfully, for the Palace of the Soviets on the site of the Church of the Redeemer near the Kremlin.

The Genevan approach was developed further here. The Moscow structures are more adventurous, though the two halls that the program demanded have roofs suspended from gigantic exposed frames, while the space between them was developed as a multilevel assembly. In Moscow Corbusier had impressive rivals: the Frenchman Auguste Perret, the Dutchman Hendrik Berlage among his seniors, Walter Gropius and a number of Soviet architects among his contemporaries.

The winner—though not outright—was Boris Mikhailovich Iofan, whose project had a similar configuration on plan to Corbusier's—but no agora, of course. It focused on a tower from which a giant worker flashed a light—recalling the Statue of Liberty, not altogether creditably. Iofan's scheme went through several transformations. The final version was an Art Déco–ornamented, stepped building—rather like a New York skyscraper—and the giant worker became an even more giant, gesticulating Lenin! That revised project was not built either, but its victory signaled that the Soviet authorities' patience with the avant-garde had run out. Iofan became well known in the West as the designer, with a woman sculptor, V. I. Mukhina, of the prominent Soviet pavilion at the Paris World's Fair in 1937, and one of the most successful Soviet practitioners, Order of Lenin and all. Meanwhile, the International Congress of Modern Architecture, which had planned a Moscow meeting in 1933, was prudently moved to Athens.

This also signaled the dispersal of the various teams that had worked on new Soviet cities in 1932–33. Northern planner-architects Ernst May and Hannes Meyer from Germany, the Dutchman Mart Stamm, and many others had gone to the Soviet Union in the hope of finding a

Socialist home compatible with rational planning and construction. By the time things had become really awkward for them under the system in which they had placed their hopes, the Nazis were taking power in Germany, and most architects of note—Gropius, Breuer, Mies, Hilberseimer—were leaving the country for the United States. Their way back to Germany had been barred.

In the Soviet Union, constructivists and productivists, and the groups around the exciting workshop schools of design, had never quite had it all their own way, of course. Powerful older architects had survived the Revolution intact; the most revered of them was Ivan Vladislavovich Zholtovski, who had been very successful before the Revolution in a pure Palladian manner, while he maintained good relations with avant-gardists, many of whom had been his pupils. His contemporary Alexei Shchusev, who had revived the "old Russian" style in which he designed the Kazan station before the Revolution, became the architect of the wooden (1923) Lenin mausoleum as well as the granite one that replaced it in 1930. Together, Zholtovski and Shchusev worked on the Moscow expansion plan for Mossoviet, the agency in charge of all planning. Groups such as the "Workshop for Socialist Classicism" were actively encouraged.

During the twenties various approaches were tolerated, and the more experimental tendencies were protected by the Commissar for Enlightenment, Anatoly Lunacharsky; nor was Trotsky out of sympathy with them. But Trotsky fell in 1928, and Stalin had no taste for any avant-garde art (his views on music are well known). By 1930 Lunacharsky had been moved into the diplomatic service and was taking his distance from the avant-garde. He even went on record as approving of Iofan's project for the Palace of the Soviets; he died in 1933.

By then Stalin was taking such matters in hand personally. In 1931 Lazar Kaganovich, a Politburo member and a Stalin faithful (later in charge of the Moscow subway system), had read a report to the Central Committee of the Soviet party that called for a country-wide rational planning policy; he also put forward the notion that Moscow was to be the model for Socialist reconstruction (this as a prelude to the Palace of the Soviets competition). Soon after, at the Soviet writers' conference of 1934, Stalin's closest "cultural" henchman, Andrei Zhdanov, laid down the doctrine of socialist realism. Culture, he decreed, was henceforth to be didactic and optimistic. Stalin further commanded that Soviet cities be high-density and relatively high-rise. Another Mossoviet-commissioned Moscow plan of 1935 provided for a number of wide thoroughfares in the city, most of which were never laid out.

Even if it was not built, Iofan's Palace of the Soviets, with its curious Art Déco detailing, would set the tone for Soviet architecture. Moscow was to be dominated by a group of six skyscrapers, not haphazardly set like the American ones, but deliberately placed at crucial points in the city. Their footprints were large and their slope gentler than that dictated by New York zoning, although they were heavily influenced by Hugh Ferris's dramatic drawings of the zoned New York buildings that Shchusev, for one, had studied. The Ministry of Foreign Affairs (the Minister's office was on top of the tower) near the Kremlin, apartment blocks on Kotelničeskaya Nabrežnaya and Vostaniia Square, the Ukraina and the Leningradskaia hotels, and a mixed-use building at Krasne Vorota were built, and another was planned. The largest building, the Lomonosov University building, was a separate enterprise. And in order to make the Kotelničeskaya building quite different from a New York skyscraper, the authorities decided to crown it with a sharp spire in imitation of the one that Adrian Dimitrovič Zakharov had built as a gate to the Petersburg Admiralty after 1806. Stalin was known to be partial to that feature. Such a spire was used on the university instead of the statue Iofan had originally wanted. The spire became a feature of Soviet high-rises and of the buildings Soviet power bestowed on its allies from East Berlin to Shanghai. Not until Nikita Khrushchev attacked ornamented structures at a Soviet Builders' Conference in 1954 was the social-realist line modified. This was long before he felt secure enough to attack the Personality Cult at the Twentieth Party Congress of February 1956.

Fortunately for them, few architects ended as suicides or in concentration camps, unlike writers, painters, and theater people, but many of the more innovative among them found themselves doing other, humbler work.

The United Nations was constituted in San Francisco in 1945, and the problem of establishing a world capital arose again. Although most of us now accept its placing in Manhattan as almost inevitable, the original choice of site for the United Nations was not a foregone conclusion: San Francisco, Boston, and Philadelphia were alternative suggestions.

Flushing Meadows—the tract of land where the World's Fair Exposition of 1940 presented an optimistic view of the future but had been such a flash in the pan (and another, less ambitiously optimistic fair would not do much better in 1964–65)—was favored by several influential Manhattanese; and a much larger group of buildings than the eventual First Avenue headquarters, including an extensive residential estate, was planned for that site. But doubts were expressed at once by the city authorities:

A remote, self-contained world-capital, like Canberra, New Delhi or the Vatican ... seems to have been the goal of the original United Nations Committee. We presented the obvious practical objections to this idea, and apparently were persuasive.[8]

Le Corbusier was involved—this time as a French representative on the organizing committee—in the design of a building for the second and by now already much-longer-lasting world government to assemble in New York. He saw the United Nations settling on the clear, green site of Flushing Meadows as another opportunity to implement his vision of the rational city, the *Ville Radieuse*, a concept that was to have various incarnations after he first outlined it in 1923, but it was not to be realized in New York, either.

As it turned out, the United Nations got its Manhattan site by a whisker. When the decision in favor of Philadelphia was imminent, a private gift of funds provided by John D. Rockefeller to buy the land on the East River, then belonging to the biggest New York property developer, William Zeckendorf, tipped the decision for New York. The deal had been brokered by the combative parks commissioner of the city, Robert Moses, and Rockefeller's favorite architect, Wallace K. Harrison, together with John D.'s son Nelson, later governor of New York State. The mayor of New York at the time, William O'Dwyer, was a passive supporter of the enterprise. It was only afterward that he would declare, "I felt that this was the one great thing that would make New York the center of the world."[9] Corbusier accepted the new site with enthusiasm. It was part of his proposal that the Secretariat building, a tall slab, should face onto the East River, giving it an obvious exposure to the city and visibility from the water, while the lower-lying Assembly and reception halls, which in his project were open to the town, provided a zone of encounter. As in Geneva in 1927, so in New York, the project was again handed to a design committee, though Wallace Harrison was its effective leader. The massing in his scheme was similar to Corbusier's—even if a second, smaller slab building was eliminated—but smoothed and somehow neutered. The main office block, though relatively modest in bulk, remains—for the time being—very telling against the Manhattan skyline. The Assembly and Security Council halls were reoriented, however, so that the passerby now only sees the flank of the Assembly building. The public entry, which had been designed to face the city, has now been turned sideways to it, and the approach is therefore semi-concealed—and, in any case, is now made even more secretive and withdrawn by security measures.

As in Geneva, the physical setting for world government was finally provided by a more or less anonymous committee that did not consider the public face for the institution any part of its brief. And following this lead, the prominent headquarters for the most famous or perhaps infamous—as it has been beset by corruption scandals—United Nations Agency, UNESCO, another world government building, has been sited opposite the Ecole Militaire in the center of Paris. A Y-shaped building, it is isolated among lawns and parking, and conceived as an even more street-hostile object by its two celebrated architects, Marcel Breuer and Bernard Zehrfuss, working with a yet more famous engineer, Pier Luigi Nervi. The large and prominent wall painting by Picasso, which was in its main hall, is one of his very worst. The UNESCO building seems deliberately planned and sited as to appear entirely internalized, and to make no real link or even gesture to the urban fabric: it has been denied any Parisian "face."

Other international agencies—the Council of Europe, the European Commission, the North Atlantic Treaty Organization—have done even worse by the cities in which they have been planted. Brussels, already ravaged by its boulevard builders in the 1860s, was further disemboweled by urbanists and traffic engineers on the occasion of the World Exposition of 1935. It was invaded by the European Community building on the site of the old Abbey of Berlaymont (known to the locals as Berlaymonstre),[10] a tasteless and commercial-looking structure, easily outclassed by the several banal late-nineteenth-century museum buildings set around the Parque du Cinquantenaire. It houses the European presidency, with all its ministries, while the Council, the European Community's parliament, is in its other capital, Strasbourg. It has not fared any better—accommodated as it is in an anonymous building that its financiers and masters called the "House of Promise" when it was first opened in 1977—though its thumping lack of distinction cannot have promised much to anybody, even when it was first "unveiled." Attempts to inject a little urban "character" into the Strasbourg complex by commissioning the English architect Richard Rogers to build another "palace"—this time law courts—were frustrating, since the building—made up of a number of linked cylindrical pavilions—has a configuration that might be fine for many purposes, but whose geometry is of its very nature faceless. It is isolated in an environment dominated by the Orangerie park, which had been laid out by the great gardener André Lenôtre, in the reign of Louis XIV. The masters of modern Europe may have thought their small continent had public spaces enough so that they did not need to increase the area given over to them. In this they were, of course, quite wrong, since park and promenade are eroded by increasing traffic lanes, and are being manipulated, reshaped in our own time, with consequences—as yet incalculable—for the urban fabric; they are therefore hardly suitable ground for the *flâneur*.

World government, the Council of Europe, or NATO all seem to have behaved in the same way: however their design was arrived at, their buildings have settled cuckoolike in various cities without making any real contribution to them. Problems about the relation between the urban fabric and the various buildings from which power is exercised have meanwhile arisen in other countries as well, and at various levels. It does not seem as if the authorities in charge of such projects are at ease with their responsibility, though in some cases they conceal their problems behind a show of insouciance as if they were unaware of the impact they are making on the city or of the relationship between the built form and the message to be conveyed, or implied. What is true of international institutions is equally evident in the case of national ones.

In Washington, D.C.—to take an important example—the original plan as it was conceived by Pierre Charles L'Enfant was centered on the two seats of power: the Congress building on Capitol Hill, and the White House. These were set at right angles to each other, legislative and executive power, the 555-foot-high Washington Monument, though erected later, acting as a hinge for the whole scheme. The White House and the Capitol are also linked by an oblique avenue, Pennsylvania, which has provided the location for more civic buildings. And L'Enfant, trained as he was in a French painterly tradition, envisaged the main public avenues lined with public and institutional buildings as well as shopping arcades. That the Treasury building and the State, War, and Navy Building (now the Executive Offices Building) are next to the White House, as well as the State and Commerce Departments (the Federal Reserve Bank and the Patent Office are all grouped nearby, much as ministries are grouped along Whitehall in London), is approximately as he wished it. Whatever their differences, and even though L'Enfant was dismissed after a year, the Fathers of the Republic saw his plan and the arrangement of public buildings as an appropriate representation of the sovereign power of the newly united states.

The Supreme Court, which originally sat in a semicircular chamber inside the Capitol, was moved in 1935 to its own porticoed marble palace, designed by Cass Gilbert, who had built the Woolworth Building in New York thirty years earlier. The Court is not located on the Mall, but east of the Capitol. The National Gallery was built—marble, domed, and porticoed—about the same time on the Mall. It is a mark of how, even at this early date, 1935–40, museums and galleries were displacing the seats of authority in the public eye.

The Smithsonian Institution, still in its quaint "Gothicky" castle, completed in 1849, is also on the Mall, though it is now divided among several buildings—museums and research institutes, some of which have been dispersed—and it claims, at twenty million a year, to have more visitors than the Disney enterprises. In 1976 one of its largest dependencies, the vast National Air and Space Museum, was opened directly facing the National Gallery of Art, which was extended in 1978 by I. M. Pei, who in 1990 designed the by now little-loved pyramid in the courtyard of the Louvre in Paris.

At the west end of the Mall, beyond the Washington Monument, on marshy ground reclaimed from the Potomac when the city was finally paved and sewers added after 1870, stands another marble-pillared temple. It is a shrine to President Lincoln built in 1922, which—like the Capitol itself—is often the focus of demonstrations. Indeed, it was in front of the Lincoln Memorial that Martin Luther King, Jr. made his "I have a dream" speech in 1963. It is also one of the curiosities of Washington that not one of these monuments is—the geology of the site is usually given as a reason—on the same axis as another, which seems to have a stimulating rather than an irritating effect on the visitor who takes note of it.

While the Mall was being regulated and built up, and a few years after the opening of the Supreme Court, Washington acquired a building much larger—both in scale and in size—than the older ministries and offices. The Department of Defense is known from the regular figure of its plan as the Pentagon. Ground for the building was broken a few weeks before the attack on Pearl Harbor, and it was finished relatively quickly. It is reputedly still the largest building in the world, and has become identified with U.S. military policy, in fact with the general notion of a great military command and vast weapons spending.[11] Now, quite normal rectangular buildings in other countries that house their military command are often called their Pentagons.

Although no rationale for the regular geometry of the Pentagon has ever been advanced, it is the best-known thing about that building. The image of it that appears on the lecterns of military press spokesmen is a schematic aerial view in which the design is evident and instantly striking. The anecdotes that circulate around it focus on its size: that its volume is three times that of the Empire State Building, for instance, or on its labyrinthine complexity, despite its simple plan. It has been said that a telegraph boy making a delivery got lost in it and emerged twenty-five years later as a full colonel.

The Pentagon was designed by a little-known Californian architect, George Edwin Bergstrom, whose name is not even mentioned in the usual tourist guides to the capital. Even if its detailed design had been striking, only those who enter it and work there would have any clear notion of its ornament and surface, since the building is surrounded by an extensive car park. There is no way for a pedestrian to walk past the building closely enough, so that the only experience of it available to the public is therefore an abstract one.

Of course, those Brussels buildings of the European Union are more obtrusively offensive than the barely visible Pentagon, and what may be seen of them is bland to the point of inanity, but until the Pentagon was inaugurated, public buildings in Washington were proud and—even when they were not very distinguished or idiosyncratic—strongly characterized.

The limestone-faced Pentagon is not unlike limestone- or granite-faced government buildings elsewhere. Enduring granite was Albert Speer and Adolf Hitler's favorite facing material for the buildings of great Germania, their re-created Berlin. Granite was also favored by the architects of the Soviet Union in the thirties, and it became the preferred institutional material used by democratic public bodies as well as despotic ones.

Stalin's regime and his taste survived World War II. Yet when the Chinese Communists were secure enough to build, the direction they would take was not clear. There was no established style, nor had the Chinese Communist party ever taken much interest in such matters. Yet the Revolution had to be seen as working from a center. Beijing, the Chinese capital city, is very ancient, and had been rebuilt on a modified grid plan by the traditionalist Ming emperors after 1402. Such grid planning had been practiced in China since the second millennium B.C.—if not earlier. Although Beijing is in the far north of the country, near the Great Wall— a position that is now seen as very problematic for the geography of the empire—the site was very acceptable to the all-powerful geomancers, the practitioners of that Feng-shui which has become so fashionable nowadays all over the world. The Forbidden City, the Imperial residence in Beijing, occupied much of the middle of the square now called the Manchu quarter. To the south of it was the fortified suburb known as the Chinese section; each one was walled.

The Forbidden City had also once been fully surrounded by moats and walls. Designed as the Imperial residence and the seat of the Imperial administration, it was occupied by the emperor and his court by 1422. The last Qing or Manchu ruler, the Xuantong emperor, Pu Yi, resided there until 1924 even though he had been deposed in 1910. The outer gate, through which the emperor—who rarely left the Forbidden City—used to be ceremoniously taken to the Temple of Heaven for the great solstice sacrifices, opens beyond the moat onto the square to the south. Over the gate before which the new Communist leader proclaimed the People's Republic in 1949, you may still—at the time of writing—see about the last publicly displayed portrait of Chairman Mao.

What was once a wide avenue called Tiananmen—after that southern Gate of Heavenly Peace—had offices or ministries grouped on either side (as on the Washington Mall, or in Whitehall in London). The ministries of Rites, of Works, War, and Astronomy were on the east, of Justice, Sacrifices, and the Court of Censorship on the west. After the Revolution, the offices were pulled down and the avenue enlarged to create the new hundred-acre Tiananmen Square. The authorities wanted to exploit the occasion and to assert the nature of their power through a series of very visible buildings that would also provide a model for all building in the New China. This happened a century and a half after Washington had been built on virgin territory, but with analogous ambitions.

While the Revolution was "traditional" in some literary ways—the granite obelisk that was set up to commemorate its heroes in the middle of Tiananmen Square, for instance, is inscribed on the side facing the Forbidden City with a poem in Mao's beautifully flowing calligraphy—the country had no architectural "style" or even canonic buildings to which the architects could appeal. During the Great Leap Forward, the Great Hall of the People was built to replace the ceremonial halls and courtyards of the Forbidden City as the main assembly point of the revolutionary powers. A style had to be created that was recognizably Chinese, yet quite free of associations with the feudal past of the country. The nearest, most sympathetic exemplar was the social realist style of the Soviets. Exported to China, it was a kind of spiky Russo-Palladian-Chinoiserie style, of which the two big Russian-built exhibition centers in Shanghai and Beijing are the overwhelming examples. At the time, the most respected architect—or at least theorist—of the New China, Liang Sicheng, had come back from the United States, where he had been trained in the principles of Durandian axial planning by a graduate of the Ecole des

Beaux-Arts in Paris, Paul Philippe Cret. Liang, who had served as the Chinese representative on the United Nations Board of Design and was the chief planner of Beijing, had been instructed to devise a new national style on Mao's orders. The Monument of the Heroes in the center of Tiananmen Square, the one to be inscribed by Mao, was his personal responsibility. His part in the design of the Great Hall of the People to the west of Tiananmen is not clear: Zhang Bo, who specialized in adding Chinese-style detail to commercial structures, is usually named as its actual designer. The Ministry of Heavy Industry facing it on the east, and the History Museum next to it, were all heavily colonnaded and corniced; they open a series of buildings that line that huge new square. Facing the gate of the Forbidden City and closing the space is the Mausoleum of the embalmed Mao, modeled, some say, on the equally colonnaded Lincoln Memorial that faces Capitol Hill rather than on the granite tumulus of the sainted Lenin. This mausoleum stands on the edge of the old Manchu city, just within the Daching-men—the gate of the great Ching—that opens into the Chinese quarter. All of these buildings are attributed to a collective, the Beijing Institute of Building Design and Research, rather than to any particular architect. The institute was tightly controlled by the Ministry of Culture, whose highest ranks were much affected by Liang Sicheng's teaching, although he had been disgraced in 1952 and not readmitted to the party until 1959. He was to be disgraced again in 1966, during the Cultural Revolution; he died, broken, in 1972.

The style of the Mao mausoleum is Chinese only in its use of stepped ramps and paneled stone balustrades. These buildings are in fact only vaguely "oriental" in such details as the corners of the roofs turned up into acroteria, the use of prominent yellow-glazed tiles, and so on. On the whole the style of the buildings—as well as of the sculptures that accompany them—is declarative but flaccid in a European-inspired social realist manner. The back chamber of the Mausoleum was, until recently, a favorite photo opportunity locale for newly married couples, but on my last visit all such levity had been repressed.

The official style cannot—apart from the upturned roof corners—survive the awful realities of late-capitalist development. In the "entertainment centers," which are sprouting all over China, it has been swept away by a turreted and castellated "orientalized" fairy-castle style, a spiky, sinified Disneyism that seems destined to mark the buildings of venture China. In this matter of a twentieth-century building style, China's misfortune has been her segregation from architectural developments in the rest of the world. While Japan and later India and Ceylon, even Korea, produced some inspired examples of architecture before the last war, China sent its younger architects to conservative American schools and has employed—as the Chinese still do—commercial, mostly American, offices for larger, prestige buildings. Not that the 1920s and 1930s, the period of the warlords and the Sino-Japanese War, were conducive to the development of a new Chinese architecture anyway. Even before the Republic, in the closing years of the empire, the last major state building in China was hardly an inspiration. After it was sacked by Lord Elgin in 1860, the vast summer palace outside Beijing was rebuilt by the dowager empress, Ci Xi, to include her folly—a white marble paddle-steamer built from funds destined for the Chinese navy.

When the Communist party took over, there were few real precedents either for architecture, or for planning. It is not really surprising that the new mayor of Beijing told the terrified Liang Sicheng (by then director of city planning there), as they were both looking south from the Tien-An gate, that "Chairman Mao wanted a big modern city: he expects the sky in front of us to be filled with smokestacks. . . ."[12] Yet already in the 1970s, the Chinese authorities were not content with what they were getting and were worried about the future. They looked outside the country. A delegation from the American Institute of Architects visited Beijing in 1974. It included Iaoh Ming Pei, who was born in China, though trained at Harvard and MIT. The development plans for Beijing were discussed, and the foreigners advised against a high-rise hotel at the center of the city, proposed by the city authorities. In fact, on I. M. Pei's advice over the next few years, high-rise development in the walled city was stopped altogether. In 1978, instead of this high-rise at the center, Pei designed the Fragrant Hills hotel to the north of the city, toward the Ming tombs. For a while his three-story building was *the* luxury hotel in the capital, though it has now been outclassed—in terms of luxury—by a number of international joint venture and concessionary ones. However, Pei's advice that high-rises be kept out of the city center has been respected, and this has saved the old city, though it has produced the Beijing of extended avenues and new traffic jams.

The new Beijing is one of the obvious results of Deng Xiaoping's economic reforms; it all started in 1979 with some fishing villages just north of Hong Kong, which were designated a Special Economic Region called Shenzhen. They were to provide an alternative to Hong Kong for foreign investment and trading. By 1998, Shenzhen had a population of nearly four million and it is still growing. It barely benefits from planning policy, and has become a landscape of wide traffic lanes and skyscrapers with shacks in the interstices and in the hinterland. It has no urban spaces, but a substitute urban experience is supplied in those "entertainment centers" and in ten theme parks spread through the city. Mr. Deng was so impressed by all this on his visit there in 1990 that a similar zone was opened in Pudong, the quiet agricultural suburb of Shanghai on the other side of the Huangpu River. High-rise buildings were thrown up like so many beanstalks. At the end of 1998 only 30 percent of the new space was occupied. This kind of speculative overproduction is not unusual at times of high development, though the scale at which this is happening in China seems unprecedented. The Jin-Mao building, currently the third highest in the world at 420 meters (1378 feet), but set in a wilderness of unfinished road surfaces and rather faceless walls, is perhaps the most melancholy witness to the strange nature of this quasi-urbanizing.

While the Chinese were asserting a character and a model for the future in their buildings—which were to sanction the presence of a national authority over the reorganized empire—and protecting their central monuments, in London the notion of both a central and a local authority made visible was being deliberately frittered away. A hundred and fifty years ago the ministries in Whitehall were built near Westminster Abbey and the Palace of Westminster, which shelters the two parliamentary chambers and the attendant offices, all on the site of the original royal palace. For all their shortcomings (the ministries were mostly built at a low point of British architecture), they form a powerful and monumental concentration of buildings in which Britain's imperial power and organization was enshrined and displayed. At the beginning of the twentieth century, the complex was enlarged across Westminster Bridge—by the London County (later Greater London) Council building, County Hall. A competition was held in 1908, and construction began in 1912, though the new building was not finished until 1931 because of World War I. The building was extended several times over the next thirty years, and covered a large area. In 1951 the derelict industrial ground to the east of County Hall became the site of a festival—a fair to mark the centenary of the Crystal Palace and the end of that postwar austerity campaign that had been imposed by the first Labour party government to repair war damage, but also to pay for an extensive program of industrial nationalization, as well as for the setting up of health—and other social—services.

The Festival of Britain was cast in very much the same mold as the better new towns. Some of those involved in it—and particularly the enormously prolific draftsman, Gordon Cullen, who was also the art editor of the London *Architectural Review*—launched a movement or slogan, Townscape, and gave a new word to the English language. They accepted the bipartisan political realities of postwar Britain, and did not quibble with the architecture of their time. Insistent on the continuity of the urban fabric, they paid close attention to the more or less picturesque grouping of buildings as well as the surfaces of the "in-between" spaces.[13]

Townscape ideas had some impact in Britain and Scandinavia, less in Europe and the United States. The teaching had a picturesque slant and presented the city as a selection of episodes; the lack of response to social or economic reality condemned it—for all the valuable things it had to say—to a local role, though it did affect the layout of some new towns and housing estates. The absence of any social or political implications characterized another British movement, Archigram, about a decade later. It enjoyed a great but brief vogue all over the world, and formed part of the many techno-utopias that were being promoted during the sixties, patronized by Buckminster Fuller, who firmly believed that reason and technology were sufficient to solve all the world's problems. Although he did build a number of domes and patented a number of technical devices, his ideas and those of his followers were pushed into the background by the energy crisis of 1973.

When Margaret Thatcher killed off the Greater London Council, the main section of County Hall was sold off to a hotel operator, while other parts were let or sold to various commercial enterprises. As a matter of fiscal expediency (but also perhaps only half-consciously, of symbolism), the government of the time wanted to show its contempt for the *gauchiste* council that had dominated local government in London, by sending a strong message to anyone who knew the city at all.

But it was not clear enough. County Hall adjoined the South Bank terraces on the river, on which stood the Festival Hall and the other subsidized public "cultural" institutions, culminating in the National Theatre. They represented the pride of Welfare-state Britain. That concentration of buildings is, as from the end of 1999, dominated by a vast and very expensive privately operated high-tech Ferris wheel that will turn the potentially "monumental" leisure zone into an inner-city fairground. Of course, the Ferris wheel is to be dismounted after four years, but the amount of concrete poured into the riverbed to stabilize it is enormous, and its foundations will remain; in any case, such temporary arrangements have a way of outstaying their allotted span. This relatively simple device is not just a modern bit of fun added to a stuffy old palace, but accurately represents Conservative contempt for local government. It is astonishing that a Labour government, committed to restoring local autonomy, has seen fit to allow this intrusion. Buildings and places—even if they do not exactly "carry messages"—do mark and inflect urban structure as well as urban texture: they signify. Moreover, the twenty-first-century dweller in the all-housing city still seems to harbor an atavistic craving for missing or concealed monuments. Perhaps this is why special, enclosed monumental display zones have been created—as a compensatory planning device rather than as a new building type: theme parks. Any number of critics have noted their peculiarly surrogate character. The geographer-urbanist David Harvey, for instance, pointed out:

> that it is now possible to experience the world's geography vicariously, as in a simulacrum . . . which . . . conceals almost perfectly any trace of origin, of the labour process that produced them, or of the social relations implicated in their production.

This notion has ripened so much that one hotel in the Nevada casino city of Las Vegas has condensed the whole nostalgic Old-New Monument World into one miniature: with the Eiffel Tower for Paris, Saint Peter's for Rome, Saint Basil's Church for Moscow, Tower Bridge for London, and the Statue of Liberty for New York. All these, overfamiliar through television advertising and travelogues, have become signposts for the "virtual" global tourists of television and cinema. I have seen mini-Eiffel towers (one-third size, I think—about three hundred feet) both in Shenzhen and Beijing. This kind of ghetto for monuments, which a number of satirists described thirty years ago as belonging to a remote future, has become a commonplace now that urban experience is no longer available in real cities.

The attempt to provide a mimetic "condensation" of another place and time is not new. Centuries ago pilgrimages to remote and sacred places were replicated for those who could not afford to leave home. The fourteen stations of the cross, which you may find in any Roman Catholic church, are a miniaturized and atrophied version of the pilgrimage around the holy places in Jerusalem. The "holy mountains," very popular in northern Italy, Spain, and Latin America, offered a more dramatic version of the same pilgrimage, while rather different and more graphic condensations were later attempted in "exhibitions," as when the Battle of the Nile was emulated—to Lord Nelson's satisfaction, it is said—with the help of painted canvas, real guns, and gunpowder in London in the early nineteenth century. Such replications were also offered in *panoramas*, popular exhibitions at places of historic interest. The event commemorated is evoked by a mixture of painting and relief, usually in a circular space entered through a tunnel. Some panoramas—as the one in Regent's Park in London in 1825–1900 designed by Decimus Burton—had included temporary installations, but most were permanent and site-specific. They were much frequented by a new category of travelers called "tourist"; but although one or two panoramas are still in working order—as the one on the battlefield of Waterloo, outside Brussels—most were put out of business by the cinema.

Walt Disney was the pioneer in the development of the theme park so eagerly adopted by the Chinese. The corporation that bears his name owns and runs a number of them—on the East Coast and on the West coast of the United States and outside Paris, and so on. They are not only the best known and most advertised, but one of them, in Orlando, Florida, is reputed to be the biggest of them all. Although these parks were designed in the first place to appeal primarily to children and teenagers, who are the commercial leaders of society, they usually have at their heart a surrogate urban experience, but one purified of all the inconvenience that living in a real town involves. As a toy town, the theme park holds up a distorting mirror to the reality of urban living. It offers an urbanity without surprise, yet one where planning has been rigidly enforced. Again, the critics have noted that Disney World is

> a viable representation of a real city, built for people from the middle classes that have escaped from cities to the suburbs and exurbs . . . like a gated residential community [that] promises to control the menace of strangers.[15]

Like some late-twentieth-century public buildings and like shopping malls, theme parks are always insulated from their surroundings by a sea of parked cars. Nevertheless, the first ingredient of urbanity specific to them is the variety of transport, of a kind unavailable in the real-life city, but which reformers are forever advocating: travelators and escalators, electric go-carts, monorails, and funiculars. The "park" often has a core of prominent public buildings: a castle, a town hall, the high (or main) street, a railway station (with a scenic railway winding its way around the enterprise). The urban caricature even has a population of highly visible figures of pseudoauthority: not only a toy king and queen, but also a toy mayor with a supporting town council, most of them elaborately masked as well as costumed. The king and queen are from a pack of cards (via Lewis Carroll's *Alice*), the prince is always a Prince Charming. There are also uniformed police and a toy fire brigade, but the uniformed officials are there for display, not to deal with real traffic, real crime, or real fires, not to mention disposal of real trash. This is effected by quite different employees in quiet, overall-type uniforms, intended to make them invisible (or at any rate, not noticeable), much like the scene shifters in a Nō play. Security, and surveillance, is behind the scenes or below the grade. "Invisible" employees also quietly deal with any troubles. The litter removal is so efficient that after my first visit to the original Disneyland at Anaheim some twenty years ago, I was surprised when almost all my Angeleno friends kept on asking if I "did not find it so very clean," as though that were the most conspicuous aspect of the surrogate, as opposed to the real urban experience of Los Angeles.

It seems that the main function of the theme park town is to assert "a national public culture based on aestheticizing differences and controlling fear . . ."[16] and so provide a common heritage for a heterogeneous clientele by recalling a fabulous and past time. It is usually that of familiar fairy tales, those of Grimm and Andersen, a sort of generalized European town of sometime before the war of 1870, a Franco-German town of top hats, frock coats, side-whiskers, and all. The towniness is an essential part of the experience and of the success, and if it is not the fairy tale of Europe, it can be a version of America with cowboys and Far West paraphernalia.

Other formulas quite different from the Disney version of the Grimm-Andersen fairy-tale world may be equally successful. Between Disneyland and the Charles de Gaulle Airport at Roissy near Paris, there is a park based on the very successful French cartoon books of Asterix and his pals, where those brave, resourceful, funny, democratic, and Celtically magical Gauls resist the much more powerful but clumsy rank-obsessed and incompetent Romans. On Oahu in Hawaii, the Mormon authorities, who sent their first missionaries to Polynesia in the 1850s, started a Polynesian Cultural Center to allow the students at their college there "to keep alive and share their Island heritage with visitors." The local college was affiliated with Brigham Young University in Utah, and the enterprise expanded rapidly as Hawaiian tourism grew. It is in this Polynesian theme park that the "experience" of a generalized "Polynesia" is offered to tourists in the form of dances, music, boat rides in carved canoes, luaus, and the appurtenances of sanitized village life, although carpenters were brought in from various islands to build Maori, Tongan, Marquesan, and Samoan houses. Those who "inhabit" it are paid in college fees for their impersonations of "generic" Polynesians, and the differences between the islands is homologized in a kind of uniform, and therefore inevitably fake, Polynesianness.

Of course, the past is not always the "theme" of any park. Even Euro Disneyland offers a science fiction village, a "futurama," while a whole theme park in the Loire Valley in France is devoted to an experience of a not-too-remote, but highly technicized city, since the theme park may be about the past and the future but must never be about the present. Only a surrogate urbanity and attendant monuments are essential to its success. The network of such enterprises, which started as more or less permanent amusement fairs, has now become one of the staples of world tourism.

Walt Disney himself, having created the very profitable Anaheim Disneyland against the advice of his associates and his bankers, had much greater ambitions. He had built it on 160 acres, and to Disney's chagrin, parasitical traders soon lodged themselves nearby, profiting from its drawing power. South of Orlando he therefore bought twenty-seven thousand acres to insulate himself against the surroundings, and he resolved to extend the theme park experience to the everyday. Not content to replicate or extend its success, shortly before his death at the end of 1966, he launched an expansionist version of the theme park, EPCOT, which stands for Experimental Prototype Community of Tomorrow. It was to be a "community" without any urban problems; there would be no economic crises and therefore nonstop full employment, and of course no trade unions. Industry would be constantly innovative. Children would be encouraged to be "creative," and there would, of course, be no beggars, layabouts, or criminals for that matter. The ways in which this would be achieved were not always made explicit, and the EPCOT that opened in 1982, long after Disney's death, had more modest aims. It has now been engulfed by Disney World, but his approach is partly realized in Celebration (another Disney enterprise), where all inhabitants are vetted, and the infrastructure is controlled by the leasing corporation—though its critique belongs to the later discussion of new town developments rather than to that of mass tourism.

Mass tourism is a late-twentieth-century development; it is said—by the estimates of accountants that may be fictitious but are nevertheless interesting—to have become the industry with the highest turnover in the world. Its demands and its lobbies are therefore hard to resist. The industry offers employment to variegated armies, and has developed novel institutional structures. Travelers became tourists toward the end of the eighteenth century; the word is not recorded in English before 1800, and it moved into other languages later. Yet even tourists were individual at first. In 1841 a temperance preacher called Thomas Cook made an agreement with a railway company to concede cheap fares to his extended congregation. The success of his early enterprises encouraged him to organize the first international group excursion, to Paris in 1855, for the World's Fair. By the 1860s he was moving farther afield.

Tourists, as travelers had done before them, always needed guidebooks, and the first ones, to Rome, had circulated as manuscripts long before printing was invented—and the Roman ones were also the first to be printed. By the time Cook was arranging his tours, the London firm of John Murray had begun the series of popular guides bound in red cloth which were soon emulated by the German firm of Karl Baedeker. The customers of Cook's Tours and the users of Murray's and Baedeker's guides were fairly well-to-do and fairly well-informed. They had other emulators: André Michelin, brother of the French automobile tire manufacturer Edouard Michelin, began printing guides around 1910 to advertise his brother's product. When that line proved very profitable, André became an important map and guide publisher.

The tourism that has grown exponentially over the past half-century is different in kind. It is a by-product of the leisure that longer holidays and shorter weeks have conferred on many workers in North America, Japan, and Europe, though the catchment area is now widening. It is therefore very different from the sight-seeing and information-gathering tourism of earlier periods. It requires a highly developed and ramified infrastructure, of which the theme parks are a fraction. A large section of the building industry in several countries is now organized to provide high-rise hotels near beaches and mountain resorts, and also in some metropolitan cities. They have become a common building type, almost the most common form of new housing. Hotels cannot rely on a permanent demand as may be created by an expanding population, and they are expensive to run and maintain. They have to have a continuous supply of changing custom. Tourism therefore requires the constant services of advertising to stimulate travel and increase numbers. Carriers are mostly the airlines, and the industry supports high aircraft production and, to smaller extent, that of commercial vehicles such as charabancs and buses. Yet it is a reliable contributor in terms of long-term benefits to any economy. Tourism is hostage to the weather, to any natural disaster: floods, volcanic explosions, earth movements, extremes of rainfall or heat, epidemics. The industry is also hostage to political instability and to terrorist attacks, as in Egypt or on the Croatian coast recently, which may lead to a wave of cancellations, followed by a deluge of bankruptcies, and it is often seen as the seductive and misleading short-term solution to long-term economic problems.

The new tourists often avoid the big cities, though anyone who moves through the center of any metropolis, such as London or Paris, Rome or New York, will have witnessed the disruption of the already congested traffic by tourist buses. In some smaller towns, the buses block traffic entirely. Visitors to monuments are jostled by disoriented excursion groups following after their guide, who is holding up a pennant or an umbrella or even a sign board.

These phenomena are new to the received wisdom of heritage planning,[17] which has concentrated on the use of "heritage sites" to attract the tourist trade that has been the motivation for so much urban renewal in the Old World at the expense of any investment in local industry or farming, or even market gardening.[18] Since, in any case, the illusory and the fanciful will always tend to get in the way of the real, the spectator will always be in the way of a worker, of someone going about his business. Such tourist presence may be absorbed without too much trouble in London and Paris or Tokyo and New York. The same is not true of places like Prague or Dresden or Venice, relatively small towns—half a million, 300,000, and 225,000 inhabitants respectively—where the centers are constantly clogged by visitors who, in the case of Venice, have actually transformed the nature of the city. Venice has concentrated on catering to tourists to the detriment of that industry (glass, fish farming, microengineering) to which it would have been suited and which would have given it some economic independence. The catering and the advertising have been so successful that the Venetians themselves are worried, and have begun to talk about limiting the number of tourists they are willing to accept, but, inevitably, such regulations are too difficult to frame, even if they could be applied.

The speed of travel has increased parabolically since the invention of the steam engine; and now space travel, though not interplanetary travel, seems within the bounds of possibility. Yet the speed to which our bodies are bound remains an insuperable hindrance. As of now, we cannot travel much faster than rockets allow us, which would mean that a journey to the nearest planet might take several years; we are assured by science fiction writers, however, that if in some as yet unforeseen way, our bodies could be dematerialized, we would be able to travel in communication channels—with other items of information—at a speed much more like that of light. Such marvels have already been shown in many novels, films, even television soap operas. Clearly, inhabitants of cyberspace need have only a tenuous hold on sensory reality, which means so much to the more commonplace humans. But to the ordinary man and woman the very existence of these complex creatures, so much above our everyday doings, suggests possible fields for immediate technological innovation.

However brilliant information technology techniques have become within this millennium, the notion that a live body might survive being sent through the wires remains in a science fiction future. If it is ever tried, I suspect that many laboratory cats will end up in some cyberlimbo before any human being volunteers for the trip. As for me, I remain a piece of hardware and can no more be sent through the wires than the serviceable but inanimate PC on which this text is composed. Still, using the computer screen is a daily experience for a large section of humanity. It is both an aid and a prop. You can already vote, play games, order plumbing fixtures, groceries—communicate with your bank and broker, or with friends all over the world. Most new buildings are designed, and practically all are drawn out on computer, which also allows the architect to image walks, to see the volume from above, and to work out many of its details. It has even been suggested that there now exist

> two "parallel universes" . . . an everyday analog universe that we inhabit and a newer digital universe created by humans but inhabited by digital machines . . . our machines manipulate the digital world directly, but are rarely aware of the analog world that surrounds their cyberspace.[19]

Computers may rarely be aware of the analog world that I inhabit, as they chew their software, nor can they operate, however complex their interchanges, without a sentient operator somewhere who will need at some point to visit the bathroom, go for a walk, see friends, and go to the theater or perhaps just sit in a café and watch other people pass. Indeed, one effect of proliferating electronic services may be

> that their prices will be driven down. At the same time, the value of manually performed services that cannot be readily automated or remotely delivered will correspondingly rise. Cooks, gardeners, nannies, and plumbers will do correspondingly well.[20]

If the screen is indeed as serviceable as we are told, then surely some of the vast office complexes implanted in our cities will suffer a shrinkage. Or, as someone said recently, each bit of electronic memory that issues from the factory has built into it, as it were, the virus that will devastate some square meters of built-up surface in a city center.[21] Can we already plan for that?

Like any technological advance, this huge one also involves an inevitable and corresponding loss, some kind of experiential deprivation, all part of that process that Plato had already decried so many centuries ago when he spoke of the loss of memory that the introduction of alphabetical writing had brought about.[22] Such change is irreversible, and those who promote its instruments need to reflect on—and if possible, supply—the "wants" that their device or inventions might provoke.

The computer is a prelude to the general electrification of information which is already in course. Further and more complex claims are already being advanced for the process: that smell and touch will be transmitted and reproduced so accurately that "satisfactory" (not more accurately defined) sexual intercourse—for instance—may be achieved over long distances. *Simstim* is a science fiction term that describes the equipment required for it.[23] Romantic observers of technology assure us further that the unlimited pleasures of the cyberworld will displace our need for the clumsy but solid analog environment that we currently occupy. That

> cyberspace [is] a consensual hallucination experienced daily by billions of legitimate operators, in every nation . . . [a] graphic representation of data abstracted from the banks of every computer in the human system.[24]

Though you may equip yourself easily to inhabit this form of digital space, you will neglect the socialities of bodily presence, its analog pleasures, at your peril. William Gibson, its most popular prophet, sees the effect of his heroes' and antiheroes' overinvestment in cyberspace as producing a crushing impoverishment of their analog environment. On a train journey one of them has to stare

> out of train windows at blasted industrial moonscape, red beacons on the horizon warning aircraft away from a fusion plant . . . The landscape . . . of broken slag and the rusting shells of refineries.[25]

The asocialities of this future life, in which housing has become a kind of personal prosthesis and public space is one of insecurity and violence set in those desolate, detritus-strewn landscapes, must be read as a warning—though like futurology it extrapolates from a present in which the implicit threat will certainly meet circumstances as yet unforeseeable.

This happened in the case of earlier claims of an equally daring nature made a generation ago, when the notion of the "global village" was launched by the late Marshall McLuhan. The continuous suburb of white-collar workers and executives, created as it was by railway technology that gave us darkest suburbia and its lasting symbol: the lawnmower

would be abolished by electronic technology, then still primitive, as would the towering office blocks that crowded the city centers. McLuhan thought that

> the circuited city of the future will not be the huge chunk of concentrated real estate created by the railway. . . . It will be an information megalopolis. What remains of the configuration of former "cities" will be very much like World's Fairs—places in which to show off new technology, not places of work or residence. They will be preserved, museum-like, as living monuments to the railway era.[26]

This forecast further suggested the rapid creation of a continuous quasi-rurality in which all business would be done by executives and even assistants and clerks at their computers—and they would not need to leave their homes. Made thirty years ago, the forecast has not been realized as yet, and many other developments have intervened to make this vision unlikely. Of course electronics have intensified the privatization of space through relatively primitive technology in one direction: the Walkman and the cellular telephone isolate their users in a private aural world however public their physical context. On the other hand, the prophecy has been falsified by real estate. When McLuhan wrote, only three American cities besides New York and Chicago had more than two buildings over twenty-five stories high: Detroit, Philadelphia, and Pittsburgh. Thirty years later, every sizable city has at least a dozen.[27] Their numbers are increasing at the time of writing in China and Southeast Asia—and even in Old Europe.

The pressures on the environment are quite different twenty years later, therefore. Privacy has been further electrified, but the suburbs are still growing. City brown sites remain desolate. McLuhan himself recorded a warning against taking the forecast too seriously:

> An astronomer looking through a 200-inch telescope exclaimed that it was going to rain. His assistant asked: "How can you tell?" "Because my corn hurts."

Urban problems cannot expect automatic solutions provided by technological advance. They can be approached only through political agency. We remain bound to location, and each one of us to his or her unique body. I suspect that even when ways will be found to turn us into information bits, we will still be the creatures of our senses, since

> *The eye—it cannot choose but see;*
> *We cannot bid the ear be still;*
> *Our bodies feel, wher'er they be,*
> *Against or with our will.*[28]

That is why the notion that at some future time cyberspace will perform the functions of the tangible public realm must remain chimerical. There is no possible appeal now, nor in the foreseeable future, from the here and now of bodily presence—the presence that has never felt comfortable, never been at ease in the city of housing. The bodily presence has demands of another kind also, demands of memory and order that have had to be supplied by such surrogates as the theme park. Already a century ago reformers were contemplating cities in which all our demands could be met.

6. The Suburbs and the New Capitals

THOSE WHO TRIED TO MANAGE CITIES in the nineteenth and twentieth centuries had to deal with such an unwieldy mass of perplexities that attacking one problem at a time—such as traffic or hygiene—seemed a useful course. Another approach was to start all over again, but not the way the utopians had done, attempting to solve all social and physical problems at once by creating a tightly knit community where they would all be resolved. No, it could be done more modestly by providing the industrial and financial conditions in which a new and rational, cooperative population would be induced to build a soundly planned town and set an example of how to live well within it.

Of course many towns since antiquity have started as mythically or historically recorded new foundations or perhaps re-foundations. Legends about Theseus of Athens, Romulus and Remus of Rome, and King David of Jerusalem were known to most people. More recent and famous foundations were the Abbasid Caliph Mansur's Baghdad or the medieval French and English *bastides*; there were the refuge cities after the Reformation, and there were the new capitals required by geographical or political realignments—Madrid, Warsaw, Canberra—and virtually all the cities of the Americas, both North and South. And there were also those new towns that were required by industry and mineral resources, like Magnitogorsk. I would like to consider those that proposed a novel urban form and invited a different settlement rather than such others as may have been directly sponsored by an industry for their workers. The growth of suburbs—apparently uncontrollable and mostly unplanned, even unpremeditated—was one pragmatic problem that prompted several reformers to propose such new foundations. Suburbs have existed as long as cities had edges or borders, the inevitable by-products of curfews, of gates shut for the night, which meant that late-comers had to find accommodation outside the walls. From the Middle Ages onward in Europe, inns catering to the stranded traveler and the imposition of import duties by towns prompted the working of a tax-free market. All this attracted obvious illicit activities, gambling and prostitution. Market and inn then generated their own settlement.

The English word "suburb" does not describe the situation as accurately as the French *faubourg* (out-of-town) or *banlieue* (corruption of Latin *banlauca, banleuca*—the distance of a league outside the limits of a town or monastery to which its rule, its *ban* would run). As medieval and later cities grew, new enlarged walls would enclose previously suburban areas that had become uncomfortably big and important. So the Faubourg Saint-Germain became, in the eighteenth century, the district of great noble mansions and consequently *faubourg* (unqualified) came to suggest high fashion (of the aristocracy) against the new-rich; the English word "suburb," meanwhile, has retained its derogatory sense, as in Lord Byron's description of an unfashionable lady looking "vulgar, dowdyish and suburban."[1]

A suburb must always be parasitic on a town or city. Even when it acquires an independent administration, it is never a financial center, or a center of power. Suburbs were rarely meant to be agriculturally or industrially productive. In the eighteenth century they began to take on a new and bourgeois aspect as citizens found the city increasingly crowded and polluted, at a time when roads and transport were constantly improving. Such citizens as could afford it therefore moved to city edges or even out into the country nearby for fresh air and a semblance of rural life while remaining within reach of their place of work. In view of the English preference for the detached house, contractor-developers then began to cater to this fashion by providing estates. Even before mid-century the extending of railway lines stimulated such growth. Londoners began to colonize Hampstead and Clapham.

In Paris, too, the railway played its part. The extension of the western suburban line just before 1850 prompted the planning of a country suburb by Alphonse Pallu, a developer, at Le Vésinet, opposite the old royal palace of Marly. He hoped to attract a mixed-income public to an estate where design and planning were carefully controlled. As it filled up, however, it soon became a middle-class enclave. Bedford Park in London, which I mentioned in the previous chapter, was also a developer's response to a new railway station. New York grew outward over Long Island, as well as over New Jersey, along new roads and rail lines; Philadelphia, to Camden over the Delaware, but also along the westward railway that ran to Harrisburg, the Pennsylvania state capital. This patrician "main line" retains both its label and some of its social cachet. Near Chicago suburbs such as the elegant Riverside, planned by Olmsted, responded to the same kind of extension of the railway.

As the lines lengthened and the journey to work took longer, so drains and the water mains also became overextended. The affluent refuge-suburb had a dark obverse of vast areas of working-class row housing and miles of densely populated sooty red brick and blue slate. More or less regulated as the century went on through increasingly stringent bylaws, the terraces spread ever wider as the density decreased, but depended on and therefore remained within reach of the factory or mine where their inhabitants worked. The factory was their center, much as the city was that of the middle-class suburb.

A number of nineteenth-century urbanists took fright at this development. Soria y Mata's proposal for dealing with it, the *Ciudad Lineal*, and the many projects of his followers were one response. But a quite different one was suggested by Ebenezer Howard, who became perhaps the most influential of the new crop of reformers. Of modest origins, he had learned stenography early in life, worked in a London law office, and even tried his luck farming in Nebraska. When that failed, he moved to Chicago, the "Garden City," where he first came across the ideas of such transcendentalist thinkers as Longfellow and Emerson. On his return to England, he began working as a parliamentary stenographer, and that remained his chief source of income. In 1881 he heard the American physiocrat Henry George lecture in London. Howard was very struck by his ideas about land ownership and his belief that the real class conflict was not between capital and labor but between industrialists and landowners.

He—unlike William Morris—read Edward Bellamy's *Looking Backward* enthusiastically when it came out in 1888, and would buy it in batches to give to prospective converts. What impressed him about the society represented by Bellamy was its spirit of cooperation and its enjoyment of technological progress, even if he was to reject Bellamy's centralism in favor of Peter Kropotkin's more humane anarchist vision. He had also met the itinerant Scots ideologue Thomas Davidson, the "guru" of a "Fellowship of the New Life," which proposed a cooperative settlement—a politicized version of Bedford Park—in the Lake District. But in 1883, some of that Fellowship was transformed into the Fabian Society, and it might now, anachronistically, be called a left-wing think tank, the intellectual arm of the Labour Party, though at the time it did not intend either to own or to settle land.

Meanwhile Howard was elaborating his project, one he considered scientific and practicable, based, in part, on James Silk Buckingham's Victoria, which I listed among the utopias. Once Howard's ideas had matured, he wrote his proposals quickly, and published them as a pamphlet in 1898: *Tomorrow: A Peaceful Path to Real Reform*. It was received enthusiastically, though not by the Fabians, and led within weeks to the foundation of a Garden Cities Association, which immediately began a quest for money and land, supported by a number of influential persons, including Lord Leverhulme and the Cadburys of Bourneville, who had built model tied housing for their workers.

In 1902 Howard enlarged his pamphlet into a book: in *Garden Cities of Tomorrow* he coined the term with which he became completely identified. The label was a little unfortunate, since "garden city" had already been associated with park-ringed Chicago, as well as with Christchurch in New Zealand. Around 1870, a suburban estate had been built by the New York drapery magnate A. T. Stewart on Long Island, and adopted Garden City as its name, and it then became a popular name for American small towns and suburbs. In England it had been used in the publicity for Bedford Park before 1880.

Howard, who was no architect and self-taught in other matters, was always very specific. Public, municipal, or cooperative, rather than national ownership of land was essential. His primary concern was the relation between urban and agricultural space. All this was detailed in the illustrations to his books, which have since become very famous. They were explicitly schematic, and clearly labeled "N.B. Diagram Only." They showed the concentric-radial organization of a region around a "Central City" of fifty-eight thousand inhabitants, which would be surrounded by six "Garden Cities," each with a population of thirty-two thousand, so that there would be 250,000 inhabitants in all. Each of these garden cities would require a site of a thousand acres, but would occupy five times as much in agricultural and common land. The boundary would be marked by a railway line within which there would be an outer industrial belt operated only by electric power—no steam. Howard is vague about its generation. Within the railway belt, there would be two concentric zones of housing separated by an avenue wide enough to accommodate churches and schools. At the center, a public space would be outlined by a town hall, museum, library, and so on, separated from the housing by a belt of parkland. A "Crystal Palace–type" gallery would provide another zone of separation between parkland and housing.

Howard was an excellent speaker and his familiarity with Esperanto allowed him to preach his doctrine internationally. By September 1904 land had been bought at Letchworth in Hertfordshire, and architects were invited to prepare designs. Raymond Unwin and Barry Parker were chosen—and in fact became the architects of the movement—and their simplified version of the Queen Anne style its trademark. After a brilliant beginning, progress was slow: at first the Association could pay for only the infrastructure, but when a railway station was opened in 1905 and several exhibition cottages were built, they attracted many visitors and inevitably more settlers. Industries moved in. By 1914 Letchworth was the qualified success it has remained. Meanwhile, inner London suburbs were growing along the extending underground lines. Some denizens of Hampstead, aware of the Letchworth experiment, proposed to build a "garden suburb" close to Golders Green, the new station. It was to have a social mix, but not the productive intentions or the agricultural surrounding of the garden city—in fact it was to be more like Bedford Park than Letchworth. Still, the main layout was by the same architects, Parker and Unwin. They invited a young architect, Edwin Lutyens, to design the churches—one Episcopalian, the other "free"—in the main square, which also had an institute and a school and was edged by two-story houses. Commerce, even small shops, were excluded, so that it always seemed a bit dead. Nor was a planned market nearby ever built, since its location was cut by a new road. Hampstead Garden Suburb was therefore never able to offer employment, and the rise in property values soon pushed out the artisans. But the housing made an alluring environment, and did much to convince the public of the charm and practicality of the garden city idea. This suburb grew much more quickly than Letchworth, and soon other such suburbs had been organized at Romford in Essex and Esher Park in Surrey.

Although the vertical suburbs of European cities had very different configurations, and rather different problems, a French urbanist, Georges Benoit-Lévy, published his *La Cité-Jardin* in 1904; it presents his plan for open suburbs as a realization of Howard's idea, which he would later attempt to graft on to Soria y Mata's Linear City in Madrid.

A rather different and much more detailed enterprise, though in many ways parallel to Howard's, was taking shape in France and Italy quite independently. Tony Garnier, a young architect from Lyon, had gained the coveted Rome prize at the Ecole des Beaux-Arts in 1898. In 1901, instead of sending the required and conventional study of an ancient site back to Paris, he provided an elaborate, highly worked out scheme for an industrial city instead, breaching not only the Ecole regulations, but contradicting its teaching that new settlements were not desirable. Inevitably, therefore, he was treated harshly by the Parisian authorities. Still, his project was exhibited in 1904, and published later, in 1917; and then republished as part of a portfolio on his work—much of it had been built by then—in 1932.[2] He remained proud of it, rightly.

Garnier's new city, which was to have thirty-five thousand inhabitants like Howard's central town, is set on a plain between the curve of a river and a chain of mountains, and though not specified, it was in fact situated just north of Saint-Etienne. A tributary, on which there is a small, older town, flows down to the main river but is dammed to provide hydroelectric power for its inhabitants and for its industry. Hydroelectric power was only about ten years old at the time, so that Garnier's suggestion was a daring novelty. This power was to work the electric smelting furnaces, which were the town's major industrial installation, as well as its secondary, textile industry. It would also run the electric streetcar line along the spine of a main street. The town is focused on a group of public buildings, which include an assembly hall, a theater, an art and craft school, and a stadium which form its core. A "health center" overlooks it, and below the escarpment that goes down to the river, there is a motor-car track and a small airport—all complete novelties. Programmatically, there are no churches, no law courts, police stations, or prisons in this town. Housing is of a higher density than in the English garden cities, but still relatively low, and the architecture is flat-roofed, colonnaded, creeper-covered—deliberately "Mediterranean."

Before he moved to Rome, Garnier became involved in a left-wing Parisian literary circle, the Amis d'Emile Zola, a support group for the great naturalist writer (a friend of Cézanne and Manet), who had become embroiled in the agitation surrounding the arrest of a Jewish army officer, Alfred Dreyfus, on a trumped-up spying charge. Zola had about this time also become obsessed with the utopian writers whom I mentioned earlier, particularly Fourier, and was beginning his four anything-but-naturalist gospel novels, of which the first, *Work*, was published in installments in 1900. *Work* tells of the foundation of a cooperative manufacturing town by a Fourierist and benevolent engineer-architect. Garnier's town may not be an exact realization of Zola's novel, but the inspiration is obvious—the reliance on electric power being one of them. Moreover, in the later versions of his project, Garnier inscribed the public buildings in the town-center with long quotations from Zola's book.

Garnier was more matter-of-fact than Zola—who foresaw solar batteries augmenting hydroelectric energy and private electric two-seaters supplementing public transport—and his project, worked out in considerable detail, would be realized in part, at least, because he had the confident backing of the Radical mayor of Lyon, Edouard Herriot. Herriot, anti-clerical, bourgeois, left-leaning, was in turn a senator and a deputy, foreign minister, as well as premier three times, though he refused to stand for the presidency of the Republic. A prolific writer, he was elected to the French Academy, unlike Zola. In Lyon his authority was absolute, and he was mayor for fifty years, until his death in 1957. Herriot was aware of German and English developments. He visited German hospitals—taking Garnier with him—in 1909 and in 1911, and went again to a planning meeting to speak with appreciation of "what the Germans call *Städtebau.*" A Lyonnais delegation, guided by Georges Benoit-Lévy and Ebenezer Howard, visited English garden cities and suburbs.

By then Garnier was employed by the city and running his atelier at the local branch of the Ecole des Beaux-Arts. He initiated his *grands travaux* in Lyon after 1905. The huge cattle market and slaughterhouse at La Mouche in the south of the city came first, then the stadium, most of a new hospital and much housing, some schools and minor public works. In 1925 he designed the Lyon pavilion at the Exposition des Arts Décoratifs in Paris, and then his last major work, the town hall for Boulogne-Billancourt, outside Paris. All these were partial realizations of that *Cité Industrielle* that had occupied his early career and was—in that sense—no utopia, but a viable new town to which he managed to annex parts of Lyon. In 1914 a great planning exhibition was housed in the abattoir building, though it did not have the impact hoped for, being overshadowed by the outbreak of war. The great Scottish biologist and urbanist Patrick Geddes thought it the best he had ever seen, and young Charles-Edouard Jeanneret—soon to become Le Corbusier—saw both buildings and exhibition; he was to meet Garnier soon after the war and always confessed himself a disciple of that stripped, yet intentionally Mediterranean architecture which purged his more Nordic inclinations.

Although their solutions *look* so different and their methods are also at variance, both Howard and Garnier were practical men and both believed in urban reform through the public ownership of the soil. Neither plan required a revolution, nor did they call for any special legal leverage, and both exercised an enormous and positive influence on the way cities were to move after 1918, though certainly not nearly enough.

Although French social thinking was highly original, even visionary, building and planning regulations were about half a century behind the British ones. A concerted effort to develop housing and planning policy was made in the 1890s through the foundation of the Musée Social, an urban pressure group, which in turn, in 1909, gave birth to the Société Française des Urbanistes. An Institut d'Urbanisme was then established at the University of Paris in 1919. Most of the members of the Société and the graduates of the new institute worked outside France—many of them in the colonies. However, in the twenties and thirties, a Socialist deputy, Henry Sellier—who was to become both mayor of the Parisian suburb, Suresnes, and later minister of health under Léon Blum—became one of the moving spirits in the office that coordinated the socially backed low-cost housing called Habitations Bon Marché (HBM), in which he also collaborated with Herriot. The earliest efforts, before 1914, were low-density housing on the English model for Lilas and Cachin—both were demolished between 1960 and 1970. Sellier did not consider that public money should support Howard's kind of experiment, and adapted the idea of the garden city to mixed-height apartment buildings grouped as dormitory suburbs, of which sixteen were built, mostly to the south of Paris: Stains, Plessis-Robinson, Pré Saint-Gervais, Châtenay-Malabry. One of the last of such schemes, La Muette at Drancy, built in 1933–35 to the northeast, became the prototype of much postwar building. Five steel-framed point blocks, fifteen stories high, were clad in prefabricated concrete panels and surrounded by an estate of similarly built three-story apartment blocks. It was immediately commandeered as gendarmerie barracks, and the adjoining buildings were the infamous assembly point for those going to their death in concentration camps during World War II. Howard's vision was lost there.

Lutyens and the other architects involved in the garden city movement represented a high point of British influence on design and planning worldwide. When, in 1910, an international planning conference met in London, Ebenezer Howard was one of the main speakers. Delegates came from all over the world. An Australian delegate reported that his government had decided that a new capital was needed. Australia had become a self-governing dominion in 1901, with its capital in

Melbourne, but that old capital had already by then been overtaken—in size as well as economic power—by Sydney. After heated and acrimonious debates, a Capital Territory was carved out of New South Wales—as had been done in the United States and in Mexico—on a straight line between Melbourne and Sydney. Since it had no name, Australian wags suggested Caucus City or even Swindleville and Gonebroke before the adaptation of the aborigine place-name, Canberra, was settled and announced.

The delegate at the London conference having hinted at the creation of a new capital, the government held an international competition in 1911 to design it. Although boycotted by British architects, it produced a high level of entries. The winner, Walter Burley Griffin, an American, had been closely associated with Frank Lloyd Wright. In spite of really nasty bureaucratic obstruction and the four years of war that followed, as well as the financial crises associated with it, the building of Canberra became one of the important achievements of interwar architecture. It made Griffin into an international figure, though strangely neglected in recent histories of architecture or of the city.

Griffin, a native of Oak Park, Illinois, and his wife, Marion Mahoney, had drawn some of Frank Lloyd Wright's best-known presentations and were both well known in Chicago. When the plans for Canberra were published, Camillo Sitte's magazine *Städtebau* found them too formal, too much like the Great Chicago Exhibition of 1893, too much the City Beautiful. Set on an artificial lake, which was not fully dammed until 1964, Canberra is conceived with many monument-centered traffic circles, and stellar avenues opening onto vistas toward Mount Ainslie and the Black Mountains. It has inevitably been compared to New Delhi, its exact contemporary. Yet the scale and the approach are entirely different. Griffin planned Canberra—Howard-style—with leasehold land, to reduce profit from land speculation and to maintain control of standards. It was to have 25,000 inhabitants, but that figure could not be maintained in a capital city. Today it has 330,000, and satellite towns have been opened since 1972. A national university, gallery, library, science museum, as well as parliament buildings (the old ones were opened in May 1927 by the Duke of York, who became George VI, to the tune of the Australian diva Dame Nellie Melba singing "God Save the King") and the High Court make up the proper furnishing of a metropolis. There has been a small influx of light industry, which has brought in a limited blue-collar population, but there are as yet no international airport, no first-class hotels. In spite of this growth, Canberra's excellent climate, a low crime rate, and all the many visiting tourists, the city lacks a metropolitan buzz. Such high-rises as have been built are still modest, but tourists seem to find the low profile of the buildings—even the new parliament is buried under a hill in a vast traffic circle and is therefore nicknamed "the fallout shelter"—a comforting framing for the vistas. The modest approaches to public buildings suggest a relaxed view of authority, while the flocks of sulfur-crested cockatoos and pink-and-gray parrots that fly about them, as pigeons do in other cities, are an entrancing variation on the garden city idea.

At the same London conference, the first suggestion was made that a new Indian capital might be established in the old Mughal center, Delhi. Calcutta had been the seat of the British government until that time, but at the Coronation Durbar—an imitation of the Mughal ceremony in which the Indian princes offered their loyalty to the king-emperor—of George V, held at Delhi in 1911, the king-emperor himself announced the move to the new capital and laid its foundation stone. Edwin Lutyens, who was at that time still working with Parker and Unwin on Hampstead Garden Suburb, was appointed architect-planner to the city the following year, and the project was ready by the time the war broke out in 1914. The buildings were not in fact finished until after 1930.

Griffin had conceived a modest center for a federal democracy in Australia, and faced all the rigors of a factional and hamstrung administration as a client. Lutyens, who designed a monumental and haughty capital for an imposed, authoritarian regime, had few such problems, since he had direct access to the viceroy and even to the king himself.

Even before Delhi was chosen as capital, Lord Curzon, the brilliant choreographer of Raj pageantry, announced the program: "To me the message is carved in granite, it is hewn out of the rock of doom—that our work is righteous and that it shall endure";[3] this in a speech relinquishing his viceroyalty in 1904. Yet his successors were to occupy the overbearing palace for a mere fifteen years, ceding it to the president of the Indian Republic in 1947. Before that handover, Gandhi had characteristically suggested that it should be converted into a hospital.

Unfortunately, by then, all the exciting arts-and-crafts energy that had made British design the envy of Europe between 1870 and 1905 seemed spent, absorbed into the spongy froth of Edwardian opulence. Lutyens, who had come out of the Queen Anne, garden-city background, changed style as well as associate for New Delhi, and found Herbert Baker, who had already built the government palace for South Africa in Pretoria, 1911–13, though he is now chiefly remembered for disemboweling John Soane's marvelous Bank of England buildings in 1921–37. In both Baker's and Lutyens's work, the old bugbear of style that the Queen Anne manner had held at bay reappeared—as it did for many of their contemporaries all over the world—as the "high game of classicism." Although they considered themselves the heirs of Inigo Jones and Christopher Wren, there was some official pressure at Delhi to make their design in an adapted Indian style. They therefore tried to graft Indian motifs onto their already ungainly "neo-baroque" style. This is evident at the climax of their project: the portico of the viceroy's palace, deeper and wider than that of any Roman emperor or Renaissance despot, is incongruously crowned by a replica of the great Buddhist stupa at Sanchi, flanked with more or less Mughal-type *chattris* in a futile attempt to indigenize the imposition. The palace and the ministries that surround it are approached by a strangely bumpy Kingsway—the Rajpath—that runs for a couple of miles through an arid open tract, edged by isolated official buildings that offer neither shelter nor interest, baked brown through the summer season and rendered sodden during monsoons. The complex only comes into its own for military parades and state funerals (Jawaharlal Nehru's, Mrs. Gandhi's). It contrasts sharply with the Maidan, the old assembly space in front of the Mughal Red Fort, surrounded by closely packed commercial buildings and bazaars.

Apart from that, New Delhi is divided by wide, tree-lined avenues—it is not a pedestrian city. Originally it was tightly zoned between different classes of princes, officers, and civil servants, and further subdivided between English and "native" occupation. And although the classification was altered with independence, the tightness has remained. The blocks between the avenues of the plan were not conceived as "neighborhoods." As late as 1960, the density of Old Delhi—Shahjahanabad—was about fifty times higher than that of the Lutyens-Baker new town, where an early attempt to introduce garden city type planning led to the rapid dismissal of the consulting urbanist.

Since Sitte and Howard are forgotten, it is back to the Beaux-Arts. Fittingly, therefore, Delhi's social center is a long way from the palace and the Rajpath—a traffic circle in effect, but made up of two concentric ranges of buildings and colonnaded shopping arcades, with a park at the center, Connaught Place. It acts as a kind of hinge between Old and New Delhi. Even if the axes, domes, and porticoes might at the time have seemed elements of a timeless way of building, the disordered, motorized twentieth century soon put paid to all notions of a purely formal solution to urban problems.

New Delhi has been given an enthusiastic revaluation by recent "postmodern" apologists. They are less inclined to offer the same justification for the even more ambitious but analogous efforts of despotic regimes in Italy, Germany, and the former Soviet Union. Compared with those—or with New Delhi, for that matter—the sort of planning represented by garden cities, however influential they can be considered in retrospect, seemed a rather milk-and-water remedy for serious urban distemper in the interwar period.

In England, after the wartime hiatus, Welwyn, another garden city, the first to be called a "satellite" town, also in Hertfordshire but on the main railway line north, was initiated in 1919–20. The first buildings went up in 1925, but Welwyn was cramped by postwar depression and the market crash of 1929. However, by 1939, the government loan was paid off, several industries were well established, and the population reached 18,500 of the planned maximum of 40,000 by 1948; that year it was officially "designated" one of the New Towns that were planned around London.

The term "satellite" came to replace "garden city" in later theory; it was coined by an American planner, G. R. Taylor, who offered the satellites of St. Louis (Granite City), Birmingham, Alabama (Fairfield), and most extensively of Chicago, as examples. He cited particularly Gary, Indiana. Many of these pre–World War I satellite towns had no land-use policies and were soon incorporated into their adjoining mother towns, but Gary, founded around steel and cement works in 1906, was an exception. It grew from nothing to a population of 30,000 in 1912 and now stands at 116,500. It was named after Elbert Gary, the chairman of U.S. Steel, and though not a company town it remained linked to one industry. Gary had regulations to prevent land speculation and the sale of alcohol (both have now lapsed) but did not become a model in planning literature; one reason for this is that its lakeside is entirely blocked by the mills. The true innovations in American planning were to come during and between the wars.

Another idea was launched in the United States about the same time as the garden city originated in England—the neighborhood principle. It was formulated by Clarence Perry, a young sociologist, who was to spend his whole career working for the Russell Sage Foundation in New York. A population large enough to support an elementary school constituted a neighborhood; it was to be bounded by arterial streets containing adequate open green space for the school and other institutions to be grouped within them; enough shopping to supply essential needs was sited around the periphery, while internal streets catered only to local traffic. These principles were published several times and given wide publicity through the Regional Plan for New York of 1929.[4]

Neighborhood and transplanted garden city often coalesced. The Black Rock development, outside Bridgeport, Connecticut, and Yorkship Village, now called Fairview, outside Camden, New Jersey, both erected for naval workers, were built during World War I. Frederick Lee Ackerman, who had visited the English garden cities, worked there with a team that included Frederick Law Olmsted, Jr., and the young Henry Wright. Although the builders of Fairview were chided at the time for providing housing of too high a standard, the district has retained its coherence, and maintained its value in decaying Camden. The curved roads and the village green with a school opening onto it have remained. One of the collaborators on the project was John Nolen, who went on to become the planner of San Diego.

These wartime and immediate postwar experiments led to the formation of a Regional Planning Association, in which Clarence Perry, Olmsted, and Wright, as well as Clarence Stein, another planner-architect familiar with the English experiments, took part. Its offshoot was the City Housing Corporation, which was formed in 1924 to create the American garden city. Its success was partial. In Queens, but with a good connection to central New York, Clarence Stein and Henry Wright built Sunnyside Gardens, modifying the New York grid by grouping houses of different height around inner greens in each section. It still exists today and flourishes as a neighborhood unit. They next laid out Radburn Village in New Jersey, which gave its name to the ordering of traffic circulation to avoid crossings, economize on road surface, and allow the separation of pedestrian and motorized traffic without cutting off access to buildings. The method was applied to a number of towns both in the United States and in Europe. Sunnyside and Radburn were both stunted by the 1929 crash and its consequence, and in any case, never developed any industry.

The effect of the crash on building was catastrophic. Housing construction around New York dropped by 95 percent. In the United States as a whole, 85 percent of building workers became unemployed. Various private measures were undertaken for pumping finance into building. Valley Stream in Nassau County, New York, was to house 18,000, and although it was not built, it became the pilot scheme for the Resettlement Administration's "green belt towns": Greenbelt in Maryland, Greenbrook in New Jersey, Greendale in Wisconsin, and private enterprises—Baldwin Hills Village in Los Angeles—a city that received its first inhabitants a few days before the attack on Pearl Harbor. All were sponsored by the National Housing Authority.[5] However, these settlements tended to be homogeneously middle class, did not develop industries, and were not always able to protect their green belts, all of which led to their association with suburbia.

Although the National Housing Authority was an arm of the New Deal, proclaimed by Franklin D. Roosevelt on his election in 1932 in answer to the huge unemployment problem in the wake of the farming crises that followed the stock market crash, it made small claims on the public purse. The bulk investment over the next decade was in roads and road transport—at the expense of railways or any other form of mass transit—and this has marked American cities much more than such limited construction and planning efforts as the greenbelt cities. Even the New Deal's greatest regional planning success has been a tragic missed opportunity: the Tennessee Valley Authority produced splendid engineering structures—power plants, dams, and roads—and galvanized a whole region, but there was no associated urban development of any consequence.

Land has never been in short supply in the United States, but analogous suburban growth worried successive British governments. There had been a baby boom after 1918, yet the official campaign to produce "homes for heroes" made little headway and was tailing off after 1925. Private developers stepped in, and picking up on the Bedford Park/Turnham Green–Hampstead Garden Suburb/Golders Green connection, found association with public transport, particularly the growing underground system, profitable. A new station would be built with a "parade" of shops nearby—often with flats over them—perhaps a cinema or two, though no church; an estate, mostly of semidetached houses, would quickly develop around such a nucleus. The layout was always determined by the main drains over which the roadways were laid, and the lots divided on bylaw minima, not on the garden city kind of layout, though the individual houses would often be a cheap version of the garden city prototype. Most of the owners were of modest means, and could not afford an automobile. A network of bus services from house to station was therefore introduced. Having been privatized in the 1980s, such services are today as run down as the rather shoddily constructed housing stock. These developments meant that the built-up surface around London was increasing at an alarming rate, invading not only green belt territory but also some prime agricultural land.

The idea of the green belt, so important to Howard, had not been formulated by him, and it did not become a familiar planning concept till later: it was Raymond Unwin who first proposed the formation of a "Green Girdle" round London about 1930. There was much agitation to form such "girdles"—before they became "belts"—and there were a number of reports to the government and the Greater London Planning Committee that urged action, one chaired in 1921 by Neville Chamberlain, who would later declare war on Germany in 1939.

All these government reports recommended some form of garden city plan as the preferred solution to urban problems, but no action followed until Lord Reith—chiefly remembered as the founding father of the BBC—was appointed minister of works in 1940. Two further reports recommended the enforcement of land-use policy—particularly for rural land—and a central agency to supervise it. A new ministry of planning and the London County Council commissioned projects, of which the most important was by the council's own chief architect, J. H. Forshaw, working with Patrick Abercrombie, a Howard disciple and by then the most authoritative planner in the country. They provided the basis for that British postwar planning policy that led to the creation of the New Towns.

But by then the garden city movement was too closely associated with a backward-looking architecture. Not only despotic, but even democratic governments in Europe and America patronized some variety of inflated classicism. The brightest of the younger architects were still smarting from their collective defeat in the League of Nations competition. When they met at the Château La Sarraz in Switzerland, they bound themselves into a society, the International Congress of Modern Architecture, CIAM for short (acronym of the French form, Congrès Internationaux d'Architecture Moderne), which aimed to reform not only the design of buildings but the whole fabric of the contemporary city; their focus was the street—incapable now of carrying a vastly increased volume of motorized traffic—as the main generator of disorder. After that foundation meeting, the next one, in 1928—dealing with minimum dwellings—was in Frankfurt, Germany. Others followed, in Brussels and Barcelona. The 1933 meeting was to have been held in Moscow, but the organizers were disconcerted by the results of another competition, that for the new Palace of the Soviets. They sent a letter of protest to Stalin, who took no notice, and it was therefore moved to a ship that traveled from Marseilles to the Piraeus and Athens, and back again. During this trip the one hundred eleven theses that together are still known as "the Athens Charter" were formulated. The charter was to provide the basis of much planning in the coming half-century. It declared that any city should be analyzed into four basic functions.

1. Dwelling—habitat—and well-spaced high-rise apartments had to be preferred to other forms.
2. Work—to include both offices and factories.
3. Recreation and leisure—the focus was on sport, and therefore on parks and stadia.
4. Circulation—it was treated as a separate zone.

Supplementary observations concede that the existence of older buildings could be important, but then the clearing out of smaller, later, and less prominent constructions clinging to them should be encouraged, which, the charter maintains, will allow the primary monuments to be presented as free objects, an approach that seems to hark back to the ideas and methods of the more brutal nineteenth-century restorers.

A study scheme, a "grid," was devised on the basis of the Charter, which could be applied to all cities. It offered a method as radical and as universal as the Beaux-Arts axialities of Lutyens and his contemporaries. One of its more drastic consequences was that it dictated a very strict functional zoning of the city. This was to have the effect of curdling that social and functional mix that gave older cities their enduring vitality.

Only once has the Athens Charter been imposed directly on a garden city project, at Chandigarh. The Punjab region had lost its old capital, Lahore, to Pakistan at partition in 1947. After much hesitation the decision to start anew was taken at the highest level, and that, in India and at the time, involved Nehru. Albert Mayer, an old collaborator of Clarence Stein on the green-belt towns, who happened to be in India, was consulted. The site chosen in the Himalayan foothills was just off the main Delhi-Lahore road, and near the confluence of two rivers. Mayer designed the city to be built in two stages: the first anticipated 150,000 inhabitants, rising to half a million in the second stage. A separate administrative center for the province was to be on the eastern edge of the town, while a business district became the focus of the plan, to be surrounded by Radburn-inspired superblocks. Mayer soon involved a young Polish architect, Matthew Nowicki, who turned his rather poker-faced garden city plan into a flowing, leaflike plant form. All this was in 1950. That same year Nowicki was killed in a plane crash, and the rupee being weak against the dollar, the Indian government began to look for European collaborators—no Indian architect at the time was thought to be of sufficient stature, which may be a comment on the educational policy of the British Raj. After some negotiations, Le Corbusier became the chief architect, together with an English couple and partnership, Maxwell Fry and Jane Drew, and his cousin and collaborator, Pierre Jeanneret. Although they maintained Mayer's general layout, they turned it, as well as Nowicki's leaf, into a rectilineal grid. The "capitol" was now set on higher ground and detailed. Government offices, parliament, the High Court—and the governor's palace—were backed by a geometrical, Mughal-type garden, which has yet to be built. The center of the layout was occupied by colonnaded civic and commercial buildings grouped around an open square, the Chandigarh Central Business District. The urban area was edged by an artificial lake produced by damming one of the rivers.

In several places throughout the town, the plan is prominently displayed, together with an image to which Corbusier would return over and over again, that of the human body articulated by the golden section, a system he devised and called *Modulor* and used in all his designs. At Chandigarh that display seems an invitation to see the town in terms of the human body. Inevitably, the state capitol "reads" as the head, the central avenue as the backbone, the city center—which has the town hall and main commercial ventures—as the stomach/heart, and the river crossing the site as a metaphor of the bodily processes.[6] Whether by happy accident or, in some part, by design, the elaborate personal symbolism to which Corbusier was partial was acceptable and assimilated in an Indian context: the "open hand," which he uses as a sign of reciprocity and generosity—and which in Chandigarh became a large, weather vane sculpture overlooking an assembly space at the side of the High Court—is interpreted locally as a *mudra,* one of the symbolic hand gestures that dancers use.

The distance between capitol and business center also means that the town is binary, and this, perhaps only half-intentionally, enforces a measure of social and income mix within the sectors, cut off as they are from the main roadways and each other by walls or hedges to create more or less working "neighborhoods." The Radburn system, which was at the basis of Mayer's plan, implied a classification of roads and movement derived from the CIAM zoning endeavors. Seven different intensities of traffic were catered for in Chandigarh, where all main crossings are traffic circles, which may be fine for cars and bicycles but is a little cumbersome for pedestrians, camels, or elephants, though both capitol and business districts have created areas for pedestrians only. Most of the housing has so far been maintained at low, two-story or three-story height. Four- and five-story business buildings are appearing, mostly at the roundabouts, but the isolation of the walled super-block still makes the streets of Chandigarh bleak and unfriendly.

The governor's palace, planned at the top as it were of the "head" of the complex, had none of the gigantism or the domineering aspect of the viceroy's palace at Delhi. It was not built, since the governor of the time preferred a more discreet and modest home, as have his successors. For the 1999 celebrations of Chandigarh's half-century, however, a full-size cloth-and-bamboo model of its façade was erected, and it had the desired binding effect on the grouping. Unfortunately, since the assassination of the prime minister of the Punjab outside the legislative chamber some years ago, the capitol has been obsessively filled with security police and metal detectors. What were meant to be open pedestrian areas have been turned into parking lots. For all that, the capitol still retains the character of an open—perhaps overextensive—pedestrian environment.

Chandigarh, while acting as a provincial capital with its own flourishing university, has also acquired a large retirement community of civil servants and army officers. The splendid climate and, for all its defects, the scale and interrelation of the buildings, and the—for India—rapid train connection to Delhi have certainly allowed its inhabitants to find an identity and a pride in the place which has something of the quality that Howard hoped his garden city residents would also feel. Those who wish nothing to change—and there seem to be many of them in Chandigarh—tend to use slogans like "hands off our beautiful city," though the threat to its configuration that growth necessarily represents is also a paradoxical measure of its success.

While Chandigarh grafted CIAM ideology onto the garden city model, the principles of the Athens Charter alone were invoked in the making of the new capital of Brazil, Brasília. Rio de Janeiro had been the colonial and imperial capital of the country, and by far its most prominent and important city, but there had always been a notion that the center of power should be moved into the interior of the country. A prophecy of 1883, attributed to Saint John Bosco of Italy—founder of the Salesian order, who in fact never crossed the Atlantic—had promised unexpected bounties if central Brazil was developed. The new Republican constitution of 1891 then required the move, and designated a Distrito Federal to accommodate the new capital. A president laid a foundation stone there in 1922—in what is now one of Brasília's satellite towns—but the actual move was not made until 1960, a decade after Chandigarh was first planned. President Kubitschek, as governor of the state of Minas Gerais, had already worked with the young architect Oscar Niemeyer, who produced some of his best work for him at Pampulha in a free-form, lyrical interpretation of Corbusier's geometry. Kubitschek appointed him outright to design Brasília's buildings but declared a competition for the city plan, which was won by Niemeyer's close friend Lucio Costa.

This plan was roughly cross-shaped and it has been metaphorically interpreted either as an arrow in a bow or as a bird with spread wings, or even an airplane. If Costa is to be believed, he was invoking the ancient cross shape that had governed the orthogonal layout of ancient cities, and the foundation ceremonies and the blessing of the site were therefore carried out on April 21, the legendary, and still celebrated, birthday of Rome. The mythology is acknowledged, if obliquely, or half-consciously.

Brasília is the most elaborately zoned of all cities, and the plan makes this quite plain. The arrow, or the bird's body of the metaphor—sometimes also called the "Monumental Axis"—is the "work" sector. It starts at the lowest point of the site, at the plaza of the three powers that groups the presidential palace—the executive; the two parliamentary chambers and their offices—legislative; and the High Court—judiciary. In one early version of the plan, the plaza was literally triangular. The axis continues up into the esplanade of the ministries, a series of slab blocks that house the civil administration of the country. To one side is the cathedral—though whether it counts as work or leisure I cannot tell—but the high point of the esplanade is a television tower. This tower has now been prefaced by the white marble, Egyptian-style mastaba tomb of the late president Kubitschek, in which his body lies under a red glass dome—a chunky granite sarcophagus labeled *O Fundador*—continuing the epic of mythical origins but making little sense in terms of the metaphor either of the bird or of the arrow.

On either side of the esplanade, arranged symmetrically, are two sectors for embassies, hotels, commerce, hospital, public services, banking—all work; and culture, which presumably counts as leisure. Only radio and television get a section of their own. All this inevitably means that most pedestrians in any zone have to walk, sometimes quite a long way, to enter a different milieu. If you are an embassy employee, for instance, and succeed in walking out of your compound (most are well defended and very motorized), it may take you half an hour or more before you see anything other than the wall of another embassy compound.

The housing goes into the bow or the wings, to continue the metaphor. It is articulated into two lots of sixty *superquadras* on either side of the main axis; each one is a square unit, 240 by 240 meters, and houses twenty-five hundred inhabitants in slab blocks of three or six stories, mostly raised on *pilotis*, and grouped around green spaces. Four of these *quadras* make a neighborhood that has shopping, cinemas, a social club, schools, and a church. Although there are some echoes of Idelfonso Cerdá's *ensanche* or even Clarence Perry's "neighborhoods" about this arrangement, Costa's aim was quite different. Within each *superquadra* roof heights and finishes were all to be uniform. This

> prevents the hateful differentiation of social classes [since] . . . all the families share the same life. . . . Because . . . of the inexistence of social class discrimination, the residents of a *superquadra* are forced as if into the sphere of a big family. . . . Thus raised [their children] . . . will construct the Brasil of to-morrow, since Brasília is the glorious cradle of a new civilization.[7]

To do away with all the evils of the class system by defining a city's physical structure, and by imposing uniform heights and finishes as a monument to that process was very quixotic—a palpable contradiction almost. It could not have the desired effect.

The original plan was explicit on another point as well: there were to be no *favelas*, no illicit settlements, but no legitimate satellites either in the Distrito Federal. Even before the building of the capital began in 1958, squatters had turned up from a distressed zone nearby, appropriated land, and called their settlement Villa Sara, after President Kubitschek's wife, supposing—as it happened, rightly—that by invoking the protection of such a powerful name, they would forestall forcible removal. Having elected a governing body, they negotiated their legal rights with the authorities. A number of other such settlements followed, some created by seizure and negotiation, others by decree, however reluctantly granted. Indeed, satellites had to be allowed from the beginning, since a city of civil administrators inevitably requires a service population of menials: operatives, cleaners, porters, and mechanics, and there was no affordable accommodation for them in the plan. The size of the city with its satellites was to be limited to 500,000 inhabitants. *Favelas* therefore had to grow on greenbelt land that the planners had zoned for agriculture, and by 1996 the vast majority of the Distrito Federal's recorded population of 1,821,000, and growing—though I suspect that this may be an underestimate anyway—was in the *favelas.* The population of the capital city on the other hand has been falling: it was 213,000 in 1990 and 199,000 in 1996.

The upper echelon of officialdom also defeated the founder's aims: as soon as they could, they abandoned their *superquadra* apartments and built houses on the other side of the lake. This inevitably led to many problems including, for all the official denials, a high and violent criminality. My own guide to the city lived in one such house—a lightly constructed stylish, Japanesy affair—but defended by two growling, slavering Rottweilers which he kept in a concrete compound at the back of the house during the day.

The criminal presence in Brasília was forcing some of its inhabitants into zoning of a different kind: into enclosing and policing sectors in which the embassies and the more expensive private houses might be built. This kind of "concentration" was also emulated in São Paulo and Rio de Janeiro. In the 1980s it appeared also in the United States, where it received the polite description "gated community," whether in California or Nevada, later in the outskirts of Chicago, and finally in the outskirts of Washington, New York, and Boston. "Secluded from the world at large, yet close to the finer things of life,"[8] whole neighborhoods were walled, and given real gates, sometimes quite fiercely armed. Gated communities have now become popular in the Middle East and in Asia—in India, in Bombay and Calcutta, papers carry advertising for "gated communities" where the large dimensions of the houses suggest that several domestics would be needed for their maintenance. And since about 1990 they have also been appearing in increasing numbers in China, where they are sometimes moated and walled. Chinese publicity shows armed guards and banks of closed-circuit security screens.[9] Individual houses and bungalows come in all styles: Georgian and Tudor, Spanish colonial and even High Tech—though the remote and coarsened derivations of Bedford Park and Letchworth seem the most popular. New forms of such "communities" are constantly springing up, more or less "gated."

With its gated communities and its chaotic *favelas,* Brasília has become a very different kind of city from the one its founders intended. Saint John Bosco's prophecy has not yet been fulfilled, and the whole development seems to have put the very concept of the zoned city into question.

A very different capital was founded at the very same time as Brasília at the other end of the world: Islamabad, the new capital of Pakistan. The country's original capital, Karachi, was a relatively modern port city—even more recent than Calcutta and Bombay/Mumbai—and considered too small and too crowded to house the government. Field Marshal Ayub Khan, who seized power in 1958 and imposed a despotic regime of martial law, rejected the plans for Karachi prepared under Patrick Abercrombie of the London Plan, and decided that government had to be distanced physically from the corrupting influence of commerce. He chose a site near the northern Punjabi city of Rawalpindi, which had been the largest British army station in India during the Raj. It had certain obvious disadvantages—being between two troubled and conflictual areas: Peshawar and the Khyber Pass, which leads to Afghanistan, to the west; Kashmir to the east.

Although Islamabad had been conceived almost as a satellite of Rawalpindi—and in the hope that their roles would be reversed—the move of the whole government machinery forced its growth, so that the population of Islamabad is now approaching 350,000. Some tourist literature claims that it is as high as half a million, far from the 2.5 million to which the plan aspired. Its planners did not have any of the reformist zeal of the Chandigarh team, yet they claimed to have rectified the mistakes of both Chandigarh and of Brasília. The plan seems nonetheless to have been a rigidly zoned one, dominated by a presidential palace on a New Delhi scale but much more banal, and without any of Lutyens's compensating grandiloquence. The hilly site was flattened by an army of bulldozers, while six-lane roads cut it into oversize, Radburn-fed square blocks, each housing thirty to forty thousand people. Unlike Brasília, Islamabad acquired satellite villages from the outset to rehouse those dispossessed by the building of the city.

The contrast with Chandigarh points another lesson. Whatever Chandigarh's mistakes and failures, it has acted as an extraordinary catalyst on Indian architecture, and the school of younger Indian architects it inspired has made a great impact on the country. Islamabad has not had any cohesive effect on building in Pakistan, and in that sense has failed in its role as a trend-setting capital.

Some three hundred fifty new towns of various shape and scope have been founded in the twentieth century. The most ambitious and perhaps earliest program was that of the English new towns. Immediately after World War II, seven were first planted around London. Welwyn served as a seed project and made the connection with the garden city movement quite explicit; indeed Howard is considered "the father of the New Towns."[10] Their number has now grown to thirty-two, and although most are in England, one was sited in Wales, three in Scotland, and four in Northern Ireland. Their creation has not been welcomed with universal enthusiasm. Critics have attacked the policy of subdividing the town into neighborhoods, the mediocrity of their architecture, and their low occupation densities, all of which seem part of the Howard heritage.[11] Nevertheless, they have become effective urban units and all have survived. Of the newer ones, Milton Keynes has been an essay in dispersal: at very low density (6 to 10 persons per acre), it presents itself as a miniature, automobile-governed Los Angeles, organized around a shopping mall. Its opposite is Cumbernauld, of 1962 (extended 1975), outside Glasgow; with 205 people per acre it has the highest density of any British new town. Unusually, 40 percent of the housing is in apartments, some of them high-rise, while many of the individual units are arranged into courtyards to provide shelter from the harsh winds. The center—which is also the first megastructure in England—was located along the main Glasgow-Edinburgh road, at the high point of the town. A half-mile, eight-level building, surrounded by lawns like a castle surrounded by its moat, its spine is a bridge over the roadway, a high-level, enclosed, interior shopping street through which you enter its main institutions: the magistrates' court, the town hall, a police station, and a sports center. While the character of the town may be dour—the prevailing gray and green of Cumbernauld is the granite (or limestone) and grass coloring you often see in Scotland—on my visits there I have found the center lively and working. When the town reached its relatively modest target figure of seventy thousand, Cumbernauld had to acquire its own satellites. It was the one attempt to provide monumental architecture for a new town in Britain, but it had no successors.

Things were done quite differently in France. The rent control act of 1948 did not help investment in housing, and the official first answer to the postwar housing crisis were the *grands ensembles,* large—twenty thousand inhabitants and higher—estates of HLM apartments. The first one, at Sarcelles—just ten miles north of the center of Paris—was begun in 1954. The particular forms of *anomie* associated with them was given the tag *sarcellitis,* and provided the substance for one of Jean-Luc Godard's best-known films, *Deux ou trois choses que je sais d'elle.*

But more than a producer of anomie, these housing estates, planned as collections of serially built slab blocks, provided a negative image of the city of housing as a warehouse for the labor market, so that they became silos of extreme left-wing votes. A ministerial decree embargoed any further *grands ensembles* in 1973, and energy was diverted to the new towns.

The new town program was also central government–sponsored, but fifteen years later. On paper the administrative decisions and the planning seemed admirable, and the siting and the communication links were certainly very well considered. But whereas British architects at the time sinned in their timidity, which looked like meanness, the French ones tended to big gestures—it was not a good moment in French architecture. Paris had already acquired five satellites, and the detailed planning and the buildings were, in the first decades, almost universally overbearing and lamentable. The fabric of these towns seemed to have been conceived as collections of discrete objects and therefore without any possibility of that functional and social mix that is essential to urban well-being. The later additions in the last decade—particularly Henri Godin's at Evry and Henri Ciriani's at Evry and Marne-la-Vallée—have raised the standard of the buildings and produced urban environments and humane surfaces. Some sense of urban texture has been restored to these new towns.

There were other less concerted new town programs: for Prague and for Budapest. Rather vindictively, Nowa Huta in Poland was planted as a working-class, industrial and polluting counterweight to reactionary Kraków, but despite its planners, it became the second center of Solidarity. The British pattern was followed in Sweden, where Stockholm acquired two satellites, Vällingby and Täby. Perhaps the most successful single one is the Finnish Tapiola—whose name was found by competition—just outside Helsinki. Not a government initiative, it was developed by a private nonprofitmaking housing association—which was responsible for financing the infrastructure as well as the industry of the new town; even if it was sited only six miles from the capital—though separated from it by a deep bay in lieu of a green belt—the founders wanted Tapiola to be a garden city in the sense in which Howard used the term. But beyond the undoubted success of the plan and its rapid occupation, the organization of the enterprise is also interesting, since it is related to analogous enterprises in the United States about the same time. All the new towns founded there since World War II—many of which invoke the name of Howard—were the initiatives of private developers. They therefore broke one of Howard's prime conditions for garden city development, a principle he owed to the American Henry George: that land would remain in public ownership, and the profits of increased value would be plowed back into its fabric.

If no private ownership in land were acknowledged . . . the occupier or user paying rent to the state, would not land be used and improved as well and as securely as now? There can be but one answer. Of course it would. . . . The complete recognition of common rights to land need in no way interfere with the complete recognition of individual right to improvements or produce. Two men may own a ship without sawing her in half. . . .[12]

In the period immediately after the war, urban organization was not an American priority. Returning servicemen were offered cheap mortgages and encouraged to buy houses—to revitalize the war-depressed building industry—and persuaded to borrow to acquire automobiles for similar reasons. This produced increasingly large estate developments on the periphery of cities, of which Levittowns—which took their name from their developer, Abram Levitt, whose two sons, William and Alfred, followed him into the business—became a type. It is also the time when Walt Disney began to think about the possibility of his EPCOT, which I mentioned in the last chapter, though it did not become a real estate proposition until 1982.

Beginning in the northeast, these quasi-urban developments sprang up all over the country until, within a decade, the motor traffic they generated could no longer be carried by existing roads. The Interstate Highway System was then established in 1956. It was in the next year that Charles Wilson, the president of General Motors, made his famous declaration: "What's good for General Motors is good for America and vice versa."[13] This was the era of the first shopping malls, which could be reached only by car, and which proliferated in the late sixties and seventies around traffic changes. As the postmodern architects were proclaiming that "Main Street is nearly all right," that same American Main Street was being ravaged by the shopping mall. It may be ironic that the American city that has suffered the worst inner-city blight is Detroit, signposted by the violent riots of 1967, only a decade after Charles Wilson's optimistic comment.

Meanwhile, countermoves were sporadic. The first major new town, Irvine in California, took over a vast colonial landholding in about 1950 made up of over thirty thousand acres in Orange County, south of Los Angeles. The University of California established a campus, and the city center was planned. The housing plots were sold relatively quickly: the plan, very much in the wake of Parker and Unwin, divided the site into introverted "neighborhoods" of very low density requiring large road surfaces; the house designs were provided by town authorities and stringent regulations forbade any major changes on individual properties, which brought in complaints that the result was even more uniform than Levittown. Although Irvine was not emulated on the East Coast, soon after its foundation, Washington, D.C., invited the first satellites. A plan published in 1961 indicated that the preferred sites were to be north, toward Baltimore, and westward, into Fairfax County, Virginia. Reston was initiated on the second site, Columbia, Maryland, on the first. Reston, some ten miles west of Washington, was to be strictly white-collar; it eschewed industry while providing elaborate leisure facilities such as a golf club and boating harbor, but was not a great success financially, and was repossessed by one of its main financiers, Gulf Oil, to become their company town. Its financial and amenity status was in any case radically changed when Dulles Airport was sited three or four miles farther west, so that it is now engulfed in the greater Washington sprawl. Yet its lumpy Market Street has a kind of urbanity absent from most strip developments, and efforts are being made to urbanize it.

Columbia, established between Washington and Baltimore, Maryland, was much more ingeniously managed. It has become the prototype for such planning. The Columbia Economic Model (CEM for short), a guide for all managed development, "has, in fact, given the new community legitimacy as a business enterprise."[14] The town has attracted major industries, particularly General Electric, and has provided housing for a mix of both income and racial or ethnic groups. It is composed of neighborhoods with twelve hundred to two thousand inhabitants, and four or five of these combine into "villages"—an organization that owes something to Clarence Perry, of course, as well as to the English new towns.

Although it has been much more successful than any other analogous development, and occupancy has been as varied as its developer hoped ("from the janitor to the corporation president" is how James Rouse, its developer, put it),[15] speculation in land values has not been avoided. In fact, a rapid rise in value has been the explicit condition for its success, as it must be for every privately financed urban foundation. On the debit side, its critics have noted deficiencies in racial and cross-income integration; inevitably, also, for all its central shopping facilities, Columbia remains an auto-dependent town that has never developed even a modest institutional center nor an adequate transport system.

Reston and Columbia were designed and begun before the New Communities Act of 1968 had been passed.[16] A somewhat insular British critic commented on the legislation: "Good new-town creation is only possible if a public body comparable with our development corporation is entrusted with the landownership and groundwork, leaving the provision of building mainly to commercial developers. They are probably right." More than a hundred plans for analogous new towns were floated following the 1968 act.

Columbia was founded a sufficiently long time after the war for the privations and tensions of that period to appear very remote; nor was it a zoned town, and its very low density and dependence on cars guaranteed that. It has remained fairly open, but of course it is not a center of power, since it was designed to be a satellite of Washington. Other more or less successful realizations of the garden city idea have been built, such as Woodlands in Texas, which had been planned since the sixties but was actually set up in September 1972 with the sort of government aid the 1968 legislation foresaw. In spite of organizational and financial problems, it has prospered moderately. Yet unlike the smaller British new towns, all of them satellites, none of the American settlements ever developed their own urbanity in terms of recognizable physical structures. In any case, after the 1973 energy crisis and the insistence of authorities in older cities that they should have priority in the allocation of scarce federal funds, President Ford withdrew new town funding just before his electoral defeat in 1976, and his Democratic successor, Jimmy Carter, did not attempt to restore it.

Another movement, associated with the term "New Urbanism," arose in the late eighties and the nineties. Its proponents also like acronyms. PP, Pedestrian Pockets, are advocated by the San Francisco urbanist Peter Calthorpe, while TND, Traditional Neighborhood Development, is promoted by Andres Duany and his wife/partner, Elizabeth Plater-Zyberk. Both appeal to the ideas of Howard, Olmsted, Perry, and Nolen; in fact they see themselves as taking up the work of these predecessors:

> Urban planning reached a level of competence in the 1920s that was absolutely mind-boggling . . . we're not up to their ankles. But what happened to these people is that they were hit by the crash of '29 and they never worked again.[17]

Unlike them, Duany and Plater-Zyberk work within normal fiscal development strategies. Indeed, Duany, who seems the most articulate of the three, is quite explicit about his preference for operating as a client in the corporate world rather than as the citizen of a country or state.[18]

Duany has himself recently bought a plot in a new town not of their designing—but one representative of their views. It is a new town that he sees as embodying some of his principles, a recent real estate speculation of the Disney Corporation called Celebration. The old EPCOT Center near Orlando and Disney World has just become another part of that theme park, but sited three or four miles south of it, Celebration has been designed to look "vernacular" by a group of New York architects working in what I have to call an indefinitely "olde worlde" style. The result is still fairly new. As has often been pointed out, the Disney Corporation has kept Mickey and Minnie out; no images of them, no souvenirs in the tourist shops—and there are already tourist shops in Celebration, selling souvenirs and reproduction furniture and toys, since this piece of olde worlde has been widely advertised and is one of the sights of Orlando; and this is also why it has an inordinate number of restaurants for its current 2,500 inhabitants (to rise to 12,500—still nowhere near the Howardian garden city).

The town lies among the "semi-abandoned strip malls and miles of decaying housing stock . . . virtually obsolete within a single generation."[19] The olde-worlde Market Street runs down from the town square to a lake. In the center there is a very low, but many-columned town hall, and opposite it the most imposing building of the whole town, with an ornate, dominant outlook tower: the sales offices. That seems to demonstrate what the whole business of "community" at Celebration is "about"—it is about real estate.

Like many such settlements when they are quickly built (and therefore verging on the gimcrack), Celebration had to rely on transient, often immigrant and untrained laborers who stay in much cheaper housing than they have been summoned to build, housing that can later be adapted for the servant population of the "new town." There is nearby a curiously named town, Kissimmee (once more earthily known, it is said, as Cow-town), where many Disney World employees also live.

The danger that settlements such as Celebration inevitably run is that they will turn into gated communities. For the time being you will see no poor people there, certainly no "street people." And if there is a police presence, it is discreet to the point of invisibility.

Since most of the architect-planners involved in Celebration have preached the importance of "making places" as the chief aim of any new building, the lameness of their Orlando efforts should imply a reassessment of their policies. It seems, after all, as if New Urbanism, for all its harkening back to Howard and Nolen, is not in the business of resolving urban problems, but offers instead a refuge and shelter from the city. Since Celebration has no communal dimension (for all the insistent reference to "community" among its proponents), but is a real estate exercise, it differs from the older American new towns—of all persuasions— which were attempts to curb and curdle suburban sprawl, to condense the Levittown effect, cut urban roadways, and defuse the megalopolitan drive toward Bos-Wash and San-San predicated on the emptying out of the urban centers.

Yet the city, for all its problems and for all the attacks on it, remains unbeaten. And the most powerful of all of them, New York, though under constant siege, has maintained its astonishing and contrary vitality. Manhattan, not Bos-Wash, is the world capital.

7. The Heart of the City and the Capital of a Globe

FROM WHEREVER IT IS SEEN—Europe or Asia, Latin America or the Pacific Rim—New York now seems to be the capital (financial, administrative—even cultural) of all the world. It is that—as I suggested at the beginning of this book—that makes arriving there such a thrill. As always happens when a new capital emerges or is established, other cities will both envy and try to emulate it. That is why the word "Manhattanization" had to be coined for the process of making towns or cities more or less like Manhattan. A compliment like that has not been conferred on any other metropolis.[1] Not even "Romanize" had that sense when its empire was at its greatest. And that means, too, that any manipulating and restructuring of Manhattan will inevitably be emulated and perhaps replicated elsewhere in the world.

It enjoys a spectacularly favorable site—an island of schist, covered with enough light topsoil to accommodate quite intensive farming. Two rivers (East and Hudson) on either side of it discharge into a bay that is enclosed by the breakwaters of Brooklyn and Staten Island. In the north, Manhattan is separated from the mainland by a third, the Harlem River. Water traffic therefore became an essential feature of its planning, its economy, and its growth.

The bay had first been located or "found" in 1524 by Giovanni da Verrazano (the commander of a Franco-Florentine ship), though he neither bothered to claim nor even to name it. Still, the excellence of the natural harbor soon became evident, and at the beginning of the seventeenth century an English traveler who surveyed the territory labeled the island variously: *Manna-hata* and *Manahatin* (presumably Indian place-names, perhaps signifying mountain isle) on his map,[2] which was used by Henry Hudson when he sailed up the river that would be named after him in 1609.[3] On that journey he was being sponsored by some Dutch merchants to look for the northwest passage to Cathay. He continued the search on behalf of the English crown two years later, and that second exploration led to the discovery of the vast Arctic bay that was also named after him, and ultimately to his death.

Few traces remain of the Dutch in their old North American possessions except for place-names and some venerable East Coast family names. Yet the Dutch East India Company established some control over the New Netherlands territory after 1620 in order to exploit a profitable trade in dried salt cod, supplemented by fur pelts. The pelts soon displaced cod to become a staple and more profitable merchandise, and this reduced furred game in the Hudson Valley drastically. With the growth of trade, some huts were built at the south end of Manhattan, settled first by a group of Walloons. It was the director of New Netherlands, Willem Verhulst—not his successor Peter Minuit as the legend says—who probably bought the island from some Indians—probably from Lenape speakers, a Delaware people, possibly from Wappinga Algonquins, though neither had any particular claim to it anyway—for sixty guilders' worth of sundry goods. The southern end of Manhattan was built over, palisaded, fortified, and called New Amsterdam. Like Albany, but unlike Boston and Philadelphia, it was a fortress with a settlement attached rather than a covenanted or corporate town. A threatened English incursion was countered by a temporary fortification, whose emplacement is remembered in the name of Wall Street. Minuit's energetic but rabidly Calvinist and unpopular successor, the one-legged Peter Stuyvesant, did not fortify the settlement securely, and had to surrender the renamed "New Yorke upon the Island of the Manhatoes"—with a population of some 1,500—to an English fleet on September 8, 1664. At the treaty of Breda in 1670, the Dutch happily swapped the island for a far more valuable one near New Guinea, Run, which produced the world's largest harvest of the then virtually priceless nutmeg. Manhattan had grown to include 2,200 inhabitants, and prospered as a trading post in minerals and foodstuffs as well as furs, and by then, in slaves also; the population was about 10,000 by 1740 and in 1760, approached 18,000, outgrowing Boston.

Yet at the beginning of the nineteenth century New York was still confined to the tip of Manhattan Island and a strip of the Brooklyn riverside, even though John Adams had recognized it as "the key to the continent." Growth would be forcefully stimulated by the building of a canal to the Great Lakes, which was first planned in 1810–11, though not operational until 1825. Meanwhile, the harbor's importance was vastly increased—first because during their 1810–15 difficulties the British traders chose it as their favorite port for "dumping" blockade goods, which was bad for home industries but good for New York,[4] and then by the deepening of steam ocean-going vessels that the harbor easily accommodated, particularly after the introduction of steel ships: the first transatlantic paddle-steamer, the *Great Western*, sailed into New York Harbor on April 23, 1838. The first railway lines, for the Union Square to Harlem Railway, were laid in the 1830s and extended over the Harlem River into the Bronx and farther north after 1840.

Regulating the potential growth of the city inevitably became a concern of the city authorities. Although expansion was certainly expected, it had not been planned for. As Manhattan grew very populous, agitation for some kind of overall design for the island started at the end of the eighteenth century. The bits that had been laid out in an orderly way were episodic, such as when, about 1790, Peter Stuyvesant's descendants laid out his large estate on a directional south-north grid. After a number of abortive and extravagant projects had been put forward, the City Fathers took action: a Street Commission was appointed, for which a young surveyor, John Randel, Jr., mapped Manhattan. On the basis of his map, a plan of twelve avenues (a hundred feet wide) and 155 fifty-foot streets was announced. It deployed a uniform grid—irrespective of the irregularities of the terrain and the rights of landowners—over the whole of the island north of Houston Street, and was immediately engraved. The plan provided for a few exceptions. Greenwich Village was allowed its old layout, as was the Stuyvesant estate on the Lower East Side, which the city inherited from his descendants in 1836. The most important one, however, was the run of Bloomingdale Road, by then called Broadway—a formal avenue following the line of an old Indian path. Sometimes it lies parallel to the grid lines, at others it is oblique—allowing for bow-tie-shaped spaces to be opened at the resulting intersections.

Between Fourteenth and Thirty-fourth Streets, Third and Seventh Avenues, there was to be the biggest cut in the original grid, a "Grand Parade," which would accommodate military exercises, displays, and the like. And there were to be four further squares. Private developers intervened early on, buying several adjoining blocks and treating them as an "estate" on the London model. Notable was one Sam Ruggles, who juggled private and city capital to create both Union Square at Fourteenth Street and Broadway, and Gramercy Park nearby. Madison Square was another such creation—at Twenty-third Street and Broadway.

For all these private enterprises, the 170 acres of public space the original plan allowed had, through various modifications and encroachments, shrunk to 117 by 1850. All this could be treated as a trivial matter at first, since the occupancy of the blocks foreseen in 1811 was—as in Philadelphia—to be mostly individual houses with gardens. But New York had grown largely by increasing immigration from overseas, Asia as well as Europe—like practically all North American cities—while European cities had grown mostly by absorbing displaced rural populations. In 1800 Philadelphia was the largest city in North America, with a population of some 70,000, while New York County—which coincided with Manhattan Island—stood at 60,000 inhabitants. A century later, by 1900, Manhattan alone had a population of 1,850,000.

As the blocks filled with ever higher and denser buildings, agitation for a large public park grew. The city fathers resisted: the rivers on either side of the fairly narrow island provided plenty of fresh air, they thought; the extensive "green" cemeteries—particularly Green-Wood Cemetery in south Brooklyn—could always serve for promenades, as other such cemeteries served many American cities.

Yet rapid growth had made New York a place of violent race and class tensions. In 1835 a great fire had burned much of the city, and the first banking crash in 1837, and another one twenty years after, devalued much property. Riots and epidemics, particularly of yellow fever, were common. In 1848, appalled by the frequent disturbances, the epidemics, and the European revolutions of that year, the first major American landscape architect, Andrew Jackson Downing, proposed the creation of a vast "lung" for the city; he was soon backed by uptown landowners.

After several abortive schemes were rejected, a competition for the design was held in 1858 and money found for the project. The resulting elaborately landscaped park on the rocky outcrops of upper Manhattan was designed and organized by Calvert Vaux (the same who had written a famous pattern book) and Frederick Law Olmsted. It became one of the models for public parks all over the world.

The high trees around its edges were planted to keep out all views of the city and maintain the illusion of rurality, since for some years the tallest houses in the vicinity were six floors high. But the presence of the park immediately attracted development along Fifth Avenue. The château-style houses of the very rich mushroomed in the 1870s and 1880s, though they maintained a relatively low height. Then the character of the edge was broken on the west side of the park at Seventy-second Street by the eight-story, mansarded Dakota apartments (so named ironically to suggest its remoteness from "civilization"), which, built in 1880–84, heralded the growth of those tall buildings that have now ringed the vast, quasi-rural green space like an out-of-scale palisade. As the naming of the Dakota suggested, the edges of Central Park would retain a suburban air until the late nineteenth century, while the lower end of Manhattan which had no such amenities, became increasingly dense.

The crowding of the new industrial centers and an urgent demand for any form of shelter had provoked different responses among developers and builders. In Britain—in London and the north principally—the result was the packed two-story row or terrace house sometimes stretching over vast areas and at a wretchedly high density which builders had found to be the cheapest form of development as land values dropped. Even the very poorest seemed attached, notionally at least, to the possession of a family home, and this kind of development was also intermittently dominant in the United States. Manhattan did begin to develop buildings that rose upward early on in the nineteenth century, however, since immigrants—even quite prosperous ones—did not seem to find apartment dwellings objectionable, although the great luxury of the American city lay in apparently unlimited and readily available open space. At any rate, as late as 1872 a New York journalist could write:

> We have all heard about the European method of living in flats . . . [sic!] It is possible for us to greatly improve upon the European method since by establishing steam communications between each floor and the street, we may carry buildings as high as we please and render the top floor the choicest of them all.[5]

Manhattan soil, with its relatively shallow topsoil over rock, allowed builders to save on foundations, so that many-story, squalid tenements went up rapidly in lower Manhattan from the mid-nineteenth century onward. In the absence of any building regulations, tenemented slums were so appalling that an "improved, reform" five-story estate, Gotham Court, which was financed by a Quaker philanthropist in 1850, became a byword for squalor and high criminality; and even though housing improved little in the second half of the century, it was condemned and demolished by 1890.

In 1876 a competition for a Manhattan apartment house on an 8-by-33-meter (25 feet by 100 feet) site was won by a surveyor who produced a scheme for a terraced plan of row houses with four apartments to a floor, served by a minimal internal light well that allowed every room to have an outer window. There were two privies on each floor, and because of its internally pinched shape, it came to be known as the dumbbell plan. When New York passed an ordinance the following year stipulating that every bedroom was to have an external window, this plan was immediately adopted by developers, and vast numbers of these tenement houses, usually five to seven floors high, were built all over the city. Taken up in other American towns, this type of structure remained the most popular one with developers and builders until it was outlawed by a Tenement House Act in 1901. By then two-thirds or more of the Manhattan population, nearly two million people, were living in such tenements, and although no new ones were built after that date, many are still standing and continue to be inhabited.

Manhattan is not all there is of New York, of course. Brooklyn (named after Breuckelen, just north of Utrecht in Holland) Heights, across the East River, was already settled in the seventeenth century, while to the north, a Danish family, that of one Jonas Bronck who farmed there, gave their name to the Bronx. The mix of Dutch and English names in New York villages—like Nieuw Haarlem, probably named about 1650 by Stuyvesant himself, though the "Nieuw" was soon dropped—reflected its ethnic composition. In the eighteenth century, other boroughs on the East River end of Long Island were organized. The westward shore of the Hudson on the other side of Manhattan—the state boundary runs through the river—was less hospitable than the East River shore. Jersey City, then called Paulus Hook, was not really settled until the eighteenth century, and was only incorporated in 1820. Nevertheless, for most of the world and for most New Yorkers as well, Manhattan was and remains the essential New York. Until recently, Brooklynites and other Long Islanders traveling to Manhattan would say that they were going to "the City." This perception is no longer dependent on either population or financial numbers. At the last census in 1993, the New York Statistical Area, which covers the old county, was counted at 7,312,000. By 1998–2000, several cities outside the United States have outgrown New York in population—Shanghai, Jakarta, Tokyo. Mexico City, the largest, has reached 20 million, but no rival has threatened the position of New York as the world capital.

As in every city, transport in Manhattan was an essential factor of city growth from the outset. Ferries across the East River to Brooklyn were already a commercial enterprise and were regularized in the eighteenth century; by the nineteenth increasing numbers of ferryboats were crossing the river. A similar traffic grew over the Hudson, linking Manhattan to the New Jersey shore; it was also regularized after 1764. By 1830 even the many ferries then operating were obviously inadequate, and the first bridges were proposed, though all such projects seemed quite daunting both technically and financially. The first one to be built, the very elegant Brooklyn Bridge, was a suspension bridge designed and organized by a German engineer, John Augustus Roebling, from 1867 onward. He did not finish construction but died leaving its completion to his son, Washington, who was nearly killed by "the bends," the condition that deep-sea divers share with the builders of underwater caissons, such as those on which the vast piers of the Brooklyn Bridge still rest. The bridge has remained in nearly constant use since it was opened in 1883, even though it had to be renovated in 1954. The link it offered contributed to the incorporation of Brooklyn as a New York borough in 1898.

Suspension bridges were not a new building type, of course. In 1819 Thomas Telford had built a bridge over the Menai Strait—between Wales and Anglesey—with a central span of 570 feet. Several bridges designed by pioneering French physicist and engineer Marc Séguin, who was a nephew of Montgolfier, the first balloonist, spanned the river Rhône in the 1820s. Roebling himself straddled the eight hundred feet of Niagara Falls with a new type of suspension bridge, in which a stiffening girder was hung from the chains to avoid many of the problems of earlier similar constructions. The Brooklyn Bridge, twice the span of the Niagara one, and with alluvial mud thickly covering the rocky riverbed, provided many more problems. Its characteristic outline, however, became, with the Statue of Liberty, the badge of Manhattan. Inevitably, therefore, it also became the model for the many successive bridges built over the two rivers, including the Verrazano, one of the very largest bridges in the world, which spans the 4,260 feet of the Verrazano Narrows, the entrance into New York Harbor. It was first suggested in 1923 and built, despite vigorous environmentalist criticism, between 1960 and 1964 to provide a bypass from New Jersey to Long Island.

By the mid-nineteenth century most of the bulky and energy-consuming industry had moved out of Manhattan: the iron foundries and chemical businesses relocated to Brooklyn, which at one point was the world's largest sugar manufacturer, using cane shipped in from the Caribbean. Other industries moved to Staten Island, attracted by a further extension of the railway network, over the Hudson to New Jersey. The industries that remained in Manhattan were mostly craft-based, of which ready-made clothes was the biggest by 1855, about the time when it was transformed by Isaac M. Singer's introduction of the foot-operated sewing machine. It quickly made him one of the richest men in Manhattan and his factory on Mott Street one of the most advanced structures in New York.

The Singer factory was designed and built by Daniel D. Badger. He was also responsible for one of the most opulent New York cast-iron buildings, the Venetian-style Haughwout department store at 488–492 Broadway on the corner of Spring Street. The store had the first commercial Otis steam-operated elevator. Badger was not the initiator of the principle of cage construction. It was James Bogardus, watchmaker-inventor-engineer (he had devised the engraving machine that produced the first English postage stamps), who first advocated the use of such cast-iron "cage" or "skeleton" buildings. Few of Bogardus's own executed projects have survived: a large 1856 warehouse on the corner of Canal and Lafayette Streets remains, a smaller one on Leonard Street, of 1860; another at 75 Murray Street is made of his patent components. Long gone is the grand office and warehouse for the publishers Harper Brothers (at Franklin Square in what would now be Tribeca), his most ambitious and most representative building. Daniel Badger exported prefabricated iron buildings to several other cities in the United States—including Chicago—as did Bogardus, and one was even shipped to Havana; the principle of cage construction that he established anticipates the skeleton construction that has dominated building ever since.

The image of the city had—and continues to have—one other important and unique element: the Statue of Liberty. It was set on Bedloe's Island in New York Harbor—once the site of a colonial-era isolation hospital—and was to have been a gift of the French to the American people on the centenary of the Declaration of Independence, though its origins are more complex than this implies. The giant statue holding a torch had first been conceived for the Port Said end of the Suez Canal—a truly Saint-Simonian monument—by Frédéric-Auguste Bartholdi, its creator, as a lighthouse with the light emanating from her forehead, not from the torch. While that Egyptian project came to nothing, the idea of such a giant statue as a gift to the people of the United States on their centennial was taken up by a group of influential French republicans who wanted it both as a piece of propaganda, for home consumption, as well as a diplomatic gesture. As things turned out, the gift was not as warmly greeted by its recipients as the donors had expected. Yet in the end, both the site and the finances were found and the technical problems resolved: the hollow statue has a surprisingly thin skin of copper sheet held in place by a rolled iron frame designed by Gustave Eiffel himself, with passages and stairways within. Her torch "of liberty" was too solid at first to have acted as a guiding light for ships, while her radial crown "of enlightenment" became a viewing gallery. The crown and torch flame were belatedly glazed and electrified and can now be illuminated. The podium was the work of Richard Morris Hunt, now chiefly remembered for having designed and expanded the Metropolitan Museum of Art on the edge of Central Park.

Before the whole construction was assembled, even before the commission was confirmed, Bartholdi made a quarter-size model of it and cast it in bronze. One of three miniatures stands at the tip of the Ile des Cygnes on the Seine, in the west of Paris. In the second half of the nineteenth century, when giant monuments were still very much in demand, it was perhaps the biggest and certainly the most famous, and the only one in a big city, since most of the others are in rural or uninhabited places. In spite of early misgivings, it became the iconic mark of New York, and any film director or airline advertiser can use it as shorthand for the city. Replicas of it in all sizes—from ashtrays to captive balloons—are standard publicity and tourist fare. It has been the subject of innumerable caricatures and of a musical comedy. Large-scale replicas were also produced and a fifty-five-foot copy—perhaps one of Bartholdi's miniatures—was placed on top of a warehouse in a bid to become the focus of Lincoln Square, where Broadway crosses Columbus Avenue and Sixty-fourth Street. With another giant statue, of Dante, they made the area a rival to Columbus Circle a few blocks south.

Neighboring Ellis Island, earlier called Oyster or Gibbert Island, which lies north of Bedloe's Island, took over in 1892 from Castle Garden in Lower Manhattan to become the great clearing place for the newly arrived immigrants.[6] Some sixteen million, having sailed around the Statue of Liberty, passed through its dour and unwelcoming sheds before air traffic and new procedures closed them in 1954. The ships from Europe disgorged their soiled, shabby, disoriented human cargo within sight of her; Emma Lazarus's poem "The New Colossus," written in 1883, rang so true for so many of them that it has now been cast in bronze and fixed to the pedestal:

> *A mighty woman with a torch . . . and her name*
> *Mother of Exiles. From her beacon-hand*
> *Glows world-wide welcome: her mild eyes command*

The air-bridged harbor that twin cities frame.
"Keep, ancient lands, your storied pomp!" cries she
With silent lips: "Give me your tired, your poor,
Your huddled masses yearning to breathe free . . .
I lift my lamp beside the golden door!"

For a while the Statue of Liberty, 305 feet high on its podium, along with the 284-foot spire of Trinity Church, rebuilt by Richard Upjohn in 1839, though only finished in 1846, and the Brooklyn Bridge, opened in 1883, with its 271-foot-high piers, were the tallest structures in New York and the dominant elements in the image of the city. But not for long. Soon after midcentury, the desire to build ever higher had seized New Yorkers, and the Bogardus metal frame and the Otis safety elevator certainly made such developments easier. This desire was only in part a by-product of the rising value of downtown land, and of the land taxes based on it, which are often quoted to justify the phenomenon. But a conservative critic writing just after 1920 about the growth of the sky-scraper outside New York was explicit:

> It has been urged that the skyscraper was forced upon New York by the narrow limits of Manhattan Island and has no place in a city like Detroit, where there is no natural limit to lateral expansion. This entirely misses the point. Men build skyscrapers because they like skyscrapers. They concentrate them in a district because they like so to concentrate them. There are plenty of places in restricted Manhattan where there is room for sky-scrapers, yet none is built. In the Western cities, where expansion is unlim-ited, the skyscrapers are none the less concentrated in small areas.[7]

Was there an element of quite uncontrollable but also shaming agora-phobia in this fear of those apparently infinite spaces that prompted all this huddling together? Perhaps at the beginning. More important, in the early days, was the powerful drive for competitive display, for which close proximity was essential. What is clear from this quotation—as from what will follow—is that there was nothing "expressive" or inevitable and therefore, in a sense, unconscious about the origin and the growth of the skyscraper. From their first beginnings, skyscrapers have explicitly been representations of the modalities of power and wealth within the city.

The first really high New York buildings—all of them using some form of metal frame—had been the new four- or five-story warehouse-like dry-goods stores, the hotels, and the insurance houses of the forties and fifties. One of the most famous and impressive to rise above all of them was the Equitable Life Assurance Society building. Insurance was a novelty in New York, where none had existed before 1830. For all its imposing height—and it was to be further enlarged in 1875 and 1889—and its steam elevators, the exterior masonry was treated in a sedate, Second Empire style, with heavy cornices breaking the height into two-story units, topped by a tall mansard roof, so that its nine stories are—visually—reduced to three stories topped by an attic. Solidity rather than ambition was represented in such business houses, particularly those of banking and insurance. For all its fireproofing and its masonry-cased iron frame, however, the Equitable building was wrecked by fire in 1912.

This approach to high building changed about 1870, when newspaper magnates, who had none of the bankers' or insurers' inhibitions, wanted to display their achievements, their new riches, and their power. The earliest of their really tall offices was the Tribune Building of 1875—designed by the same Richard Morris Hunt of the Statue of Liberty podium and the Metropolitan Museum of Art—which in its day was looked askance at as a folly because of its overbearing, if not showily expensive, exterior. In spite of that the Tribune Building turned out to be a great commercial success. Like the Equitable Life building, the Tribune still mitigated its height with two- or three-story mansard roofs, as did the Western Union building, which was begun in 1872 by George B. Post, who had trained as an engineer, and was to become the most important designer of New York high-rises. Because it defied its urban context, the Western Union building has recently been called "New York's first skyscraper," even though at the time it was built the term had not yet passed into common speech.

The high building that became the familiar "type" of skyscraper did not at first flourish on the rocky base of "historic" Manhattan, but on the much less propitious clay, sand, and gravel soil of new and rapidly growing Chicago, where bedrock may be 125 feet below ground level. During the Civil War it had become the capital of Midwest farming exports—principally of wheat and meat—from the Mississippi Valley. Cincinnati had been the first city to claim the title of hog capital of the world, but it was too close to the fighting, and too far from the transport that the new railway (after 1852) and the lake-to-sea canals, such as the Erie (and after 1848 the Michigan and Illinois) could offer. In 1830 Chicago had the population New York had two centuries earlier, but it then grew astonishingly fast—from four hundred to thirty thousand inhabitants by 1850; and in the twenty years that followed it increased tenfold. By 1865 the stockyards, which quickly became the world's biggest meat processing and packing center, were opened. About the same time, steel production became a factor in Chicago's wealth; even though the rolled-steel joist that would make the skyscraper possible was not devised until after 1870, by 1880 the United States had become the world's greatest steel producer. Nor was Chicago, unlike Cincinnati, touched directly by the Civil War.

In October 1871 its relentless growth was catastrophically halted by a vast fire that consumed more than three and a half square miles of buildings—very many of wood, and tinder-dry after a rainless summer. Cast iron had also proved ineffective in the disaster: in fact, molten iron was one of the carriers of the fire. Reconstruction was rapid, and in Chicago, as in London after 1666, a concern with fireproofing became the primary consideration. Since the fire coincided with the industrializing of steel construction, steel became the prime building material, but one used in conjunction with fireproofing masonry, and later with concrete. As the buildings grew, in spite of the economic depression of 1873–74, so their foundations had to become more extensive. Only masonry stepped pyramidal footings seemed appropriate to provide support for the increasingly massive buildings arising on Chicago soil. Masonry construction would culminate in the vast and austerely smooth sixteen-story Monadnock Building that Daniel Burnham and John Wellborn Root designed and constructed in 1889–91. Iron and steel are used here for interior support and wind bracing only, and the building rests on a huge platform foundation. But by then the whole trend of Chicago building was developing in a different direction.

Sophistication and public spirit do not spring to mind when one considers the combination of stockyards and grain elevators on which the economy of Chicago depended, yet the city saw itself as the most "cultured" in the United States—outdoing New York in the patronage of the arts and the high education of its population—to which the number of bookshops, libraries, and private book collections are called to witness. In spite of inevitable rivalries Chicago architects were a fairly cohesive group. *The Inland Architect*, their magazine, shows that these architects were a very articulate lot as well. The ebullient economic upsurge of the city in any case smoothed the edges, since there really was a vast amount of work. The concentration of intelligence and talent among Chicago architects as well as among their patrons is therefore an important factor in the formation of the skyscraper. They were all aware of the importance and grandeur of their primary task: to provide an urban image that would represent the ambitions and the achievements of the "American Dream" through soaring forms. The "Loop," a central area of the downtown that was to be ringed by an elevated railway as well as by a wall, was the heart of the city, and most (though by no means all) of the high-rise buildings in the decade between 1880 and 1890 went up inside it.

Of the Chicago group, none was more prolific as draftsman, writer, as well as practitioner, than Louis Sullivan. Like many of his contemporaries he was both inspired and challenged by the energy and the greed of his clients. It is hardly surprising, therefore, that he provided the clearest account of what the architects would do; they would impart

> . . . the graciousness of those higher forms of sensibility and culture . . . to this sterile pile, this crude, harsh, brutal agglomeration, this stark, staring exclamation of eternal strife,

by which he meant, of course, the new skyscraper form. When Sullivan published "The Tall Building Artistically Considered" (from which this remark is drawn) in *Lippincott's* in March 1896, most of the famous Chicago skyscrapers had already been built; the word had made its entry into the English language fifteen years earlier—at any rate in America. Having been used for anything tall or high up, including tall— i.e., exaggerated—stories, after about 1885 the word came to be applied exclusively to tall buildings, especially those of skeleton construction. It was a wholly original, wholly American building type, the skeleton construction perforated by a service "core," in which plumbing, wiring, stairs, and elevators were set more or less centrally in the building.

The primary innovator was Major William Le Baron Jenney, the son of a Massachusetts whaling contractor, who had acquired an engineering degree in Paris and had served in the Union army under Grant and Sherman, hence his military rank. On being demobilized, he set up a partnership in Chicago specializing in railroad engineering: he even collaborated with Frederick Olmsted and Calvert Vaux on the planning of Riverside, which was to be a suburban "community" in Illinois. Having changed partners in 1869 and written an architectural handbook, he became the first master of steel-and-masonry fireproof construction in the decade following the Chicago fire. His office acted as the training ground for a whole new generation of architects and engineers that included Daniel Burnham (though not his partner, Root), as well as Louis Sullivan; William Holabird and Martin Roche worked for him as well. Jenney often combined iron—cast-iron columns and rolled-iron I-beams—with masonry and was the first to use the metal members as true structure and the masonry only as dressing and fireproofing. Success was quick; after building more or less conventionally with these materials, he designed his first near-frame building—the Leiter store in 1879—whose seven-story iron structure is encased by fireproof brick piers, while the façade is almost entirely of thinly mullioned glass. He was even offered some steel beams—whose manufacture had only just begun in the United States—when the frame of his Home Insurance Company Building was about half up in 1884. And that was the true beginning of the skyscraper skeleton.

Le Baron Jenney was not very interested in architecture, either in the detail of the skin or even in the planning and the volumes of the interior—he left such matters to his assistants. The variety of garnish with which he served his Chicago office buildings might be a curiously bare permutation of "classical" themes (the second Leiter building of 1889, for instance) or the opulent rustication of the Fair Building, which he designed in the same year. Yet he was no philistine; on the contrary, he presented himself very much as a cultured man. His French, if Louis Sullivan is to be believed, was execrable, but he spoke it. And he was very much the socialite and the *bon-vivant*.

Another, very different demobilized Union army engineer who set up practice in Chicago was Denkmar Adler, who was the son of a German rabbi; he was the first to use timber piles and timber and steel sleepers in concrete foundations, a system that was perfected by John Wellborn Root, who extended and reinforced the footings with rails and so ensured that a building would not settle out of true alignment. These raft foundations, later also known as "mat" or "floating" foundations, displaced the older pyramidal footings of masonry, and were henceforth used for all tall buildings in Chicago.

The taciturn and austere Adler was the perfect foil to the brilliant and rhapsodic Louis Sullivan, his partner, arguably the greatest, and certainly the most inventive American architect of the century. Until the breakup of the partnership during the 1895–96 recession, the combination of the ingenious engineer and professional with the inspired designer was an unqualified success. Their first major building, the Auditorium, built in 1889–91, was dominated by a tall tower—not quite a skyscraper yet—whose top stories were occupied by their office. Stylistically the Auditorium was a brilliant development of H. H. Richardson's *Rundbogenstil*.

Sullivan realized most clearly what the new type had to offer. The office building, this tall building (of which he wrote in the essay I quoted earlier):

... is lofty. This loftiness ... is its thrilling aspect. It must be ... the true
excitant of the [artists'] imagination. It must be tall, every inch of it tall.
The force and power of altitude must be in it. The glory and pride of
exaltation must be in it. It must be every inch a proud and soaring
thing ... the unexpected, the eloquent peroration of most bald, most sin-
ister, most forbidding conditions.[8]

Although this formulation may seem radical as well as grandiloquent,
Sullivan's skyscraper had a rather traditional five-fold division: a working basement, a strong base, a *piano nobile*, a slender trunk that was
emphatically vertical, and a "specific and conclusive" capital or attic,
though he rejected with contempt any idea of the skyscraper being made
to look like a column.

By the time he formulated his ideas so explicitly, the Chicago skyscraper had reached its canonic form; it was not a Sullivanian tower but
a rectangular or square block with a prominent cornice and an internal
light well; sometimes, as in the Rookery of 1888, the street level
entrance is a large two- or three-story glazed staircase hall, a luxurious
internal courtyard. The Chicago skyscraper then peaked with the steep
mansard-roofed Masonic Temple of 1889, designed, like the Rookery,
by Daniel Burnham and John Wellborn Root and at twenty-two floors
briefly the world's highest occupied building. The tallest building in the
world still remained the transparent and skeletal Eiffel Tower in Paris,
which had been built for the Paris World Exposition of 1889, the centenary of the French Revolution.

The end of the 1880s and the early 1890s in Chicago were clouded by
financial problems and by violent labor troubles. It is also the moment
when American architectural development was cramped by the great
World's Columbian Exposition of 1893, which commemorated the four
hundred years since Columbus's voyage with a huge display, organized
again by Daniel Burnham and landscaped by Frederick Law Olmsted
(John Wellborn Root had died young in 1891, soon after work on the
Exposition began). This Exposition provided a canvas-and-plaster anticipation of the "classicism" that was to dominate American official architecture for the next half-century. It owed more to French academic
planning and the rigid axialities of Durand than to the relaxed, parklike
approach of L'Enfant in Washington. Burnham himself thought the exhibition would usher in an era of architectural grandeur to rival antiquity:

We have been in an inventive period ... but action and reaction are
equals. ... designers will be obliged to abandon their incoherent original-

ities and study the ancient masters of building. It will be unavailing here-
after to say that the great classic forms are undesirable. The people have
the vision before them here, and words cannot efface it.[9]

Burnham, with Charles McKim and his new Chicago associate, Edward
Bennett, who had recently returned from his Parisian studies at the
Beaux-Arts, extended these implications over a decade in a series of
ambitious projects for "the city beautiful." The first important one was
the general development plan for Washington—with the ailing Frederick
Law Olmsted, who was already relying much on his son, Frederick
Junior—but he also devised plans for St. Louis and San Francisco. His
and Bennett's plan for Chicago, prepared in 1906–8 and published officially under the auspices of the Chicago Commercial Club in 1909, was
adopted by the city only in 1917. Much of the street widening and planting as well as some land-use regulations followed its recommendations.
It was the first American "metropolitan" plan to consider the city and its
hinterland and it forecast a population rise to 13,200,000 by 1950, a figure it still has not reached.

Burnham was a keen driver: he possessed three motorcars himself,
and was on friendly terms with Henry Ford, with whom he had discussed the production of cheap and popular automobiles (the Model T
was launched in the same year as the plan). This vast project to Hauss-
mannize Chicago, make it friendly to the coming motor traffic, and even
grander than Paris, fittingly illustrates Burnham's best-known dictum,
"make no small plans." The scheme culminated in a domed city hall
much taller, if not larger, than the Congress building in Washington, and
axially dominant over a city whose primary emphasis was in any case
horizontal. Even now Chicago's lakefront is strangely monotonous, or if
you prefer, harmonious.

This horizontality was in part a product of the financial crisis of
1893–94. It coincided with the breakup of the Sullivan and Adler partnership and the end of the primacy of the Chicago skyscraper, since there
was already a glut of office space. Cornice height was then capped at
130 feet for a decade; it was revised in 1902. After further ups and
downs, the limit was finally removed altogether in 1955.

By then the development of the tall building had been taken over by
New York. A portent of this New York ambition was the Tower Building of 1888–89; this was not a skyscraper in the usual sense at all, but a
very tall, narrow slab running through the width of a whole block. One
of the narrow ends, the one on its Broadway façade at no. 50, was

designed by Bradford Lee Gilbert to look like an independent tower, hence the name: a heavily rusticated base was pierced by a cavernous Chicago-style archway that carried the stone-and-glass body of the building. Strong, pilastered corners and thin mullions that looked like vertical structural elements carried a cornicelike attic and a pyramidal roof—almost like a miniature of Sullivan and Adler's Auditorium building in Chicago, which was finished just as the "Tower" was begun. Within months it was followed by a new headquarters for the *New York Times,* and the Western Union Building farther up Broadway, both designed by George B. Post. Tall though they were, these mansarded and towered buildings still did not reach the height of the Trinity Church spire; nor did the next few buildings around lower Broadway and City Hall Park. This was the time when a clutch of newspaper offices and agencies—the *New York Sun,* the *New York Tribune,* and the *New York Times* (on the corner of Park Row and Nassau Street, overlooking the crossing that came to be called Printing House Square, where it had settled in 1851 when it was founded), as well as the American Tract Society—were all rising in sharp rivalry within a few yards of each other. Park Row was renamed "Newspaper Row." The *New York Herald, New York Aurora, Evening Mirror,* and *Knickerbocker Magazine* all had buildings in the close neighborhood. Unlike the mansarded or flat-roofed Chicago buildings, whose patrons were mostly developers, the spiky or domed New York newspaper and business buildings, most of them crowned by a flagpole sporting a banner, were overtly advertising devices. There was something stern and almost collective about the representation of its energy that Chicago exhibited on its lakeside, while the New York skyline toward the end of the nineteenth century was a carnival of competition.

That competition created the New York downtown skyline which, when people still arrived by boat, was a dramatic and lasting image of the city. The lakeside view of Chicago was not as important if only because most people arrived there by train. The New York skyline became the subject of much comment, of pride and some embarrassment, to which Henry James famously bore witness:

> The "tall buildings," which have so promptly usurped a glory that affects you as rather surprised, as yet, at itself, the multitudinous sky-scrapers standing up to the view, from the water, like extravagant pins in a cushion already over-planted, and stuck in as in the dark, anywhere and anyhow, have at least the felicity of carrying out the fairness of tone, of taking the

sun and the shade . . . and they are triumphant payers of dividends; all of which uncontested and unabashed pride, with flash of innumerable windows and flicker of subordinate gilt attributions, is like the flare, up and down their long, narrow faces, of the lamps of some general permanent "celebration."[10]

The Trinity Church tower, having been an unstated but respected regulator of height, now became a challenge. The first building to overtop it was the *New York World* building that George Post designed for the paper's owner, Joseph Pulitzer. It went up on Newspaper Row in 1889–90, next to the *Tribune,* and although Post still maintained an insistent horizontal articulation, he topped it with a gilt dome on a tall drum (in which Pulitzer had his private office), which raised it, with its flagstaff, to 349 feet, and made it the tallest occupied building in the world. The *Tribune* responded by adding more stories to the offices that Hunt had designed for them, but it did not reach record height.

In lower Manhattan, business was localized, with banking, insurance, transport, and management forming the primary or central business district, or CBD, as geographers say. Although Newspaper Row had the tallest buildings, lower Broadway and Wall Street had by then some of the bulkiest, notably the Produce Exchange at the very bottom of Broadway, facing Bowling Green, and designed, again, by George Post.

The depression in the mid-1890s was one of the first examples of the pattern of achieving a record for a high building followed by financial recession, something that has been repeated in the history of urban building in the twentieth century. With the *Tribune* tower as a challenge, the bid for the tallest building became a race—overtly.

Record-breaking high-rises everywhere were finally outclassed in 1906 by the Singer building, an elaborate and opulently Frenchified confection. At forty-seven stories, 612 feet high, it was—as it set out to be—the tallest skyscraper not just in New York but in the world, more than 250 feet higher than Pulitzer's *World* building, but still far shorter than the thousand feet—three hundred meters—of the Eiffel Tower. This record was beaten only a year later by the 700-foot *campanile,* emulating and doubling the size of Saint Mark's in Venice, which the Metropolitan Life Insurance built in Madison Square. Its unusual form was due, so various accounts have it, to the company's chairman nurturing a passion for the great Venetian precedent. As a new millennium begins, the Singer building still holds the record for the tallest building ever to be knocked down, which happened in 1968.

Apart from the Metropolitan Life Building, all the ones I have considered were south of Houston Street, very much downtown. "Uptown" and "Downtown"—the specific terms of the Manhattan layout—have come to mean "periphery" and "center" in the English language generally, and they are another symptom of Manhattan's dominant position, much as "West End" or "East End" (derived from the layout of London) used to mean "upper class" or "middle and working class." "Uptown" first implied "suburban," and referred to the avenues running on either side of Central Park, while "downtown" came to mean the business district—downtown because it was downstream of the rivers, and because it was the south end of Manhattan. Coined in New York—Herman Melville gave it first literary airing—it was to be used for all sorts of very different locations—for the Loop in Chicago, which is in fact at the town's east end, or for an equivalent district in Los Angeles. It is the mark of New York's status that the word has crossed the Atlantic and is now applied to many European, Asian, and African cities. It has remained part of the nomenclature of New York, although many of the downtown functions have moved north, and this movement has, by a series of fits and starts, transformed the geography and profile of Manhattan.

Speculative developers rather than companies were the chief players in this game. Triangular sites, the "bow ties" created by the oblique run of Broadway against the orthogonalities of the grid, intrigued several of them. The Flatiron Building, at the intersection of Twenty-third Street, Fifth Avenue, and Broadway, at Madison Square, was designed in 1901–3 by the Chicago office of Burnham and Root for a Chicago developer. At twenty stories, it was for a while the highest building that far north, until it was dwarfed by the Metropolitan Life Tower five or six years later. But there was another site of the same bow-tie kind where Broadway crosses Forty-second Street and Seventh Avenue. The *New York Times* would move in 1906 from Newspaper Row into another Italianate "flatiron" tower, which was to recall Giotto's *campanile* for Florence Cathedral. "It touches higher clouds than anything within twelve miles—extreme height of 476 feet" wrote a special issue of the paper celebrating the move from City Hall Plaza, though the building was to be "renovated" out of recognition in 1965. The open space in front of it, Long Acre Square, has since then been known as Times Square, but until World War I, not much tall building went on north of Thirtieth Street, and the Times Tower was isolated.

As the effects of economic gloom waned, the city itself also became a developer. In 1907, a new municipal building, directly north of Newspaper Row, was built by the most prestigious of the Beaux-Arts group of architects, McKim, Mead & White. But just before it was finished and occupied, the spikily Gothic Woolworth Building went up directly facing it, on Broadway, in 1913, topping the previous champion, the Metropolitan Life Insurance *campanile*. It was Frank Woolworth himself who decided that his tower—to rise 794 feet and one inch above the sidewalk—would be the tallest in the world. Designed in a terracotta version of flamboyant Gothic, it was soon called "the Cathedral of Commerce" and held the record for height until the 1920s boom. Cathedral or not, Woolworth's own room at the top of his tower was entirely lined with Napoleonic memorabilia, and his desk faced a life-size copy of a portrait of the emperor in his coronation robes.

This need to hold the record for the highest building never affected the Chicagoan patrons or their architects in quite the same way, but the New York rivalries led to the establishment of an office that actually keeps records for the highest building.[11]

Around 1910 the New York City authorities were becoming concerned that the Equitable Assurance Company proposed to replace its modest old building with a sixty-two-story colossus of 909 feet, just short of the Eiffel Tower. Unlike its predecessors, this record was not to be set by a Sullivan-type tower, rising from a wider podium, but its full height was to occupy the entire surface of the block. Owners of adjoining properties protested (". . . it will cause several irremediable losses to many neighboring property owners . . . shuts off the light on four streets and brings into existence an amount of rentable space that is disproportionate . . .").[12] In the end it was built to a mere thirty-eight stories, but it did occupy the whole of its site. Subsequent agitation was then channeled into the height and zoning regulations of 1916. Zoning was familiar as a horizontal division of the city according to use; in New York, because of the Equitable Building, it acquired a new sense, that of dividing the city vertically according to the density of built occupation so that the building would effectively be stepped and reduced to a tower shape as it went up; this virtually imposed Sullivan's preferred silhouette on bylaw regulations. The image was expected to be so striking, that a New York graphic artist, Hugh Ferris, produced a series of dramatic drawings illustrating the result—though they were not published until the effect was already shown in buildings all over the city, just before the 1929 stock market crash. Begun in 1913 and finished in 1915, the Equitable Building was to be the last unzoned New York high-rise, and brought about a brief construction hiatus. In any case, competition was also dampened by the First World War.

During that hiatus, in 1922, the English architect and urban planner Raymond Unwin—by then well-known as the designer of Letchworth and for his agitation on behalf of Howard's ideas—visited New York. On a fact-finding trip he saw, as some native observers like Burnham did not, that the city would soon have to deal with a wholly unprecedented pressure, which even the earlier high-rise buildings would exacerbate—namely the problem presented by the production of the cheap automobile. The saturation point had not, he realized, been reached yet, and he attributes this view to "Mr. Ford, who has contributed more than anyone else to the supply." Seen from Europe, the phenomenon could not really be appreciated, he goes on:

> Owing to the fact that the motor car is used in America by people who do not employ a chauffeur, the question of parking cars already presents an unsolved problem.[13]

He made his point with a case study of the Woolworth Building, still the highest in New York at the time. He calculated that if the fourteen thousand people who worked there were to walk out, ten abreast, they would require a mile and a quarter of pavement; and if one-tenth of these workers had automobiles, they would require six to seven miles of roadway to collect their passengers. His paper was intended as a warning of the consequences of such traffic conditions in European urban environments, but it took thirty years to see them applied to Europe. His English listeners thought him unduly alarmist at the time. There would never be skyscrapers in Europe, they thought, and such traffic conditions as Unwin observed in New York would never be realized. Manhattanization was still very remote and improbable.

A few years after Unwin's visit, the skyline would be altered by another growth of skyscrapers. Downtown acquired the vast Standard Oil Building in 1926, and the New York Telephone Building in the same year. But a new nucleus was growing at Times Square, around Forty-second Street. The New York Times Building had heralded that development, and Park Avenue had been closed off by the Grand Central City Tower at Forty-fifth Street in 1928–29; General Electric had also built a Gothic skyscraper on Lexington Avenue nearby. For all that, the record set by the Woolworth Building had not yet been broken, but the first initiative to do so came from a new kind of tycoon. The automobile magnate Walter P. Chrysler was determined that his new building would be the tallest in the world. He knew that the Bank of Manhattan downtown had commissioned H. Craig Severance to break all records at 40 Wall Street. That proposed tower, at 925 feet, was to beat the Woolworth Building and to be two feet higher than the already projected Chrysler Building. Walter Chrysler incited his architect, William van Alen, to conceal a telescopic spire in the jagged and curved crowning element of the building. As soon as 40 Wall Street was completed, the Chrysler team raised the spire-spike to 1,046 feet, beating not only the Wall Street giant but even, finally, the Eiffel Tower. It held the record until the Empire State Building was completed in 1931 at 1,250 feet to become the tallest building in the world, and it remained so for over forty years. All these skyscrapers were commissioned and their building begun in a state of high optimism. The stock market crash of October 1929 came as a horrible shock, and its effects were long-lasting. The Empire State Building was nicknamed the "Empty State" Building, as much of the space was unlet for some time and it took twenty years for it to declare a profit.

The articulation of all these buildings—whatever their style—Gothic, Renaissance, Art Déco—was consistently vertical. Louis Sullivan was obeyed in this if not in his other injunctions. Raymond Hood won the most publicized architectural competition, for the *Chicago Tribune,* with a vertically articulated Gothic project crowned by a spire, rather absurdly "supported" by pinnacled flying buttresses. Just before the market crash, he had designed an almost "style-less" but emphatically vertical building for the *New York Daily News,* but broke the mold himself the following year in the headquarters for the McGraw-Hill company which, though stepped as zoning required, was a skeleton cage whose garnishing, in a modified Art Déco—almost Expressionist—manner, gave the building a horizontal emphasis. But he went back to verticality with his most successful disciple, Wallace K. Harrison, when he began the planning of Rockefeller Center in 1931, even if his contribution was solely limited to the outline plan (he died in 1943).

John D. Rockefeller had bought a tract of land between Fifth and Sixth Avenues at Forty-eighth Street from Columbia University. An enthusiastic melomane, he wished the new Opera House to be relocated on his land. That was only one small part of an ambitious plan drawn up by Hood and Harrison on a scale unprecedented even in New York. But although Rockefeller Center did include two theaters, neither of them ever housed the Metropolitan Opera, which had to struggle throughout the thirties to weather the Depression unprotected. Rockefeller pressed ahead with the development of his land: a group of thin slab near-skyscrapers was grouped into a complex that was to be, as journalists

New York. The Guggenheim Museum. Designed by Frank Lloyd Wright from 1943 onward, first as a ziggurat but finally as an inverted spiral in defiance both of the New York street grid and of the orthogonality of the painted canvas. It was finished in 1959.

New Delhi. The Rajpath, or Kingsway, from the Presidential Palace looking toward the "India Gate," which Edwin Lutyens designed as the "All India War Memorial Arch," 1917–1931. The site was laid out in 1913. The buildings—the palace by Edwin Lutyens and the ministries leading up to it, on either side of the Rajpath, by Herbert Baker—were occupied in 1929. Gandhi wanted to turn the palace, now known by its Hindi name Rashtrapati Bhavan, into a hospital, a role for which it was completely unsuited.

New Orleans. Piazza d'Italia by Charles Moore. One of the first postmodern projects. A recent office block in the standard commercial modern manner is in the background. The ironic treatment of historical themes is almost a caricature. The classical columns have solid metal capitals, which are in fact shower nozzles so that the column shafts produce jets of water when the fountains are working.

General view of the entry into the Piazza, showing its context.

Euro-Disney. Sleeping Beauty's castle, in the spiky manner favored by the Disney designers. It does not have much of an interior, since it is used primarily for daily ceremonies such as the arrival and reception of Prince Charming. (Courtesy of Index Stock Imagery/Terry Why)

Celebration, Florida. The Outlook Tower, right. Designed by Charles Moore, it is the tallest building in central Celebration and proclaims the sales and real estate office as its dominant landmark.

Canberra. The Parliament buildings, designed by Ehrman Mitchell and Aldo Giurgola; the "umbilicus" of the country, the huge flagpole was planted when the city was planned. The green sward, in fact, a huge traffic circle, is contrasted with rather formal entrance forecourts, which cut into the hill and present appropriately monumental façades to the capital.

Brasília. Praça dos Três Poderes, The Square of the Three Powers. The Presidential Palace (executive) and the High Court (administrative) buildings are not visible, only the towers of the Congress buildings (legislative). The towers are linked by walkways to make an H for "humanity," according to the official booklet.

Brasília. The tomb of President Kubitschek. Sited at the high point overlooking the town, it takes the form of an Egyptian pharaonic tomb, a mastaba, and like a mastaba, or a pyramid, has no visible entrance. Access is by a tunnel. Kubitschek's body is entombed in a stone sarcophagus on the upper floor, under the dome and simply impressed "O Fundador." Surrounded by memorabilia, it has effectively become a museum rather than a monument.

Paris. The Dalle, the vast slab laid over the infrastructure of subways and parking garages 1964–1969, focused on the Grande Arche. The Arche, designed by Danish architect Johan Otto von Spreckelsen in 1982, now acts as the climax of the axis from the Louvre, through the Champs Elysées and the Triumphal Arch at the Etoile.

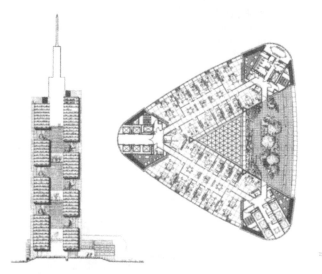

Frankfurt, Germany. Commerzbank tower by Norman Foster, the first
large-scale building planned and designed on ecological principles.
Ventilation is largely based on unforced natural air movements and the
open volumes are used as greenhouses. (Courtesy of Foster Associates)

Córdoba, Argentina. A Communal Participation Center for one of the outlying
municipalities, designed by Miguel-Angel Roca. All these centers are variations on
very similar elements to make the group of buildings immediately identifiable, even
to a passing driver. This particular center is designed to be a gate to the city, since it
bridges over the main motorway into it. (Courtesy of Miguel-Angel Roca)

The Guggenheim Museum, Bilbao, designed by Frank Gehry, 1998. It has had a tonic effect on the economy of the rather depressed Basque capital and has become a model for many cities hoping for economic regeneration through tourism.

London. The London Eye, designed by David Marks and Julia Barfield, near the Houses of Parliament. It has been a great financial success, and a number of other cities—Toronto, Boston, Johannesburg—have made bids to build copies.

Shanghai, Pudong. The Jin-Mao tower, far right, designed by Skidmore, Owings and Merrill in a SinoArt Déco manner. The Chinese references are rather token: the designers' claim that the tower resembles a pagoda seems mystifying, though the Art Déco spike on top is a clear enough signal.

London. The Docklands area on the Thames, where much building is going on; One Canada Square, center, was designed by Cesar Pelli

Berlin, viewed from the roof of the Reichstag; since *1990*, millions of square feet of new buildings have been added to the city.

would say later, "a city within a city"; the construction was organized as a street spectacle—startling even for New York—and the last of its estimated ten million rivets was ceremonially driven in on November 1, 1939, exactly two months after the Second World War had begun in Europe. Rockefeller—and the Center—had to wait until well after the end of the war, nearly a decade, for it to become the great financial success it has remained.[14]

To date it has established itself as the visible heart of New York, if there is such a thing. A number of quasi-ceremonial functions seem to have gradually accrued to it. The city's sixty-to-eighty-foot-high Christmas tree, which started as an initiative of the building workers in 1934, has been illuminated there every year, and the lights are usually switched on by some notable. In 1942, when America entered the war, the flags of the Allies were displayed around its main open space, and when the United Nations was founded, this was extended to include the flags of all the member nations. The central space was to have been an upscale shopping arcade, but about 1945 was converted to a large ice rink among the towers. That the city should have a heart of ice may well be entirely appropriate. Appropriate, too, that various attempts to develop a cultural center to the north of it, involving the Guggenheim Museum, the Opera House, and the nearby Museum of Modern Art were, in spite of support from Mayor La Guardia and the powerful Robert Moses, his parks commissioner, stymied by the inability of the Rockefeller family to buy the northward land.

The unofficially "international" nature of the complex, established by the United Nations flags, is reaffirmed in such popular lore as the allocating of the buildings on either side of its principal boulevard—which leads from Fifth Avenue down to the piazza with its ice-skating rink—to England and France, so that the avenue is inevitably nicknamed "the Channel." It opens not far from Saint Patrick's Cathedral—a building architecturally inferior to several other churches on that stretch of Fifth Avenue but much loved—whose steps serve as a kind of unofficial reviewing platform for the Saint Patrick's Day parade, giving the location a centrality and prestige that other, scaffolded reviewing platforms, strung out along the edge of the park on Fifth Avenue, never acquired.

None of these developments inflected the image of the city as much as the first high-rises. The downtown tip of the island, with its concentration of sky-scrapered financial institutions, was and indeed still is interpreted as "the head" of Manhattan. By the mid-nineteenth century, New York had also acquired those vast, easily identifiable lungs—Central

Park—down the middle of the island, from Fifty-ninth to 110th Streets. The corner where Broadway crosses Fifty-ninth Street and Eighth Avenue, marked by a statue of the eponymous hero, was to become Columbus Circle. The polarity of head and lungs already implied the corporal image of Manhattan.

The image, the metaphor, starts as if the body was primarily head and lungs; if it may be extended, then the next essential point would need to be the heart. The problem of New York was that its heart, or core, was a wandering one. Although it is now more or less fixed at Rockefeller Center, this fixing is, as I have suggested, fairly recent. The original heart, in the seventeenth and eighteenth centuries, was the Town Hall on Parade Square, now part of Battery Park, facing the fort. It was replaced by a more regular and stately City Hall, where Broad Street runs into Wall Street. This building was transformed by Pierre L'Enfant into the Federal Building where the first elected Congress met and where, on the balcony, George Washington was sworn in as the first president of the United States. When the government was moved to Washington, it reverted to its role as City Hall, only to be demolished after 1812 when a replacement was opened a little uptown, on the Civic Square at the crossing of Broadway at City Hall Park.[15] By about 1860, the gracious three-story building with its lanterned dome was crowded in by the much taller offices of Newspaper Row. By 1900, it was entirely dwarfed by the neighboring elevated railway, and after 1914, reduced further when it virtually disappeared below the vast Municipal Building, even though the new giant made a gesture to its diminutive, aged neighbor by being crowned with a similar lantern.

By then the city already had another alert and sprightly heart anyway: Madison Square Garden, on Madison Avenue at Twenty-sixth Street. It was not a municipal building but a vast entertainment palace, the biggest in the world if its publicity is to be believed. Its main auditorium was designed to house more spectators than the Albert Hall in London or the Paris Opera, and its bulk—a kind of classicized version of the Palace of the Doges in Venice—was overshadowed by an enlarged 304- as against 295-foot version of the Giralda, the bell tower of Seville Cathedral. Its fame was enhanced when its designer, Stanford White, was murdered by his mistress's husband in one of its restaurants in 1906; this gave it the rather louche notoriety that it has retained in popular memory. But its dominance was brief in any case. The Metropolitan Life Insurance Company's 700-foot Venetian *campanile* across the square dwarfed the Madison Square Garden's Giralda. When the developers of the Garden declared bankruptcy in

1925, the buildings, with all their luxurious interiors and scandalous bachelor apartments in the tower, were destroyed. But this was not all. Nearby, between Seventh and Eighth Avenues, the Pennsylvania Railroad had commissioned the same firm of architects, McKim, Mead & White, to build a terminal—in emulation of the huge baths of Caracalla in Rome—in 1904-10. Its destruction in 1963 triggered a series of furious protests leading to the New York movement for historic preservation—which, like everything that happens in Manhattan, was repeated all over the world, sometimes merely reinforcing existing enterprises like the Society for the Protection of Ancient Buildings in England. Only the names of these two grandiose buildings have survived, attached now to an anonymous office block and station concourse with a circular amusement arena attached to them, built in 1967[16] on the site of the old terminal. The positive result of all this agitation came very late: in 1998 the majestic (but underused) Post Office building behind the station, which the same architects designed about the same time, was proposed as a new and spacious terminal building for the railway.

And uptown was where the heart of the city removed—farther north—and after 1918 it seemed to be located at Times Square, where Broadway crosses Forty-second Street and Seventh Avenue. It was the obvious center of "entertainment." New York, with few public buildings—and the world's biggest billboard display—prompted G. K. Chesterton's famous comment: "What a glorious garden of wonders this would be, to anyone who was lucky enough to be unable to read."

Toward the end of World War II, Times Square received, temporarily, yet another Statue of Liberty replica. Around it—and the teletext news display—a vast crowd waited for President Truman's announcement of the surrender of Japan in August 1945. The buildings of Times Square, concealed as they were by their electrified hoardings, were in any case already dwarfed—and their role would also be displaced. The "revitalizing" of Times Square in the last years of the twentieth century began when the Disney Corporation bought into Forty-second Street, so that "family entertainment" displaced the strip-joints, pornographic peep shows, and S & M clubs that had taken over the old burlesque theaters. In the last years of the twentieth century, new and very tall buildings just north of Forty-second Street on Broadway have attracted publishers and newspapers—even law offices. "Family entertainment" may not seem quite a cardiac function, but the entertainment offered in Times Square for the millennium celebrations reasserted its old centrality and its new-found commercial vitality.

The spread of the city northward up Manhattan required some other, more central, and perhaps definitive "heart." Many in authority, especially Robert Moses, the parks commissioner who was the dictator of New York's environmental changes, had hoped that by implanting the old opera house, which used to stand at Fortieth Street near where Broadway crossed Seventh Avenue and therefore close to Times Square, and locating some concert halls on West Side slum-clearance land, the attraction they would exercise would be powerful enough, since the city was not wholly easy with a privatization of its heart.

An attempt was therefore made, soon after World War II, to turn Columbus Circle into a nexus that would include an opera house and a philharmonic hall, a convention and exhibition center as well, and to give it a high-rise focus that would rival Rockefeller Center. There was hope, too, that this would stimulate development of the rather derelict territory on the West Side. It was not to be. A series of misjudgments and mishaps dogged the project so that neither the Philharmonic nor the opera house ever participated in it. Now, a new consortium has been put together, and it may well be that a year or two after this book is published, a convention center and other promised attractions will make Columbus Circle a new focus in the city. However, in the 1950s attention was diverted up Broadway to Sixty-fifth Street. By 1955 the slum-clearance project west of Lincoln Square became a possible candidate for a city center; the site was an infamous and overcrowded slum district where—as often happens with slum sites—a number of artists had also lived. Rehabilitation by building much-improved low-cost housing had started in the 1940s, and in 1955 the city authorities announced a plan to provide a home for the New York City Opera and the Metropolitan Opera, as well as the New York Philharmonic and the Julliard School, together with several other subsidiary institutions. Lincoln Plaza was raised on a high podium and frequented by a limited and fairly prosperous public so that it came to be seen as an enclave of privilege. It is not quite clear why this happened: the exclusion of retail trade (except for museum shops and museum restaurants, which do not count in such stakes) may have been a factor; the disruptive character of the surrounding buildings and the threatening lines of traffic that cut it off from pedestrian thoroughfares have also played their part in defeating any civic role. Perhaps New York has not yet established itself as a musical world capital. Not only London, Berlin, and Paris but Chicago, Cleveland, Boston, and Los Angeles might challenge the primacy of New York.

New York is now, on the other hand, dominant in the visual arts. The gradual decade-long process by which American artists came to dominate the world scene after 1950 and free themselves of a European, Paris-oriented hegemony of taste has often been examined. Certainly, a newly confident patronage in New York and in the rest of the United States was looking to native artists as a badge of success and accomplishment, as well as of emancipation from European dominance. The patrons' willingness to pay substantial sums for their work determined the artists' celebrity and valuation in the world art market. This has happened even though the auction houses (which in fact fix the constantly rising prices of all works of art) are still attached to Europe (London especially).

During the sixties, the configuration of the skyscraper altered decisively. Those that had adhered to the zoning laws acquired a silhouette similar to the Eiffel Tower: a wide base, rising in steps to a sharp point, their sides approximately paraboloid. They may be read as representing the vast energy of the rising economy, the striving and the ambitions of a new dominant class, the pride of their developer or manufacturer-builders. The new generation of high-rises, however, no longer rose through steps to follow the zoning "envelope," but met the ground abruptly, and were often isolated from the street by a plaza or square. In a sense the underuse of land became the showiest expression of wealth in the city. The Lever Bros. company was a case in point. They had bought 390 Park Avenue before the war; the main structure of the building, which was finished in 1949, was a square *cortile* enclosed by a single story of offices on high columns that opened that square to the street. One side rises as a relatively thin slab, all of it air-conditioned and enclosed in a glass cage.

Another skyscraper is the 1954 three-story Manufacturers Hanover Trust Company building on the corner of Forty-third Street and Fifth Avenue. Although zoning regulations may not have allowed a very high building on that site, the three-story transparent cage impudently showing the door of a gigantic safe toward the avenue as its signboard became an instant landmark and a great success. Both of these were the work of Skidmore, Owings & Merrill, which then became, and remains, perhaps the largest architectural firm in the world. Across Park Avenue, however, the Canadian distiller, Seagram, had bought a site, and after some hesitation commissioned Mies van der Rohe to design their headquarters in 1954. The building was prefaced by a half-acre, travertine-paved open space, and recessed from the street line in a lordly way; it rose vertically, marked by bronze mullions holding the curtain wall of topaz (or bronze-tinted) glass.

These were prestige buildings, in which the raw considerations of money were secondary. But about the time Rockefeller Center was completed, the elevated railway that ran through the middle of Sixth Avenue was torn down, sending surrounding land values up, though the exploitation of an obvious commercial potential was checked by the war. Many splendid plans were made for the area—the period coincided with New York's capture of the primacy of the art world, after all—but in the end a group of bland and faceless towers, undistinguished emulations of the Seagram Building and, like it, drawn back from the street line, were built between Fiftieth and Fifty-eighth Streets and occupied by clients such as Time-Life, Exxon, Celanese, and even McGraw-Hill, who were persuaded to expand there from the building Raymond Hood had designed for them. But while the buildings did nothing for the prestige of the landlords or their tenants, neither were they as profitable as had been hoped at that time.

In any case the floor-to-area ratio calculation, known by its acronym FAR, had to be reworked when Chicago abolished its height limitations in 1955 and New York's zoning rules of 1916 were heavily revised in 1961. Various new technologies had prompted these changes. Air conditioning and fluorescent lighting, for instance, made the distance from exterior walls and windows less critical, and framing construction was very much refined. The calculations of cost and profit had soon to be updated, since it had become obvious that, as the head of one of the most profitable practices of the time, put it:

The ideal building, from the functional point of view, calls for a square plan with each of its sides . . . approximately 145 to 175 feet.[17]

The World Trade Center in New York has two such towers, and briefly (1972–74) took the title of "the world's highest building," though it lost it two years later to a more sophisticated example of the type, the Sears Tower in Chicago. At the time of writing, it remains the highest building in the Western hemisphere, and it was finished just in time for the energy crisis provoked by the Yom Kippur War, October 1973, and the recession that followed from it.

The New York skyscraper's relation to the street was radically modified ten years later when the Citicorp Center was built between Lexington and Third Avenues and Fifty-third and Fifty-fourth Streets in

1976. The difficulties of its planning were focused on a church on the site that could not be persuaded to move. The building was therefore raised on ten-story-high pylons and cantilevered over the church, and a shopping mall—called a market—was accommodated in the huge lobby area. The new church building opens out to the "market." Since it was deliberately designed as a criticism of fifties buildings on Sixth Avenue, the approachability that it practiced was an important part of the lesson it taught. Although still a square-plan block, the Citicorp Center substituted a horizontal alternation of glass and aluminum siding for the vertical emphasis of many earlier buildings. The top was cut off at 45 degrees southward, and designed to include sun accumulators that would power the air-conditioning system—though these were never installed. Nevertheless, the plume of air-conditioning vapor rising from the sharply angled roof gives the building an almost iconic quality.

Although the Citicorp Center is sometimes seen as a mere subcategory of the shopping mall species, just another outpost in the northward march of the skyscraper, it seems to me a powerful and novel visual marker of the skyline. It was certainly meant to put the passerby in mind of new concerns:

> We must use the resources of big business, reinforced by moral and social ideas, to develop a new generation of office buildings planned for the community and expressive of the humanity of the individuals who use them. . . . Such a building might even be a source of inspiration for other cities.[18]

So the architect, Hugh Stubbins, wrote to one of the bankers. But his approach was not emulated. And the market, though moderately successful, has drawn criticism for its exclusiveness.

The northward skyscrapers were no longer clustered in groups now, but were sporadically dispersed towers, rising here and there out of the city fabric like the skyscrapers of Houston or Fort Worth. This new generation of high-rises, built mostly in the late eighties and nineties, differ from their predecessors by their thinness and small footprint—they are sometimes known as "pencils"—as well as by their pattern of single use, since they are primarily residential. The ultimate grotesque is the Trump World Tower, still building at the time of writing. At ninety stories, the square smooth block, sheathed in bronze mirror glass, advertises itself as "one of the most visible and architecturally significant additions to the Manhattan skyline." Since it is merely a taller version of the Pedersen formula for profitable investment, "significant" hardly seems the *mot juste*. But it does add an important feature to the skyline. The naked moneymaking machine will tower over its two most important rivals at this point: the seat of world government, the United Nations, on one side, and the Citicorp Center, which is an attempt by capital to make a return to the city.

This last group of buildings represents accurately the situation of postindustrial society, whose prosperous elite they house, since they are effectively vertical "gated communities." Their penthouses, like the offices of the robber barons of the first decade of the twentieth century, offer a view all over the city and monumentalize the newly established inequalities of the Communication Age. They offer, as another real estate advertisement puts it, "a commanding residence for the privileged few."[19]

New York may have a wandering heart, but its boundaries are more or less permanent. The actual shoreline has suffered various modifications as the result of harbor building, reclamation, and dumping, but the integrity of Manhattan, outlined by its three rivers, has inevitably remained fixed. Nor has the manifest immobility of its boundaries really been compromised by the increasing number and surface of bridges, tunnels, and funiculars. And in this it may be unique among North American cities.

Within this outline the citizens of Manhattan, perhaps those of outlying boroughs too, can know themselves to be members of that colossally articulated body. The power of this image alone could never have made Manhattan the capital of the world, but it has certainly made it feel that it was the city that could assume this role, one it will probably keep for the foreseeable future.

All world cities, all capital cities—I am even tempted to say *all* cities—have a special character, a slang or dialect, a form of humor, which sometimes has a special label unrelated to its name: like *Porteño* in Buenos Aires, *Carioca* in Rio de Janeiro, *Cockney* in London, and so on. The inhabitants of Vienna and Paris, Munich and Berlin, Shanghai or Bombay or Moscow will assure you that their particular one is especially savory, even if it may seem tasteless to outsiders. But Manhattanites are unique in this matter, since their locutions, their particular humor, and their fashions—even their particular, not always toothsome, delicacies—have been distributed worldwide by the cinema and the musical, by advertising, and by fast-food concessions.

So they are being imitated, and this mimicry would not need the support of any special commercial pressure, though it gets plenty, but would happen anyway because the world, as I keep on saying, now looks to New York in general, but Manhattan in particular, as its political and even its cultural capital, and rightly surmises that it may also be its economic one. The cultural hegemony of New York seems, at the moment, more total than those of Paris or London ever were. Paris dominated the scene once through its language, urbanism, women's fashions, and cuisine. When English took over as the dominant language, London also set the tone for industry and engineering, men's fashions, even, briefly, for design. By 1950, it was the English spoken in New York, and even more so in Hollywood, that was the imperial one.

Countries where there are "second cities" have always had a problem: Milan with Rome, Lyon with Paris—Los Angeles and Chicago (which calls itself "second city," after all) with New York. The world hegemony of New York means that imitation will inevitably fail, since the greater the effort, the more explicit is the submission—it shows merely that all the world's "first" cities are second to it. The peculiar circumstances that have made Manhattan, never the capital of any country—or even of any state of the Union—into the capital of the whole globalized world are unique to it. They are not, in themselves, positive powers or virtues, but they present one of the great challenges to any urban development over the next century.

8. For the New Millennium?

IT HAS BEEN SAID OF MANHATTAN that even if it had not been a capital city, it certainly is *the* city of capital. Its famous skyline has graphed the fluctuations of land values as well as tycoon ambitions ever since New York took the lead for high building from Chicago after 1890; and it has continued to be constantly transformed by speculation and rivalries.

The Manhattan skyline is a collective product, of course, but it is also an aggregate of individual and corporate decisions, driven by the conviction that building high will not only show the builders' power and achievement but also enshrine all the energy and enterprise that fuel the American dream. As the dream was "available" to everybody, so the pre-1914 skyscrapers and those of the twenties had one thing in common: the wide bases from which their towers rose were porous, riddled with semi-public and commercial spaces of various kinds. Their sometimes sumptuous entry halls, meant for public display, were therefore more or less openly accessible to the street; they could be read as the building's enriched and ornate extensions.

By contrast, the "pencil point" climbers that have sprung up all over Manhattan during the 1990s rise abruptly from the sidewalks, even though many include some shops at their base. Their foyers may be elegant, but they are also forbiddingly guarded. I suppose the message they convey about the American dream is that if you want to dream it now, you had better have enough income to sleep on.

For two centuries the American dream was dreamed by the poor in many countries, including the United States. They flocked to New York, to Manhattan, to get rich, to succeed: the whole world thought that Manhattan streets were paved with gold. The majority of the millions who crowded into the city got neither success nor riches, and the outer New York boroughs are filled with them and their progeny. It is said that Newark once had many inhabitants whose English remained so poor that they mistook their new home for New York.

Today, Manhattan's prosperity is built on the power of Wall Street, the operations of the real estate market, and, increasingly, on communications technology, not on the dreams of the poor. Yet all that is built not only obeys some internal rules of gain and loss but also becomes a counter in a rather different game—a game in which those very dreams and imaginings are an important factor. Perhaps planners and architects are insufficiently aware that the forms they produce will inevitably be assigned metaphoric value by the general public. Metaphoric projection is, after all, an elemental human activity, as advertising people know all too well. Earlier in the book, I suggested how the human figure may be adapted (as with Chandigarh) or popularly projected (as with Manhattan) to interpret the abstract, apparently neutral grid of a plan. It never ceases to astonish me that all concerned—developers, planners, and architects, even architectural schools—continue to ignore this fact.

Take the example of the World Financial Center building in the Pudong section of Shanghai, designed by Kohn, Pedersen and Fox, and unfinished at the time of writing. It is to be the very tallest occupied building in the world at ninety-five stories or 1,509 feet (460 meters), and much smoother and slicker than the neighboring knobbly Chinese-style Jin Mao tower, which will then be demoted from third to fourth place. From a small square footprint, surrounded by a group of low, horizontal entry pavilions at its base, the World Financial Center building will rise, a prism of office space, while its upper, hotel part, is chamfered, becoming increasingly thinner until it narrows to a blade at the top. To help with wind pressure a 50-meter (164-foot) circular opening has been cut through its top stories. The top is about the same diameter as the spherical central cabin on the nearby television tower, officially dubbed the "oriental pearl" but known to the locals, because of the three thin struts on which it stands, as "the chicken leg."

On the publication of the project, which is backed by Japanese developers, the Chinese public—ignoring the architects' claim that their unifying of square and circle embodied a Chinese cosmogram—read the building as the image of the Japanese sun rising over Shanghai once more, this time through the power of capital. The architects reacted to the rumors by crimping the circle: a bridge cut a segment off the bottom of the sun, and there is now misguided talk about a Chinese moon-gate. That bridge inevitably damages the smooth look that is the building's main formal virtue, but it has added little in associative appropriateness. The unwary designer and developer anywhere may offer material for such a misreading simply by applying bits of local or "national" style to an otherwise neutral commercial building, or even invoking a piece of local lore ornamentally, while neglecting the metaphoric value of the overall form.

The development of Pudong, over the river from the Bund which was the waterside promenade of Shanghai as a special area or zone where high-rises are concentrated, emulates certain patterns in Paris and London rather than Manhattan. An area for intensive economic activity is created where an older center already exists and continues to be active, rather like La Défense in Paris. Whatever the structural differences in the plan, that forest of skyscrapers will always be seen as an emulation of Manhattan, carrying with it the promise of excitement, power, and wealth.

The Central Business Districts of both Paris and London had local authorities who exercised some control over land use and building heights. However, the nature of that authority was different in each city, as was their relation to central government. Parisian developments were stimulated by the appearance of the Tour Montparnasse, a high-rise near the center of the city, at Montparnasse Station. This second Parisian sky-scraper—the first was the anonymous but less central tower of the science faculties of the University of Paris—was begun in 1958 when the station was remodeled as part of a general updating of railway access to Paris. The Tour Montparnasse, which dominated the southward vista of the rue de Rennes, was designed by French architects working with American engineers for an American developer. Though it was not popular with Parisians or with the press, Paris needed office space and it was eventually occupied.

The threat that Montparnasse might be replicated throughout central Paris promoted the rapid development of an area to the west of the city that extended the Axe de Paris from the Louvre, through the Champs Elysées and the Arc de Triomphe, to Neuilly and beyond. The scheme was not a new one. In 1931 the City of Paris had promoted a competition to develop that very axis, and some of the best architects of the day—Auguste Perret, Robert Mallet-Stevens, Le Corbusier—had taken part in it. The prize, as in so many competitions of the time, went to an academic, Paul-Arsène Bigot, a new-minted professor at the Beaux-Arts.

Nothing more was done until 1950, when a government-financed plan to develop the site around a monument to the 1870 war which was known as La Défense and lay at the west end of the *Axe,* was initiated. Though the corporation to run the planned business center was not set up until 1958, the year of the Montparnasse tower, the first public building went up immediately. It was a large, relatively low triangular and vaulted concrete exhibition hall. Final plans for the district of La Défense were approved in 1964, and the enormously expensive infrastructure installed at state expense, including—as it did—a terminus for the new high-speed east-west underground line (RER), which has had Euro-Disney at its eastern terminal since 1990. By then there was also underground parking for twenty-six thousand cars and a huge shopping complex. All this was covered by a windswept carless platform a mile long and three hundred feet wide—known as the *Dalle,* or the "Slab"—which was too wide to be a promenade and too long to be a square. Soon several other high-rises surrounded that infrastructure. The modest densities allowed in the original plan unfortunately could not provide income enough to justify the public investment, and in 1972 building heights were raised. There was still very little housing, and workers came from other neighborhoods. Like any single-use development, the area tends to be deserted after office hours.

General de Gaulle, during whose presidency most of the complex was done, deferred to others in matters of building—though in very little else. He favored the La Défense project, since it would not only save the heart of the city, but also, he thought, allow Paris to offer planned and orderly rivalry to the chaos of Manhattan. He had noted that in Rockefeller Center, "you see a church at its feet, but in France, you see a church from below."[1] In his view, Paris should be developed as a basin, the heights progressively rising with distance from the center. The general's ideas were incorporated in the Paris planning bylaws and reinforced and modified by quotations from the Athens Charter concerning the freeing of the street. The city that resulted from this policy sometimes looks like a seedier, messy version of *La Ville Radieuse,* Le Corbusier's much-attacked and ridiculed 1925 project, which proposed that Paris be reduced to a grid of high-rise blocks into which all the working space would be concentrated, and among which the monuments of the city would provide a random network of cultural institutions. As if to emphasize the preciousness of the old buildings, de Gaulle's minister of culture, André Malraux, promoted an energetic program of cleaning and restoring historical monuments.

Various administrations had meanwhile realized that their *Grands Travaux,* all housing and offices, could not replicate either the texture or the prestige of Paris. For that, new public buildings and new public spaces were essential. The first major enterprise was the building of a library and museum-gallery of the type that came to be called a *Centre Culturel* on the Plateau Beaubourg, an unsanitary, overcrowded district, condemned in 1931 (the *îlot insalubre* no. 1). The Centre Pompidou, 1971–77, designed by Renzo Piano and Richard Rogers and named after the general's presidential successor, whose design had been the subject of a much-discussed international competition, was to act as a focus for cultural bustle in the northern part of Paris, much as Les Halles, that cast-iron market built by Napoléon III, had done for commercial activity a century before. The planned move of the market functions took place in 1961–69, and the much-admired cast-iron buildings were destroyed in 1971 after much protest. Their replacement is a rather graceless sunken shopping mall, officially known as "the Forum," over which a blank concrete ninety-foot-high transformer station towers. Though it was later masked by apartments, its ominous bulk did not bode well for the space, and even as enterprising a mayor as Jacques Chirac, who became president of the Republic in 1995, was not able to impose a pattern on it. The Centre Pompidou, meanwhile, troubled though it is—both structurally and institutionally—has performed the role in northern Paris for which it was intended.

Meanwhile, in 1982, a new President, François Mitterand, was determined to leave his mark on all Paris through some *Grands Projets* that, unlike the *Grands Travaux* of previous regimes, were to be for public buildings and public spaces, not for housing. The first was an attempt to give the La Défense development the cohesion it lacked by installing some "feature" at its head (it was actually known as *La Tête de la Défense*) that would close the very long vista from the Louvre. The building was to focus the public areas of the *Dalle,* where various "works of art" had been placed without much effect either on the configuration of the space or—it would seem—on its users. The winning project, by Johan Otto von Spreckelsen, a Danish architect, was for an open, boxlike cube object, the *Grande Arche,* 106 meters (348 feet) square, rising to 110 meters (361 feet), ornamented with modish wire-stretched sails and set on a podium that had to be twisted 6 degrees off axis to get its foundations clear of the RER lines. This strictly noncommemorative and ornamental "arch," which was completed in 1989, is nevertheless dwarfed by the surrounding anonymous office blocks. Various political changes have modified its details, so that the glass pavilions around it were not built nor the roof-gardens planted as Spreckelsen had envisaged. The arch has one disagreeable and unforeseen effect: for anyone walking up the Champs-Elysées, its roofline cuts the view through the Arc de Triomphe in half. Although the Grande Arche does not welcome the modern *flâneur,* it is much loved of skateboarders, and the glass-enclosed elevators have become a focus for organized tourists.

Many of Mitterand's projects involved the revamping of old institutions like the Louvre or the Jardin des Plantes. But while the disproportionately rich western part of the city was growing rapidly, the administration became concerned about the eastern section, which provided a quarter of its jobs though only half its housing.[2] A concerted effort to revitalize the southeast began in local government and planning offices about 1970, and soon involved politicians who inevitably disagreed. For all that, it seems that Socialists and Gaullists were acting in concert when the eastward growth of Paris was visually articulated by a long Ministry of Finance building, designed in 1982 by a group headed by Borja Huidobro and Paul Chemetov, that ran like a bridge between the Gare de Lyon railway lines and the river. Beyond, a new covered sports stadium, the Palais Omnisports, built in 1984, became the best-equipped sports stadium in France. Associated with those buildings is a mixed housing project that contains some of the more interesting recent architecture in France. At the Place de la Bastille there is a new Opera House, and a park has been laid out along the northern riverbank.

Most notable and controversial has been the last Mitterandian enterprise, the new National Library, known as the Très Grande Bibliothèque (TGB for short), across the river from the Finance Ministry. Demoralized by disaffection and labor problems, by inept book stack towers, and disgraced by sterile, unhappy public spaces—both within and without—it seems a perfect candidate for a revised edition of Peter Hall's book *Great Planning Disasters.*

If some entirely faceless skyscrapers now crowd the banks of the Seine both eastward and westward out of central Paris, as well as on the peripheries, the fabric of the center has remained intact, and this can be seen as a qualified victory for de Gaulle's vision of the city. London on the other hand has no triumphal way, no Grande Axe, and its government, disorganized and balkanized after 1980, could not afford any *pro-jets,* certainly no *grands* ones. There is no British technocratic tradition, nor was there an inter-party consensus on planning. There was, however, a healthy and well-established pattern of local consultation on central planning decisions which was sometimes effective and successful. The one major national building project the Conservatives inherited from previous administrations, the proposal for a National Library in Bloomsbury—near the British Museum, of which it had originally been a part—started out grand enough, but successive governments moved the site and reduced its scale and therefore its capacity.

As the longest-serving prime minister, Margaret Thatcher relied on private enterprise to provide the monuments of her regime. Downstream of, but adjoining the overcrowded "square mile" of the City of London, lay the "brown" area of mostly abandoned nineteenth-century docks and warehouses. By 1970, Docklands offered a prime site for development, but only if there was a huge investment. The government agreed to fund an elaborate infrastructure in 1987—roadways, rail links, and mains services on a large scale—much as the French had done at La Défense. As the Communist regime of Mr. Deng would designate Shenzhen and Pudong a little later, Mrs. Thatcher's government made Docklands a special Enterprise Zone exempt from planning regulations, an area controlled by a development corporation ironically modeled on those that had promoted the New Towns.

The main Docklands developer was Canadian, so that Canada Square became the hub of a district dominated by a square-plan, pyramid-topped office tower—at 800 feet the tallest occupied building in Europe—so tall that on a clear day it could be seen from Heathrow Airport and Windsor Castle on the far west of London, some twenty miles away. The New York architect Cesar Pelli built the tower, and several other North American architectural firms did the adjoining buildings.

But things did not go smoothly. The tower was finished just as another recession began in 1991 at a time when the City of London itself relaxed planning restrictions. Vacancies were at their peak, as they also were in midtown Manhattan. The development failed, owing some $2 billion (£1.3 billion). By 1999 the government had put, according to ministerial authority, about $6 billion into the scheme (this includes infrastructure and credit guarantees), which is three or four times more than the developers had invested originally. Having reorganized themselves, the same developers returned and bought back the entire Docklands development in 1999, by which date most of the main tower was occupied. Two new square towers, only slightly smaller, went up that year, and one was already leased to the Hong Kong and Shanghai Bank.

Although it was visible from the Louvre and along the Grande Axe, La Défense had no towering focal buildings—nor did it absorb or directly affect any of the older Parisian monuments. In London, Docklands faced one of the most splendid architectural complexes in Britain, Greenwich Hospital, part palace, part hospice for naval veterans. The three great seventeenth-century architects, Inigo Jones, Christopher Wren, and Nicholas Hawksmoor, had all worked on the buildings. The Greenwich Meridian—zero longitude—passes through it. The view from it across the river had been appropriately crowded with ships and harbor buildings, while behind these lay the East End, a derelict and impoverished area of London into which poor immigrants had crowded throughout the nineteenth century; as late as 1980, one British parliamentarian had called the area "the squatter capital of the Globe."[4]

Expensively finished high-rise office buildings would now dwarf the more or less gated new housing to make an even sharper contrast with a blighted hinterland. After two decades, the district of Tower Hamlets, which contains Docklands, has remained as socially confused as La Défense. The view from Greenwich Hospital is now of a stubby square across the river, the overwhelming Docklands tower a permanent reminder of the association of very high building with recession and of the impotence of corporate capital to generate a socially cohesive environment.

In some circumstances the choice to build high may even have disruptive political implications. The Petronas twin towers in Kuala Lumpur, designed by the same New York office that produced the Docklands colossus, are still the tallest buildings in the world in the year 2000. They were shown in a 1998 film called *Entrapment,* with Sean Connery, rising from a miasma of slum dwellings, which—so the Prime Minister of Malaysia, Mahathir Mohamad, announced while publicly banning the film—were located in southern Malacca, "hundreds of miles away."[5] Wherever that scatter of slums was located, what really provoked Mohamad's ire was the reading of the twin towers as an image of social inequity, since, of course, Kuala Lumpur has plenty of slums to show.

Those twin towers might also be read as a warning symptom of the approaching Far Eastern financial crisis that struck Thailand and then Malaysia in 1997, before spreading to the rest of Southeast Asia—a crisis that broke the worldwide momentum of the financial markets, even if not for long. "International propagation of bubbles and crashes seems not to be an economic law as much as a tendency,"[6] after all.

The interdependence of bubbles and crises will almost certainly increase with creeping globalization. But I am no futurologist, and my concern is with what ought to—not with what will inevitably—be.

If there is one "ought" about the city, it is that it has to ensure that justice be done by its citizens. What that might mean in detail and how it is to be achieved will, of course, be disputed. Whose justice? It is a question that is often asked nowadays. A few people would take the argument further and demand that their city should also *look* just—and would know what you meant should you suggest it. Justice, as the old legal saw has it, must not only be done, it must be seen to be done.[7] The implications of that saw in terms of architecture and of public space, and its present difficulties, need to be spelled out.

High building, which is the source of many urban problems, is with us for the foreseeable future. In spite of the Pedersen formula, which calculates that a square plan is the most profitable form of investment building, this is not always followed, as the cylindrical Petronas Towers have shown. And indeed at the end of 1999, two new bids have been entered in these competitive stakes: the World Financial Center in Shanghai, which I have already mentioned, and a cylindrical building on a small footprint, to be built in Chicago, at 7 Dearborn Street, which at two thousand feet when it is finished in 2003 will be the highest building in the world.

The business of high buildings, though, has really passed out of the hands of architects, because a wholly new kind of designer has now come into being. Although many still use the title "architects," others prefer to be styled "design professionals"; they operate in large offices that handle many millions' worth (in various currencies) of work a year. Such offices offer financial advice, quantity surveying, and structural and service engineering, all of which determine the actual configuration of the building, but the architects' and decorators' actual designing is limited to advice on the surface dressing (mirror glass or Gothic or Renaissance or Chinese or some sheathing details derived from Art Déco patterning). This change was conveniently theorized by Robert Venturi and Denise Scott-Brown. They exalted the "decorated shed," a straightforward rectilinear structure whose outside surfacing might be in any of the styles I have just listed or in no style at all. This shed was to supersede the old "modernist" building shaped from the inside by its program and warped by its symbolic requirements. As an ironic instance of this mistaken approach, they noted a duck-shaped roadside shop in New England that sold dead oven-ready ducks and duck eggs. The opposition between the duck and the decorated shed became a slogan during the seventies and eighties.[8]

For a while, the application of assorted patterns on high-rises passed as an avant-garde movement, when it was called postmodernism. Postmodern, as I suggested earlier, is a term that has changed meaning over the last two decades of the twentieth century, and has been applied to everything from food or fashion design to philosophy.[9] Practically marginalized in Western architecture, it has been zealously taken up in China, and with less enthusiasm also in India. Local derivatives—from Mughal to Ming—have all been mined to provide ornament for commercial builders there, though by now any kind of historical detail will do. Chinese apartment blocks—I have seen them in Shenzhen and Guanzhou, in Shanghai and Beijing—rise from the mass of two- or three-story tenements haphazardly, in a pathetic imitation of Manhattan. As in India, so in China, local or national echoes are being pushed out by variations on a coarsened, barely identifiable westernizing "classicism."

In such a situation the architect is no longer playing the part of an independent adviser who can, for instance, counsel a client to abandon or modify a project he may consider against the public good or even against the client's self-interest. He is no longer the positive contributor to the shaping of the inner and outer volume of the building, which he then sets in its surrounding. This new kind of architect, in any case, designs only a tiny fraction of what gets built. If the world building stock doubled in volume between 1918 and 1945, as has been estimated, it has multiplied several times more in the half-century that has followed. Being a relatively powerless group, architects are a convenient scapegoat for the more forceful generators of the city's ills.

The city has never been short of critics, but sharper than usual dissatisfaction with the man-made environment began to be voiced aggressively around 1970 by spokesmen who claimed to speak for the "common man" and his woes: they were as different as Tom Wolfe and Prince Charles. Although they primarily attacked architects, the buildings they despised had been produced by those large commercial offices I have described, who, undeterred, have gone on manufacturing the same huge structures, even though they are now decked out with pseudohistorical ornament in deference to their critics.

Many people were indeed dissatisfied with the modern city and its buildings and their environment, but this had little to do with "style" or "ornament"—as their self-appointed spokesmen maintained—but a great deal to do with the frustration that the alienation of merely rent-producing and characterless building induced. Questions of style and ornament, which may seem harmless, become dangerously misleading when they stop at the surface and consequently mask problems of social structure and of context.

Public frustration has been channeled into various forms of community action directed at corporate or municipal abuses, which are on the increase. Jane Jacobs, a lover of cities and of Manhattan—particularly of its downtown section—has described, for example, in *The Death and Life of Great American Cities,* how popular pressure avoided the potential destruction of Washington Square by a city-sponsored project to run a major road through it. That was in 1958.[10] More recently, citizens have taken matters (if not the law) into their own hands. Derelict riverside land in the borough of Wandsworth in London belonging to the Guinness Corporation was seized by an acronymic group, TLIO (This Land Is Ours), who invited the landlords and the authorities to a land-use seminar in the summer of 1999.

These are isolated examples, but popular opinion, forcefully organized, can and often has diverted bureaucratic urban blunders. This phenomenon is not particularly new therefore, though it is not always effective. The blunders of corporations or developers are often more difficult to detect early—and delay or prevent—than municipal or civic follies. Community action also has its downside, described by the acronym NIMBY—"Not In My Back Yard." That label usually applies to the rich and politically powerful who want to prevent the location of a drug treatment center, a homeless shelter, a traffic lane—or some other inconvenience—near their homes. Such an action was taken in 1999 against Donald Trump's proposed tower, 861-foot-high and ninety stories, on First Avenue and Forty-eighth Street in New York, which I mentioned in the previous chapter. It failed, perhaps because it could be presented as a NIMBY—the rich and powerful blocking the action of the enterprising plebeian; nevertheless, that community action is leading to yet another reconsideration of the New York zoning laws.

Community action, citizens' initiatives, have at times been heroic. The collective power of such protests against various government, municipal—but above all corporate—agencies has grown much more powerful. Business has responded with thousands of lawsuits against individuals or organizations concerned with the environment or other public policy issues, which usually involve accusations of defamation, conspiracy, and nuisance. Sporadic vexatious lawsuits have been incorporated into a technique called, acronymically, SLAPP—"Strategic Lawsuit Against Public Participation." Most of these cases have been thrown out by the courts, and more than three-quarters of those that are tried are won by the accused. However, they can give rise to three years or more of litigation, ruinous costs, as well as much anxiety and loss of time for individuals or small groups. Government agencies or business corporations, on the other hand, simply absorb the legal costs into normal business expenses. The answer is a more recent technique, SLAPP-Back. One of the most famous examples of this is the libel accusation brought by McDonald's against a former post office employee and an unemployed gardener, both vegetarians and members of a small anarchist group, London Greenpeace (not connected with the much more famous Greenpeace International). The couple had distributed pamphlets alleging that McDonald's was responsible for destroying rainforest, was cruel to animals, a bad employer, and that the food served was not nutritious or healthy. The case, inevitably called McLibel, began with a writ in 1990, was heard in June 1994, and judgment was given in June 1997—the longest libel case ever fought in Britain. As long as it lasted, it was a splendid free sideshow, and British libel laws made the prosecution easier than it would have been in the United States.

The defendants had counterclaimed that they had been libeled as liars, and this complicated and extended the case. Although many of their accusations were found unjustified, enough in the pamphlet was found to be true for the awarded damages to be small. The negative publicity for McDonald's was vast, particularly as the trial was seen by many as being "about the globalization of culture and belief systems." Since "McDonald's is the most important institution of our time . . . [which] has utterly changed eating, the most elemental of commercialized human activities . . . [it has] turned plates into paper and polystyrene, dispensed with crockery and deleted the cook." The journalist who wrote this sees, rightly, that this particular case "will resolve nothing."[11] It may seem a puny victory in a war which may have been lost, though it will surely provoke similar and repeated guerrilla action elsewhere.

Some intimation of future developments at an international level came at the Earth Summit in Rio de Janeiro in 1992 when a number of pressure groups were strong enough to compel an agreement on the emission of greenhouse gases. In 1994 a group of protesters disrupted the fiftieth birthday celebrations of the World Bank. In December 1999 people power was demonstrated in an even more public and global way by the disruption of the World Trade Organization meeting in Seattle.

These cases have had one positive effect at least: they have directed public opinion toward much that is wrong with our society and our environment. Such groups, acronymically called NGOs—nongovernmental organizations—can also use information technology to work on a worldwide scale, and combine internationally to become what some economists have called NGO swarms; indeed, they have acted savagely against global powers, as a swarm does, as well as governments.[12] The acronym now covers vast and powerful aid groups—which may be government-funded fully or in part, like the Red Cross—as well as minute ones that deal with a particular shortage or injustice. With the help of some governments, they have succeeded in getting land mines banned and are now agitating for the remission of the debt incurred by poor countries. In an urban context, their actions have been primarily negative: they can obstruct and prevent to brilliant effect, provide revitalizing street action in a moribund neighborhood, but they cannot propose and project physical presence or new formal inventions. Or as one "activist" put it: "people don't organize or fight for something, but they organize to fight against something."[13]

Much of what has been said by various activists working in the city has been overtaken by events. The argument set up by Jane Jacobs in the case of Washington Square, for instance, proposed a vital, spontaneous city of variety in opposition to the sterile one of planning and order. The revitalizing of 125th Street market in Harlem during the 1980s and its forcible suppression in 1994 make a good story of the same kind.[14] Activists oppose the tidy city of various "disurbanists" and utopians— who range from Ebenezer Howard to Le Corbusier—to the messily vital city of "communities." But the realities of the late twentieth century in fact oppose a "designed" city, where the first consideration is urban form and some dialogue with the citizens, to the much more pervasive and insidious city of networks "arranged" by the traffic and sanitary engineers whose interstices are to be filled by the developer and the speculator—the city of efficiency guiding profit. Attempts to revivify those parts of such a city that have been degraded by speculation and economic change always require an injection of capital (with an expectation of some financial returns), a process that came to be called urban renewal.

Urban renewal is not a new slogan; it was coined in the United States in 1954. The idea is very much older than the slogan; the process whereby the poor were simply removed to a more outlying and derelict district was explicitly condemned by the British Royal Commission on the Housing of the Working Classes of 1884–85, which I quoted in my third chapter.[15] American satire puts the same criticism more pithily: "Urban renewal means Negro removal," as a Philadelphia wit quipped when Society Hill—a riverside district, once grand, but fallen on bad times by 1945—provided a prime instance of a process now more commonly called "gentrification."[16]

Other forms of renewal were initiated sometime after 1945 in certain badly bombed German cities, mostly at the behest of architects and planners—notably in Cologne, in Essen and Bremen. Vehicular traffic was excluded from some parts of the city centers often against the protests of traffic engineers and of shopkeepers, though they later discovered that the exclusion of motor traffic actually produced an upturn in trade.

Pedestrianization in crowded urban areas has now been adopted as policy in a number of countries: England, France, Italy. Following the success of Covent Garden in London, cars may be excluded from Trafalgar Square as part of a large scheme put forward by Norman Foster and is one of the recommendations backed by the recently convened British Urban Task Force. In Paris, pedestrianizing started earlier. Fast traffic lanes have been sunk on both sides of the riverbed of the Seine, while the most showy sector of the Grande Axe, the Champs-Elysées, has been repaved and motor traffic rerouted. These fragmentary essays suggest a different kind of urban renewal in city centers from that practiced by the gentrifiers.

To many, any projects involving even the partial exclusion of the car may seem unrealistic. From the time of its introduction, certainly since the appearance of the Model T Ford, the automobile has been presented, and is probably still generally accepted, as a universal symbol of freedom. In the United States and in most of the Western world, the car is ubiquitous. It is only in the last few decades, particularly after the energy crisis of 1973, that its universal benefits have come into question.

In the city the automobile has been a dominant player. Its manufacture and marketing represent a large slice of the world economy, and its lobbies are proportionately powerful; they have a long history of resisting any government regulations to restrict free road access or polluting emissions. More perniciously, the car lobby acts to depress mass transportation; sometimes small railway and bus companies are even bought up to stimulate the demand for an increase in road surface. This has (as in the case of Los Angeles) led to an acute hypertrophy of highway and the destruction of existing and vital neighbourhoods.[17]

Building roads, bridges, tunnels, multilevel junctions, and freeways is presented as normal public expenditure, while any form of financial investment in mass transit is treated as "subvention" and therefore an insidious form of "creeping socialism." Since manufacturers depend on constant demand, and on road-building programs—not only in North America but also in Europe—highways have become the dominant form of public works.

That situation is now being replicated in Eastern Europe and even more radically in China, where for many decades the roads of the main cities have been choked with shoals of bicycles. A bicycle takes up less space than a tenth of a small car; despite the frantic road building and road widening, Chinese city roads today are chronically bottle-necked with cars and trucks, some produced by the growing Chinese car industry. Much the same is true in the countries of Southeast Asia. No measures are being taken to prevent and mitigate the catastrophe. On the contrary, Thai commuters, for instance, are being advised to make their car "a little home on wheels," since they spend so much time in it, and traffic police are trained in emergency midwifery; brightly colored portable plastic urinals can also be bought at gas stations.[18] An elevated monorail has finally been introduced in Bangkok, though the fares are very high, and it is a private, profit-making enterprise.

The demand for alternative modes of transportation is still a minority one. The travelator, which has become a fixture of airports, the monorail, and the light electric railway are all consistently discouraged by motorcar manufacturers,[19] who are some of the most powerful agents of globalization. That word—and the notion, as I said earlier—has been around for half a century or more, but its effects are being increasingly felt as Japanese executives find it cheaper to play golf in Australia or Thailand than on the home turf, while German car manufacturers prefer to have parts made in Korea or Indonesia. Microchips for a Japanese computer may be produced in Washington State or Massachusetts, Cambridgeshire or—even more cheaply—in Bangalore. All this has been interminably ventilated.

What is less often discussed is efficiency, the justification for globalizing. In fact, globalization cannot be about quality, but is very much about quantity. Efficiency is, of course, calculable and its quantifiable benefits, in industrialized countries, include a higher life expectancy and a rising average income. Its true index, however, is corporate profit, which may in turn be translated equally easily into the market value of company shares. Like all social processes, globalization is neither impersonal nor inevitable, but the product of a number of decisions, choices, and transactions by individuals, even if they often hide behind the acronymic shields of international bodies.

In spite of its demonstrable benefits, globalization, with its imposition of the automobile culture and its homogenizing of customs, diet, and clothes, is unsettling. Of course, the calculation of the rising average income can be derived from the mushroom growth of a new managerial-executive elite rather than the improvement of the lowest incomes. As Zygmunt Bauman put it, "New fortunes are born, sprout and flourish in . . . virtual reality, tightly isolated from the old-fashioned rough-and-ready realities of the poor. The creation of wealth is on the way to final emancipation from its constraining . . . connection with making things, processing materials, creating jobs and managing people. The old rich needed the poor to make and keep them rich. That dependency at all times mitigated the conflict of interest. . . ."[20] Prosperity is promised to the poor as the result of investment, and the condition for investment is social stability, which, if it cannot be obtained by negotiation, may be imposed by force.

In spite of all assurances, we still have the poor with us. But poverty now has new faces: the loss of identity that an increasing mobility imposes is one of them, and the increasing prison populations in many seemingly prosperous lands is another. In the meanwhile, protests against the World Trade Organization and the NAFTA Agreement are further attempts to assert economic independence, though probably not powerful enough to have a real effect on policy.

The reassertion of local or just ethnic identity is an essential weapon of these poor against the uncertainties of the globalized labor market. The insistence on Hispanic identity in New York or Los Angeles is an obvious instance of this process. In another world, the French Academy's attempts to maintain the purity of the French language—against the hegemony of English—may seem quite futile as long as young Parisians sport Yankees caps and listen to American rap. It is a modern instance of the process that already absorbed much energy in the nineteenth century, when the great bourgeois provincial cities guarded their economic vitality by affirming their identity against a capital: Lyon had to emphasize and cultivate its particularity against Paris, Milan had to stand out against Vienna first and Rome later, Munich against Berlin, or more recently Kyoto against Tokyo.

The urge for independence is proportionately more violent as globalization increases. The Iranian fight against "Satan" was one, and the nationalist fragmentation of the old Soviet Union, of the Balkans themselves, are other symptoms of the resurgence of smaller groupings asserting their identity against global leveling. There is a renaissance of the regional languages that late-nineteenth-century nationalism engendered: Catalan, Galician, Provençal, Breton, Basque, Lithuanian, and Latvian in Europe, various Indio languages in Latin America. All this has led to curious imbalances: English has almost disappeared in Quebec, French from northern Belgium, while the Danish language struggles to survive a powerful onslaught of media-English.

The paradoxical obsession with a local past that these linguistic phenomena illustrate has had its impact on the city, particularly on city centers, and it has led to the enhancing and renewing of various historical relics. The restoration of old buildings, which is often also misleadingly called urban renewal, is based on the assumption that there are relics from the past that are worth visiting almost everywhere. Where none exist, such as in Las Vegas, a past can always be imported or invented. This is a form of urban renewal, even revival, which is closely tied to the stimulation of varieties of tourism, and it has created a new architectural demand.

The museum has now become the only universally recognized institutional building, and it has therefore assumed an unprecedented importance as a type in modern cities. In that modern sense, "museums" have existed for three hundred years or so. They were more or less assiduously visited by schoolchildren, artists, and culture-tourists. However, a new kind of museum/art gallery is developing as a landmark and a city magnet. All over the world—China, India, Russia, Brazil and Argentina, or Canada—museums are packed, especially at weekends. Many collections are fast outgrowing their building's capacity to house them, and museums are therefore fissuring. However locally anchored, they have become cult buildings of a global religion that offers the advantage and the disadvantage of imposing neither doctrine nor any rule of life.

Museum interiors have undergone a radical transformation. Like the older institutions, modern museums are dependent on gifts and bequests that form their capital, but they are able to raise an increasing income from restaurants, bookshops, and the collectibles trade. This has also transformed their context and potential. Museum shops offer not only casts but also replicas, and so popular have they become that they have opened branches—as the New York Metropolitan Museum did in midtown and Soho. What is more, shops have grown up that are not connected to any institution anywhere but use the label "museum shop" to suggest refinement and quality.

The architecture of the princely collection open to the public, the "improving" and paternalistic taste-raising nineteenth-century institutions, have had to be completely reoriented. The old versions—from Schinkel's crisp, precise but also generous Altes Museum in Berlin, to the ham-fisted Sainsbury wing of the National Gallery in London, with the Washington National Gallery at a midpoint—presented themselves as dignified, somewhat antique, perhaps a bit fuddy-duddy. This image was first challenged by the Guggenheim Museum. When Frank Lloyd Wright designed the original structure in New York between 1950 and 1955, he broke the mold of the New York grid with his huge spiral.

Today the Guggenheim, enlarged and partly deaccessioned though it is, has sprouted colonies in downtown New York, Venice, Salzburg, and Bilbao, making it also a global phenomenon. The Bilbao Guggenheim, designed by Frank Gehry, is the best-known building in the world at the end of the twentieth century. His concrete and titanium shell dominates a bend in the Nervion River which divides the medieval from the dour nineteenth-century town, an important port until sea trade declined and its mines became uneconomical. For the last thirty years of the century, Bilbao was also the epicenter of sporadically murderous Basque separatism.

Some of the trustees of the New York Guggenheim, when it was first opened, had scoffed at visitors who had come to see Wright's building and not the art. All this has changed, however. The city of Bilbao was so concerned to have the museum—as well as its collection, mostly of American art—that it was glad to share construction and running costs with the New York Guggenheim. It also had Norman Foster build a new subway system, and Santiago Calatrava build a bridge and an airport. So far the risk has paid off splendidly. Separatism is on the decline, and Bilbao has received a huge injection of what the Bilbaoans themselves call high-class tourism—not cruise-trippers with packed lunches, but people who want to stay in comfortable hotels and eat well, and who will also buy local luxury products. They look at the exhibitions and the collection, but the primary attraction is the building itself.

Following that example, other museums have decided that their buildings should themselves be showpieces, attracting a new audience. The Victoria and Albert Museum in London has commissioned a very different fractal-spiral building by Daniel Libeskind, whose Jewish Museum in Berlin, not filled at the time of writing, has already become a landmark and a monument. No doubt his building for the Manchester branch of the Imperial War Museum will also have a revitalizing effect on the town, much as Salford hopes to gain from the new Lowry Centre opened in April 2000. In Rome, civic authorities decided to build a gallery of recent art in a run-down northern part of the city, and in 1999 chose a project by the Anglo-Iraqi Zaha Hadid in the hope that it would also act as such a catalyst, since there is not much of a collection to fill it.

This enthusiasm for the museum is in sharp contrast to the hostile reaction that works of modern art sometimes encounter in public places.

The sculpture of Richard Serra has been attacked and institutionally vandalized in New York, while his huge *Clara-Clara* was moved from the Tuileries Gardens in the center of Paris to one of the outlying parks in the depressed eastern part of the city. Set in the Bilbao museum, however, his work has become its most magnetic attraction. What may be considered an offensive imposition in a working environment is transformed into an integral piece of the mosaic of modernity in a museum like the Guggenheim.

Gehry's Bilbao museum is in sharp contrast to the drab stolidity of the mining and foundry town. It is not quite the harbinger of the new type—its mother institution in New York was that—but it has focused attention on the city in a way no other building has done, and emphasized the fact that the institution of the museum can create a new kind of public ambience. The sheltering of civic institutions, and by that I mean law courts, town halls, schools, universities, and even railway stations, must now receive the sort of attention that can give them an analogous drawing power—that is, if the great spectacle that the Guggenheim has offered Bilbao can be emulated in the life of the city.

Another Spanish—rather, Catalan—town, Barcelona, adopted a completely different approach. It had never been a "museum" town, since its principal monuments were relatively modest, though having been the dominant center of industry in the peninsula, it had had its share of international fairs. Barcelona had been scarred by the Civil War and was regarded with disfavor by the Franquist regime as a center of separatism. In the new democratic-federal Spain, the capital of the Catalan region now sees itself as an independent metropolis, and even before bagging the Olympic Games, embarked on a policy that the Catalan architect and politician Oriol Bohigas, who is most responsible for the transformation, has described as one of "monumentalizing the suburbs and sanitizing the center," an invocation of and an improvement on Soria y Mata's catchword—that he wanted "to urbanize the country and ruralize the town."[21] In 1981–82 spaces were found in the most remote and anonymous housing estates, and both American and European artists were invited to articulate the public squares and parks. Almost the first to do so was the same Richard Serra, whose rather polite plastered curved wall—even if it now looks a bit bedraggled—did not provoke the kind of hostility generated in Paris and New York. Many more artists—the Basque Chillida; the two Catalans, Joan Miró (posthumously) and Antoni Tapies—were involved in projected monuments and having squares organized around their sculptures.

More important from the point of view of the inhabitants was the freeing of the seafront, which had long been a waste of harbor-installations and warehouses like the London Docklands. Barcelona did have a famous promenade—the Ramblas—a wide, overcrowded pedestrian boulevard with relatively little traffic at the western edge of the Barrio Gótico, the nuclear medieval city, around which, as I have had occasion to note, Cerdá planned his *ensanche*. Just off the Ramblas, the Casa de Caritat, a roomy old poor-hospice, was turned into a lecture and exhibition center. A new Museum of Modern Art, the inevitable fixture of urban renewal, adjoins it. This is also by an American architect, Richard Meier. However, the harbor boulevard to the south of the Barrio, lined with cafés and restaurants and with traffic sunk in a throughway, has become the liveliest public space in the city.

The Barcelona planners also brought over the work of several New York artists (Oldenburg, Lichtenstein, Ellsworth Kelly), but many of the others were local. The program has certainly been a success for the image of Barcelona, as the world recognized at the time of the 1992 Olympic Games.

It is Berlin, however, that has gone through the greatest upheaval in the last decade of the century. Previous efforts at rebuilding—two "exhibitions," which were in fact large-scale construction programs—harnessed public enterprise to private investments. The first *Interbau,* in 1957, created a number of high-rise housing developments, some on the scale of the Parisian *Grands Travaux,* while the second, in 1980–84, proposed smaller-scale interventions in those parts of the urban texture that had not quite healed after wartime destruction. The Wall had run on the old border between the Soviet and the American sectors, and by it a new *Kulturforum,* more ambitious than any French *Centre Culturel,* was built: it was begun in 1963 and included a concert hall for the Berlin Philharmonic and the National Library, both designed by Hans Scharoun, as well as the National Gallery, designed by Mies van der Rohe. In spite of the huge reputation of the orchestra and of the two architects, the *Kulturforum* was too shapeless, too contradictory, too out of the way ever to become the heart of West Berlin. When the Wall was destroyed with jubilation in 1989, as the Soviet Union imploded, the provisional nature of this "cultural" planning became apparent. If the city was to weld together, something had to be done about the derelict areas adjoining it, the Pariser Platz with its Brandenburg Triumphal Gate opening onto the Tiergarten, the Reichstag and its forecourt to the north, as well as the Potsdamer and the Leipziger Plätze with their nexus of roadways to the south. In 1999 the Reichstag, now re-domed in glass by Norman Foster, became the home of the German parliament, newly moved there from Bonn. Pariser Platz, which links the old city through its main avenue, Unter den Linden, and the adjoining streets, will now have their quota of grand hotels and embassies restored. The most ambitious rebuilding will be between the *Kulturforum* and the Potsdamer Platz, where some of the world's best architects, by some providential freak, will produce some of their least interesting work.

The Wall has left many scars. The city was so shaken, its institutions so transformed, that it was unable to reshape itself for some time, while a mistrust of planning, perhaps all too understandable given the megalomania of the past, has meant that its government was not able to promulgate, much less embody, a plan for reconfiguring all Berlin. It is to become the communications center for a new European railway network, though. Of course, Berlin has its traffic problems as well, but the strength—intermittent though it is—of the Green party in Germany has led to a pressure for reinforcing the railways rather than the freeways. In Germany their pressure has also had a direct impact. Norman Foster won the competition for a new triangular skyscraper for the Commerzbank in Frankfurt in 1991. Completed in 1997 as the tallest building in Europe, its form departs radically from the square-plan-with-a-central-core American formula. The services, elevators, and stairs are in a tower at each angle, while the main accommodation spans between the towers. Every block of offices (most are eight stories) carries a three-story greenhouse in a broken pattern. The interior of the tower is hollow and acts as the main thermic duct and the lightwell for the offices that face onto it, and so allows the use of natural ventilation rather than air-conditioning. This approach has not yet had emulators in Europe or in America, but in Malaysia Ken Yeang has designed a "green" or ecologically correct high-rise in Penang, the Menara Umno tower, which was finished in 1998 and has spawned a number of other high-rises—including a 600-meter (2,362 feet) tower (twice the height of the Eiffel Tower) for the Expo planned in Nagoya for 2005. Making high-rise buildings ecosensitive may solve no urban problems but is a shrewd move at a time when ecology has become part of mainstream politics.

"Green parties" have entered into ruling coalitions in Germany and in some other countries; they are no longer NGOs, nongovernment pressure groups. That may weaken their thrust in direct action, but it also compels them to move from protest to project. I am not sure that the coopting into government is the only way in which that rather important step may be accomplished. Nevertheless, that move from protest to project is a crucial passage, one that all the slogan-shouting and McDonald's-smashing demonstrators at the break of the century have not, it seems to me, yet considered.

This change is more urgently needed than ever. You can hardly pick up a paper in the Northern Hemisphere without reading about some case of catastrophic overcrowding, traffic bottleneck many miles long, or pathological pollution. Yet the same newspaper will carry triumphalist accounts of ever-higher buildings and ever-larger and ever-more-distant supermarkets, as if the two kinds of phenomena were unrelated. There are other sources of urban unease: though repeated statistical surveys show that urban crime is on the decline, anecdotal experience shows otherwise, and this has led to a noticeable trend in America, which will inevitably be followed in the rest of the world. "More and more gated communities, consumer-determined city services, and suburbs built to ensure isolation from those who live across city borders is the almost inevitable consequence of accelerating privatization."[22]

Many of those who do not care for suburbia or gated communities but have no interest in high-rise apartments are tempted by the alternative offered by the "New Urbanists," of whom I spoke in chapter six. Although this revival and movement, which has grown out of post-modernism, invokes the Garden City as an ideal, it has quite abandoned the primary planning principle that Howard (a "creeping socialist" if ever there was one) preached: the public ownership of land.

The New Urbanists' emphasis on private transaction for planning procedure does point up the most important deficiency in public projects: that local government, if starved of funds and low in public estimation, cannot give good service to any community. Still, although the New Urbanists are totally committed to working through corporate business, they have introduced an important feature into their practice: the *charrette*.

This French word refers to the cart that used to go around the dispersed ateliers of the Ecole des Beaux-Arts in Paris collecting student drawings for submission. If you did not make it in time for the cart, you could not submit, and the consequences were dire. For designers and architects, *charrette* has therefore come to mean all urgent work and, by extension, brainstorming. So the French word has been borrowed for the New Urbanists' brainstorming sessions with financiers and residents as well as local officials. Something of that kind was done in the English New Towns, and planning appeals—common in Britain—do take the *charrette* form. Perhaps the *charrette* should become an accepted part of planning practice, since civic authority must learn to involve all citizens in the city or town as a continuous project, in the modeling and the changing of its fabric. Unfortunately, such transactions are often quasi-secret, so that the majority of residents in any given city learn of important changes from the real-estate pages of "quality" newspapers—assuming they look at them—and by that time the new structures are building anyway. City councilors, sitting in discreet session in association with traffic advisers, sometimes allow major changes in road patterns to bypass the inconvenience of community involvement. Recourse to a *charrette*, time-consuming though it is, may turn out to save time in the long run.

In any case, the *charrette* is an important instrument for the "airing" of the planning process, whether it is initiated by a private developer or a public authority. Choice and freedom from "interference"—that is, from government control—is, after all, a constant advertising slogan, lest we believe that the force of the multinationals is not as great and as insidious as that of any government, and that the freedom to choose a brand of hair spray, washing detergent, or dog food represents a real victory for the human spirit.

For all their ridiculous overstatements, advertisers only harp on what most of us accept anyway: that manufacturing must be a private business, even if its hold on certain fields—pharmaceuticals, genetic engineering, weapons—can never be entirely free of government supervision—nor indeed can urban planning. The limits of its operations may be difficult to define, but most of us would acknowledge that they need to be explicitly marked out and respected.

Residual participatory democracy—if it can still be called that—is passing from voters to shareholders and customers. In this, too, the New Urbanists are correct. The prime business of shareholders is to look for the largest possible return on investment. The proper concern of all statutory bodies—inevitably advertisers are not keen on this side of the process—is to set limits on investors' profit-making proclivities, to make sure they do not conflict with competitive freedom (as in cartels and mergers) or the blatant pursuit of profit, as was the case with tobacco consumption and carbon dioxide emission, and so damage the constituents they have been elected to serve and to protect.

If the limits between the two estates become confused, the number of voters, already low in national and even lower in local elections in many countries, will certainly and rightly fall. In itself, voting is not a measure of participatory democracy, though a very low voter turnout almost certainly shows a lack of confidence in the power of elected officers. The remedy is not to concentrate power in ever bigger units or to impose ever-more-frequent voting decisions (though a profusion of plebiscites seems to work quite well in Switzerland) but, on the contrary, to decentralize and to increase the services that the region or the city offers. Every vote can then be seen to matter. Local government can extend its activities by taking many small, even apparently trivial steps in the direction of public involvement.

Two Latin-American municipalities have attempted just that: first, La Paz, the squatter-invaded capital of Bolivia, and then, more extensively, Córdoba, Argentina's second city. In both of them, the same architect, Miguel-Angel Roca, has also acted as planner. In both cases, the tactic has been to give as much importance as possible to the seats of local government and to merge administrative and representative activities with communal ones: a small theater, ballrooms, libraries, a bar—all run as a part-private, part-public enterprise. This is a more assertive version of the Barcelona program, that of monumentalizing the suburbs, but it is carried through with a political subtlety matched by formal invention.

Working on a less ambitious level, a city can find an almost Fourierist solution to its street people by giving them employment and smart, brightly colored uniforms, as Philadelphia did successfully from 1995 onward, rather than expelling them to poorer outlying areas as was done in New York. It can sponsor and even own sports teams and so claim gate money and the loyalty of such citizens as are fans, instead of merely providing the expensive infrastructure for games.[23] Cities can also enter cooperative food supply and provide markets for where food might be grown within a given distance of its location, as is done in Santa Monica and other California towns, as well as some French ones. Even in New York—not in Manhattan itself but in Queens and Flushing—there are flourishing farms.[24] More generally, there was an increase from 30 percent to 40 percent in the dollar value of metropolitan food production in the United States. Allowing for much local variation, this has almost become a global phenomenon: in Dar es Salaam in Tanzania, currently one of the fastest-growing cities in the world, the proportion of families involved in farming rose from 18 percent to 67 percent in recent years. In Moscow the rise was particularly drastic: from 20 percent in 1970 to 65 percent in 1991. Selective tax rating can encourage the formation of this kind of urban agriculture—a movement that has, in fact, already taken root in England, where London alone has twenty such farms.[25]

Any discussion of urban farming also implies that the vast baggage of zoning regulations needs careful unpacking, since zoning may actually hamper its development. Certainly the very simplistic rules instituted by the original Athens Charter, by which so many of the planners and architects reconstructed Europe after 1945, have long been recognized as damaging. Another document was drawn up in 1998 (in Athens, again) by a European Council of Town-planners, under the aegis of the European Union, to replace the sixty-year-old original charter. Much of the new document was devoted to conventional pieties, but it also contained hard, substantial suggestions contrary both to the spirit and the letter of the original document:

"For most citizens and visitors," the charter says, for instance, "the character of a city is defined by the quality of its buildings and the spaces between them. In many cities, the urban fabric, including many heritage assets, have been destroyed by inappropriate plans for spatial reorganization, road construction, and uncontrolled actions by the property industry."

This dogmatically sums up what I have been arguing so far. The new charter warns against the increase in traffic densities in Eastern Europe and calls attention to the implications of the telecommunications revolution. It calls for an increase in mixed-use zones, and an insistence that they serve the public interest. Above all, the new charter insists that land use and transport planning cannot be separated, that mixed-use zones must also have an impact on transport needs, that pricing and taxing can and should discourage the private vehicle, that the development of non-polluting public transport is now urgent. Rightly, I think, this new Athens Charter insists that "the application of strict zoning policies has created monotonous patterns of land uses, which have broken the continuity and diversity of urban life."[26]

This last quotation amounts to a planner's confession. It is too early to see the results of such repentance, and the acceptance of responsibility for many past failures. Of course, planners are not the only ones responsible for this state of affairs. All of us—public authorities, investors, and professionals such as architects—have connived to produce the cities in which we now live.

The way we approach the business of building and what we expect of it needs to be reconsidered. We can no longer afford to read the city as an amorphous stringing out along freeways into conurbations as futurologists once did. The city can be understood only in the context of its landscape, as part of its inalienable region, but also as an entity with one or more designated centers, with marked edges—if only on the map. If there is one thing that the computer has added to the designers' resources, it is the facility to see the city not as a two-dimensional figure-ground image but as a three-dimensional construct, which is, after all, how it is experienced by its inhabitants.

As for architects, they must bear their share of popular complaints against environmental depredation and against the formal and sensory poverty of the buildings that constitute the city, and this has now made a revision of their position urgent. For far too long they had been content to be thought of as men of taste, only to transform themselves in mid-twentieth century into managers and specialists who "made buildings work," and then added the "aesthetic" factor.

There are two unfortunate aspects to such an attitude: taste is notoriously difficult to argue about, and the aesthetic factor, whatever it is, is not something that can be added to or taken away from anything but is what the visitor and spectator feel about a building (or picture or poem) once it has been put before them. The architect's primary duty, his true art, is to give *form* to the way in which the building works. To make it work is, often, not all that difficult; but to make legible form out of the working, that is the secret of his craft and skill. That and his ability to manipulate and govern the metaphoric intensity of those forms so that some of the charge that the artist or architect puts into it, the spectator may take out. The architect's specific role in making the fabric of the city needs to be reasserted.

All action to do with planning and with building is inevitably political. It is therefore an action for which all builders and planners must be held publicly accountable. That is why I find the use of the term "space," as common currency in the discussion of the city and its planning, worrisome, as I pointed out in the introduction. All worthwhile building is done without reference to such abstractions. It must involve the making of places, that is, enclosures that people can inhabit and appropriate without doing themselves violence.

Historians and sociologists can interpret as culture and space the accretion of these artifacts and their workings and the results of these actions. But understanding the world I inhabit, and which I want to be able to alter, must begin with the recognition that

> Our field of perception is made up "things" and the "voids between things" . . . at first I see as things the objects which I have never seen in motion: houses, the sun, mountains. . . . If we consider as things the intervals between them, the outlook on the world . . . will be appreciably altered.[27]

To understand the city and to be able to work on it and with it, we need to see it as a concatenation of man-made, willed things—things that add up to a texture of places. Places in turn are composed of buildings and streets and parks, which are ordered and decided upon by more or less empowered individuals for varying, often incompatible reasons. Power may be theirs by popular vote, by professional authority, or because they have been able to buy it. This means—or it should mean—that all those involved may be approached with objections and criticism, and may be influenced by arguments or pressure.

Constant community participation and involvement are needed to shape our cities and to make them communicative, and this notion seems tragically to have been forgotten by the various bodies that govern us. To understand the city as a dynamic and three-dimensional figure, to follow and inflect its process of self-generation, to knit and extend its fabric requires a humane discipline, an understanding of how built forms are transformed into image by experience. "Make no small plans," Daniel Burnham, the author of the vast Chicago plan of 1909 is quoted as saying, "they have no magic to stir men's blood."[28] It is not intoxication and grandiloquence we need now, but sobriety and effective action. Therefore, make little plans, say I—and lots of them.

If I could identify an NGO able to achieve that kind of understanding and move to propose solutions—not merely to block the worst excesses of the city spoilers, but make that crucial passage from protest to project—then such a group would command my loyalty. The political and intellectual effort to make a real impact on our cities requires the action of one or more such groups. It requires, too, a historical reassessment of the city and its institutions—to which this book has, I hope, made some contribution.

Epilogue

AT 8.46 AND 9.03 AM OF SEPTEMBER 11, 2001 two Boeing 767s, their tanks full of high octane fuel, crashed into the twin towers of the World Trade Center to flare into a spectacle of devastation only seen in movies. Not only the towers, but five buildings around them were totally wrecked. A third plane, a Boeing 757 was rammed into a side of the Pentagon building in Washington. Even though the fourth strike—probably aimed at Capitol Hill or the White House—was aborted, the three that hit their targets made them the most showy act of terrorism ever. The world—or so commentators and journalists kept on saying—had changed forever. Certainly, our perception of urbanity had been given a cruel jolt by the terrorists' choice when towering and inviolate metaphors of power collapsed into twisted, charred ruins.

The terrorists had chosen their targets well: when the Twin Towers were built, some twenty years earlier, a cartoonist swathed them in an "S"-shaped cloud to make them look like the two bars in the $ sign; according to that jibe I quoted earlier, they looked to some like the boxes in which the Empire State Building might have been packed.

But with time, their size and position established them as the masthead of the Manhattan skyline—which now seemed bereft, so that their absence inspired a wave of nostalgia. Their lightly-corrugated, glistening surface had given them a kitschy charm—especially at sunset and sunrise—but their vaguely gothicky detail merged the sterile over-simplifications of modernism into a glib, finicky historicism. Their lack of architectural distinction was matched by their damaging impact on the urban fabric: their volumes were inert, and the plaza between them was hostile to any lingering humanity. They stood for the triumph of the cash nexus. The jibes I reported contrast ironically with the architect's declared aim that the buildings should "become a living representation of man's belief in humanity, his need for individual dignity . . ."[1] As for the Washington pentacle, its arbitrary geometry had made that remote and intangible building with the biggest footprint in the world (pp. 6, 144) into a universal emblem of occult power. By striking at those two most prominent emblems of world-domination, financial and military, terrorists inflicted a psychological wound on their apparently invincible enemy that may be more festering than any physical damage they wrought.

Still, of the five sides of the Pentagon, only one was wrecked, and that was fully and ceremoniously restored within two years. Lower Manhattan was very different. In the immediate aftermath of the catastrophe, some even said that New York could not survive the mutilation of its image. The demand was heard that the Towers be rebuilt as they were—or even thirty stories higher—so as to underline the endurance of their symbolic power. Others, more emotively, asked for a tangible, visible monument to the three thousand victims, or yet wanted to leave the void in the skyline as a negative commemoration of the tragedy. Meanwhile, the Towers were temporarily replaced by two upward searchlight beams recalling Albert Speer's "Cathedral of Ice" at Hitler's Nürnberg party rallies.

Developer and landlord between them soon produced a number of schemes drawn up by large architectural practices for an equivalent rent-able volume, with a concessionary public park by way of a monument. They seem to have been taken aback by the violence and the scale of public disdain for what looked like callousness. An invited "ideas" competition in 2002 produced five ambitious projects, a great deal of discussion—perhaps the most vital discussion of an architectural issue anywhere—but no resolution, though it was won by the office of Daniel Libeskind, who has now been yoked to the vast machine of Skidmore Owings and Merrill to produce, on the latest showing, a gradu-ated group of buildings, of which the highest, the "Freedom Tower", to be a symbolic 1776 feet high, is in fact crowned by an empty cage. The struggle between the different interests—developer, landlord, survivors, architects—will continue before a passionate concerned public certainly until construction, which is due to begin in 2007, and probably well beyond that date. In mid-2003 another competition, specifically for a "monument" to mark the event, was declared by the same Lower Manhattan Development Corporation. It attracted over five thousand entries and was judged in October of that year. The rather tenous results provoked the expected and unresolved controversy.

In real estate terms, the site is precious. New York has lost ten million square feet of office space, seven times the area of the Empire State Building. The towers themselves were never easy to fill, nor did they have services adequate for the information age. Their masters may not want to broadcast pride in the financial domination they symbolized quite so brazenly now, and their absence from the skyline will become less offensive as time goes on. Should the buildings which will take their place not allow for more humane public spaces and for the creation of a civic center which might rival the pulsating energies of uptown?

The Mayor's office of New York has made known its recommendation about the minimal public space required; yet in the absence of any informed policy about such space, or any concern with it in our architectural culture, the resolution will, I suspect, become a trade-off between landlord (the Port Authority), the leaseholder, and the city when the complex insurance claim is settled. It will fix the funding available for the project, and allow the developer the luxury of building without incurring loans. Those involved must surely hope that the architectural discussion will meanwhile have died down. If it does not, New York may yet serve as a model of public participation in the planning process for the rest of the world.

The problem of that site is not just architectural or economic. Eighty-one years earlier—almost to the day—on September 16, 1920, a dynamite charge had blown up outside the Morgan Guarantee Bank on the corner of Wall and Broad Streets, a quarter of a mile away, killing 33 and wounding hundreds. The perpetrators were never found nor were their motives unravelled. The Twin Towers themselves had been attacked before: Moslem fundamentalists exploded a car-bomb in the basement parking garage on February 26, 1993—some fifteen years after they were finished, presumably with the intention of toppling one tower against the other—which would have wrecked a larger area and caused vastly more casualties. The attempt was botched even if it closed the Towers for a couple of weeks. But the second assault worked. Concentration of power invites violence.[2]

Those last attacks brought an old anxiety to the surface: half a century ago E. B. White already sensed it " . . . in everyone's mind. The city, for the first time in its long history, is destructible. A single flight of planes no bigger than a wedge of geese can quickly end this island fantasy . . . In the mind of whatever perverted dreamer might loose the lightning, New York must hold a steady, irresistible charm . . . "[3]

Now that White's prophesy has been so flamingly fulfilled, there are complaints from the worried workers in the higher reaches of the Sears Tower in Chicago, which succeeded the World Trade Center as the world's highest building and was in turn overtaken by the Petronas Towers in Kuala Lumpur. It is also rumored that plans for the forthcoming champion in the "world's tallest building" stakes, which had been projected at 7 South Dearborn Street in Chicago (doubling the height of the Eiffel Tower), may have been abandoned. Nevertheless, in February 2003, work started on an alternative tallest building, the World Finance Center in Pudong, Shanghai (p. 221), its design modified by an addition of 32 meters to make it, at 460 meters, the current title holder when it is complete. In July, 2003 it was announced that yet another champion tower to a height as yet undisclosed is to be built in 2004 on the sands of Dubai; it has been contracted to Skidmore Owings and Merrill, who once held the record with the Chicago Sears Tower.

In London, the construction of the glass-faced obelisk or needle (nicknamed "the shard") at London Bridge, which promises to be the tallest building in Europe, at 313 meters, has been approved. Recent planning enquiries have pushed the demand for licenses to build a number of other high rises in London. In spite of all the brave words about the inevitability of these—or other—skyscrapers, that September morning catastrophe has thrown a shadow over the investment value of any future height champion. Perhaps only hindsight can suggest that it was not prudent to concentrate power intensely in very tall buildings which take on a symbolic function—that, after all, is the bait for violence. Terrorism has already had another short-term impact on the physical environment all over the world. The growth of barriers in the expectation of suicide attacks puts another obstacle between institutions and the public they are supposed to serve. This has also prompted rulers to put the various political and economic "summit" meetings beyond the reach of potential bombers, as well as the anti-globalization gatherings which have become increasingly crowded, noisy, and violent, so that our leaders no longer have the opportunity for those smiley walk-abouts with hand-shaking and baby-kissing which nourished public relations. These restrictions may limit the usefulness of such expensive jamborees to their participants.

Whatever the fate of projected skyscrapers, the world population has continued to grow and emigration from the countryside to the cities and from poorer countries to the richer has not slowed. This will increase pressure on both urban work- and housing space, high or low rise, high or low density, all over the world. The building stock has been sporadically decreased by destruction—particularly of housing—where dangerous splinters have broken off the deceptively homogeneous fabric of global civilization: central Africa and the Balkans have fragmented further, Kabylia has rebelled against pan-Arab Algeria, and other separatist nationalist movements—in Africa, the Crimea, and Spain, in Southeast Asia, on the Pacific Rim—have proliferated. Splintering fury and factional conflict contrast with weak political involvement in two of the oldest and most powerful democracies, the United States and Britain. In their last national elections, each of them has registered the lowest voter turnout in their histories—about half of the electorate—which confirms the recurrent accounts of political and economic alienation in such 'developed countries'.

Yet nothing has altered the status or context of world cities in the five years since this book was finished—nor has anything substantial been done to mitigate, let alone resolve the problems I had outlined. People still require safe, easily accessible, and interconnected spaces, but motorized traffic demands increasing road surface and parking lots which cut swathes from the city fabric. Traffic and transport are a big factor in the emission of greenhouse gases moreover—and they are entirely dependent on oil. The politics of oil may indicate one way to read our situation. Its concentration in specific regions has swollen selective pockets: the rulers of Iraq and Iran, the sultans—of Brunei, of Qatar and Oman, the emirs of the Gulf States and the royals of Saudi Arabia; these last converted some of their oil-dollars into missionary activity, exporting their particular Wahabi home-brand of militant fundamentalism to Egypt and Afghanistan to fuel the Al-Quaida terrorists; it has enriched the oil barons of Texas even more. Houston and Dubai (in the United Emirates) are among the cities with the highest incomes in the world, and they are cities which are growing quickly, as is al-Kuwait, the homonymous capital of the emirate. Its victim status in the first Gulf War has only been a glitch in its growth. It remains the personal realm of its emir, while Houston, though it was the metropolis of the President of the United States whose commitment to the oil-and-gas lobby is a matter of general knowledge, has become the fourth city in the USA, as well as its second port.

The Houston city fathers seem to harbor the ambition to make it into a world city, like London, New York, Tokyo. Although I have (I hope consistently) avoided any temptation to forecast, I might break my rule here and venture to guess that they will not succeed. My skepticism can be reduced to a question of metaphor. The fabric of Houston, it seems to me, has none of the figurative characteristics required for such a role. It has no kind of center—fixed, as in London or Mexico—or mobile, as in New York. Being set on fairly level ground, it also has no feature—river or mountain range—which might suggest an edge condition. Even its lakes and coastline or its extended suburbs that stretch to Galveston Bay are too far from the main inhabited area (and likely to remain so in the foreseeable future) to provide such a reference.

All this was illustrated for me last time I visited it. I wished to reach a museum, well known to anyone in the world with the slightest interest in art, and gave its address to the cab driver who picked me up at my hotel. He took the address confidently and delivered me to the Galleria, a rather nasty piece of real estate development, a suburban shopping mall (just outside the loop, the inner ring-road) masquerading as an urban feature. He was surprised, too, that I would not accept it as fair exchange for the museum. That, he explained to me, is where *all* foreign tourists wanted to be taken—my reluctance seemed mere caprice to him.

I have not visited Houston since the annex of the Museum of Fine Arts doubled its volume, but I doubt if even that noble building can make much of an impact on the existing structure. If I now gave a taxi driver the Museum address, I might well do better, but there is no guarantee that I would.[4] Museums, churches, universities, municipal halls, law courts— Houston has had all such institutions in appropriate, even generous quantities. Its hospitals are some of the most extensive and best-equipped in the world. But none of them are so grouped as to provide the city with a heart; it does not even have the kind of surrogate, electric pacer that the Strip provides for Las Vegas. By now, I suspect, its fabric has developed so extensively that no insertion can perform the animating trick. In any case, the city remains, in spite of any later developments, based on one industry—energy—and especially on oil. Its economy is therefore too closely tied to the fluctuations of oil prices to support civic cohesion.

Though it cannot act as its "heart", Houston has a kind of downtown, a cluster of high-rise office buildings. The streets between them tend to be underpopulated because many of the buildings are interconnected by underground passages which are as much part of the private, the "armed" environment as the luxurious, but security-guarded lobbies of the sky-scrapers. Houston has a wretched climate in the summer, as humid and stifling as any in the United States, and it may be argued that such air-conditioned streets are an essential for its operation. Yet Montreal, which has a climate almost as forbidding—if cold rather than hot—has also developed a system of underground streets in stark contrast to the

Houston ones. They connect points on the public transport system, are only policed like a normal street, and like normal streets are lined by retail outlets. Though sheltered, they even offer a certain amount of entertainment.

Houston has no planning constraints. High-rise buildings have pushed up wherever a developer thought fit (and/or profitable) to build one, usually sticking out of the sea of two- or three-story sprawl. Sprawl and skyscraper coexist uneasily in brutal juxtaposition. Since public transport is fragmentary, the siting of skyscrapers in the street pattern is unimportant. For several years in the early 'nineties the most popular soap opera in the world, *Dallas*, was played out in such high-rises and in the exurban mansions of the oil-drilling, helicopter-driving (since cars cannot circulate easily in such cities—certainly not at rush hour) magnates of a smaller Texan city. Its configuration, which served as a setting for (and metaphor of) the way the cash-nexus overcomes the most powerful loyalties of blood and kin held up a fascinating, if distorting, mirror of our society to us. I use the slightly anachronistic term exurban advisedly.[5] It was coined half a century ago and has been rather neglected since—but still seems useful to me. It describes those mansion dwellers who occupy land well beyond the suburbs, beyond the taxing power of any local government (at least in the US), and require—on occasion—a helicopter to reach their office in a mid-town high-rise. At the time, the bulk of that group were various kinds of communication-wallahs. Though it remains accurate locationally—to describe those who live beyond the suburbs—the group now has a very different vocational and social make-up, composed as it is of venture bankers, currency brokers, and bond dealers; if it still has its ratio of communication wallahs, they are now mostly computer specialists, some of whom tend anyway to live in restricted, widely dispersed colonies (gated suburbs, in effect) with their own campuses. They rarely need to come into town.

But I am more concerned with the physical structure of exurbia than with its social mix. The texture of exurbia thins out gradually as it moves further from its suburban hinterland, so that it becomes an unregulated green belt. It has no visible or legally determined boundary, and is a loose network of large houses in extensive grounds, even estates; among them are golf courses, country clubs, and private woodland. Since it is quite unregulated, suburbia seeps into it gradually. The motor for this movement is not simply the population increase but the constant deterioration of suburban infrastructure (particularly its road surface). As depopulated city centers are abandoned by beggars and petty criminals, who move to the suburbs following the population on which they prey, so the suburbanites move further out, impinging on *exurbs*. Something like this has even happened in the case of the Philadelphia Main Line, which had been the exclusive preserve of WASP exurbanites at one time, but has gradually become a byword for suburban development and taken on a definite ethnic—if not a social—mix.

Such growth has been constant and gradual; withdrawal or shrinkage has been rare in our time, and the invasion of exurbia by suburbia will merely remove it yet further from the city center until it begins to edge towards the exurbia of a neighboring town—at least in North America. This seems to be happening already in the case of Baltimore and Washington. And yet the shapeless sprawl has not led to the formation of that continuous conurbation which the futurologists foretold. It almost seems as if there were some atavistic drawing power in every urban nucleus which maintains its dominance against the sprawling odds.

The Baltimore-Washington case may be crucial. The particular status of Washington is displayed by its powerful central configuration of public buildings around the Mall and on the banks of the Potomac, which form the largest cluster of monumental buildings and spaces in the United States. The Potomac is the border of the Federal district, though not of the conurbation, and it is an essential limiting feature. The capital should therefore have absorbed Baltimore which, though bigger and more populous, has a much more modest monumental downtown (its Cathedral, Washington Column, etc.), as well as a university campus and a newly developed "leisure center" around the old harbor. Extended though this tripartite complex may be, it is sufficiently strong to give central Baltimore a definite identity, which the sprawl of suburbia and exurbia has not stifled.

Still, the exurban sprawl on the East Coast and around the Great Lakes is restrained compared to the new suburbs of the South and the Southwest of the United States where a city like Phoenix covers (at any rate administratively) an area larger than Los Angeles. Los Angeles, for all its canyons and ridges, has nearly seven times the population of Phoenix. Sprawl, with its direct impact on traffic levels and consequent pollution, impinges relatively little on the structure of the land in North America, whose great luxuries (as I have been insisting) are wide, open spaces and cheap oil. It does not provide a good model for Europe or Asia, where densities are sometimes extremely high, arable land at a premium and oil highly taxed.

The abandoned industrial buildings and the disused railway-shunting yards that abound in many European and American cities do not seem very attractive to most developers, who want to build new and build uniform—and if they can, build high. Brown sites, as they are now called, are considered by many authorities to be the essential staple of growth in many a large city—but often involve conflicts with or between previous owners. Such sites may be irregular and older buildings on them may attract conservationist enthusiasm; for all these reasons, developers have contributed heavily to the destruction of landscape and of arable land— and will go on doing so unless inducements are offered them to consider brown alternatives.

The adaptation of disused industrial buildings—warehouses, department stores, factories—into flatted dwellings started in New York, in the nineteen-fifties. It is now general in North America and in some European cities, and has generated the "loft" model which combines the advantages of a central urban location with uncluttered expanses of floor area. It is still considered chic. But larger-scale adaptation of existing industrial equipment and even whole "brown sites" has not really followed. In fact when two European students of mine visited the City Engineer's office in Philadelphia (where loft living had not really caught on) to inquire about a reuse of industrial buildings policy, they were met with incomprehension. The city had no such policy then, nor did it adopt one until much later when its administration also started to rehabilitate abandoned city properties for low-cost housing. The European situation is rather different—in this matter at least. Rotterdam and Hamburg have large areas of derelict harbor installations which are being integrated gradually into the existing fabric.

In France, Lille has made a bid to become a new European metropolis, a communications super-link on the vastly improved, speedy intercity railway, but there seems to have been a metaphor slippage. The old center, upgraded heavily in the nineteenth century (especially after the Franco-Prussian war of 1870), has been overwhelmed by a miniature instant Houston-by-design which seems to have had limited appeal. In any case, the link does not appear to have attracted as much activity as its backers hoped—at least in part because—since 1989—the railway center of Europe has moved sharply eastward. But the brown sites of Northern Italy have set the pattern for a different kind of management. The Pirelli tire-manufacturing company, who moved their works (the Bicocca) from a large site to the north of Milan, staged a planning competition for its reuse which was won by the Milan office, Gregotti Associates, in 1986/7. A number of other architects, including some of the competitors, were awarded contracts for buildings within the plan. The conditions had stipulated mixed use, and the projects included a new university complex specializing in scientific subjects, a theater suitable for opera which could house one of the world's great companies, La Scala (while its own theater is being rebuilt), as well as a number of public and private offices whose employees would be accommodated in the many housing developments both inside and outside the development area. There are a park and sports facilities. Most of this development has already been built and is occupied, and the university has awarded degrees. The Pirelli company has kept some office space for its headquarters, as well as experimental laboratories, and the project includes a technical innovation—an energy and heat-producing plant using controlled oxygen and hydrogen fusion—which began operating in the summer of 2001. Unfortunately, the covered market building that was originally part of the proposal got lost in the course of development.

The Milanese project is the result of the determination on the part of the main landowner, Pirelli, to develop a profitable scheme on land they owned that would also provide a civic service and act as excellent if indirect publicity. The plan does not aim to rival—or even deflect—the old center, but is very much its satellite, almost in the sense in which Ebenezer Howard used the term. In spite of the chronic political instability of the Italian central authorities, the development has had the decisive backing of local government.

A very different turn of events has created more threatening satellites in three old cities of which I wrote earlier: Paris and La Défense (pp. 223 ff), London and Docklands (pp. 227 ff.), followed by Shanghai and Pudong, the new commercial development on the other side of the Huangpu river (pp. 221 ff.). In each case a large group of high-rise buildings is set outside the central historic zone; and each time a local or central government has to provide a heavy subsidy in the form of infrastructure and/or generous tax waivers as well as—in the case of London Docklands (the only one involving a brown site)—the redemption of developer bankruptcy. The justification of such—sometimes vast—expenditure of public money is more employment, higher revenue from increased property values, and the prestige which emulating the "Manhattan model" seems to confer on the city which adopts it. In the particular case of London this has led—since the book was published—to a spate of projects for very high-rise buildings not apparently related to the existing street pattern nor to the configuration of the already overburdened public transport system.

The 1997 change of government in Britain promised restraint on private profiteering, the restoration of public services and of local administration to London (the one promise which was certainly maintained), but instead of returning London's reconstituted authority to the alienated County Hall at Westminster, the new mayor was shunted off to a rather disagreeable circular box tucked in under Tower Bridge. The mayor has now declared his enthusiasm for the coming high-rises, though there are rumors that some form of policy is to be adopted by his administration. In particular, it is said that the building of high-rise office space is to be linked to subsidized, low-rental (and not high-rise) housing. As a short-term financial measure, London has introduced a congestion charge, a tax on automobile entry into the city center—the first one in any large city. It has been an unqualified success financially, and it has reduced inner-city crowding to a remarkable degree. In a parallel development, more of the center is also being closed to vehicular traffic: particularly, in 2003, Trafalgar Square.

Such restrictions should be balanced by an improvement in public transport. That, in Britain, depends on central government which seems to have decided that transport should be a business and not a public service—which is out of tune with the rest of Europe. Meanwhile the projects for which developers seek licenses have entailed a series of public inquiries which should certainly promote more debate about the city—if carried out openly enough. They are standard procedure in Britain, though the recent one about a fifth terminal proposed at Heathrow Airport has turned out to be notoriously long (and therefore expensive) and has ended ambiguously. A business-friendly government is therefore gesturing to developers about limiting future planning inquiries so as to make them more favorable and both cheaper and quicker—and so taking most of the debate out of the public domain. Because analogous inquiries in the United States are more limited (and their character differs from state to state), American projects do not need to pass through quite such a mangle; objections to development are sometimes improvised therefore—and have on occasion (as in the case of Washington Square) been very effective.

No inquiry at all was needed for the decision to develop Pudong. The central Chinese government decided to make it a control-free and tax-privileged Special Enterprise Zone, just as the Conservative government of Mrs. (now Lady) Thatcher in Britain exempted Canary Wharf in Docklands from planning restrictions by offering its builders large tax benefits. Shanghai had been a small country town until the East India Company made its base there between 1750 and 1760. It was then planned through the nineteenth century as a series of strips, stretching westward from the Huangpu river, each "owned" as a concession by one of the Imperial powers (America, Britain, France, Germany). It became the largest town in China before the conflict with Japan—and remained that, though its population had been gently falling since about 1995. Its new prosperity led to the upgrading of the People's Square—once a parade-ground—which now has a National Museum (its contents moved from an older building on the Bund), and a swish new Opera House, as well as the dowdy but forbidding Municipality building. Across the river was Pudong, a stretch of market farmland.

Pudong was given development status and a planning competition was held in 1992. Had any one of the projects submitted been adopted, I suspect that the result would have been preferable to what did in fact happen: traffic and sanitary engineers laid out vast roadways above ground, and equally capacious drains below, while the "left-over" land was sold off to developers, each one of whom has put up detached object-buildings surrounded by roadway and wasteland. More of them will follow, making Pudong a city with no fabric.

Wide roadways are essential in China; some statisticians foresee a tenfold increase in car numbers over the next decade. They will be supplied by a growing Chinese automobile industry, and the consequence of that, a Chinese automobile lobby, is a really frightening prospect. What it will do to the cities in terms of pollution and traffic blocks is hard to imagine. Meanwhile China is building office and housing accommodation everywhere and on a vast scale.

If Pudong is Manhattan on the Huangpu, much of more recent building in the older sections of Shanghai resembles Houston, with high-rise apartment blocks sprouting here and there among the low-built housing areas, the result of the haphazard and sometimes capricious policy changes of the Communist Party. In the early days of the regime high-rise communes were built in Beijing and Shanghai, but housing remained scarce everywhere. During the "Great Leap Forward" various low-cost and autarchic building methods were tried. They produced instant and dangerous slums. Shanghai, the birthplace of the Communist Party, was privileged and some of the best housing, using inner courtyard planning (in Fuanguanong and on Tianmu and Minhang Roads) was built just before the Cultural Revolution which coincided with another great population move into the towns. Experiments in light panel construction of the kind tried in Europe about the same time produced further high-rise dwellings (especially in Beijing and Shanghai—North Caoxi Road). As the regime was generally hostile to attempts at "refined" planning, a large crop of vast and uniform groups of parallel slab-blocks were built in the second half of the 1970s. The fall of the Gang of Four brought a renewal of selective housing standards and a few ingenious projects. Chinese architects and planners, who suffered like all professionals during the Cultural Revolution, did not begin to emerge as a force until about the year

2000, and since the introduction of commodity building there, urbanism and housing standards have been left to the mercies of the market,[6] while much capital is generally available in profits from forms of licit as well as more or less illicit trading. Investment in immobile property is a traditional Chinese way of securing it.

China is certain to pass through financial upheavals—no prophetic gift is required to realize that entry into the World Trade Organization and the freeing of imports will trounce the Chinese economy, particularly at the lowest level, that of subsidized farming. A spate of bankruptcies in recently de-nationalized state industries will bring about a corresponding rise in unemployment levels. This may entail a shift in the political system, which may—or may not—be peaceful. Economic journalists everywhere have long been writing about it, and the crisis is in fact already beginning. The spate of public executions for corruption and drug-dealing is merely a symptom of its unfolding and the Party's determination to hold on to central power.

In Shanghai or Guanzhou, and of course in Shenzhen, the figure of the new Chinese city may be emulating Houston rather than Manhattan, but Beijing, where the center has not been distorted yet, is modeled after the Parisian "basin" (above, p. 223). Beijing has at its venerable center the Forbidden City, with Tiananmen Square to the south and Beihai Park to the north. They form a really powerful complex which is the city's heart, and no very high building is allowed too close as a matter of planning policy settled long ago (above, p. 147) and reinforced in 2003. Moreover, the awarding of the 2008 Olympic Games to Beijing has thrown the city authorities into a frenzy of enterprise. The main sporting events will be in the northeastern section of the city which includes the Beijing University campus. Nearly nine billion dollars (on current estimates) is to be spent on new rapid transport, on reducing carbon dioxide emission, on purifying the water supply, on clearing the reservoirs, and on nearly doubling the green areas. This will certainly affect the urban fabric—though some skepticism about any long-term benefits to the city may be legitimate.

The very size of Beijing suggests that the effect of the games on the city fabric may only be marginal. The planning decisions of the immediate post-war period had respected the very low-rise center, even if the road patterns were geared to traffic and height increases, but the growth of the building stock threatens to overwhelm it. Two or three years ago central Beijing was still supplied by fresh-food markets, though as the city has mushroomed, the supplies seem to be cut off; even if they were to be maintained, I suspect the district will become museified. The other capital of a planned economy, Moscow, has an even more powerful central core:

its fortified palaces and cathedrals crowning the Kremlin hill, the vast Red Square stretching below it, and the embanked river winding past show the autocratic nature of the power that created it. During the Stalin regime the dominance of this nucleus was reinforced by the concentric nature of several plans commissioned by the government as Moscow's population trebled in the decade after the Revolution. It has been growing since, but the six skyscraper spires I mentioned earlier (pp. 138 f.) still emphasized the centrality of the Kremlin. That Stalinist network formed such a powerful structure that the implanting of "Houston" elements—haphazardly-sited high-rises decked out in more or less post-modern fancy dress—had little impact on it, and its stability closely reflects the social and political reality of the new Russian state.

The implosion of the Soviet Union was, in part, provoked by bureaucratic gridlock of which the central regulation of urban—as well as economic—planning was a part. Release from central regulation may seem good in itself to some Eastern Europeans, as well as to some Chinese, but such perceptions change as quickly as any fashion, and the chaotic growth of Moscow or Beijing, Shenzhen or Kiev will invite its own reaction.

It is a tragedy of our times that the seesaw between centrally regulated planning and a free-for-all growth (with its occasional crash) plows into city fabric, allowing only contractors or speculators to be the winners. The extreme resolution of this dilemma—to make every city an independent economic entity (even minting its own currency)—was advocated some time ago by Jane Jacobs.[7] Such an extreme measure may not be practicable or even effective, but there are many smaller steps that any relatively autonomous city can take without provoking state intervention. One of them may be a quasi-protectionist market policy. This does not demand any legally unsustainable ban on food imports, which may run counter to international free trade agreements, but the establishment of markets where everything sold would have to be made or grown within a set distance from the city center: indeed it is done in several cities in the United States, and I have seen the locality of produce advertised more or less discreetly in France and Italy. Regulating the "place of origin" label—as has always been done with wines (and is now done with olive oil) anyway—should be a relatively simple matter.

Demand for locally grown food is allied to a similar pressure for organic farming. Customer insistence on the supply of organic food became urgent about 1960, when it could be bought only in a few specialized shops, though some religious societies—the Anthroposophists in Europe, the Amish and Mennonites in the United States—had always rejected machine and chemical husbandry. The demand increased dramatically as information about pesticide residues on fruit and vegetables became more widely available. Small markets were soon opened in Britain and in the United States to provide only "organic" foodstuffs. Big supermarkets soon saw it as a new source of profit, and once the corporate multinationals get hold of such a matter, it is compromised since marketing promotes the standardizing of food production, while intercontinental food transport promotes monocultures (which some economists see as the indirect producer of sporadic famines). It incidentally puts constant, heavy pressure on air and overland truck routes, swelling the hothouse-gas cover. When supplies are brought from countries where the definition of what constitutes "organic" varies, the "organic" label becomes virtually meaningless since there is no agreement about which pesticides or additives can be used. A "local produce" line inevitably soon appeared in corporate supermarkets.

Yet some crops can only be grown and processed in specific regions: rice, some fruit, spices, wines, tea, and coffee. Though its consumption has been increasing worldwide, coffee futures, to take one instance, dropped in about 2000 to their lowest price for more than a decade and continue to fall. This cannot be blamed on any multinational corporation, but rather on the decision of the World Bank to promote huge new coffee plantations in Vietnam, turning that country into the second-biggest producer in the world and so undermining African and South American growers—which last have turned to their trusty (and much more profitable) crop, coca leaf, in turn depressing the street price of cocaine in North America. It was not what the World Bank intended, but illustrates how the delicate balance of the world economy can be easily upset, and also reinforces the case for local control over agricultural production.[8]

The association of "organic" agriculture and "sustainable" ecology also translated into a constant pressure by environmental groups that has produced a growing movement among both developers and architects for energy-conscious buildings. This movement also goes back to the nineteen-sixties. Green Party politics were hardly conceivable then, but various "alternative" technologies—energy from the sun and from the wind, heat storage, natural ventilation, recycling of water and of waste—were all being explored at that time, though as technical devices and with no thought of integrating them into the design process. All this occurred in the absence of any governmental or even local directives on such matters. Architects in Austria and Germany and in the United States—notably the groups SITE and "Jersey Devil"—produced the first essays in application which turned the technology into architecture, so that a number of younger architects realized that alternative energy sources could also inspire new formal inventions. Perhaps the most influential was the Argentinian-born Emilio Ambasz, whose first successful major building, the Fukuoka prefecture in Japan (begun in 1989), has become a kind of flagship for this tendency. By then major design offices took up the cause: Norman Foster's Commerzbank tower (see p. 240) is the most conspicuous example of it so far, though I think it is important to stress that however green your building, it may still not be making much of a contribution to the lay and texture of the city.

Yet seemingly minor issues, such as the "green" adaptation of high-rise buildings, do show how small-scale pressure can work against corporate grasping and government indifference. Many such small steps will be needed before citizens will be able to reclaim their environment, some of which I have mentioned in the body of the book, steps such as the increasing municipal control of such "facilities" as local sports teams or banks or television stations—at least in the United States. City authorities can buy and become the more or less commercial landlords of existing housing stock—something of the kind is proposed in Philadelphia—and it could own and manage the sort of markets for locally grown produce that I have proposed.[9]

It will require many steps for local government to assert itself against central authority. A strong local administration provides one possible way in which citizens can regain control of the urban fabric. This will only be possible if we can convince those whom we elect to represent us that the form of the city, however changeable, is not the product of impersonal forces. It is also not merely a matter of taste and 'aesthetics' which can be left to underemployed royals or to ministers of culture, but is built into the city's economic life. When citizens are asked their views on such matters in planning inquiries and investigations, it is essential that they express them and examine the way in which proposals reinforce or weaken their own vision of the city.

Their views often conflict and can be circumvented—and usually are. Such discussion is a political matter, of course. A final decision is often in any case dictated by central, not local government, which may or may not take note of them. Of course, it does not obtain in "tied communities" like Seaside or Celebration which I discussed earlier, nor in gated suburbs generally, where politics are replaced by management, and where a real public space of disagreement and even quarrel has no place. Such a space is not required in the settlements proposed by the New Urbanists. In fact, the remarkable feature of the gated suburbs is that they are, in a sense, cut off from the open, the liberal society whose citizens we all seem to be, and

therefore assume the characteristics of a closed one. In many cases, pur-
chasers willingly sign an agreement which alienates their civic privileges
within the gates.

My emphasis on civic pressure must not obscure the importance of
asserting locality and autonomy politically. One of the few districts in
England which had a turnout very much higher than the national average
in the lethargic 2001 elections also had a winning no-party candidate, a
physician with a local practice who was fighting against the indifference
of the major political parties to a local issue—the closure of a hospital
which most of the constituents wanted maintained—by the central
authority.[10] It is often on such local issues rather than arguments of high
finance or national foreign policy that electors sense that they control
their own fate—and by aggregation, influence that of the country.

That vote was cast against government policy for a particular reason—
and most pressure groups are negative in their motivation, which is the
urbanists' problem. It is always easy to unite against some grievance—but
difficult, sometimes harrowingly so—to form alliances in favor of a clear
policy without crippling it by compromise. This has recently been shown
by the painfully extended negotiations to implement the 1997 Kyoto
treaty to limit atmospheric pollution. In mid-2001 a partial agreement
lowered the already modest figures originally set, and now it is a dead
letter. Or look at the report on urban renewal sponsored by the British
Labour government just before its victorious re-election in 2001. Its
recommendations (called "objectives") were couched in a monitory
tone—part prophecy, part command: "There will be substantial increase
in recycling ... There will be urban repopulation ... There will be
increased quality of life ... (By 2021) England will have become the
leading international location to acquire urban development skills ..."
Which is fine as a pious hope, but the motor on which the report relies for
achieving these aims is improvement in design.[11] Even remembering the
"Bilbao" effect (p. 237) whose benefits have gradually weakened and the
less spectacular Manchester/Salford one, to propose "a design-led renaissance of British cities" begs the question of when design is good and who
decides on its quality. That there is no agreement is clear from the number
of cases where buildings which some think beautiful and adventurous are
judged unsuitable or offensive by many citizens, and often by planning
authorities. It is difficult to see how any form of urban renewal could
be arrived at without a powerful economic and political struggle—yet
politics do not come into the report.

It is essential, of course, that citizens express their views and scrutinize
proposals in order to consider how they might reinforce or weaken their

own vision of the city. Even if their views are then set aside, debate and disagreement are essential if the urban fabric is to be returned to them. Loud voices are one weapon that may convince those we elect to represent us that the form of the city—however changeable—is not subject to impersonal forces. That is why the metaphoric power of the city as social representation seems to me the comment in the book which most needs reasserting. Some of my readers and critics found me too inflexible in the application of principle. In London I was repeatedly told that there was, after all, no harm in the "London Eye" which I had treated rather harshly earlier (p. 149). Some of those who see "no harm" in the giant Ferris wheel and admire it as an "elegant structure" will agree that building is not just a matter of "function plus aesthetics" but must in some way be seen as a representation (and therefore also a comment) on the ways of society. It is not, after all, an isolated object but must be considered within its physical context so as to appreciate the metaphoric implication of a tourist attraction towering over Parliament, much as the new black-glass Trump Tower in New York looms above the United Nations headquarters.

I invite my readers to take the next step with me, and agree that the metaphoric faculty is essential to the way we occupy the world; metaphors work so well in language precisely because they are part of our innate conceptual equipment. Only metaphor can offer us the clues to negotiate with our physical environment. It is the business of architecture—and to some extent of the other arts also—to captivate and nourish that faculty. To neglect or frustrate it is to invite the sort of discredit that has been the part of developers and their architects in the popular imagination and the popular press, and is encapsulated by the label "modern monstrosity" often applied to any sizable new building.

The metaphoric function has little or nothing to do with an aesthetic one, since we experience its power both constantly and unconsciously in our negotiation with our environment, as we expect a pattern of meaning in the sounds made by fellow humans. They may sing us beautiful songs or scream vulgar abuse at us, but we construe man-made sound whenever we hear it and we experience it rationally, taking into account what the memory holds. Unlike "aesthetics" or even by implication "design quality" (a managerial term for the same thing), metaphor can be a matter for reasonable discussion. We may never be able to agree whether the Pentagon building in Washington is beautiful or ugly, but we can certainly discuss, with some hope of consensus, what its all-too-solid presence on a vast parking lot surrounded by security suggests about its place in the city fabric, or indeed what its irrational geometry might convey to the viewer.

Take the London Eye again—because it is both recent and shows this conflict clearly. The vaunted elegance of the structure is that of a much enlarged bicycle wheel, to which the cabins—called "pods"—are attached. I might take nugatory pleasure at the lightness of the structure, at the fine surface of the steel and the neatness of the joints, at its smooth movement. But such minor satisfactions seem to me neutralized by the knowledge—which may be merely conceptual, though in my case it was certainly experiential—of the heavy bulk of concrete that had to be poured into the river bed so as to support it. The lightness of the visible is in disagreeable contrast to the known or deducible, if concealed. Even more disturbing is the consideration that an object appropriately associated with a light, temporary structure at a fairground has been turned into a semi-permanent feature of the monumental city center. What is to be done with the bulk of the foundations if it is removed? Will they just stay on the river bed?

As the Eye was beginning to operate in London, a fair to celebrate the millennium was opened in the Place de la Concorde in Paris. It was just off the axis that joins the Palais-Bourbon, the seat of the Chamber of Deputies, and the Madeleine, one of the largest Parisian churches—and its most visible feature was a Ferris wheel, brightly coloured and with none of the pretensions to high-tech elegance of its big brother in London. But its relatively modest scale and its patently temporary nature never did cause the sort of metaphoric unease I still experience at Westminster. In spite of some opposition, the Mayor of Paris ordered its dismantling which began on January 24, 2002.

The fairground effect of the wheel has been emphasized by recent developments in London. County Hall has been hired for various purposes—most conspicuously for an exhibition of freakish art-objects collected by the advertising agent who orchestrated Mrs Thatcher's election triumphs (embalmed animals, disembowelled automobiles, giant portraits of serial murderers, madonnas painted in elephant turds, etc.). As an expression of contempt for the authority once housed there, it seems to me almost too explicit.

I ended my book originally hoping that I had made some contribution to the way we assess the city and its institutions—its fabric and all its power over us. Yes, the city can never be a static formal organization—it is in constant movement, at present in particularly violent movement. But in that process of change, we must not consider ourselves the passive flotsam which the impersonal swirling of great forces can toss about as it will. In so far as we are rational creatures, we can exercise our resistance as voters, as consumers, as agitators and as publicists. Let the swirl not be quite so smooth and fluid. Reason can make little dams, can staunch or divert the flow. Or, if you like, we can stop the smooth grinding of the managerial wheels. Remember the old saw: it is only the squeaky wheel that gets the oil. So, get in the way.

But all that remains negative. Taking thought and giving voice loudly and publicly can still be a powerful weapon and can operate at many levels. Never mind your political candidates' views on abortion and gay rights—or any other factional interest, however important. Quiz him on his stand about matters of city texture and ask him if he knows that the fabric of the city is a metaphor for the society which you and he or she want to bring about. Demand to see any urban project, and consider its implications for energy consumption, for retail trade, for the provision of public space, or its adequacy for demonstrations and for public gatherings, not just for parks for leisure activities. Demand mixed use, and space for urban markets and urban farming in conjunction with housing. Insist that rapid urban transport be a public service, not a business enterprise.

Many such issues have surfaced in the (often acrimonious) discussions about the various different futures being thrust at Ground Zero in Lower Manhattan, the site opened by the catastrophe of nine/eleven when terrorists cruelly but unwittingly reaffirmed the metaphoric power of building. Many voices oppose the absolute power of the cash-nexus over the rebuilding. The return to the skyline of a form that would proclaim the developer's right to draw the maximum profit from the site would do just that. They therefore urge the claim of a memorial to commemorate the dead—and perhaps more positively—the assertion of civic pride and public utility over private gain. Because Manhattan remains the world capital, these debates and their outcome will matter beyond New York to the whole world.

Notes

Finding Some Place in All the Space

1. Joseph Rykwert, *The Idea of a Town*.
2. Italo Calvino, *Le Città Invisibili*, p. 50 ". . . Anche le città credono d'essere opera della mente o del caso, ma né una né l'altro bastano a tener su le loro mura."
3. Plato, *Republic* 4.422e. Also Kratinos in *Comicorum Atticorum Fragmenta*, ed. Theodor Kock, 1:29 (frag. 56). Czesław Bielecki has based his treatment of urban form on this notion in his *Gra w Miasto* (The Town Game) (Warsaw, 1996).
4. "Toute nation a le gouvernement qu'elle mérite," Joseph (-Marie) de Maistre, *Letter to the Chevalier de Rossi* "on the Constitution of Russia," August 27, 1811, in his *Oeuvres Complètes* (Paris, 1886), vol. 12, p. 57. He adds that this truth, which has cost him a great deal of trouble to arrive at, has the force of a mathematical proposition. However good the law, he adds, it is of no value unless a nation is worthy of it.
5. The primary text on the production of space is Henri Lefebvre's, *The Production of Space*, trans. Donald Nicholson-Smith (Oxford, 1992), pp. 38 f, 68 ff. The plant-city analogy is too common to call for specific reference.
6. "Natura enim in suis operationibus non facit saltum." Perhaps a proverb. First recorded by an antiquarian, Jacques Tissot, reporting on some reputed

giant's bones in 1613, but insistently repeated by Linnaeus, in *Philosophia Botanica,* 2d ed. (Vienna, 1763), sec. 77, pp. 31 ff.

7. Thomas Jefferson, "Notes on the State of Virginia" (of 1785), in *Writings,* ed. Merrill D. Peterson (New York, 1984), p. 291. An explicit recantation in the letter to Benjamin Austin, January 9, 1816 (*Works,* 1984), pp. 1370 f.

8. Emile Durkheim, *The Elementary Forms of the Religious Life,* pp. 24 ff.; Claude Lévi-Strauss, *Tristes Tropiques,* pp. 227 ff.; Claude Lévi-Strauss, *Anthropologie Structurale,* pp. 147 ff.

9. Modified. Hesiod, *Works and Days,* trans. Richard Lattimore (Ann Arbor, Mich., 1959), 1.170 ff.

10. *Critias* 110c–121; *Timaeus* 23d ff. *Laws* 737–60, 848 ff.

11. Pausanias, *The Travels,* X, 4, (i).

12. Herman Kahn and Anthony J. Wiener, *The Year 2000.* The preface is by Daniel Bell. The term "global village" was much used by Marshall McLuhan.

13. Daniel Bell, "The Year 2000—The Trajectory of an Idea," in *Daedalus* 96, no. 3 (summer 1967), 640 ff.

1. How We Got There

1. *Business Cycles* (New York, 1939), p. 177.

2. Jean-Jacques Rousseau, *Les Confessions* (1778), ed. Francis Bouvet, vol. 1, (Paris, 1961), pp. 260 ff.

3. Sir John Sinclair.

4. "The Village Minstrel," ¶107, in *The Early Poems of John Clare,* ed. Eric Robinson and David Powell, vol. 2 (Oxford, 1989), p. 169; and "The Mores," in *John Clare,* ed. Eric Robinson and David Powell (Oxford, 1984), pp. 168 ff.

5. Brian Inglis, *Poverty and the Industrial Revolution,* pp. 86 ff.

6. Oscar Wilde, *A Woman of No Importance,* act 1, in *Works,* ed. G. F. Maine (London, 1948), p. 422.

7. "The Deserted Village," in *The Works of Oliver Goldsmith with a Life and Notes,* vol. 1 (London, 1854), p. 96.

8. Adam Smith, *An Inquiry into the Nature and Causes of the Wealth of Nations,* vol. 1 (Oxford, 1904), p. 3.

9. It really meant artifact in the widest sense: Cicero quotes Cato on the stoic philosophical system: "What has nature, what have artifacts to show that is so well constructed?" (Quid enim aut in natura. . . . aut in operibus manu factis tam compositum . . .). *De Finibus* 3:74. The meaning had so changed in the nineteenth century that the mathematician Andrew Ure could write, ca. 1835: "The most perfect manufacture is that which dispenses entirely with manual labor."

10. Attributed both to Vincent de Gournay, French minister of commerce in 1751, and to François Quesnay, and quoted by Adam Smith, *The Wealth of Nations*.

11. See Pierre Barrière, *La Vie Intellectuelle en France*, pp. 382 ff. Peter Gay, *The Enlightenment*, pp. 347 ff., 493 ff. But see also Fernand Braudel, *The Identity of France*, vol. 2, pp. 378 ff.

12. His criticism of their system in *The Wealth of Nations*, vol. 2, pp. 292 ff.

13. Jacques Vaucanson (catalogue of Exhibition), Musée National des Techniques (Paris, 1983), passim; Vaucanson's looms are nos. 55–60; Jacquard's, nos. 61–64; Siegfried Giedion, *Mechanization Takes Command* (New York, 1955), pp. 34 ff.

14. "Mill" from the Latin *molere*, to grind; the Indo-European root is **mar*. But variants of *molino* early produced "mylne," corrupted to "mill." On the introduction of the windmill, see Jean Gimpel, *La Révolution Industrielle du Moyen Age*, pp. 11 ff.

15. Simon Schama, *Landscape and Memory*, pp. 162 ff.

16. Schama, pp. 173 ff.

17. Bertrand Gille, *Leonardo e Gli Ingegneri del Rinascimento*, pp. 114, 184; the invention is sometimes attributed to Aristotele di Fioravanti and seems to have been first described by Leon Battista Alberti (a distant kinsman) in his *de Re Aedificatoria* 10:11.

18. Martin Kemp, *Leonardo da Vinci*, pp. 232 ff.

19. The effects of Turgot's reform were not immediate, of course; yet by Napoléon's time, the mail coaches were circulating in spite of war operations. F. Braudel, pp. 480 ff.

20. The great seventeenth-century work on Roman roads, *Histoire des Grands Chemins de l'Empire Romain*, by Nicolas Bergier, was given a splendid reprint in Paris in 1728, and another in Brussels in 1736; it is this last edition that Gibbon possessed and used.

21. Terry Coleman, *The Railway Navvies*, pp. 20 ff.

22. M. J. B. Davy, *Aeronautics*, pp. 15 ff, 29 f.

23. William Wordsworth, *The Excursion*, first published in 1814; bk. 8, "The Parsonage," in *Poetical Works*, vol. 6 (London, 1874), pp. 249 ff.

24. Ms. in Halifax Public Library quoted by E. P. Thompson, *The Making of the English Working-Class*, p. 547.

25. First published in Siegfried Giedion, *Space, Time and Architecture*, pp. 125 ff.

26. Although up to May 1851, the duke of Wellington persisted in calling it "the Glass Palace" (in his letters to Lady Salisbury, quoted by Christopher Hobhouse, *1851 and the Crystal Palace*, pp. 177 ff.). But the official "Crystal" was used that same year in the title of *The Crystal Palace, Its Architectural History and Constructive Marvels* (London, 1851) by Peter Berlyn and Charles Fowler.

27. S. G. Checkland, *The Rise of Industrial Society in England, 1815–1885*, pp. 27 ff.

28. William Gilpin, *Observations on the River Wye*, p. 37.
29. Now in the Science Museum, London. But see Stephen Daniels, "Loutherbourg's *Coalbrookdale by Night*," in John Barrell, ed., *Painting and the Politics of Culture*, pp. 195 ff.
30. *The Great Day of His Wrath*, painted in 1851–52 and now in the Tate Gallery. The conversation with his son is quoted by Francis D. Klingender, *Art and the Industrial Revolution*, pp. 132 ff.
31. *Frazer's Magazine*, June 1844; quoted by Andrew Wilton, *Turner in His Time*, p. 233. The two pictures are nos. 377 and 409, in Martin Butler and Evelyn Joll, *The Painting of J. M. W. Turner*. Both are in the National Gallery, London.

2. First Aid

1. Karl Friedrich Schinkel, *The English Journey: Journal of a Visit to France and Britain in 1826*, ed. David Bindman and Gottfried Riemann, pp. 174 ff.
2. Alexis de Tocqueville, *Oeuvres*. vol. 1, pp. 501 ff.
3. "Socialism Utopian and Scientific," in K. Marx and F. Engels, *Collected Works*, vol. 2 (Moscow, 1962), p. 119.
4. *Observations sur l'Architecture*, by M. L'Abbé Laugier (The Hague, 1765), pp. 321 ff.
5. On these and others, see John Hale, *The Civilization of Europe in the Renaissance*, pp. 413 ff.
6. A. R. Sennett, *Garden Cities in Theory and Practice*, pp. 125 ff., 193 ff.
7. The full title gives its flavor: *La Découverte Australe par un Homme Volant ou le Dédale François: Nouvelle Très-philosophique* (Paris, 1781). Sade's exotic utopias were described in *Aline et Valcour, ou le Roman Philosophique: Ecrit à la Bastille un an avant la Révolution de France* (Paris, 1793). 8 vols.
8. *Seine höchst komplizierte Organisation erscheint als Machinerie—die Verzahnungen der Passions sind primitive Analogiebildungen zur Machine in Material der Psychologie.* Walter Benjamin, "Paris, die Haupstadt des XIX Jahrhundert," in *Illuminationen*, p. 187.
9. *The Correspondence of Thomas Carlyle and Ralph Waldo Emerson*, vol. 1 (London, 1888), pp. 308 ff.
10. William Morris, *News from Nowhere*, p. 31.
11. Unlike *outopia eutopia*, ευγενεια is an authentic Greek word, which means nobility of birth, however, not biological perfection.
12. The Oxford English Dictionary also cites it as *Cacotopia*; first used by Jeremy Bentham in 1818 as the imaginary seat of the worst government to be discovered and described.

3. House and Home

1. It is the title of one of his most famous essays in *Illuminationen*, p. 185, which I quoted earlier.
2. For the documentation of housing as a type, see Ulf Dirlmeier et al., eds., *Geschichte des Wohnens*, 5 vols.
3. Jeannot Simmen and Uwe Drepper, *Der Fahrstuhl*, pp. 29 ff.
4. F. Engels, *The Condition of the Working Class in England*, tr. W. O. Henderson and W. H. Chaloner (Oxford, 1958), pp. 47ff.
5. May 13, 1848; quoted by J. H. Clapham, *An Economic History of Modern Britain*, vol. 1, p. 545.
6. James Hole, *The Homes of the Working Classes*, p. 54.
7. An uncritical account by Phebe A. Hanaford, in *The Life of George Peabody*, pp. 124 ff, without mention of the architect.
8. Benjamin Disraeli, Earl of Beaconsfield, *Tancred, or the New Crusade*, vol. 1, pp. 146ff, in *Works*, vol. 15, part 2.
9. George Gilbert Scott, A.R.A., *Remarks on Secular and Domestic Architecture*, pp. 6 ff.
10. Report of the Royal Commission on the Housing of the Working Classes, pp. 19 ff. Quoted in Donald J. Olsen, *Town Planning in London: The Eighteenth and Nineteenth Centuries*, p. 208. Both "slum" and "rookery" (used to describe human habitation) were words of nineteenth-century coinage.
11. Friedrich Engels quoting the Spanish periodical *La Emancipación* of March 16, 1872. Karl Marx and Friedrich Engels, *Collected Works*, vol. 23 (New York, 1988), pp. 329 ff.
12. Quaranta, Cavalier Bernardo, et al., *Napoli e le Sue Vicinanze* (Naples, 1845), vol. 2, pp. 581 ff. Paolo Sica, *Storia dell'Urbanistica. Il Settecento* (Bari, 1981), pp. 197 ff. Italian silk-weaving methods were first emulated or imitated in Britain by the Lombe Brothers of Derby after 1717. Although their works, powered by the River Derwent, could claim to be the first factories, silk throwing and weaving remained a secondary industry and seemed to have no direct impact on later spinning and weaving machinery. *See* Paul Mantoux, *The Industrial Revolution in the Eighteenth Century* (New York, 1961), pp. 192 ff.
13. *See* Christian Devillers and Bernard Huet, *Le Creusot*, pp. 164 ff.
14. Benjamin Disraeli, Earl of Beaconsfield, *Works*, vol. 14 (*Sybil*, part 1), pp. 259 ff.
15. Charles Dickens, *American Notes and Pictures from Italy* (London, nd), pp. 30 ff.
16. *Industrial Housing*, published by the Aldin Company in Bay City, Michigan, in 1918. Quoted by Gwendolyn Wright, in *Building the Dream*, p. 184.

17. Nicholas Bullock and James Read, *The Movement for Housing Reform in Germany and France,* pp. 31, 110 f. I have relied on this book for much information in this chapter.

18. Arthur Raffalovich, *Le Logement de l'Ouvrier et du Pauvre,* pp. 249 ff., 264 f.

19. Nicholas Bullock and James Read, pp. 472 ff.

20. Gwendolyn Wright, *Building the Dream,* pp. 141 ff.

21. The word "urbanize" in English has had the sense of making people more polite and refined; in Cerdá's sense, it appeared in the United States about twenty years after his book was published. However, it did not have the same fortune in England and in the 1920s an English journalist could still call "urbanism" a "new-coined word."

22. Quoted by Françoise Choay, *The Rule and the Model,* p. 236.

23. *Aérodomes, Essai sur un Nouveau Mode de Maisons d'Habitation* was published in Paris in 1865; the only recent reference is in Françoise Choay's *The Modern City,* p. 20.

24. *Le Corbusier, Oeuvres Complètes,* ed. Willi Boesiger, 1924–1934 (Zürich, 1935), pp. 138 ff., 174 ff., 1938–1946 (Zürich, 1946), pp. 44 ff. His version of the linear city is on pp. 66 ff., but he makes no reference to Soria.

25. On the importance of Magnitogorsk for the NEP and Stalin's "industrial revolution," see Isaac Deutscher, *Stalin,* pp. 329 ff. But see also Selim O. Khan-Mahomedov, *Pioneers of Soviet Architecture* (London, 1987), pp. 335 ff., 392; and Andrei Gozak and Andrei Leonidov, *Ivan Leonidov,* pp. 86 ff.

26. Remembered now for having beaten up a prominent Georgian Bolshevik who called him a "Stalinist arsehole." Orlando Figes, *A People's Tragedy,* p. 799.

27. Pierre Patte, *Monumens érigés à la Gloire de Louis XV* (Paris, 1765), pl. 17.

28. See Richard Sennett, *The Fall of Public Man,* pp. 14 ff.

4. Style, Type, and Urban Fabric

1. First published in 1817, it went through many editions.

2. Augustus Welby Pugin, *The True Principles of Pointed or Christian Architecture* (London, 1853), p. 1.

3. Quoted in Klaus Döhmer, *In Welchem Style Sollen Wir Bauen?,* p. 27, n. 150, as being drawn from the *Royal Architectural Institute of Canada Journal* 12 (1835): 159 ff., but as given, the reference cannot be correct.

4. Barry Bergdoll, *Léon Vaudoyer,* p. 207.

5. Published in London, 1851–53, pp. 413, 394, 362. Elaborately illustrated.

6. Charles Parker, *Villa Rustica, Selected from Buildings and Scenes in the Vicinity of Rome and Florence and Arranged for Rural and Domestic Dwellings* (London, 1848). The seventy-two plates were published in sixteen monthly installments in 1832–41 and reprinted.

7. Calvert Vaux, *Villas and Cottages. A Series of Designs* (New York, 1857), p. 19.

8. It was destroyed, in spite of much protest, in 1962. See Alison and Peter Smithson, *The Euston Arch* (London, 1968).

9. *Illustrated London News* (May 4, 1844).

10. Account given in Sir George Gilbert Scott, *Personal and Professional Recollections*, pp. 179, 271 ff.

11. Letter to Hawksworth Fawkes, January 31, 1851, in A. J. Finberg, *The Life of J. M. W. Turner, R. A.*, pp. 430 ff.

12. Perhaps after the mansion flats in Queen Anne's Gate, built in 1875; though, in fact, it is such an eclectic mix that it could almost be considered a non-style.

13. Anonymous ballad, published in the *St. James's Gazette* (December 17, 1881). Quoted from *Richard Norman Shaw* by Sir Reginald Blomfield, R.A. (London, 1940), pp. 34 ff.

14. G. K. Chesterton, *The Man Who Was Thursday, a Nightmare* (London, 1908), p. 10.

15. *Der Städte-Bau nach seinen Künstlerischen Grundsätzen* had a long subtitle and was published in Vienna.

16. The episode is told in detail by H. Allen Brooks, *Le Corbusier's Formative Years*, pp. 200 ff. Corbusier confesses to his disenchantment in *Quand les Cathédrales étaient Blanches* (Paris, 1937), p. 58.

17. See David Harvey, *Condition of Postmodernity*, pp. 276 ff.

18. *Entartung*, almost immediately translated as *Decadence*, an international best-seller by Max Nordau, was published in 1892–93; *The Decline of the West* by Oswald Spengler summed up this attitude; first published (as *Untergang des Abendandes*) in 1918.

19. I am deliberately echoing Serge Guilbaut's title: *How New York Stole the Idea of Modern Art*.

20. See Manfredo Tafuri, *The Sphere and the Labyrinth*, pp. 129 ff.

21. Lines 11 and 12 of *Zone*, a long poem written in 1912. In *Oeuvres Poétiques* (Paris, 1956), pp. 39 ff.

22. Guillaume Apollinaire, *Les Peintres Cubistes: Méditations Esthétiques* (Geneva, 1950; reprint of Paris edition of 1913), fig. 1. Alfred J. Barr, *Picasso: Fifty Years of His Art* (New York, 1946), p. 68; John Richardson, *A Life of Picasso* (New York, 1996), vol. 2, pp. 128 ff. Apollinaire dates it 1909, the other two 1910.

23. The situation was already set out by El Lissitzky and Hans Arp in *Die Kunst-Ismen/Les Ismes de l'Art/The Isms of Art* (Zürich, 1924; reprinted Baden, 1990).

24. Adolf Loos, "Ornament und Erziehung (1924)" in *Trotzdem: 1900–1930* (Vienna, 1931), pp. 200, 205.

25. As in the offensive glib *From Bauhaus to Our House* by Tom Wolfe (New York, 1981).

26. That is where I saw it; others had seen the same one outside Paddington Station; Nigel Rees, *Graffiti Lives O.K.*, p. 37.

27. Norman Mailer, *The Faith of Graffiti* (New York, 1974); quoted in *Vandalism and Graffiti: The State of the Art* by Frank Coffield (London, 1991), p. 64.

5. Flight from the City: Lived Space and Virtual Space

1. Joel Garreau, *Edge City*, p. 452.

2. Kevin Lynch, *The Image of the City*, p. 5.

3. As the word "chip" is being displaced in UK English by "French fries," it has been adopted by the French (pronounced *cheeps*).

4. Kevin Lynch, *What Time Is This Place?* pp. 66 ff.

5. Quoted from a lost play, *The Woman from Boeotia*, by Aulus Gellius, *Noctes Atticae* 3.3.v.

6. "The headquarters city of the League of Nations will be looked upon as the Capital of the world," Major David Davies, M.P., "Constantinople as the G.H.Q. of Peace," in *The Architectural Review*, November 1919, p. 148. (Special issue commemorating the signing of the Versailles treaty and largely devoted to an account of the Andersen-Hébrard proposal.)

7. Corbusier's own view and explanation of the scheme are presented in the book *Une Maison—Un Palais*, "A la recherche d'une Unité Architecturale" (Paris, 1928). See Hannes Meyer's scheme in Claude Schnaidt, *Hannes Meyer*, pp. 22 ff.

8. Robert Moses, *Working for the People*. p. 127.

9. Quoted by Robert A. Caro, *The Power Broker*, p. 771.

10. Cesare de Seta, *Città verso il 2000*, p. 54.

11. So a recent book edited by Andrew Kirby, *The Pentagon and the Cities*, does not mention the building, but is entirely concerned with the impact of military spending on local urban economies in the United States.

12. Wilma Fairbank, *Liang and Lin*, p. 170.

13. The best source is Gordon Cullen's *The Concise Townscape*.

14. David Harvey, *The Condition of Postmodernity*, p. 300.

15. Sharon Zukin, *The Cultures of Cities*, p. 53.

16. Zukin, p. 49.

17. Gregory J. Ashworth, "Heritage Planning," in *Heritage Landscape*, ed. Jacek Purchla (Kraków, 1993). Yvonne Ridley, "Have We All Got Heritage Fatigue?" (on the falling tourist figures in British Heritage Sites in 1999), in *The Independent on Sunday*, August 29, 1999, p. 11.

18. Ashworth, *ibid*.

19. Paul Saffo quoted by William J. Mitchell, in *E-Topia*, p. 33.

20. Paul Krugman quoted by Mitchell, in *E-Topia*, p. 124.

21. M. Carpo, reviewing William J. Mitchell, *City of Bits*, in *L'Architecture d'aujourd'hui* 317 (June 1998), p. 26.

22. Plato, *Phaedrus* 275 a.
23. William Gibson, *Neuromancer*, pp. 71 ff.
24. Gibson, pp. 67, 106.
25. Gibson, *ibid.*
26. Marshall McLuhan and Quentin Fiore, *The Medium Is the Message*, p. 72.
27. See Carol Willis, *Form Follows Finance*, p. 9.
28. William Wordsworth, "Expostulation and Reply," lines 16–20, but see McLuhan and Fiore, *The Medium Is the Message*, p. 44.

6. The Suburbs and the New Capitals

1. *Beppo, A Venetian Story*, from *The Complete Poetical Works of Lord Byron*, ed. Jerome J. McGann, vol. 4 (Oxford, 1986).
2. *L'Oeuvre de Tony Garnier*, ed. Albert Morancé and Jean Badovici.
3. Lord Curzon's speech on relinquishing the viceroyalty in 1904, quoted by Sten Nilsson, *The New Capitals*, p. 82.
4. Clarence Arthur Perry, *The Neighborhood Unit*, Monograph 1 in vol. 7, Neighborhood and Community Planning. Regional Plan of New York and Its Environs, New York 1929. Reproduced by Clarence Arthur Perry, in *Housing for the Machine Age*, pp. 49 ff.
5. Clarence S. Stein, *Toward New Towns for America*, pp. 96 ff.
6. Norma Evenson, *Chandigarh*, pp. 55 ff.
7. Report on living conditions in the new capital from *Brasília* (Journal of the Companhia Urbanizadora da Nova Capital do Brasil—NOVACAP), 1963, quoted in James Holston, *The Modernist City*, pp. 20 ff.
8. Sales advertisement for Downs of Hillcrest, near Dallas. Quoted by Jane Holtz Kay, *Asphalt Nation*, p. 31.
9. Thomas J. Campanella, "A Welcome Alternative: China's Suburban Revolution," in *Harvard Architectural Review* 10 (New York, 1998), pp. 112 ff.
10. Frank Schaffer, *The New Town Story*, p. 7.
11. Lloyd Rodwin, *The British New Towns Policy: Problems and Implications* (Cambridge, Mass., 1956), pp. 85 ff.
12. Henry George, *Progress and Poverty: An Inquiry into the Cause of Industrial Depression and of Increase of Want with Increase of Wealth. The Remedy* by Henry George (London, Fifty-second anniversary edition, 1931), pp. 283, 284.
13. Quoted in Jane Holtz Kay, *Asphalt Nation*, p. 233.
14. Mahlon Apgar IV, *Managing Community Development: The Systems Approach in Columbia, Maryland* (New York, 1971), p. 24.
15. "We wanted to provide a full residential, educational, cultural, recreational and vocational life within the city. There should be as many jobs in the city as there were dwelling units. It should be possible for anyone to work and live there, whether he was a janitor or a corporation executive. . . . Secondly, the plan should respect the land. Thirdly . . . we have an enormously

'examined' society in which ministers, doctors, psychiatrists, psychologists have learned a lot about people's ability to live together in an urban environment." So, James Rouse, in "Columbia, A New Town Built with Private Capital," *Occasional Papers* 26, Institute of Economic Affairs (London, 1969).

16. Signed by President Johnson on August 1, 1968; it is in fact Title IV of the Housing and Urban Development Act. See Shirley F. Weiss, *New Town Development in the United States* (Chapel Hill, 1973), p. 5.

17. Interview with James Howard Kunstler, May 10, 1990, reported in his *The Geography of Nowhere*, p. 255.

18. Reported by Andrew Ross, in *Celebration*, pp. 306 ff.

19. Ross, *Celebration*, p. 7.

7. The Heart of the City and the Capital of a Globe

1. "Manhattanization" had not appeared in dictionaries until 1999, when it was listed in the new Encarta dictionary, for instance.

2. Forty-six versions of the name—from Manachatas to Munhaddons—are registered. Dingman Versteeg, *Manhattan in 1628*, p. 205.

3. I have followed Michael Kammen, *Colonial New York*, pp. 24 ff. But alternative versions exist. See Edwin G. Burrows and Mike Wallace, *Gotham*, pp. 14 ff.; and of course the burlesque version given by Washington Irving in his *Knickerbocker's History of New York*, which first appeared in 1809. The sale and the price are reported to the Dutch West India Company in a letter of November 5, 1626, quoted in Dingman Versteeg, *Manhattan in 1628*, p. 186.

4. Janet Abu-Lughod, *New York, Chicago, Los Angeles*, pp. 23 ff.

5. Quoted by Larry R. Ford, in *Cities and Buildings*, p. 21.

6. The reception center was closed in 1954—by then most immigrants arrived by air.

7. G. H. Edgell, *The American Architecture of Today*, p. 358.

8. Louis Sullivan, "The Tall Office Building Artistically Considered," first published in *Lippincott's* 17 (March 1896), pp. 403 ff., and reprinted several times; here quoted from Sullivan's *Kindergarten Chats and Other Writings*, pp. 202 ff.

9. Daniel H. Burnham quoted by Montgomery Schuyler, often reprinted. Here quoted from Carl W. Condit, *Chicago 1910–1929*, p. 60.

10. Henry James, *The American Scene*. Quoted in *Writing New York*, by Phillip Lopate, ed., pp. 372 ff. James was in New York in 1904, his book was published in 1907.

11. The Council on Tall Buildings and Urban Habitat. It is located at Lehigh University, Bethlehem, Pennsylvania.

12. *Record and Guide* 86, of July 2, 1912, p. 8. Quoted by Sarah Bradford Landau and Carl W. Condit, *Rise of the New York Skyscraper*, p. 394.

13. "Higher Building in Relation to Town Planning," in *RIBA Journal* 31, no. 5 (January 12, 1924), p. 125 ff.
14. See Merle Crowell, ed., *The Last Rivet*.
15. Designed by John McComb and Joseph Mangin.
16. An intermediate, second "Madison Square Garden" was built on Eighth Avenue and Forty-ninth Street in 1927, but was destroyed, unmourned, to make way for a parking lot.
17. William Pedersen (of Kohn, Pedersen and Fox). Quoted by Carol Willis, in *Form Follows Finance*, pp. 142 ff.
18. Letter to Henry J. Muller, senior vice president of Citicorp in 1970. Quoted in Robert A. M. Stern and others, *New York 1960*, p. 492.
19. All advertising information and slogans quoted from the *New York Times*, October 24, 1999, Magazine section, advertising supplement.

8. For the New Millennium?

1. Quoted in *De Gaulle et Son Siècle*, ed. Institut Charles de Gaulle, vol. 3 (Paris, 1992), p. 534.
2. "Plan-Programme de l'Est de Paris," *Communications au Conseil de Paris*, November 23, 1983. Quoted by H. V. Savitch, *Post-Industrial Cities*, p. 152.
3. Ross Davis, *Evening Standard*, May 28, 1999, p. 8.
4. Ibid.
5. Reported in *China Daily*, June 22, 1999.
6. Charles P. Kindleberger, *Manias, Panics, and Crashes*, p. 125.
7. Although it seems immemorial, the maxim has a recent origin: "A long line of cases shows that it is not merely of some importance, it is of fundamental importance that justice should not only be done, but should manifestly and undoubtedly be seen to be done." Lord Justice Heward (1870–1943) in R. v. Sussex Justices, November 9, 1923.
8. Robert Venturi, Denise Scott-Brown, and Stephen Izenour, *Learning from Las Vegas*, pp. 64 ff.
9. Perry Anderson, *The Origin of Postmodernity*, p. 133.
10. Jane Jacobs, *The Death and Life of Great American Cities*, pp. 360 ff.
11. "In the U.K., the McLibel Case is a McDisaster." Reported in *Inside PR and Reputation Management*, 1996.
12. *The Economist*, December 11–17, 1999, pp. 19 ff.
13. Gerald Silver of the Encino Homeowners' Association. Quoted by Mike Davis in *City of Quartz*, p. 205.
14. Sharon Zukin, *The Cultures of Cities*. pp. 238 ff. But see Jane Jacobs, *The Economy of Cities*, pp. 224 ff., on earlier Harlem revitalization problems.
15. See above, chapter 3, note 10.
16. Not in the 1971 OED supplement, but dated 1954 by Merriam-Webster.
17. Told in outline in *Traffic in Towns: A Study of the Long-term Problems*

of Traffic in Urban Areas. Report of Working Group, chaired by Colin Buchanan and known as the Buchanan Report (London, 1963), pp. 182 ff.

18. Seth Mydans in the *New York Times*, December 6, 1999, p. A3.

19. Mike Davis, *City of Quartz*, pp. 122; Jane Holtz Kay, *Asphalt Nation*, pp. 117 ff.

20. Zygmunt Bauman, *Globalization, the Human Consequence*, p. 72.

21. My chapter 3, p. 97.

22. Gerald E. Frug, *City Making*, p. 220.

23. This argument is advanced in greater detail by Gerald E. Frug, *City Making*, pp. 215 ff.

24. Tony Hiss, *The Experience of Place*, pp. 104 ff.

25. Martin Hoyles, "Hints of the Open Country," in Tim Butler and Michael Rustin, eds., *Rising in the East*, pp. 240 ff.

26. *The New Charter of Athens: The Principles of . . . for the Planning of Cities*, European Council of Town Planners (Athens, 1998).

27. Maurice Merleau-Ponty, *Phénoménologie de la Perception*, p. 23. (My translation.)

28. Often quoted, the remark is now considered apocryphal.

Epilogue

1. Minoru Yamasaki interviewed by Paul Heyer in *Architects on Architecture* (New York, 1993), p. 194. It is very difficult to see how the building could have been interpreted by anyone except its architect to carry such a message.

2. On this, and the earlier "controlled" dynamiting of the Pruitt Igoe housing, also designed by Minoru Yamasaki and destroyed as the Twin Towers rose, see pp. 128 f.

3. E. B. White, *Here is New York*. With a new Introduction by Roger Angell (New York, 1999 (1st edition, 1949)), p. 54.

4. The extension to the Museum of Fine Arts, designed by Rafael Moneo, was opened in 2000.

5. It first appeared as the title of a racy, journalistic study by A. C. Spectorsky: *The Exurbanites*m (New York, Street & Smith), 1955.

6. I have relied on the new survey, *Modern Urban Housing in CHINA*, ed. by Lü Junhua, Peter G. Rowe and Zhang Jie, Prestel, Munich (London and New York, 2001), which was not available until after the book was published.

7. In her book, *Cities and the Wealth of Nations* (New York, 1984), pp. 156 ff., 215.

8. 'World takes caffeine hit' by Nick Mathiason and Patrick Tooher in *The Observer*, 12 August 2001 'News Focus', p. 3.

9. Following Gerald E. Frug (1999) pp. 214 f.; which I have already quoted earlier, p. 243 and n. 23.

10. Dr. Richard Taylor was elected for Wyre Forest, Worcestershire, by a majority of 17,630—one of the largest in that election, taking votes from both major parties, to defend Kidderminster Hospital. He has now become a spokesman on health issues.

11. *Towards an Urban Renaissance. Final report of the Urban Task Force Chaired by Lord Rogers of Riverside*, London, 1999, p. 11, 'The Key Proposals'. The report was published between the completion of my manuscript and the publication of the book.

Bibliography

Abu-Lughod, Janet. *New York, Chicago, Los Angeles: America's Global Cities*. Minneapolis, 1999.

Adriani, Maurilio, et al. *L'Utopia nel Mondo Moderno*. Florence, 1969.

Anderson, Perry. *The Origins of Postmodernity*. Oxford, 1998.

Aymonino, Carlo, et al. *Le Città Capitali dell XIX Secolo*. Rome, 1975.

Bairoch, Paul. *Cities and Economic Development: From the Dawn of History to the Present*. Trans. Christopher Braider. Chicago, 1988.

Balfour, Alan. *Berlin: The Politics of Order 1737–1989*. New York, 1990.

Banham, Rayner. *Los Angeles: The Architecture of Four Ecologies*. Harmondsworth, England, 1971.

Barnett, Jonathan. *The Fractured Metropolis*. New York, 1995.

Barrell, John, ed. *Painting and the Politics of Culture*. Oxford, 1992.

Barrière, Pierre. *La Vie Intellectuelle en France*. Paris, 1961.

Bauman, Zygmunt. *Globalization, the Human Consequence*. New York, 1998.

Benevolo, Leonardo. *Le Origini dell'Urbanistica Moderna*. Bari, 1963.

Benjamin, Walter. *Illuminationen*. Frankfurt, 1969.

Benoit-Lévy, Georges. *La Cité-Jardin*. Paris, 1904.

Bergdoll, Barry. *Léon Vaudoyer: Historicism in the Age of Industry*. Cambridge, Mass., 1994.

Berton, Kathleen. *Moscow: An Architectural History*. London, 1990.

Bindman, David, and Gottfried Riemann, eds. *Karl-Friedrich Schinkel: Journal of a Visit to France and Britain in 1826*. New Haven and London, 1993.

Bird, Anthony. *Roads and Vehicles*. London, 1969.

Bonnome, C., et al. *L'Urbanisation Française*. Paris, 1964.

Boyer, M. Christine. *Dreaming the Rational City*. Cambridge, Mass., 1983.

———. *The City of Collective Memory*. Cambridge, Mass., 1994.

Bradford Landau, Sarah, and Carl W. Condit. *Rise of the New York Skyscraper 1865–1913*. New Haven and London, 1996.

Braudel, Fernand. *The Identity of France*. New York, 1990.

Brooks, H. Allen. *Le Corbusier's Formative Years*. Chicago, 1997.

Brooks, Richard Oliver. *New Towns and Communal Values, A Case Study of Columbia, Maryland*. New York, 1974.

Buder, Stanley. *Pullman. An Experiment in Industrial Order and Community Planning 1880–1930*. New York, 1967.

Bullock, Nicholas, and James Read. *The Movement for Housing Reform in Germany and France 1840–1914*. Cambridge, 1985.

Burchard, John, and Albert Bush-Brown. *The Architecture of America*. Boston, 1961.

Burrows, Edwin G., and Mike Wallace. *Gotham: A History of New York City to 1898*. Oxford and New York, 1998.

Butler, Martin, and Evelyn Joll. *The Painting of J. M. W. Turner*. New Haven and London, 1977.

Butler, Tim, and Michael Rustin, eds. *Rising in the East: The Regeneration of East London*. London, 1996.

Calthorpe, Peter. *The Next American Metropolis*. New York, 1993.

Calvino, Italo. *Le Città Invisibili*. Turin, 1972.

Carini, Alessandra, et al. *Housing in Europe, 1900–1960*. Bologna, 1978.

Caro, Robert A. *The Power Broker: Robert Moses and the Fall of New York*. New York, 1974.

Castells, Manuel. *The City and the Grassroots*. Berkeley and Los Angeles, 1983.

———, ed. *High Technology, Space and Society*. London, 1985.

Castells, Manuel, and Peter Hall. *Technopoles of the World*. London, 1994.

Checkland, S. G. *The Rise of Industrial Society in England, 1815–1855*. London, 1964.

Choay, Françoise. *The Modern City*. New York, 1969.

———. *The Rule and the Model*. Cambridge, Mass., 1997.

Ciucci, Giorgio, Francesco Dal Co, Mario Manieri-Elia, and Manfredo Tafuri. *La Città Americana dalla Guerra Civile al New Deal*. Bari, 1973.

"Civitas/What Is a City." *Harvard Architecture Review* 10. New York, 1998.

Clapham, J. H. *An Economic History of Modern Britain*. Cambridge, 1926.

Coleman, Terry. *The Railway Navvies*. Harmondsworth, England, 1968.

Condit, Carl W. *Chicago 1910–29. Building, Planning and Urban Technology*. Chicago and London, 1973.

———. *Chicago 1930–70. Building, Planning, and Urban Technology*. Chicago, 1974.

Crowell, Merle, ed. *The Last Rivet: The Story of Rockefeller Center.* New York, 1940.

Cullen, Gordon. *The Concise Townscape.* London, 1961.

Davis, Mike. *City of Quartz.* New York, 1992, and London, 1990.

Davy, M. J. B. *Aeronautics.* London, 1949.

De Magistris, Alessandro. *La Costruzione della Città Totalitaria.* Milan, 1995.

Dethier, Jean, and Alain Guiheux, eds. *La Ville, Art et Architecture en Europe, 1870–1993.* Exhibition catalogue. Paris, 1994.

Deutscher, Isaac. *Stalin.* Harmondsworth, England, 1966.

Devillers, Christian, and Bernard Huet. *Le Creusot: Naissance et Développement d'une Ville Industrielle 1782–1914.* Seyssel, France, 1981.

Dirlmeier, Ulf, et al., eds. *Geschichte des Wohnens.* Stuttgart, 1997–98.

Disraeli, Benjamin, earl of Beaconsfield, *Works,* edited Edmund Gosse. London, 1904.

Döhmer, Klaus. *In Welchem Style Sollen Wir Bauen?* Munich, 1973.

Domosh, Mona. *Invented Cities.* New Haven and London, 1996.

Downs, Anthony. *New Visions for Metropolitan America.* Washington, D.C., 1994.

Duany, Andres, Elizabeth Plater-Zyberk, and Jeff Speck. *Suburban Nation: The Rise of Sprawl and the Decline of the American Dream.* New York, 2000.

Duby, Georges, ed. *Histoire de la France Urbaine.* Paris,

Durkheim, Emile. *The Elementary Forms of the Religious Life.* New York, 1961.

Edgell, G. H. *The American Architecture of Today.* New York and London, 1928.

Eliot, Marc. *Walt Disney: Hollywood's Dark Prince.* London, 1994.

Ellin, Nan. *Postmodern Urbanism.* Oxford, 1996.

Evenson, Norma. *Chandigarh.* Berkeley and Los Angeles, 1966.

———. *Paris: A Century of Change, 1878–1978.* New Haven, 1979.

Fairbank, Wilma. *Liang and Lin: Partners in Exploring China's Architectural Past.* Philadelphia, 1994.

Figes, Orlando. *A People's Tragedy: The Russian Revolution 1891–1924.* London, 1996.

Finberg, A. J. *The Life of J. M. W. Turner, R. A.* Oxford, 1961.

Ford, Larry R. *Cities and Buildings.* Baltimore and London, 1994.

Frug, Gerald E. *City Making: Building Communities without Building Walls.* Princeton, N.J., 1999.

Galantay, Ervin Y. *New Towns: Antiquity to the Present.* New York, 1975.

Gans, Herbert J. *The Urban Villagers.* New York, 1982.

Garreau, Joel. *Edge City: Life on the New Frontier.* New York, 1991.

Gay, Peter. *The Enlightenment: An Interpretation.* London, 1973.

Geist, Johann Friedrich. *Arcades: The History of a Building Type.* Cambridge, Mass., 1983.

Gibson, William. *Neuromancer.* London, 1995 (1984).

Giedion, Siegfried. *Space, Time and Architecture.* New York, 1941.

Gille, Bertrand. *Leonardo e Gli Ingegneri del Rinascimento.* Milan, 1972.

Gilpin. *Observations on the River Wye . . . Made in the Summer of the Year 1770.* London, 1782.

Gimpel, Jean. *La Révolution Industrielle du Moyen Age.* Paris, 1975.

Glass, Ruth. *Clichés of Urban Doom.* Oxford, 1989.

Glazer, Nathan, and Mark Lilla, eds. *The Public Face of Architecture: Civic Culture and Public Spaces.* New York, 1987.

Goldberger, Paul. *The Skyscraper.* London and New York, 1982.

Gordon, W. Terrence, *Marshall McLuhan.* New York, 1997.

Gottmann, Jean. *Megalopolis: The Urbanized Northeastern Seaboard of the United States.* Cambridge, Mass., 1961.

Gozak, Andrei, and Andrei Leonidov. *Ivan Leonidov.* Edited Catherine Cooke. London, 1988.

Graf, Arturo. *L'Anglomania e l'Influsso Inglese in Italia nel Secolo XVIII.* Torino, 1911.

Grout, Catherine, and Tsutomu Iyori, eds. *Le Paysage de l'Espace Urbain.* Enghien-les-Bains, France, 1998.

Gruen, Victor. *The Heart of Our Cities, the Urban Crisis: Diagnosis and Cure.* New York, 1964.

Guilbaut, Serge. *How New York Stole the Idea of Modern Art: Abstract Expressionism, Freedom and the Cold War.* Chicago and London, 1983.

Hale, John. *The Civilization of Europe in the Renaissance.* London, 1993.

Hall, Sir Peter. *Managing Growth in the World's Cities.* Lecture given in Toronto, October 1990. Published March 1991.

———. *Cities in Civilization.* New York and London, 1998.

———. *Great Planning Disasters.* London, 1980.

Hanaford, Phebe A. *The Life of George Peabody.* Boston, 1870.

Harvey, David. *The Limits to Capital.* Oxford, 1982.

———. *The Condition of Postmodernity.* Oxford, 1990.

———. *Justice, Nature and the Geography of Difference.* Oxford, 1996.

Hatt, Paul K., and Albert J. Reiss, Jr., eds. *Cities and Society.* New York, 1957.

Hayden, Dolores. *The Power of Place.* Cambridge, Mass., 1997.

Heertje, Arnold, ed. *Schumpeter's Vision: Capitalism, Socialism and Democracy after 40 Years.* New York, 1981.

Hilberseimer, L. *Entfaltung einer Planungsidee.* Berlin, 1963.

Hiller, Carl E. *Babylon to Brasília: The Challenge of City Planning.* Boston, 1972.

Hiss, Tony. *The Experience of Place: A New Way of Looking at and Dealing with Our Countryside.* New York, 1991.

Hitchcock, Henry-Russell, et al. *The Rise of an American Architecture.* London, 1970.

Hobhouse, Christopher. *1851 and the Crystal Palace.* London, 1937.

Hobsbawn, Eric, and Terence Ranger, eds. *The Invention of Tradition*. Cambridge, 1983.

Hodgson, Godfrey. *A Grand New Tour*. London, 1995.

Hole, James. *The Homes of the Working Classes with Suggestions for Their Improvement*. London, 1866.

Holston, James. *The Modernist City: An Anthropological Critique of Brasília*. Chicago, 1989.

Hübsch, Heinrich, et al. *In What Style Should We Build?* Introduction and translation by Wolfgang Herrmann. Santa Monica, Calif., 1992.

Huxtable, Ada Louise. *Architecture Anyone?* Berkeley, 1986.

———. *The Tall Building Artistically Reconsidered*. Berkeley, 1992.

Inglis, Brian. *Poverty and the Industrial Revolution*. London, 1971.

Institut Charles de Gaulle. *De Gaulle en son Siècle*. Paris, 1992.

Jacobs, Jane. *The Death and Life of Great American Cities*. New York, 1961.

———. *The Economy of Cities*. New York, 1969.

Jefferson, Thomas. *Writings*. Edited by Merrill D. Peterson. New York, 1984.

Jordy, William H. *American Buildings and their Architects*. Vol. 4, 5. Oxford, 1972.

Kahn, Herman, and Anthony J. Wiener. *The Year 2000: A Framework for Speculation on the Next Thirty-three Years*. New York, 1967.

Kammen, Michael. *Colonial New York: A History*. Oxford and New York, 1975.

Kay, Jane Holtz. *Asphalt Nation: How the Automobile Took Over America and How We Can Take It Back*. Berkeley and Los Angeles, 1997.

Kemp, Martin. *Leonardo da Vinci*. London, 1981.

Kindleberger, Charles P. *Manias, Panics, and Crashes: A History of Financial Crises*. New York, 1996.

Kirby, Andrew, ed. *The Pentagon and the Cities*. Newbury Park, Calif., 1992.

Klingender, Francis D. *Art and the Industrial Revolution*. London, 1947.

Kunstler, James Howard. *The Geography of Nowhere: The Rise and Decline of America's Man-Made Landscape*. New York, 1993.

Ladrière, Jean. *Vie Sociale et Destinée*. Gembloux, Belgium, 1973.

Le Corbusier (Charles-Edouard Jeanneret). *Oeuvres Complètes*. Edited by W. Boesiger. Zürich, 1935.

Lefebvre, Henri. *La Vie Quotidienne dans le Monde Moderne*. Paris, 1968.

———. *Du Rural à l'Urbain*. Paris, 1970.

———. *La Production de l'Espace*. Paris, 1974.

Lévi-Strauss, Claude. *Tristes Tropiques*. Paris, 1955.

———. *Anthropologie Structurale*. Paris, 1958.

Lopate, Phillip, ed. *Writing New York: A Literary Anthology*. New York, 1998.

Lynch, Kevin. *The Image of the City*. Cambridge, Mass., 1960.

———. *What Time Is This Place?* Cambridge, Mass., 1972.

McLuhan, Marshall. *Understanding Media: The Extensions of Man*. London, 1968.

McLuhan, Marshall, and Quentin Fiore. *The Medium Is the Message: An Inventory of Effects*. Harmondsworth, England, 1967.

Magistris, Alessandro De. *La Costruzione della Città Totalitaria*. Milan, 1995.

Manuel, Frank E., and P. Fritzie. *Utopian Thought in the Western World*. Oxford, 1979.

Merleau-Ponty, Maurice. *Phénoménologie de la Perception*. Paris, 1945.

Merlin, Pierre. *Les Villes Nouvelles*. Paris, 1969.

Merlin, Pierre, and Françoise Choay, eds. *Dictionnaire de l'Urbanisme et de l'Aménagement*. Paris, 1988.

Merrifield Andy, and Erik Swyngedouw, eds. *The Urbanization of Injustice*. New York, 1997.

Mitcham, Carl, and Robert Mackey. *Philosophy and Technology*. New York, 1972.

Mitchell, B. R., ed. *International Historical Statistics*. London, 1998.

Mitchell, William J. *E-Topia: "Urban Life, Jim—But Not As We Know It."* Cambridge, Mass., 1999.

———. *City of Bits*. Cambridge, Mass., 1995.

Moore, Charles. *Daniel H. Burnham: Architect, Planner of Cities*. New York, 1968.

Morancé, Albert, and Jean Badovici. *L'Oeuvre de Tony Garnier*. Paris, 1932.

Morris, A. E. J. *History of Urban Form*. New York, 1979.

Morris, William. *News from Nowhere.* London, 1890.

Moses, Robert. *Working for the People: Promise and Performance in Public Service*. New York, 1956.

Mumford, Lewis. *Technics and Civilization*. London, 1934.

———. *The City in History*. New York, 1961.

Nicholson, Max. *The Environmental Revolution*. Harmondsworth, England, 1972.

Nilsson, Sten. *The New Capitals*. Lund, Sweden, 1972.

Olsen, Donald J. *Town Planning in London: The Eighteenth and Nineteenth Centuries*. New Haven and London, 1982.

Overholt, William H. *China: The Next Economic Superpower*. London, 1993.

Parsons, Kermit Carlyle, ed. *The Writings of Clarence S. Stein*. Baltimore, 1998.

Pearson, S. Vere. *The Growth and Distribution of Population*. London, 1935.

Perloff, Harvey S., ed. *Planning and the Urban Community*. Pittsburgh, 1961.

Perronet, Jean-Rodolphe, et al. *Ecrits d'Ingénieurs*. Paris, 1997.

Perry, Clarence Arthur. *Housing for the Machine Age*. New York, 1939.

Pétonnet, Colette. *Espaces Habités: Ethnologie des Banlieues*. Paris, 1982.

Phillips, Peggy A. *Modern France: Theories and Realities of Urban Planning*. Lanham, Md., 1987.

Power, Anne. *Hovels to High Rise: State Housing in Europe Since 1850*. London, 1993.

Quilici, Vieri. *Città Russa e Città Sovietica*. Milan, 1976.

Raffalovich, Arthur. *Le Logement de l'Ouvrier et du Pauvre*. Paris, 1887.

Rees, Nigel. *Graffiti Lives O.K.* London, 1979.

Reps, John W. *The Making of Urban America*. Princeton, N.J., 1965.

——. *Monumental Washington*. Princeton, N.J., 1967.

Reulecke, Jürgen. *Geschichte des Wohnens*. 3 vols. Stuttgart, 1997.

Robinson, Eric, and A. E. Musson. *James Watt and the Steam Revolution*. London, 1969.

Rojek, Chris. *Ways of Escape: Modern Transformations in Leisure and Travel*. Basingstoke, England, 1993.

Ross, Andrew. *Celebration: Life, Liberty and the Pursuit of Property Value in Disney's New Town*. New York, 1999.

Rykwert, Joseph. *The Idea of a Town: The Anthropology of Urban Form in Rome, Italy, and the Ancient World*. Hilversum, Netherlands, 1960; London and Princeton, N.J., 1976; Cambridge, Mass., 1980.

——. "Reflections on the Continent as a Museum." *Times Literary Supplement*, Dec. 8, 1989.

——. "Rebuilding Europe's Bombed Cities." *Times Literary Supplement*, May 11, 1990.

——. "Für die Stadt—Argumente für ihre Zukunft." In *Die Welt der Stadt*, ed. Tilo Schabert. Munich, 1991.

——. "Off Limits: City Pattern and City Texture." In *Constancy and Change in Architecture*, edited by M. Quantrill and B. Webb. Texas A&M University, 1991.

Sadler, Simon. *The Situationist City*. Cambridge, Mass., 1999.

Sassen, Saskia. *The Global City*. Princeton, N.J., 1991.

Savitch, H. V. *Post-Industrial Cities: Politics and Planning in New York, Paris and London*. Princeton, N.J., 1988.

Schaffer, Frank. *The New Town Story*. London, 1970.

Schama, Simon. *Landscape and Memory*. London, 1996.

Schnaidt, Claude. *Hannes Meyer*. Teufen A/R, 1965.

Schumpeter, Joseph. *Economic Doctrine and Method*. London, 1957.

Scott, Allen, J. and Edward W. Soja. *The City: Los Angeles and Urban Theory at the End of the Twentieth Century*. Berkeley, 1996.

Scott, Sir George Gilbert. *Remarks on Secular and Domestic Architecture.* London, 1858.

——. *Personal and Professional Recollections*. Edited by Gavin Stamp. Stanford, 1995.

Seabrook, Jeremy. *The Leisure Society*. Oxford, 1988.

Sellier, Henri. *Une Cité pour Tous*. Edited by Bernard Marrey. Paris, 1998.

Sennett, A. R. *Garden Cities in Theory and Practice*. London, 1905.

Sennett, Richard. *The Fall of Public Man*. London, 1978.

——. *Flesh and Stone*. New York, 1994.

Seta, Cesare de. *Città verso il 2000*. Milan, 1990.

Siegel, Arthur, ed. *Chicago's Famous Buildings*. Chicago, 1965.

Sies, Mary Corbin, and Christopher Silver. *Planning the Twentieth-Century American City*. Baltimore, 1996.

Simmen, Jeannot, and Uwe Drepper. *Der Fahrstuhl: Die Geschichte der Vertikalen Eroberung*. Munich, 1984.

Sitte, Camillo. *City Planning According to Artistic Principles*. London, 1965.

Skinner, B. F. *Walden Two*. Toronto, 1948.

Smiles, Samuel. *James Brindley and the Early Engineers*. London, 1864.

Smith, Adam. *The Wealth of Nations*. Oxford, 1904.

Sorkin, Michael, ed. *Variations on a Theme Park*. New York, 1992.

Stein, Clarence S. *Toward New Towns for America*. Liverpool and Chicago, 1951.

Stern, Robert A. M., Thomas Mellins, and David Fishman. *New York 1960*. New York, 1997.

Stewart, Murray, ed. *The City: Problems of Planning*. Harmondsworth, England, 1972.

Sudjic, Deyan. *The Hundred Mile City*. London, 1992.

Sullivan, Louis H. *Kindergarten Chats and Other Writings*. Reprint, New York, 1947.

Sutcliffe, Anthony. *The Autumn of Central Paris*. London, 1970.

———. *Towards the Planned City*. Oxford, 1981.

———. ed. *Metropolis 1890–1940*. Chicago, 1984.

Tafuri, Manfredo. *The Sphere and the Labyrinth*. Cambridge, Mass., 1987.

Tallmadge, Thomas E. *The Story of Architecture in America*. London, n.d.

Taylor, Graham Romeyn. *Satellite Cities: A Study of Industrial Suburbs*. New York, 1970.

Thompson, E. P. *The Making of the English Working-Class*. London, 1963.

Tocqueville, Alexis de. *Oeuvres*. Edited by André Jardin. Paris, 1991.

Trachtenberg, Marvin. *The Statue of Liberty*. New York, 1986.

Tunnard, Christopher. *The City of Man*. London, 1953.

Van der Ryn, Sim, and Stuart Cowan. *Ecological Design*. Washington, D.C., 1996.

Venturi, Robert, Denise Scott-Brown, and Stephen Izenour. *Learning from Las Vegas*. Cambridge, Mass., 1977.

Versteeg, Dingman. *Manhattan in 1628*. New York, 1904.

Vidler, Anthony. *Claude-Nicolas Ledoux*. Cambridge, Mass., 1990.

Ward, David, and Olivier Zunz, eds. *The Landscape of Modernity*. New York, 1992.

Warner, Sam Bass. *The Urban Wilderness: A History of the American City*. Berkeley, 1972.

Watkins, Perry. *The Rise of the Sunbelt Cities*. London, 1977.

Whyte, William H. *City: Rediscovering the Center*. New York, 1988.

Williams-Ellis, Clough, ed. *Britain and the Beast*. London, 1938.

Willis, Carol. *Form Follows Finance: Skyscrapers and Skylines in New York and Chicago*. Princeton, 1995.

Wilton, Andrew. *Turner in His Time*. New York, 1987.

Wright, Gwendolen. *Building the Dream: A Social History of Housing in America*. New York, 1981.

————. *The Politics of Design in French Colonial Urbanism*. Chicago, 1991.

Yelling, J. A. *Slums and Slum Clearance in Victorian London*. London, 1986.

Zukin, Sharon. *The Culture of Cities*. Oxford and Cambridge, Mass., 1995.

Index

Lightning Source UK Ltd.
Milton Keynes UK
UKOW06f2323040316

269616UK00001B/31/P